Past and Present Publications

Towns in Societies

Past and Present Publications

General Editor: T. H. ASTON, *Corpus Christi College, Oxford*

Past and Present Publications will comprise books similar in character to the articles in the journal *Past and Present*. Whether the volumes in the series are collections of essays – some previously published, others new studies – or monographs, they will encompass a wide variety of scholarly and original works primarily concerned with social, economic and cultural changes, and their causes and consequences. They will appeal to both specialists and non-specialists and will endeavour to communicate the results of historical and allied research in readable and lively form. This new series continues and expands in its aims the volumes previously published elsewhere.

Volumes published by the Cambridge University Press are:
Family and Inheritance: Rural Society in Western Europe 1200–1800,
  edited by Jack Goody, Joan Thirsk and E. P. Thompson
French Society and the Revolution, edited by Douglas Johnson
*Peasants, Knights and Heretics: Studies in Medieval English Social
  History*, edited by R. H. Hilton
*Towns in Societies: Essays in Economic History and Historical Socio-
  logy*, edited by Philip Abrams and E. A. Wrigley

Volumes previously published with Routledge & Kegan Paul are:
Crisis in Europe 1560–1660, edited by Trevor Aston
Studies in Ancient Society, edited by M. I. Finley
The Intellectual Revolution of the Seventeenth Century, edited by
  Charles Webster

Towns in Societies

Essays in Economic History and Historical Sociology

Edited by
PHILIP ABRAMS
E. A. WRIGLEY

CAMBRIDGE UNIVERSITY PRESS

Cambridge
London · New York · Melbourne

Published by the Syndics of the Cambridge University Press
The Pitt Building, Trumpington Street, Cambridge CB2 1RP
Bentley House, 200 Euston Road, London NW1 2DB
32 East 57th Street, New York, NY 10022, USA
296 Beaconsfield Parade, Middle Park, Melbourne 3206, Australia

First published 1978
First paperback edition 1979

First printed in Great Britain by
Western Printing Services Ltd, Bristol
Reprinted in Great Britain at the
University Press, Cambridge

Library of Congress Cataloguing in Publication Data

Main entry under title:

Towns in societies.

(Past and present publications)

Bibliography: p.

Includes index.

1. Urban economics – Addresses, essays, lectures.
2. Cities and towns – Addresses, essays, lectures.
I. Abrams, Philip. II. Wrigley, Edward Anthony.
HT321.T69   301.36'3   77–82481
ISBN 0 521 21826 8 hard covers
ISBN 0 521 29594 7 paperback

Contents

Contributors

Philip Abrams is Professor of Sociology at the University of Durham; his recent publications include *Communes, sociology and society*, and he is currently engaged on research into the sociology of altruism. He is the editor of *Sociology*.

M. J. Daunton was educated at the Universities of Nottingham and Kent, and has been Lecturer in Economic History at the University of Durham since 1973. His previous publications have been on the economy and society of south Wales in the nineteenth century, principally *Coal metropolis: Cardiff 1870–1914* (1977). At present he is working on a study of urban property in Victorian England.

Mark Elvin is Lecturer in Chinese History at the University of Oxford, and a Fellow of St Antony's College. His chief interests are the economic history of pre-modern China and China's historical demography. Author of *The pattern of the Chinese past*, and editor (with G. W. Skinner) of *The Chinese city between two worlds*.

Christopher R. Friedrichs is Assistant Professor of History at the University of British Columbia in Vancouver (Canada). His field of research is the social, economic and political history of German cities during the early modern era. In addition to the paper reprinted here, he has published articles in the *Business History Review* and *Canadian Historical Papers*, and is currently completing the manuscript of a social history of the city of Nördlingen between 1580 and 1720.

David Herlihy is Professor of History at Harvard University. He has recently completed, in collaboration with Mme Christine Klapisch of the École des Hautes Études, Paris, a two-volume study of Tuscan households, entitled *Les Toscans et leurs familles: une étude du Catasto florentin de 1427*, which is now in the course of publication.

A. B. Hibbert is a Fellow of King's College, Cambridge.

Keith Hopkins is Professor of Sociology at Brunel University. He has edited a book called *Hong Kong, the industrial colony* (1971) and has two books in press: *Conquerors and slaves*, and *Succession and descent*; both are sociological studies in Roman history and will be published in 1978.

J. J. Lee is Professor of Modern History at University College, Cork. His publications include 'Administrators and agriculture: aspects of German agricultural policy in the First World War', in J. M. Winter (ed.), *War and society: essays in memory of David Joslin* (1975) and 'Labour and German industrialisation', *Cambridge Economic History*, vol. vii. He is at present completing a book entitled *Economic history of Germany, 1750–1939*.

Charles Phythian-Adams is Lecturer in the Department of English Local History at the University of Leicester. Publications include 'Ceremony and the citizen: the communal year at Coventry 1450–1550', in P. Clark and P. Slack (eds.), *Crisis and order in English towns 1500–1700*, and two units for the Open University Course no. A322, Urban History 1500–1780, 1977; he is currently completing a book on the depopulation of medieval Coventry. Other publications include an analysis of Anglo-Saxon Rutland in *Mercian Studies*, ed. A. Dornier; *Local history and folklore: a new framework*, Standing Conference for Local History, 1975, and a study of rural kinship patterns in early nineteenth-century Leicestershire is in preparation.

E. A. Wrigley is a Director of the S.S.R.C. Cambridge Group for the History of Population and Social Structure and a Fellow of Peterhouse, Cambridge. His publications include *Industrial growth and population change* (1961), and *Population and history* (1969), and, as editor, *An introduction to English historical demography* (1966), *Nineteenth century society* (1969), and *Identifying people in the past* (1972).

Introduction

PHILIP ABRAMS

Classical political economy, whether represented by Smith or by Marx, took it for granted that the foundation of the progress of the division of labour lay in the separation of town and countryside. Yet most of the rather delphic formulations of that theme still await empirical clarification. In *The country and the city* Raymond Williams has done something to explain the cultural resonance of the idea. But its economic and sociological significance remains oddly obscure. No theoretical elaboration of the relationship of town and country with any degree of general application has yet emerged. Many interesting claims have been made. Sombart held that by systematically consuming more than they could afford early modern capital cities fostered the growth of capitalism. By contrast, Weber argued that the very same patterns of consumption in some cities were a principal obstacle to capitalist development. Pirenne and later Postan, interpreting medieval towns as non-feudal islands within the feudal order, saw them as a primary source of change and economic growth. Most younger English historians – represented in this volume by Charles Phythian-Adams and Martin Daunton – have chosen to emphasize the ways in which the persistence of essentially feudal patterns of social control within towns acted as a decisive disincentive to economic innovation, stressing the rural rather than the urban origins of capitalism. But in sociology and urban geography there has been a contrary tendency; a consensus of opinion has been inclined to see towns as playing a positive role in the process of economic growth. The formation of towns is treated as both an indicator and a multiplier of industrialization. Yet even here there are important qualifications and uncertainties. The growth of towns is variously seen as a condition, a consequence or at least a concomitant of more intensive productive exploitation. But cases are observed with troublesome frequency in which urban growth, in the third world as in medieval Europe or classical antiquity, is in fact a significant or decisive obstacle to industrial and other forms of economic development; long stretches of the history of Rome, Seville, St Petersburg or Peking, to say nothing of a host of modern colonial cities, came to prove highly problematic in this sense. Even in the fairly crude, averaged-out language of

1

social indicators it appeared that although levels of urbanization do, in gross, correlate with levels of industrialization, urbanization alone is quite a poor predictor of any sort of economic growth; the relationship between them – and in turn any general relationship between town and country – remained opaque.

It became apparent, in other words, that to give the idea of the separation of town and country, or theses about the role of towns in economic growth, any firm analytical value one would need a much tighter grip, theoretically and empirically, on the variations in specific structural forms of urbanism within specific types of society than had yet been achieved. By 1975 it seemed reasonable to hope that the elements of such an understanding might have to exist beneath the surface of the great volume of work that had been done in urban history and urban sociology in the several generations since the general problem of the role of towns within the framework of the separation of town and country had been posed. It was in that hope that the Past and Present Society organized its Conference for that year around the theme 'Towns and Economic Growth'. This volume in turn has its beginnings in that Conference. Four of its chapters – Friedrichs on early modern Germany, Hibbert on the urban patriciate, Hughes on medieval Genoa and Wrigley on London – appeared originally as articles in *Past and Present*; the remainder spring from papers and discussions at the 1975 Conference.

But the book is at best only in part concerned with the theme that gave the Conference its title. As indeed was the Conference itself. In an unexpected way the Conference did reveal a new sense of how urban history might proceed. And it was one which involved a quite radical redefinition of the town as an object of study; a redefinition which sought to undo the conceptual separation of town and country and re-unite the town with its larger social environment. The hopes of the organizers of the Conference of being able to draw a body of synthetic generalizations about the role of towns in economic growth from a review of recent empirical work were thus largely frustrated. Most of the contributors were so obviously reluctant to talk that sort of language. The debates of the previous decade about 'generative' and 'parasitic' towns and the accompanying concern to tease out an 'urban factor' in economic and social history seemed to have lost their momentum – at least in their familiar terms. The tendency, rather, was to move away from any attempt to treat towns as variables in themšelves – whether dependent, independent or merely intervening – and also from the attempt to regard the town as a generic social reality, and to see cities and towns instead as fields of action integral to some larger world and within which the interactions and contradictions of that larger world are displayed with special clarity. The town was now treated – the implicit agenda of the Conference seemed to suggest – mainly as a resource for the understanding of the structures and processes of a more inclusive reality it expressed and epitomized, and in which its inhabitants were in interesting specific ways actively engaged.

In effect the problematic had been changed. The dualistic tendencies implicit in the idea of the separation of town and country had led earlier urban historians to an increasingly explicit conception of a dual economy, the rural and the urban. They had set themselves the task of identifying each of these and then tracing the action of one upon the other. That model and that task – at their clearest in the work of historians such as Pirenne and Postan – seem now to be being, consciously or unconsciously, abandoned. The issue of the role of towns tends to lose significance and to be replaced by a concern to understand towns as sites in which the history of larger social systems – states, societies, modes of production, world economies – is partially, but crucially, worked out. The separation of town and country is seen as a *social* division of labour within an encompassing economic or political whole; the relative unity of town and country in political or economic terms tends to be stressed.

Of course the dual economy model was never that well established as an orthodoxy and the retreat from it has been going on for some time. A. B. Hibbert's analysis of the origins of the medieval urban patriciate voiced a strong challenge to it as long ago as 1953. And E. A. Wrigley's study of London is an influential example of the way in which the dual economy approach had always tended to collapse in practice when applied rigorously to the careful analysis of a single town in a specified period. It is in fact a study of the intimate and pervasive involvement of London in the whole economy and social structure of English society and *vice versa*; and London's 'importance' is shown to be inseparable from that not at all 'simple' involvement. Then again, Martin Daunton in discussing English provincial capitals in the eighteenth century reviews several possible applications of a number of different versions of the dual economy thesis to his subject and finds that, while some case can be made for each of them, nothing that could be accepted as empirically constituting a dual economy can actually be found – rather there is a single, variously stratified economy and society constructed and reconstructed historically through the interaction of diverse functions, occupations and powers. He goes on to explore the rise and fall of towns, within and as part of that single socio-economic system, in terms of the ways in which appropriations of power associated with economic or cultural innovation in one epoch become ossifications of power as an obstacle to change in another – echoing here Charles Phythian-Adams' elegant analysis of a similar category of towns in the later Middle Ages.

Daunton's paper together with Wrigley's concluding chapter and my own contribution are the nearest this collection of studies comes to offering a programmatic or formal justification for a new view of urban history. As it happens an extended statement of that sort did appear concurrently with the *Past and Present* Conference in an article by John Merrington.[1] It is of interest that so few of the authors whose contributions are published here seem to have felt the need for such theoretical and methodological exegesis. The shift of emphasis away from the dual economy model of urban history is, rather, taken for granted in their work. We find it, for example, in Keith Hopkins' important discussion of the Roman Empire. Here the particular form of parasitism that is conventionally attributed to Roman towns – Goliaths of luxury living off the taxation of many fragmented rural economies – is replaced not by a different dualism but by an insistence upon the unity of an international Roman market and upon the integration of Roman towns into that market through processes of production and consumption and exchange. The unity was enforced politically to be sure, but the possibility of political enforcement was itself contained within the special relationships of that market. In this sort of treatment the town becomes less visible as a distinct social object, but the social relationships – of production, trade, exploitation and control – that bound the inhabitants of the Roman world to one another in town and country are more clearly seen.

The same movement of attention and analysis is evident in David Herlihy's study of Florence in the early fifteenth century.

---

[1] Merrington, *New Left Review* (1975).

Here again we have a study of a town in and inseparable from its environment; Florence is understood through its implication in the regional economy of Tuscany. At the same time the entity 'Florence' is rediscovered as a matter of 'a remarkably few patrician households within it' and their historically constructed relations with both an urban and a rural world. The separation of town and country is again reworked concretely in terms of very precise functions and powers embedded in relationships which unite the urban and the rural economically, even as they divide them culturally. Diane Hughes' study of medieval Genoa points in the same direction in its insistence on the differences between Genoa and Florence, on the impossibility of catching both towns up in any single urban generalization and on the need to explain the peculiarities of Genoa's 'urban reality' in terms of the historical working out of a particular set of class and status relationships within an increasingly competitive larger economy. Even in nineteenth-century Germany the close interconnections between cities and their hinterlands stand out. J. J. Lee's analysis of urbanization and economic development demonstrates the importance of the contingent and coincidental even where in hindsight there appear to be some notably clear patterns in urban growth.

But if the dual economy approach to the understanding of urban history is slowly being abandoned what is to take its place? What then is the problem about towns? In what alternative framework of analysis is urban history to be pursued? In one sense these papers reflect a rather eclectic searching for answers to such questions. But they also suggest some tentative answers. Under the influence of writers such as R. E. Pahl and Manuel Castells urban sociology has increasingly moved away from the ecological determinism that once characterized it and has come instead to treat towns as fields of social power; 'whose city?' becomes the distinctive question. And the papers collected in this book suggest that a parallel development may be occurring among urban historians. Thus, Christopher Friedrichs, in tracing the way in which the putting-out system enabled entrepreneurs in Nordlingen to establish an overall control of the process of production and reduce the craft workers, through indebtedness, to a permanent dependency, exemplifies the way in which the resources of urban history can be used to bring to light the dynamics of class formation and, thence, of economic transition. Several other papers in the volume also seize on the internal class relations of towns as the key to unlock an understanding of social and economic change. Characteristically, one feature of work of this kind is the discovery of the connectedness of town and country – at least insofar as the dominant strata are concerned. Thus, Hibbert, Hopkins, Herlihy and Elvin are all in quite different settings concerned to emphasize the continuity of social stratification between town and country, and the extent to which the town needs to be understood as the social realization of power created in the countryside. These studies are not of course definitive; but they do emphasize the fruitfulness of an approach to urban history which concerns itself with towns as sites for the study of inequality rather than as self-contained social structures.

At the same time they raise a further possibility of innovation. If the town ceases to be treated as a self-contained unit of analysis, a question must arise as to the nature of the wider context in which, alternatively, towns should be examined. The contributors to this volume are perhaps less certain of their direction in this respect and certainly less unanimous. The tendency is to place the town in the setting of some larger economy. But the boundaries of economies are not easily fixed – they plainly do not coincide with the boundaries of political systems whether regional, national or international. There seem to be important unresolved questions, too, about the extent to which towns can be typed and classified, and about the appropriate nature of any possible classifications. An emphasis on the connectedness of town and country, and on urban social relations as points of access to the history of social stratification, tends to cast doubt on the usefulness of many conventional ways of classifying towns – the attempt to identify 'parasitic' towns for example. The ambiguity and mutability of towns from such a point of view is strongly brought out by several of these papers – perhaps especially in the work of Phythian-Adams. At the same time, some other long-standing classifications do seem to have a continuing value; Hopkins and Wrigley, for example, both find Sombart's notion of the 'consumer city' helpful and pertinent. What they have done of course is to substitute relatively precise economic categories for relatively vague moral categories. And that, too, seems a sensible if modest step forward.

It would be wrong, however, to overstate either the novelty or the comprehensiveness of this collection of studies. There is a sense of movement and innovation implicit in them. And more immediately, although the volume does not include all the contributions to urban history that have appeared in *Past and Present* or all the papers that were read at the 1975 Conference, it does reflect the distinctive interest which the journal has taken in this field since its foundation. Representative, too, is the combination it offers of substantial scholarly articles, thoroughly researched and focused on a single theme or topic, and shorter, speculative, critical or frankly polemical pieces designed to raise questions or stimulate debate. No less appropriately the book ends with an agenda as much as with a conclusion. It is worth emphasizing though that this is an agenda not for new concepts and theories of the town but for further historical investigations.

Editors' note. Since we have prepared a consolidated bibliography, references to published work in footnotes are given in an abbreviated form.

1. *Towns and Economic Growth: Some Theories and Problems*

PHILIP ABRAMS

Urban history, and to a greater degree urban sociology, have been haunted by the idea of generalizing about the town. To an impressive extent both types of work have rested on the belief that, as Braudel has it, 'a town is a town wherever it is'.[1] The material and especially the visual presence of towns seem to have impelled a reification in which the town as a physical object is turned into a taken-for-granted social object and a captivating focus of analysis in its own right. Thus Harris and Ullman began an influential paper on the nature of the city by reacting in just that way to the immediately given urban phenomenon: 'As one approaches a city and notices its tall buildings rising above the surrounding land and as one continues into the city and observes the crowds of people hurrying to and fro past stores, theatres, banks and other establishments, one naturally is struck by the contrast with the rural countryside.'[2] In differing ways and degrees Marx, Sombart and Weber, Dopsch, Maitland and Pirenne were all indeed struck by that contrast and tempted by the possibility of treating the town as a generic social structure. And the credibility of the notion of the town as a social entity *sui generis* has become extraordinarily well-established. To formulate an understanding, even a theory, of the town in those terms has been proclaimed an ideal by sociologists such as Hoselitz no less than by historians such as Braudel. Yet actual urban history, and to a lesser degree actual urban sociology, have proved graveyards of generalizations about the town. Fidel Castro remarked that the town is a cemetery of revolutionaries and resources; it seems to me it has been no less fatal to the idea that a town is a town.

The insistence on the possibility and desirability of treating the town, generically, as a social entity in itself and for itself that we find in so much of the literature is both natural and odd. It is natural in that the town is a striking phenomenon, odd in that the town is so plainly nothing more than a phenomenon. The trouble, perhaps, is that the town is a social form in which the essential

[1] Braudel, *Capitalism and material life*, p. 373.
[2] Harris and Ullman, *Annals Am. Acad. Pol. and Soc. Sci.* (1945), p. 7.

9

properties of larger systems of social relations are grossly concentrated and intensified – to a point where residential size, density and heterogeneity, the formal characteristics of the town, appear to be in themselves constituent properties of a distinct social order. Thus the western industrial city confronts us directly and forcibly with the contradiction Marx discerned within capitalism between the social and the industrial division of labour. But unless one's frame of reference already includes the idea of that contradiction what one 'observes' in such cities will be the apparently distinctively urban problems of segmental role relationships, anomie, vandalism, public squalor and the slum, or the less well-defined but seemingly no less urban processes by which the town accelerates, blocks or co-varies with economic growth. Faced with this intensification and dramatization the tendency to attribute analytical significance to the form at the expense of the relational substance becomes very powerful. Even historians who theoretically should have known much better succumb, often in the face of the evidence of their own research, to the plausible hypothesis that the town as such, or the quality of urbanism abstracted from it, must surely be an independent social structural reality and a decisive agency or variable in the process of social change. The fact that, within limits at least, interesting and often quite strong correlations can be identified between modes or levels of urbanism and other attributes of social systems such as *per capita* GNP, or industrialization or rates of crime has lent a good deal of force to this style of thought. Works such as Reissman's *The urban process* or Lerner's *The passing of traditional society* are entranced by such patterns of co-variance and build ambitiously upon them and the general relations that can be induced from them.[3] Nevertheless it is as true now as it was when Wirth wrote 'Urbanism as a way of life' that, as he put it, 'in the rich literature on the city we look in vain for a theory systematizing the available knowledge concerning the city as a social entity'.[4] It may be that one reason for this is that in an important analytical sense the city is *not* a social entity; that we have been victims of the fallacy of misplaced concreteness in treating it as such; and that one object of urban history and urban sociology now might be to get rid of the concept of the town.

An interesting example of the way in which even very perceptive

[3] Reissman, *Urban process*; Lerner, *Passing of traditional society*.
[4] Wirth, *Am. J. Soc.* (1938), p. 8.

historians can be distracted by the idea of the town is to be found in the work of Maurice Dobb. Quite a substantial part of *Studies in the development of capitalism* is devoted to assessing the role of towns in the transition from feudalism to capitalism.[5] Dobb's approach to this issue is loosely governed by the assumption of a general relationship between 'the decline of feudalism and the growth of towns', and more precisely by the proposition that 'so far as the growth of the market exercised a disintegrating influence on the structure of feudalism and prepared the soil for the growth of forces which were to weaken and supplant it, the story of this influence can largely be identified with the rise of towns'.[6] Read strictly rather than impressionistically such governing statements are of course remarkably weak and opaque. By implication towns are treated as a generic social entity and attention is directed to the possibility of an important relationship between what might be called 'townness' and the dissolution of feudal social relations. But neither the structure and dynamics of the implied relationship nor the specific properties of townness are ever articulated in clear and unambiguous general terms. By contrast particular towns are shown to have been involved in the growth of a market economy in all sorts of different, particular ways. The initial obscurity about the general nature of townness and its implications for feudalism is thus compounded as the discussion proceeds – but without the governing general ideas ever being overtly repudiated. The overall effect is thus profoundly disconcerting and ambiguous – as became clear in Dobb's subsequent debate with Paul Sweezy, in which the latter was able to find in the *Development of capitalism* a theory of the externality of towns in relation to feudalism, which Dobb in his turn could deny having held.[7] Having taken up (from Marx perhaps as much as from Maitland or Pirenne) an essentially mystifying conception of the town, Dobb does not reach the point of completely freeing himself from it, but he does resist it to the extent of refusing to reach the conclusion that there was anything specifically urban about the dissolution of feudalism, and indeed of not in the end presenting the issue in that way at all. But this leaves an odd tension beneath the surface of his analysis of the

---

[5] Dobb, *Development of capitalism*, pp. 33–127.
[6] *Ibid.* p. 70.
[7] Sweezy in Hilton (ed.), *Transition from feudalism to capitalism*, p. 40; and Dobb in *ibid.*

decline of feudalism. On the one hand there is the lurking belief that in principle the town as a generic social object must surely have a place in the story of the erosion and collapse of feudal social relations. On the other hand there is the increasingly firm knowledge that in practice it is the town as that sort of object that collapses when the workings of feudalism are examined.

The difficulty is that if one begins by defining feudalism as 'virtually identical with serfdom' as Dobb does,[8] rather than with a definition which stresses the internal contradictoriness of feudal exploitation, towns are virtually bound to appear as 'in a sense alien bodies whose growth aided in the disintegration of the feudal order' and so to invite attention.[9] But when attended to, the town disappears to be replaced first by numerous particular towns and then by a complex of market, political and cultural relations which are as it were enacted in towns but not in any exclusive sense of the town. Thus, it quickly emerges that one cannot, for example, regard the existence of towns as 'necessarily in all circumstances a solvent of feudal relations'.[10] Rather, it becomes clear that what looked to be an entity separable from the feudal world is in fact most ambiguously entangled with that world, 'half servants of and half parasites upon the body of the feudal economy'.[11] Moreover, no one relationship can be found to prevail between the town and feudal society so long as one treats the town as a special social object. Thus, Dobb begins by looking at the rise of towns in the early medieval period. He considers four theories of urban origins, emphasizing variously feudal military administration, the geography of long-distance trade, the concentration of agrarian production and the continuity of Roman urban settlements through the Dark Ages. It turns out that the origins of all the actual medieval towns discussed conform to several and conversely to no one of these theories and that accordingly 'we shall probably have to be content for the present with an eclectic explanation'.[12] But perhaps a complete eclecticism can be avoided and at least a modified version of the idea of the generic significance of the town preserved by distinguishing between some broad types of towns. A distinction is suggested between the feudal town, initiated by some feudal authority for military and administrative reasons, and the free town, emerging either from emancipated village communities or from the clustering

[8] Dobb, *Development of capitalism*, p. 35.   [9] *Ibid.* p. 71.
[10] *Ibid.* p. 71.   [11] *Ibid.* p. 71.   [12] *Ibid.* p. 75.

of unattached merchants around a market. Alas, 'no sharp line of demarcation...can be drawn' between such types; a large number of towns prove to be 'of intermediate type'.[13] And at this point the phenomenon of the town as a primary object of analysis begins to recede, giving way to the problem of the incapacity of feudal social relations to contain the processes of petty commodity production and exchange which feudalism itself generated. The transition from feudalism to capitalism ceases to be a change explained in terms of the rise of towns and is steadily more explicitly a matter of the struggle of different groups within the feudal order to dominate small-scale production and to appropriate the profits of trade. Particular towns are the political setting for particular versions of this struggle. The distinctive outcome of the struggle is explained not by the nature of the town but by the working-out of the contradiction between the social division of labour and the productive division of labour permeating feudalism as a whole and merely realized most acutely in the relatively concentrated social world of the town. In his later discussions with Sweezy and others Dobb completes the intellectual passage which is already implicit in the *Development of capitalism* and arrives at the view that far from towns being alien entities developed alongside feudalism, 'the rise of towns was [at least to some extent] a process internal to the feudal system'.[14] What has happened here is not that the town has moved from being an independent variable to become a dependent variable but that it has ceased to be an intrinsically problematic social object at all. The debate henceforth is about the specific ways in which feudal authorities were or were not dispossessed of control of petty production in town and country by groups and interests which feudal exploitation was of its own accord bound to create.

The flirtation of Marxist history with theories of the independent social reality of the town would seem, at least in this case, to have been quite short-lived. And yet the fact that it occurred at all, and the particular pattern of the way it occurs in Dobb's work, are both indicative of the much more serious involvement that is to be found in most other varieties of social and economic history. Marxism does after all involve assumptions and strategies of analysis which make it inherently unlikely that the town would prove to be a distinctive social structure. From this point of view the significant

[13] *Ibid.* p. 78.
[14] Dobb in Hilton (ed.), *Transition from feudalism to capitalism*, p. 60.

thing about Marx himself is not that he contributed to our stock of characteristically vague and distracting theoretical generalizations about towns but that, having said that the whole economic history of society is summed up in the movement of the antagonism between town and country, he went back to the analysis of whole systems of production, firmly ignoring the mirage of the 'separation between town and country': 'we pass it over, however, for the present', he says – and never returns to it.[15]

Elsewhere, however, the credibility of the town as a generic social object has survived undiminished. But curiously what has happened to attempts to theorize about the town in urban history and urban sociology, or even to formulate relatively definitive conceptions of urbanism, has really only been an extended and more elaborate version of what happened in the *Development of capitalism* – a retreat from the general to the particular, followed by a more or less explicit change in the terms of analysis. The belief in the possibility of treating the town as a special social entity has not always been as overt and deliberate as it was in Lampard's instruction that 'the urban historian should focus ever more sharply on topics and themes that are generically rather than incidentally urban', or in Sjoberg's assumption that 'certain structural elements are universal for all urban centres'.[16] But implicitly it has, for all its difficulties, won remarkably wide acceptance. Davis and Golden, for example, find no difficulty in maintaining that 'the city makes its own peculiar contribution to the process of economic development', or in asserting the existence of a direct relationship between urbanization and industrialization in which the former both indicates and stimulates the latter, even while they regret the fact that 'there is as yet no general science of cities'.[17] Wallerstein, whose remarkably ambitious attempt to construct a general economic history is notable for its ability to dispense with any direct attention to the phenomenon of the town, cannot resist a passing concession to an important body of urban theory, in the form of an argument that symbiotic or creative cities make no appearance in economic history until the late sixteenth century.[18] And even Finley, whose treatment of the ancient economy is for the most part firmly cast in terms of the

---

[15] Marx, *Capital*, i, p. 352.

[16] Lampard, *Econ. Dev. and Cult. Change* (1955), p. 81; Sjoberg, *Pre-industrial city*, p. 34.

[17] Davis and Golden, *Econ. Dev. and Cult. Change* (1955), pp. 7, 20.

[18] Wallerstein. *Modern world system*, p. 266.

relations of production of slave societies, tackles the question of town and country in the light of the idea of the ancient city as 'essentially parasitic'.[19]

The work of Wallerstein and Finley is representative of a large school of writers who, although they reject the idea of the unity of the urban phenomenon, still try to save the essential notion of the structural reality of the town by distinguishing between types of town. From Weber to Sjoberg and from Pirenne to Braudel this has always been the favoured procedure of relatively sophisticated devotees of the urban idea. As it appears that <u>the only characteristic which any significant number of theories of the town agree in identifying as distinctively urban is heterogeneity</u>,[20] and that for the rest no objective referent applicable to the town in general has been found, it is not surprising that those historians and sociologists who were nevertheless unwilling to surrender the concept of the town should have resorted to the idea of urban types. Hoselitz distinguishes between generative and parasitic towns; Weber contrasts the patrician and the plebeian city; Pirenne compares towns of the Liege type with towns of the Flemish type; Braudel, correctly observing that the value of such distinctions lies largely in the precision with which they point to specific variations in the social relations within towns, or in the form of division of labour between town and country, recognizes the possibility of an indefinite extension of types (which is to skate on very thin ice) but actually emphasizes three which he calls <u>open towns, closed towns and subject towns.</u> Perhaps the best known and certainly among sociologists the most influential exercise of this type, and one that well exemplifies both the attractions and the difficulties of the procedure as a whole, is Sjoberg's distinction between the industrial and the pre-industrial city. I shall discuss this in a little detail shortly, as one purpose of this paper is to suggest that, for all their relative sophistication, attempts to save the idea of the structural autonomy of the town by distinguishing between urban types are really no less mystifying, and only a little more fruitful, than the attempt to treat the town as a unitary social object or urbanism as a uniform social tendency. First, however, some aspects of the latter attempt deserve attention.

Few if any now defend the most ambitious and thoroughgoing version of the effort to constitute the town as a social object

[19] Finley, *Ancient economy*, p. 140.   [20] Dewey, *Am. J. Soc.* (1960).

– Robert Redfield's notion of the folk–urban continuum.[21] Yet a great deal of the criticism of Redfield rests on the view that what was wrong with the continuum was not its formalism but the fact that because Redfield chose to treat the town as merely the opposite of the village he failed to grasp the really distinctive features of the town as a social entity. Thus Reissman, after conceding the general irrelevance and incompetence of the folk–urban continuum as a basis for the close analysis of urban social relations, still concludes that the problem for urban theory is mainly to identify the city more precisely: 'An urban theory cannot consider the city only by way of contrast with the small town, but has to cope with the city as a phenomenon in its own right.'[22] And Hillery, for whom again 'the city is first and foremost a social system' in its own right, remains even closer to the procedural core of Redfield's work, seeking to make a series of conceptual deductions about the city from a comparison between a formal model of the city and a formal model of the folk village.[23] Abandoning the idea of an empirically given continuum he succeeds in abstracting 'the city' still more completely from the actual social setting of any actual cities. The city is characterized by frequent direct and indirect interaction, by the presence of co-operation, competition and conflict, by a territorial integration based on economic and political and spatial arrangements, by geographic segregation, centralization and decentralization, by unstable boundaries, by a combination of localistic and cosmopolitan activities, by mobility and continuance, by some degree of ethnocentrism and self-consciousness among its inhabitants, by an extensive division of labour marked both by the plurality and variety of norms prevailing in different sectors and by a preponderant emphasis on contractual norms. This is to spell out the idea of heterogeneity with a vengeance. The distinctive construct in terms of which these traits are co-ordinated in the model of the city is the proposition that 'the city is a localized system integrated by contracts and families', the folk village by contrast being envisaged as a 'localized system of families cooperating by means of mutual aid'.[24] The immediate pay-off from all this conceptual clarification is hardly very startling: both New Orleans and Timbuctoo are cities, but New Orleans has less in common with

[21] Redfield, *Folk culture of Yucatan*; and cf. Miner, *Am. Soc. Rev.* (1952).
[22] Reissman, *Urban process*, p. 138.
[23] Hillery, *Communal organizations*, pp. 252–311.   [24] *Ibid.* p. 48.

the folk village. The larger and longer term purpose of the exercise on the other hand remains, as seems to be invariably the case in this sort of work, curiously unfulfilled. Hillery's intention was to develop a theory of communal organizations, that is of social systems which although 'heavily institutionalized...lack defining goals'.[25] The city is a particular type of communal organization typified by the distinctive manner in which it functions in respect of three components – space, co-operation and the family. And the point of theorizing is said to be to be able to move from data to prediction and back to data again. But this is not what happens at the end of Hillery's book. Instead we have a familiar list of as yet unresolved problems raised by the conception of the city as a social entity – does the city spur technological change or *vice versa*, how can one specify the relationships between communal organizations, how can one possibly determine in any theoretically adequate way where the city ends and other communal organizations begin – followed by a recognition that there is for the present little prospect of 'an acceptable ideal type of the city', and by an equally familiar final call for the development of new general perspectives on the ways in which cities are integrated and, in particular, for more 'careful socioanthropological studies of communities over several generations'.[26] It is striking to see how persistently attempts to constitute an urban entity as an object of analysis in history or sociology do end by evaporating in this way. I have little doubt that had Braudel actually followed up his proposal to treat the 'town in itself, outside the economy or civilisation containing it' he would, despite his confident claim that 'all towns have certain common characteristics and that such characteristics more or less persist from one period to another', have reached the same irresolute and confused final state.[27] The fact that even before this he has already referred to towns as at once 'so many electric transformers', 'oppressive, parasitical formations' and 'accelerators of all historical time', certainly suggests as much. And in fact his generalizing efforts are very quickly set aside in favour of a quite different kind of analysis: the attempt to discover 'one basic language for all the cities of the world within their very depths' simply does not materialize.[28]

[25] *Ibid.* pp. 148, 186.   [26] *Ibid.* pp. 191, 196.
[27] Braudel, *Capitalism and material life*, p. 373.
[28] *Ibid.* p. 374.

Reissman by contrast travels a good deal further along the path of Hillery and Redfield before effectively abandoning the idea of the reality of the town.[29] He begins in a quite modest and sensible way by recognizing the absence of 'an adequate urban theory' and the extreme complexity of the phenomena such a theory would have to explain.[30] However, having noted these difficulties, he moves briskly on to state what in the circumstances must be regarded as a highly ambitious major assumption: 'that urban development in the West and in the underdeveloped countries today is the same process', and to seek on that basis to construct 'a theory of urbanization' and a 'theory of urban society'.[31] His purpose is to 'gain an understanding of how underdeveloped nations might move' and 'equally important, . . .of the dynamics of growth for Western cities as well'.[32] This project does not of course require a concept of the city as a discrete social entity, and it becomes increasingly unclear as Reissman's argument proceeds whether he has such a concept or not. He certainly starts out with one. But in the event the experience of a large number of societies is compared in terms of the relationship between four components within the 'whole process of social change'.[33] These components are urban growth, industrialization, the power of the middle class and the rise of nationalism. If we ignore such passing remarks as the claim that 'urbanization created a massive social revolution that eventually transformed the whole of society', what we are then offered is an analysis of the relationship between these components, which indeed suggests that variations in that relationship are interestingly and significantly related to variations in other aspects of 'the whole process of social change'.[34] Reissman has in fact moved towards a general analysis of social change, which is a theory of urbanization only because he chooses to use the term urbanization as a synonym for general social change. The place of the urban factor within that analysis is in the end really quite obscure. At the very least we have moved from the idea of a theory which would 'encompass a wide range of social phenomena as products of the industrial city', and from ideas of city as an actor 'imposing its ways' or 'achieving dominance', to a view of the nation rather than the city as 'the meaningful unit for the analysis of urbanization' and to an attempt to 'see the city

---

[29] Reissman, *Urban process*, pp. 122–94.   [30] *Ibid.* p. 148.
[31] *Ibid.* pp. 167–8.   [32] *Ibid.* p. 168.   [33] *Ibid.* p. 169.
[34] *Ibid.* p. 169.

through an analysis of industrial society' as a whole, since 'the path to urban analysis must run through a broader societal analysis' – even though the industrial city is still thought of as 'the dominating social feature of the society to which it belongs'.[35]

The explicit uncertainty here is of course very reminiscent of the implicit uncertainty we found in the work of Dobb. The concept of the city is preserved although it is less and less clear what the city is or does. By contrast, the idea of the industrial city as a field of action created as a 'social consequence' of struggles for power on the part of some sort of middle class, is specified with real force and precision. But if the emergence of the city is a consequence of particular social conflicts, why can we not continue to see the whole pattern of social change in those terms instead of succumbing to the idea that other aspects of that process are somehow consequences of the city? There is at best an uneasiness and ambiguity about the structure of urban theory here which make it difficult to know what relationships are really being proposed as decisive. The fact that conscientious historians and sociologists, who have accepted the conception of the town as a social entity or agent in its own right, do end up in ambiguities of this kind, suggests that the relevant issues might be a good deal clearer if we could stop ourselves surrendering to that conception in the first place. Faced with the reification of the town it is difficult not to recall the words Marx applied to the phenomenon of the reification of value: 'The philistine's and vulgar economist's way of looking at things stems from the fact that it is only the direct form of manifestation of relations that is reflected in their brains and not their inner connections.'[36] It is the capacity of a sense of inner connection, to break through conceptions derived from the form of manifestation in the history and sociology of towns, that makes attempts to derive an urban theory from an undifferentiated conception of the town as a social entity typically inconclusive.

I should say at this point that I am not necessarily questioning the pertinence of attempting to trace patterns of concomitant variation between forms of urbanism or levels of urbanization and other formal or substantial properties of social systems – or the value in an indicative sense of some of the patterns that have been observed on that basis. In particular I would accept the value as indicators

---

[35] *Ibid.* p. 198.
[36] Marx in Marx and Engels, *Selected correspondence*, p. 230.

of the correlations established by Gibbs and Martin between urbanization and the division of labour, level of technological development and dispersion of objects of consumption within societies.[37] I would even accept their inference that urbanization 'depends on' those factors. What I am suggesting is, first, that such relationships are often much more opaque, and when investigated much more spurious in a substantive sense, than they appear at first sight – so that when one attempts to establish them in closer and more exact terms they tend to lose their apparent autonomy, and be rediscovered as elements in some much more extended and ramified train of relationships. One of the best known examples of this outcome is S. K. Mehta's very convincing demonstration of the way in which the theory of the 'primate city' as an obstacle to economic growth, and indeed as a distinct type of city for any other analytical purpose, does not stand up to empirical scrutiny; instead the mobilization of a series of rather good measures of both urban primacy and economic growth sustains a series of negative or, at best, extremely weak conclusions about the existence of any sort of relationship between these features.[38] Secondly I am suggesting that, even where relatively strong statistical relationships are found between forms of urbanism on the one hand and modes or stages of economic growth on the other, we are not justified in treating such relationships as in any way self-explanatory, nor can we satisfactorily explain why these relationships exist or even how they came to exist by postulating an urban factor, the town in itself, interacting in its own right with such other factors, abstract as they are. An interesting demonstration of this difficulty is provided by Epstein's effort to make something of Gluckman's version of the urban reification – the claim that 'an African townsman is a townsman' whose behaviour is accordingly to be understood in terms of the distinctive 'needs of urban life'.[39] What emerges from the attempt to discuss the development of African societies on that basis, as Epstein rather modestly puts it, is a rather pressing 'need for sharper and more varied conceptual tools'.[40] Not only does a conception of the needs of urban life derived from European experience persistently get in the way of an understanding of African

[37] Gibbs and Martin, *Am. Soc. Rev.* (1962).
[38] Mehta, *Demography* (1964); and cf. Jefferson, *Geog. Rev.* (1939).
[39] Epstein, *Current Anthropology* (1967); Gluckman, *Cahiers d'études africaines* (1960).
[40] Epstein, *Current Anthropology*, p. 277.

townsmen, but generalizations about the effects of the town based on the experience of one African people are, Epstein shows in case after case, persistently falsified by consideration of the experience of other African peoples, often in neighbouring communities. An African townsman turns out to be very definitely not just, and certainly not decisively, a townsman, but very much a Barotse townsman, a Bemba townsman, a Yoruba townsman, or something equally specific and equally differentiated on a non-urban basis. Nor is the situation very much improved if we try to distinguish between types of towns – although this has now become an ortho-dox device in urban analysis both among historians and among sociologists.

The logic impelling a move towards a typology of towns has already been discussed in looking at the work of Dobb. It is particularly evident in the work of Hoselitz, as is the deeper pull of good sense away from making the town an object of study at all. Thus, in the first of his two major papers on this theme, 'The role of cities in the economic growth of underdeveloped countries', Hoselitz begins with a fairly standard attempt to list the things that towns 'do' for economic growth – the provision of a cheap labour, the creation of a labour force 'committed to industry', the cultivation of a spirit of functional rationality and so forth.[41] Questions are asked about the extent to which 'urban culture' is a vehicle for changing values and beliefs; towns are described as both the chief locus and the main force for the introduction of 'new ideas and new ways of doing things'.[42] At the same time it becomes clear that one of the most decisive new ways of doing things, in Hoseltiz's general view of economic development, has to do with the creation of a working class obliged to sell its labour for wages in a formally free labour market – and it is not suggested, and would of course be very hard to show, that this sort of innovation is in any really specific sense a product of urbanism. Again, although a number of effects are initially attributed to the town, it is quickly noted that the 'high correlation' between urbanization and these effects is in fact far from perfect and by no means indicative of a self-explanatory closed relationship – thus it is actually not the case that a suitable labour force for economic growth can be produced 'only in the town or city', as had been

[41] Hoselitz, *J. Pol. Econ.* (1953).
[42] *Ibid.* p. 199.

claimed at the outset.[43] As the paper proceeds the author allows, in a progressively more explicit way, that there are radical differences in the way different cities 'function' and in the 'effects' they have from the point of view of economic growth.[44] The idea of distinguishing between types of towns follows naturally from this concession, first in the form of a consideration of Pirenne's distinction between towns of the Liege type and towns of the Flemish type and then, in Hoselitz's second paper, in his own much more ambitious and sweeping distinction between parasitic and generative cities.[45] Meanwhile, the far more fundamental revision hinted at in his passing reference to towns as a locus for change and as a force for change (which might have led to the view that towns are significant merely as a locus and not as a force) is not attempted. The idea of the town doing things (such as developing 'new sets of ideas and practices') persists, and the plausibility of his idea of the town as a social force is accordingly undiminished by the proposal to distinguish between types of towns in terms of their positive or negative relationship to economic growth.[46] Hoselitz merely moves now from the proposition that 'the growth and development of cities is a necessary condition of economic development', to an attempt to explain, on the basis of the contrast between generative and parasitic types of town, why and how it is that the formation, existence and growth of some towns has a favourable impact on economic growth, while that of some others plainly has 'an opposite impact'.[47]

The problem is refined by the introduction of a further distinction between economic and cultural change, so that a town may for example be thought of as culturally generative but economically parasitic, and by a recognition that towns have histories and that the degree to which a town is generative or parasitic may change over time. But the problem at the heart of the exercise is still the wrong problem. The introduction of the idea of urban types does not allow Hoselitz to break with the central misconception of the town as a social agent, or with the consequent view that the appropriate question to ask about, say, Rome is whether 'it' was 'a factor contributory to the economic decline and stagnation of Italy'.[48] Nevertheless – as with Reissman and Dobb – a quite different and

[43] *Ibid.* p. 197.   [44] *Ibid.* pp. 200–3.
[45] Hoselitz, *Econ. Dev. and Cult. Change* (1955).
[46] *Ibid.* pp. 279, 281.   [47] *Ibid.* p. 280.   [48] *Ibid.* p. 283.

much less mystified type of problem is also present in Hoselitz's work. This is particularly evident in his discussion of colonial capitals. Little or no attempt is made to demonstrate the 'effects' of Batavia or Rangoon as exemplifying the impact on economic growth of any particular type of city. Increasingly the treatment of these cities is swallowed up in the analysis of a 'culturally generative but economically parasitic process of urbanization' associated with colonialism, and at times the focus moves away from the city as an object of study altogether.[49] Thus, Rangoon is in the end presented as 'the main locus at which the culture of Burma became affected and modified by that of the West'.[50] What is interesting about Rangoon has ceased to be the way in which it as a city acts on economic history, and is now the way in which its particular cultural and structural forms and experiences can be shown to embody the relations of domination and subordination of a variety of indigenous and foreign groups and, in particular, to enact the process of colonial penetration and rule. What has happened here is, once again, not that the city has moved from being an independent variable to become a dependent variable in the analysis of economic growth, but that the study of economic growth has been effectively detached from the whole idea of the city and cast in other terms − except in the sense that particular cities constitute sites within which more general structures of power and struggles for power are very dramatically expressed. But again this move is not achieved explicitly. Hoselitz's essays are in the end as indeterminate in this respect as those of the other writers I have discussed. Like them he discovers the unsatisfactoriness of a reified conception of the town, but like them he cannot bring himself to reject it and start again.

The work of Braudel, Sjoberg and Max Weber comes much nearer to making this necessary break. I have already touched on Braudel's admirable failure to keep any of the promises with which he starts his discussion of early modern towns. The bulk of that discussion turns out to be a characteristically well-observed analysis of the implication of a series of particular towns in particular societies. And even at this level the town is often not treated as an object in its own right − what has to be said about the way London generated economic growth turns out to be a matter of the ways in which powers and interests within British society as a whole

---

[49] *Ibid.* pp. 285–90.   [50] *Ibid.* p. 285.

worked on one another within London. It is a matter of London as an arena for a particular system of class and status and party, as an embodiment of decisions about who was to exploit whom or who would be relatively free from exploitation, realized in particular patterns of social mobility and social closure – not at all of London as an urban entity. In the same way, it is not Venice's urbanism but the caste-like stratification achieved by the Venetian nobility, not St Petersburg as a town but the social consequences of a particular kind of political domination realized in St Petersburg, that occupy Braudel's attention. And his general conclusion, insofar as he offers one, is not surprisingly almost wholly at odds with his introduction; the town in the end is seen as 'what society, economy and politics allow it to be'.[51] Implicated in a nodal manner in these larger systems, towns are stages on which their distinctive propensities and contradictions are uniquely well acted out – thus St Petersburg marvellously demonstrates an 'almost monstrous structural disequilibrium'.[52] What is at issue is 'growth in the economy of the ancien regime' as a whole, and the historical interest of the towns of the ancien regime is found, not in any specifically urban contribution to economic growth or stagnation, but in the ways in which they can be shown to display the 'deep-seated disequilibrium, asymmetrical growth and irrational and unproductive investment' of each particular national version of that social order.[53] Braudel's distinction between open, closed and subject types of town fades away as his essay proceeds. But unlike some urban typologies it manifestly does do some useful work. And it does so because it is a typology based, not on presumed variations in some intrinsically urban factor or even on varying relationships between such a factor and other properties of social systems, but on variations in the relations of social power within and between urban and non-urban social groups. In the open town no-one has detached any significant power from the structures of an agrarian world. The subject town by contrast is decisively shaped by the political ascendancy of an equally external state power. The closed town represents a distinctive appropriation of power by those within a town in relation to both farmers and princes. The secret of western economic growth is to be found in the relative success of attempts to create and maintain closed towns. In this sense 'the towns caused the West to advance'.[54]

---

[51] Braudel, *Capitalism and material life*, pp. 439–40.
[52] *Ibid.* p. 418.   [53] *Ibid.* p. 439.   [54] *Ibid.* p. 411.

But what does this mean? Not that we have found a special type of town, 'free worlds', in which economic growth *ipso facto* is encouraged, but that the structures and anomalies of western feudalism permitted open towns to be turned into or replaced by closed towns and that those who seized this opportunity were, in those circumstances, able to create closed towns strong enough to allow them to institutionalize the social relations that suited them in a relatively secure and enduring way. And what were these social relations? To whom did the distinctive freedoms, opportunities and profits of the closed town accrue? Not surely to 'the towns', as Braudel says at one point, but, as he says almost immediately afterwards, to their 'authorities and merchant entrepreneurs'.[55] It was not really the towns that caused the West to advance but the peculiar inability of western feudalism to prevent these people from maximizing their advantages which they did typically within the institutional form of the closed town. The move from open to closed towns was a move to consolidate the power of such groups against feudal and landed authorities and against the artisans and labourers within the towns. Both internally and externally the town is an institutional expression of power. It is this cross-cutting perception of power that Braudel has in common with Sjoberg and Weber, although it is least explicit in his case, and the continuing tension between urban and more usefully social categories is accordingly most apparent in his work.

Sjoberg's distinction between the pre-industrial and the industrial city is grounded in two principal variations, in technology and in social and especially political power.[56] The town is seen as a dependent variable, its type being determined by these major variations. In fact Sjoberg's break with earlier urban theory is not quite as radical as that; the town is still treated as a real social entity ('we see the city per se as a variable to be reckoned with'); and in some contexts it is still seen as an autonomous social agent ('despite our criticism of the Wirth school of thought, we recognize that the city is a factor "determining" selected types of social phenomena').[57] Moreover, there is a considerable uncertainty in Sjoberg's work as to the relative importance of his two non-urban determinants of urban type. Thus in *The preindustrial city*, 'we take technology as the key independent variable',[58] whereas in a

---

[55] *Ibid.* p. 404.   [56] *Sjoberg, Preindustrial city*, p. 17.   [57] *Ibid.* p. 15.
[58] *Ibid.* p. 7.

theoretical article written a few years later, when the empirical strength of the relationship between technology and urban types had already been vigorously questioned, especially for Asia, urban patterns are held to 'result mainly from. . .changes in the political or power structure on the societal level'.[59] This quite overt change of emphasis is very important in permitting Sjoberg to treat human activities rather than social forms as the real source of economic growth or stagnation. In this context the core of his contribution to urban history is not the typology of cities at all, and certainly not the rather shaky construct of the pre-industrial city, but the notion of 'contradictory functional requirements which in turn give rise to contradictory structures'.[60] The requirements are those of groups variously engaged in maintaining or usurping power and the structures are the institutional forms within which power is appropriated or challenged – including the structures of urbanism. Available technology creates limits of possibility for the extraction of surplus within a society. Within those limits what happens to and in towns is a matter of the ways in which surplus is indeed extracted, appropriated, consumed or re-invested by particular social groups – which in turn is a matter of their relative power to define and pursue their own interests. Within such a framework it clearly should be possible to explain, not only the conformity or non-conformity of given towns to particular constructed types of town, but more usefully to say something about the involvement of particular towns in particular processes of economic growth. A remarkable feature of *The preindustrial city*, however, is the contrast between Sjoberg's ability to explan the general parasitism of pre-industrial cities, and his noticeable inability to account for the historical transformation of some pre-industrial cities into transitional or industrial cities. His success in the first case is largely a matter of his insistence on treating the city as an enactment of class and political power relationships. His failure in the second case is perhaps equally a matter of his insistence on treating technology as an independent variable. To a lesser degree it is also a matter of his dependence on the notion of urban types. The pre-industrial city is seen as paralysed by the contradictory requirements of the social groups, and especially the 'bifurcated' class structure, which its distinctive institutional forms and its distinctive history express.[61]

[59] Sjoberg, *Internat. J. Comp. Soc.* (1963), p. 107.
[60] Sjoberg, *Preindustrial city*, pp. 13, 140, 330.
[61] *Ibid.* p. 110.

Where, then, does economic growth come from? Either some actual pre-industrial cities must be allowed to be significantly unlike the type of the pre-industrial city in some rather important respect, or the notion of contradictory functional requirements within pre-industrial societies must be assigned even greater importance and specified more variously as an internal source of change, or technological development, the history of technology, must be invoked as an essentially external factor in terms of which the appearance of new urban forms can be explained. Sjoberg's initial emphasis on technology leads him to the last of these possibilities; transition 'is associated with certain crucial advances in the technological sphere'.[62] Either of the first two possibilities would seem to me to be more plausible. Both of course would involve one in effectively abandoning the notion of urban types, as well as that of the town as an entity *per se*, as one's decisive framework of analysis. The whole point about technology is that it is a resource not a determinant – this is explicitly so for Sjoberg who repeatedly rejects any sort of technological determinism. The question must therefore arise of how technological resources are created and of why they are used or neglected. And the answer to these questions can surely only lead us back to the world of contradictory social requirements and differential social powers from which we started. Nevertheless, although he is ultimately still a prisoner of the concepts with which he began, Sjoberg has come closer than any of the other writers so far considered to what might be called an authentic sociology of the town – that is, to a sociology that rejects the idea of the social reality of the town.

All this is not of course to deny that many people apart from sociologists and historians do treat towns as social realities – just as they treat magic as a real force and the national interest as a real interest. But the task of social analysis is to say something about why and how such seeming realities are constructed socially, which is not likely to happen if they are accepted at their face value. Like the rabbit produced from a conjurer's hat, the ramparts of the town identify an enterprise not an entity; the material presence is not enough to prove that the apparent process of materialization actually occurred. Attempts to get behind the presence of the town have been couched most effectively in terms of encompassing relations of social power which towns embody and in which they are

[62] *Ibid.* p. 329.

deeply and thoroughly implicated; in different ways all the authors discussed in this paper (who in this respect represent a far greater body of urban historians and sociologists) have moved with different degrees of self-consciousness in that direction. The one writer who conspicuously starts from the point towards which almost all other writers on towns seem to be uneasily or easily moving is Max Weber.[63]

The town appears in *Economy and society*, not as an empirical entity such as the party or the sect, not as a necessary analytical construct indicating a distinct type of social action such as the traditional legitimation of authority or rational economic action, but because Weber believes that an episode crucial to the development of capitalism in the West occurred within a particular category of towns. This was the establishment of 'non-legitimate domination'.[64] The concept of non-legitimate domination governs the whole of Weber's long discussion of towns and the point of that discussion is to establish the uniqueness of the western medieval town as an institutionalization of a type of usurped power peculiarly conducive to the intensive pursuit of rational economic action. Non-legitimate domination and rational economic action are the important points of reference of the argument, not the town. This point has not always been clearly seen because Weber is here, as always, excessively fascinated by concepts, models, ideal types and other formal devices of analysis. As a result he frequently appears to be engaged on the construction of a theory of towns and their relation to economic growth based on a set of elaborate distinctions between types of towns. Numerous distinctions of type are deployed: the princely city and the plebeian city; the consumer city and the merchant city; the occidental city; the medieval city and the patrician city of antiquity. Nevertheless, three features of Weber's thought stand out quite clearly behind this screen of concepts. First, the screen itself is a distraction: 'it is not our intention to produce casuistic distinctions and specialization of concepts. . .nor do we need to stress that actual cities almost always represent mixed types'.[65] Secondly, the classifications of type he proposes are all clearly grounded in a single type of empirical variation – in the mode of power within given towns – and are used to focus in an increasingly specific way on the peculiar and historically unique

---

[63] Weber, *Economy and society*, pp. 1212–1367.
[64] *Ibid.* p. 1212.   [65] *Ibid.* p. 1217.

constellation of power embodied in the towns of medieval Europe. Power is of course a complex multi-dimensional type of relationship for Weber, varying at least in terms of class, status and office, and it is this sense of the complexity of power that guides what appears to be the construction of a complex conception of types of town. Thirdly, Weber does clearly distinguish between what he regards as a genuinely sociological conception of the town and a variety of economic, political and other conceptions. The essential feature of the former is that it seizes on the process of usurpation. Social activity is concentrated spatially in a town or city for the purpose of constituting or evading some form of power. The point about the medieval European towns is that they reveal a pattern of domination in which the burghers, having broken their dependence on the legitimate traditional (feudal) authorities of the societies around them, imposed themselves equally illegitimately upon artisans and peasants, who were forced now to depend upon them. More specifically still, Weber suggests, the social instrument of this illegitimate domination was 'usurpation through an act of rational association, a sworn confraternization of the burghers'.[66] And conversely, 'it is quite indicative of what strata were the driving power behind such acts of usurpation that in Cologne even at a much later time the guild of the rich, which from the point of view of legitimacy was nothing but a private club of wealthy citizens, could successfully assert the right to confer citizenship'.[67] The form as distinct from the substance of such usurpation was typically the creation of the town as a legal person – the first and perhaps the most consequential reification of urban experience. The *coniurationes* could thus be said to have 'conjured' the town into legal existence to legitimate their non-legitimate domination.

It is Weber's claim that this particular usurpatory outcome of the struggle for power embodied in all towns was, at once, uniquely permitted by the conditions of European feudalism and uniquely conducive to the building of the cultural and economic base from which capitalism eventually took off. It is an odd irony that although cities figure in Weber's own analysis only as legal and institutional expressions, forms of manifestation, of real and very concretely organized impositions or usurpations of power on the part of very clearly defined social groups, his discussion of these processes

[66] *Ibid.* p. 1250.   [67] *Ibid.* p. 1251.

should have been commonly interpreted as though it was a contribution to a theory of the city involving a peculiarly simple notion of the essence of urbanism as a matter of communal association. He has thus been treated as an arch perpetrator of an error about towns which he almost uniquely avoided making. It is indicative of the strength of the urban reification that the piece of work Weber envisaged as a discussion of non-legitimate domination should have been published after his death under the title *The city*, and that it should have taken forty years for the mistake to be corrected.[68] It is of course true that, if Weber is not misinterpreted in this way, he cannot possibly be invoked as in any way authorizing the treatment of the town as a social agency in itself, but would have to be read as directing attention, especially so far as students of economic growth are concerned, away from the phenomena of the town and towards the activity of the social construction, maintenance and usurpation of power. Insofar as this process is the proper context for the history and sociology of economic growth we need many studies of towns – because that is where the process in its many varieties occurs. But we can do without studies of the town.

The town, then, is an *explanandum*, not an *explanans*. Within the analysis of a chosen social system the relationships concentrated spatially in towns present themselves for explanation. But, if we are to avoid mystification, they should present themselves specifically in relation to our understanding of the system in which they occur and not as exemplars of an autonomous urban reality. Many of the historians I have discussed – Pirenne, Wallerstein and Finley, for example – whose concern is in effect only with a particular social system within a defined period of time, do substantially accept that limitation and their indulgence in the imagery of urbanism and urban types is to that extent misleading. There is, however, a large – and for the sociologist a preponderant – literature in which that measure of scepticism in urban analysis has still to be achieved. Taken as a whole the record of urban history and urban sociology suggests that it is extraordinarily difficult to resist the idea that 'a town is a town'; and that strong measures need to be taken to protect the scholar from that sort of fantasy.

The relevant measures would have to consist not just of contrary assertions but of a grounded demonstration that some framework of analysis other than the idea of the town itself, or of urbanism,

[68] Weber, *The city*.

will make better sense of the history of towns and prove to possess that explanatory power which the urban unit itself so regularly turns out to lack. The frameworks of analysis characteristically used by urban historians and sociologists who do not surrender to the mirage of the town itself are commonly the 'society', the 'culture', the 'economy' and the 'mode of production'; or more narrowly *ad hoc* specifications of those categories, such as 'medieval Europe', 'Renaissance Italy', 'feudalism', 'capitalism', 'imperialism', 'pre-industrial England' and so forth. It is perhaps an open empirical question which of these larger analytical contexts will prove most useful to us. But for my own part I would suggest that considerable progress might be made in understanding the social nature and historical functions of towns if we took to considering them in relation to a larger social context which, following Weber, we might call the complex of domination. By a complex of domination I understand an ongoing and at least loosely integrated struggle to constitute and elaborate power. The conception has a certain dynamism, and it points directly towards the analysis of social action and relationships and to the construction and destruction of institutions through action and relationships, without intruding spurious social entities between the researcher and the world he is trying to understand. From this point of view towns become interesting as moments in a process of usurpation and defence, consolidation, appropriation and resistance; as battles rather than as monuments.

Such an approach has the advantage of emphasizing both the singularity and the fruitfulness of the contribution of Max Weber among urban sociologists. More to the point, it also allows us to draw together, in something that might begin to add up to a body of useful middle-order generalizations about towns, a good deal of the work of those urban historians who have seen beyond the illusion of urbanism to the real relationships out of which towns are constituted. On inspection many of the best case studies and many of the most convincing general commentaries in the field of urban history prove to be, often implicitly, studies of and commentaries on action and relationships within a complex of domination; the town or towns in question are treated as expressions and realizations of that sort of struggle. The world of Pericles or of Burgomaster F. H. Oestens appears to have at least that much in common with the world of Joseph Chamberlain or of T. Dan Smith.

The notion of a complex of domination is deliberately a vague, unspecific, highly generalized one. It is offered as an indication of what it might be useful to look for, not as any kind of precise account of what will be found. It is not in any sense merely another version of the idea that 'a town is a town', but an orienting device suggesting a profitable way in which towns could be used as sites for historical and sociological analysis. The conception thus points towards certain types of relationship as being especially likely to help us understand the structure and functions of a town in relation to its larger setting in time and space. It points towards the dialectic of power and freedom; towards the imposition of power as law and the usurpation of power as freedom; towards a world of regulation and resistance, incorporation and escape and reincorporation. Such patterns vary greatly in their detail and are highly complicated and many-sided; almost invariably, for example, the champions of freedom in one relationship within such a complex are practitioners of oppression in other relationships. What I am suggesting is just that it is such patterns that towns pre-eminently invite us to identify and disentangle; that the history of towns commands attention as a history of appropriation and resistance, internal and external war, defiance and monopoly, a history in which resources are concentrated for the pursuit of some struggle, for the enhancement of power. Alfred creates the English burghs as an instrument of war. The settlements of the Venetian lagoon coalesce to impose restraints on the trade in salt and fish, to destroy Commachio as an alternative commercial centre and to mount an effective force against the pirates of the Adriatic.[69] Within European feudalism as a whole the making of a town was a means of breaking both the status and the class prescriptions of feudal social relations, of establishing fiscal autonomy, appropriating the products of labour more directly, rooting personal freedom in power over property (burgage tenure for example), and collective freedom in the larger power of the trade or craft monopoly. What happened to such projects seems to have been bluntly and often brutally (witness the fates of San Gimignano or Duurstede) a matter of the relative powerfulness of the feudal and non-feudal parties to them. Or again, the history of Amsterdam throughout the seventeenth century is the record of a ruthless attempt to protect the business of the Bicker family and the other great trading houses that composed the city's government against

[69] Lane, *Venice*.

all comers, Spanish, Swedish or French; the Stadholder, the province of Holland or the Dutch Republic; or of course *het grauw*, the mob.[70] It was not entirely playfully that the merchants of Amsterdam chose to have themselves painted as soldiers.

In sum, once one is alerted to it the Hobbesian quality of urban life – a war of all against all contained within a contrived and precarious domination – reveals itself everywhere. And a suitable task for urban historians and sociologists seems to be to unravel the specific complexes of domination in which particular cities are embedded and which they restlessly express.

[70] Burke, *Venice and Amsterdam.*

2. *Economic Growth and Towns in Classical Antiquity*

KEITH HOPKINS

Was there economic growth in classical antiquity? If we take the Bronze Age at the end of the second millennium BC as our base line, the answer is definitely yes. In the early Homeric world, weapons and sacrificial ornaments were usually made of bronze; iron was an object of treasure, and so it remained in north-western Europe until much later.[1] Greek myths of the world's evolution from the Age of Gold to the Ages of Silver, Bronze and finally Iron, reflected real changes in the material base of culture. But by the beginning of the last millennium BC, the transition to iron as a cutting edge had begun; among Greek weapons found by archaeologists, the great majority were made of iron not bronze.[2] Over the next thousand years, the Athenians, Macedonians and Romans successively conquered empires with the cutting edge of iron swords, and increased the productivity of land by tilling it with iron-shod ploughs. It was this increase in agricultural productivity which made the growth of towns possible.

But if we ask whether there was economic growth between Periclean Athens at the end of the fifth century BC and the age of the Antonines in the second century AD in the Roman Empire, then the answer is more complicated. We take Periclean Athens as our base because it represented the peak of economic development in the classical city-state. Let us first exploit the distinction between *aggregate* and *per capita* growth.[3] If we take the whole Mediterranean basin, or the Roman Empire at its largest extent, as the area of our study, then the growth in aggregate produce is again beyond

[1] Archaeologists have found hoards of hundreds of iron bars in Britain (Tylecote, *Metallurgy*, p. 207). In Gaul iron bars were used as currency, which suggests rarity (Caesar, *Gallic War*, 5, 12).

[2] Snodgrass, *Proc. Prehist. Soc.* (1965), found that of 88 surviving cutting weapons and knives from northern Greece datable to 1050–900 BC, 77 were made of iron and only 11 of bronze.

[3] My discussion at this point owes a lot to Gould, *Economic growth in history*; I found Hicks, *A theory of economic history*, provocative, though often wondered how far his model coincided with historical realities. Throughout this essay I am in repeated debt to and continuous debate with Finley, *The ancient economy*, especially pp. 123ff.

doubt. The gross product of the whole Roman Empire significantly exceeded the gross product of the hundreds of tribes and city-states which existed in the same area in the fifth century BC. Settled agriculture, flourishing towns, impressive monuments, the whole panoply of classical culture and of archaeological evidence from north Africa to the north of Britain provide convincing demonstration that a sizeable surplus was being produced and consumed throughout the Roman Empire, and that the average standard of living was higher over a wider area than ever before. But if we compare *per capita* product in classical Athens with *per capita* product in any prosperous provincial town in the Roman Empire, then the differences (which may have existed) are extremely difficult to trace.

Our overriding problem here is of course shortage of data; we know a huge amount about the ancient world, especially in the realm of ideas and culture, but rarely enough to give sophisticated answers to problems of economic history. The historian or social scientist who wants to trace economic developments back to an earlier age will find to his dismay either unco-ordinated details of archaeological finds, fragments from historical sources, or theories of economic growth retrospectively applied. The rest of this paper is devoted to a discussion of the role of towns in economic development. Inevitably it ranges beyond towns, because their contribution to economic change can be understood only in the context of the political system in which they existed, and of the rural hinterland on which they depended. I shall concentrate on the Roman Empire, because that is what I know most about.

My first main point has already been implied: major changes in aggregate product in the Mediterranean basin in the centuries close to the birth of Christ occurred as a result of the diffusion of productive techniques and of political organization in the wake of conquest. Techniques of agricultural production and of manufacturing spread roughly along the axis south-east to north-west, that is from the Middle East to Greece to Italy and north-west Europe. Or put another way, changes in the size of the surplus were a function of changes in political organization as well as of technical innovation. By innovation, I mean the adoption of techniques previously invented. Historians of technology, bedevilled by romantic notions of originality, have concentrated on inventions, on the problem of who discovered what first. In doing this, they have neglected the process of innovation and have underestimated the difficulty of getting inventions accepted and used over a wide area. But that is what matters for economic development. In this sense, classical antiquity was not a period of important inventions but of widespread innovations, spread by conquest.

Conquest by the Greeks, particularly under Alexander the Great, by the Carthaginians and finally by the Romans created larger and larger states. Indeed, one of the most striking changes in the Mediterranean basin during classical antiquity, that is from about 1000 BC to AD 400, was the growth in the size of political units. At the beginning of this period, in the world of Homer, warring Achaean chiefs formed an uneasy alliance in a piratical expedition to Troy. Egypt was the only kingdom of any size and consequence; Italy, Spain and north-western Europe were a melée of warring tribes, with a low level of material culture.[4] By the end of the period, the Roman Empire stretched from the north of England to the Red Sea and had a population which is conventionally estimated at fifty to sixty million, roughly the same as China at the same time; each had about one-fifth or one-sixth of the world population.[5]

A Homeric visitor to the Roman world would have been amazed by the extent of settled agriculture; arable land had replaced large areas of woodland, scrub and pasture. It supported a correspondingly larger population. And a significant proportion of this population (perhaps 10 per cent, though that is only a guess) fed off the surplus produce and lived in towns. The visitor would have been struck by the frequency, size, and similarity of these towns.[6] But if he had visited the city of Rome, he would have been overawed as even ancients were, by its size and by the splendour of its public monuments. It had a population which is best estimated at about one million; the city of Rome in the first century AD was as

---

[4] This statement appears to coincide thoughtlessly with an outdated stereotype, according to which barbarians, such as Celts or Iberians, produced very little before they were conquered by the Romans. I realize that archaeologists have long admired the artefacts of the Celts, and that their iron works, for example, were as advanced as those of the Romans. That said, I still think that their general level of production was lower than in Roman times.

[5] Beloch, *Bevölkerungsgeschichte*, p. 507; Heer, *Society and population*, p. 2.

[6] Pausanias, writing in the second century AD, dismissed the claims of a town to be a *polis*, that is a true 'city', because it had 'no public buildings, no gymnasium, no theatre, no market-square, no water conducted to a fountain' (Pausanias, 10, 4). Like the rectangular layout, these public buildings became the expected uniform of Roman towns.

large as London in 1800.[7] The Coliseum to take but one example is
still admired today for its size and boldness. But the less spectacular
system of public aqueducts (nine aqueducts brought water to Rome
from up to 91 kilometres away), fountains, baths and drains were
more useful, and made it possible for a large population to live
together in one city without them all succumbing to infectious
diseases.[8] To be sure, the city of Rome was a special case; but
most cities worthy of the name also had baths and aqueducts; some
had main drainage; the cities of Alexandria, Antioch and Carthage
each had a population of two or three hundred thousand, and so
were as large as any European town except London before the
nineteenth century.[9]

Our Homeric visitor would have been amazed by two other great
advances which had taken place in the last millennium BC: the
spread of literacy, and the invention of coinage. We do not know
how literate the masses were in the Roman Empire. The Greek-
speaking East remained largely impermeable to Latin, except
among the upper classes, and local languages, such as Syriac,
Aramaic, Punic and Celtic, everywhere survived centuries of Roman
rule.[10] But in the West, Latin eventually permeated popular speech
and so helped mould modern French, Spanish and Rumanian.

[7] The best account of the ancient evidence on Rome's population is still
that of Beloch (*Bevölkerungsgeschichte*, pp. 392–412), though Kahrstedt in
Friedländer and Wissowa (eds.), *Sittengeschichte Roms*, adds something. The
estimated population is based on the recorded number of male citizens who
received free wheat doles (320,000 when Julius Caesar held power); to these
we should add women, children and slaves. We also know the area of the
city (1,373 hectares), the number of houses listed in a fourth-century topography, and unreliable figures on the amount of wheat consumed in the city.
Even when all these are taken into account, we still have to guess: but the
best guesses are at the level of 800,000 to 1,000,000 inhabitants. It does seem
very large.

[8] Frontinus, *On the aqueducts*, 1, 1; Frontinus boasted of the usefulness of
aqueducts, compared to the idle pyramids or the inert but famous works of
art of the Greeks (*ibid.* 1, 16). By no means all Roman towns had aqueducts
or drains.

[9] On the size of smaller towns see Duncan-Jones, *Economy of the Roman
Empire*, pp. 259ff., which goes through the ancient evidence but draws some
questionable comparisons and conclusions. However, the free population of
Alexandria at 300,000 (Diodorus, 17, 52), and the similar size of Antioch
(Strabo, 16, 2, 5), and of Carthage, though at a later date (Herodian, 7, 6 but
see 3, 5, 7), are quite well attested, even if somewhat vague. But the number
of slaves deduced from the single passing reference in Galen (*Opera omnia*,
5, 49) is very doubtful.

[10] On vernacular languages see Brunt in Pippidi (ed.), *Assimilation et
résistance*, pp. 170–2.

Evidence from Pompeii, school-boy exercises scribbled on walls, election slogans and advertisements for gladiatorial games daubed on stucco walls, price-lists displayed in common taverns, all show that the capacity to read extended well beyond the elite. The success of Christianity, a dogmatic religion based upon holy writings, and on their orthodox interpretation from one end of the empire to the other, in circles outside the ruling elite, provides yet further evidence of the revolution in literacy which the Roman Empire had fostered. The word pagans (*pagani*) means countrymen; the orthodoxy of Christianity spread first between towns and among townspeople.

The diffusion of coined money as a general medium of exchange (after its invention in western Asia Minor in the seventh century BC) made possible the unification of the whole Roman Empire into a single monetary economy. Figure 1 shows that an increase in the volume of money in any one province was accompanied by a rise in the volume of money in other regions of the empire within the same short period.[11] It is based upon the analysis of over 90,000

[11] Figure 1 has been drawn so that each line on the graph represents the volume of silver coins found in a region. Some of these regions are very large, and the lines presented here comprise several strands from sub-regions, such as Britain, northern Gaul and southern Gaul. Where possible I have checked before compression to make sure that I was not mixing markedly different patterns; the patterns which I found in the sub-types seemed sufficiently similar to justify compression. I have kept hoards (strictly twenty or more coins found together) and other excavated coins separate as far as possible, because hoards may have been collected over long periods with a bias towards better coins and therefore may not correctly represent the coins in people's purses. The coins from museum collections, surveyed by Reece, may have been collected over long periods and their provenance is uncertain. It is extremely interesting that the singly found coins, carefully listed in modern German sources, produce a line which is similar to the line from the same region based on hoards.

The graph is based on a ratio scale. The base (100) is the number of coins from each region and of each type (singly found, hoards) dated AD 96–180, divided by 84 years. This period was the most stable period in the Roman economy. The average number of coins per year found in any one regnal period (for example, AD 96–117, 193–217, 217–38) for each line was then expressed as a ratio of this base. For example, of 3,812 singly found silver coins from southern Germany, an average of 5.3 were minted per year in the period AD 96–180; 5.3 therefore equals 100; in the period AD 117–38, the average number of coins found per year was 4.9=92.

The sources for this figure, about which I shall publish more in due course were; Reece, *Britannia* (1973) (Dr Reece very kindly reworked some of his data, so that I could split the reigns of Domitian from Vespasian and Titus); Bolin, *State and currency*, supplement; Bellinger, *Dura-Europus*; Kellner and

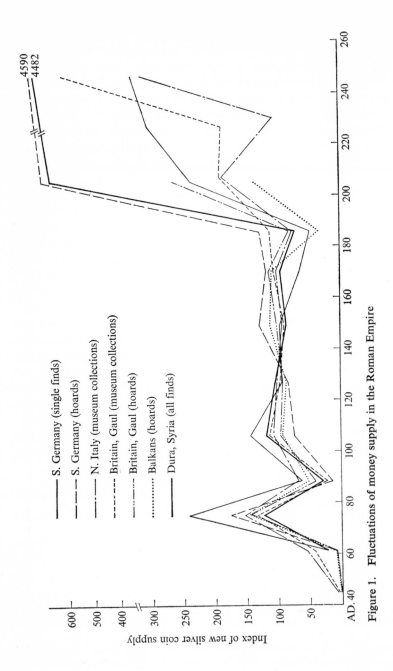

Figure 1. Fluctuations of money supply in the Roman Empire

— S. Germany (single finds)
-- S. Germany (hoards)
-·- N. Italy (museum collections)
--- Britain, Gaul (museum collections)
-··- Britain, Gaul (hoards)
···· Balkans (hoards)
— Dura, Syria (all finds)

Index of new silver coin supply

4590
4482

dated silver coins found in five regions of the Roman Empire. The prime cause of this monetary unification of the empire was the complementary flow of taxes and trade. Some of the richest provinces of the empire (Spain, Syria, Greece, southern Gaul, Asia Minor) paid taxes in money, most of which were exported and spent, either in Italy or in the frontier provinces where the armies were stationed. The rich core provinces then had to gain their tax-money back, by selling food or goods to the tax-importing regions. Towns in this network of taxes and trade acted as (1) intermediate markets for collecting staple foods (grain, wine, oil) and (2) as processors of primary products (wool, flax, hides) which, through the activities of townsmen, could be transformed into goods of higher value but lower volume (cloth, leather, dies, ropes, etc.) for sale in the chief markets of the empire. Thus the prime stimulus to long-distance trade in the Roman Empire was the tax demands of the central government and the distance between where most producers (tax-payers) worked and where most of the government's dependants (soldiers and officials) were stationed.

The unity of the Roman market also depended on the fact that the inhabitants of the Roman Empire could treat the Mediterranean as their own internal sea, free from pirates, from rivalries between competing states, indeed free from the magical dangers which for so long obstructed Odysseus' reunion with Penelope. The Homeric visitor would have been amazed at the size of the largest Roman ships (as indeed some ancients were).[12] But even the average merchant ship had increased significantly in size over the last millennium BC.[13] These larger ships carried both the increased

Christ (eds.), *Die Fundmünzen*, volumes on the Saar, Pfalz, Schwaben, Oberbayern, Süd-Baden and Süd-Württemberg.

[12] The classic description of a large ship is by the Greek satirist Lucian in his essay *The ship*, which some scholars have taken too seriously, but see the sceptical account of Rougé, *Recherches sur l'organisation du commerce maritime*, pp. 66ff. For an apologistic account, Casson, *Ships and seamanship*, pp. 170ff.

[13] We have no accurate evidence on the average size of Roman merchant ships. The minimum tonnage which would give a shipowner tax immunity for bringing wheat to the city of Rome was 325 tonnes burden, but that could be split among several ships, provided none was less than 65 tonnes burden (*Digest.* 50, 5, 3). This gives an idea of ship size on the empire's biggest supply route. Casson's assertions (*Ships and seamanship*, pp. 183ff.) about the normal size of ancient sea-going ships are mainly based on an inscription (*Inscriptiones Graecae*, xii (1939), supplement no. 348), which has been both

volume of trade, and the taxes levied in wheat which fed the city of Rome. The increased security of the seas helped shipowners risk owning bigger ships, as did the system of partnerships and maritime loans known from classical Athens and Rome, which split the risk of loss among participating investors. Improvements in steering and in rigging also helped bigger ships arrive at their intended destination.[14] From the first century AD, Roman ships regularly sailed with the monsoon almost 2,000 sea-miles from the Red Sea ports directly across the Indian Ocean to southern India. Accurate estimates of the earth's circumference (by Eratosthenes in the third century BC), maps, gazetteers, astronomical sophistication all bear witness to the slow accumulation of intellectual knowledge, and its percolation from the elite to the level of practical seamanship.[15] That said, the size of ancient ships, the seamanship, the rigging all fell short of what was achieved in Europe by the fifteenth century. Ancient ships had no magnetic compass, no stern rudders, and big ships to a great extent relied on square (instead of fore and aft) rigging which limited manoeuvrability; they always had difficulty in tacking against a wind. The recent growth of underwater archaeology owes its success to Roman ships' frequent failure. From fear of sinking, Roman merchantships did not as a rule set sail during four winter months, from November to March. During this long winter, sea trade was at a standstill, and state post usually went round the Mediterranean coast by road.

Roman roads are impressive monuments to the Roman Empire. Within Pompeii or on the outskirts of Rome itself, one can still see whole stretches of road paved with great flat stones. In Britain, the line of Roman roads is still visible especially in aerial photographs, running straight as a die through the countryside. According to some estimates, there were 90,000 kilometres of main paved roads in the Roman Empire.[16] A fourth-century pilgrim has left a record

doubtfully restored and mistranslated (but see Launey, *Bulletin de correspondance hellénique* (1933), pp. 394ff.).

[14] Rougé, *Recherches sur l'organisation du commerce maritime*, pp. 44ff. Roman ships had rudders near the front of the ship, and it now seems agreed that such steering was quite effective, although the projecting protective covers would have impeded a ship's progress.

[15] Thomson, *Ancient geography*, pp. 176ff. and 298ff.; Taylor, *The haven-finding art*, pp. 52ff.; and the anonymous *Circumnavigation of the Red Sea* (trans. Schoff). See also Pliny, *Natural history*, 6, 102–4.

[16] On Roman roads see Forbes, *Ancient roads*, and his *Ancient technology*, ii, pp. 140ff. (Forbes' work should be treated with caution); Margary, *Roman*

of his journey from Bordeaux to Jerusalem via Milan and Constantinople, a distance of about 5,000 kilometres; the roads he travelled were equipped with regular state posting-stations and rest-houses; he passed through three hundred of them on his journey.[17] The foundations of Roman roads, discovered by archaeological cross-sections and described in Roman literature[18] were deep (deeper than for many modern roads) and correspondingly expensive. In Britain, roads were often raised on causeways $1-1\frac{1}{2}$ metres above the level of the surrounding country. One gets some further idea of the scale of Roman road-building from the fact that the Alps were pierced by seventeen roads; great efforts were apparently made to keep the gradient less than one in six. Rivers were bridged in wood or stone; obstacles were overcome by tunnels, embankments or by retaining walls. As monuments then Roman roads remain very impressive. But was the cost of their construction justified by the traffic they carried? Politically, the answer must surely be yes. Straight high roads grandiosely demonstrated Roman dominance, and as in other pre-industrial empires, the roads and the horses in the post-stations enabled messages of state to be transmitted swiftly from the edges of the empire to the capital. But the cost of maintenance must have been huge.

From a commercial point of view, Roman paved roads were less useful. The current orthodoxy makes great play of the high cost of ancient road transport and of the high ratio of cost between land, river and sea transport.[19] The surviving ancient evidence is thin. The Emperor Diocletian's Edict on Maximum Prices (AD 301) made a land journey by ox cart for 1 kilometre cost the same as transporting the same weight 57 kilometres by sea on a long voyage, for example, from Syria to Spain.[20] From such evidence we can

roads, and Goodchild and Forbes in Singer (ed.), *History of technology*, ii, pp. 502ff.

[17] The normal distance between posting-stations was between 7 and 20 kilometres; these distances had apparently been reduced since the second century AD. See the itineraries of different date in *Itineraria romana* (ed. Cuntz). On the Bordeaux pilgrim's route, by my count there were 67 towns, 77 large posting-stations and 164 relay stations (*mutationes*).

[18] Statius, *Silvae*, 4, 2, 40ff.

[19] Jones, *Later Roman Empire*, pp. 841–2; Finley, *The Ancient economy*, pp. 126–7. These two are the authors of what I shall call the new orthodoxy, as distinct from the previous modernizing orthodoxy of Rostovtzeff, *Social and economic history*.

[20] For Diocletian's Edict the convenient text and English translation in Frank, *Economic survey of ancient Rome*, v, pp. 307ff., is now seriously

deduce rough price ratios per tonne/kilometre of about 600 price units for land transport, 60 for river transport and 10 units for sea transport per tonne/kilometre, with considerable variation around these figures. These price ratios are roughly concordant with the price ratios for transport found in other pre-industrial societies.[21] That is exactly the point I wish to make: the cost of Roman land transport was not significantly higher than in many other pre-industrial societies. But in medieval Europe, significant amounts of goods were moved from one region to another by road. And so they were in the Roman Empire.

Land transport was important for trade in the Roman Empire; the truth of this proposition can be illustrated but not proved. Let us take pottery as an example; but first some words of caution. The sheer survival of pottery has sometimes tempted archaeologists and economic historians of the ancient world to exaggerate its importance in the ancient economy. The most noted case is the rise and decline of Arezzo as the centre of manufacture of medium-priced table ware in the last century BC and the early part of the first century AD. Rostovtzeff put Arezzo among 'the large industrial centres of the ancient world', and then, when the manufacture of such pottery was moved to southern Gaul, he commented on the decentralization of Italian industry and took it as symptomatic of Italy's economic decline. It is this view which M. I. Finley has so effectively quashed.[22]

---

incomplete. Even Lauffer, *Diokletians Preisedikt*, is outdated by recent discoveries. I follow Duncan-Jones (*Z'tschr, f. Pap. u Epig.* (1976) in taking the military *modius* as equal to 1½ ordinary *modii* (each of 6.5 kg wheat). The prices given for sea transport in the Price Edict varied considerably (per tonne/km) and were particularly inaccurate in the western Mediterranean. Apparently the Byzantine administrator who fixed the prices was working from an old map or gazetteer and took no account of winds or traffic on routes. Therefore these legally fixed prices can be used only as very rough guides to actual practice. The price ratios between sea, river and land differ slightly from those given by Duncan-Jones, *Economy of the Roman Empire*, p. 368.

[21] A list of comparative data can be found in Clark and Haswell, *Subsistence agriculture*, pp. 196–8. The use of well-fed and well-bred and economically harnessed draught horses in the eighteenth century in north-western Europe along improved roads eventually made land transport costs much lower than comparable costs on Roman roads by ox cart. Pack-mules and donkeys were cheaper than ox carts, faster, and did not need roads.

[22] Rostovtzeff, *Social and economic history*, pp. 36 and 172; Finley, *The ancient economy*, p. 137, 'as for Lezoux and La Graufesenque they flourish only in archaeological manuals', beautifully but unfairly dismissive.

The point which I want to make is different. Arezzo lies deep inland, 100 kilometres from the sea and, although it is fairly near the head-waters of the Tiber and near a tributary of the Arno, it is not near a sizable navigable river. Yet Arretine pots have been found all over the Roman Empire, and as far away as India. The inconvenience of Arezzo's inland location was overcome. When Arezzo declined, its place was taken by potteries at La Graufe-senque, on a tributary of the Garonne which flows into the Atlantic Ocean. Yet La Graufesenque's main markets were the Roman army on the Rhine and Danube, and in Italy. For these, its riverside location was of little use. Most of its pots, which were bulky, heavy and not particularly valuable, must have been taken by road to other river heads. The volume of production was very large: we know the names of several thousand potters, and have lists of products, some of which run to over 700,000 items.[23] My point here is, not that the Roman economy depended on the manufacture of pots, but that, as the Greek geographer Strabo stated,[24] a consider-able volume of goods (of which pottery is but one example) was transported by land, between rivers or from sea port to river port, for considerable distances; for example, from the Rhone to the Loire, a distance of about 140 kilometres, and from Aquileia, near modern Trieste, through the Alps to Nauportus on a tributary of the river Save (75 kilometres).[25]

Distance overland was not then a decisive determinant of all trade or choice of route. Two further examples may be useful. First, lead ingots. The distribution of lead ingots from Roman Britain shows that lead mined in Derbyshire was taken sometimes to Brough on Humber, a nearby seaport, but at other times was taken long distances overland to Southampton.[26] The second example is at the opposite extreme: medium quality pottery cups found in the Roman military fort at Usk in south Wales and dating from the middle of the first century AD. These cups came from seven different regions of the Roman Empire, stretching from the lower Rhine, which was

---

[23] Hermet, *La Graufesenque*, pp. 291–355; Stanfield and Simpson, *Gaulish potters*. Another example of the volume of production and trade involved can be cited; dredging work at Chalon on the river Saone in 1869 revealed 24,000 wine amphorae from southern Gaul discarded near the river port (Déchelette, *La collection Millon*, pp. 155f.).

[24] Strabo, 4, 1, 14.

[25] Strabo, 4, 6, 10.

[26] Tylecote, *Metallurgy*, p. 87.

the nearest of these sources, to southern Italy. The great majority of the cups (82 per cent, N=214) came not from the most convenient source, but from Lyons, in spite of the cost and inconvenience of long transport by road, river and sea.[27] Obviously, the trade in cups was of negligible importance to the economy of the whole empire; but cups have survived and can reasonably stand proxy for all the more perishable items of medium value which were traded throughout the Roman Empire for considerable distances even overland, in spite of the cost of transport.

Up to now, we have been dealing with manufactured articles; let us now deal with staples. It was impossible to move large quantities of cereals for long distances overland, unless the transport was organized by the government and the cost imposed on taxpayers. If there was a famine in an inland district, there was little that anyone could do to relieve it, and the central government seldom intervened. Two classic cases illustrate this point. The first concerns the town of Caesarea in central Asia Minor, which is about 350 kilometres by road from the nearest Mediterranean port, and considerably further by river from the Black Sea. The following account is given by Gregory Nazianzen, a fourth-century divine.

There was a famine, the most terrible in the memory of man. The city languished but there was no help from any part, no remedy for the calamity. Cities on the sea coast easily endure a shortage of this kind, importing by sea the things of which they are short. But we who live far from the sea profit nothing from our surplus, nor can we produce what we are short of, since we are able neither to export what we have nor import what we lack.[28]

The second case is a famous famine in Antioch in AD 362–3, which was relieved by the Emperor Julian when he came there. He had 2,600 tons of wheat, about 6,700 cartloads, brought by road from two towns 80 and 160 kilometres distant where there was a surplus. Private entrepreneurs had been unable to draw upon the same source, probably because they could not command transport (oxen and donkeys) on that scale, over those distances. But the cost of land transport was probably not the main obstacle, since at known transport prices, the cost of bringing wheat 160 kilometres would

[27] Greene in Detsicas (ed.), *Romano-British coarse pottery*, pp. 23–5.
[28] Gregory Nazianzen, *Patrologia Graeca*, ed. J. P. Migne, xxxvi, col. 541.

have raised its price only by about 50 per cent, which is well within the range of wheat prices charged at Antioch during that year.[29]

The arguments which I have just advanced, namely that there was a signficant volume of inter-regional trade, much of it overland, diverge from the current orthodoxy.[30] This new orthodoxy, if I may call it that, runs somewhat as follows. Because most regions of the Mediterranean basin have a similar climate, in Roman times they grew the same produce. What was not grown locally, the masses of peasants and townsfolk could not afford. Therefore there was no large-scale inter-regional trade in staple foods (wheat, barley, wine and olive oil). To be sure, there were exceptions. The capital cities of Rome and later Constantinople, and perhaps the other great cities of the empire, Alexandria, Antioch and Carthage, were too large to be fed from their immediate hinterlands. But all large ancient cities were near the sea, and/or on rivers. The armies of the High Empire (300,000 men strong) also received some of their supplies from a distance; for reasons of supply as much as for defence, most of them were stationed in garrisons along rivers (Rhine, Danube and Euphrates). In any case, the army and the capital cities were largely fed by taxes, levied in wheat, so that their supply was not part of a pattern of exchange, but of taxation.

Local self-sufficiency in agriculture went hand in hand with self-sufficiency in manufacture. The Romans never developed systems of manufacture which substantially cut the costs of production through economies of scale or capital investment in equipment. The units of production were small. The largest recorded factory was a shield factory worked by 120 slaves in classical Athens; some forty government arms factories established in the fourth century AD may also have been large.[31] But as far as we know the concentration of workers in these factories did not apparently involve any sophisticated division of labour. In the arms factories, for example, each armourer was responsible for the whole process of making helmets

---

[29] See Finley, *The ancient economy*, pp. 126–7 for the contrary view; see Jones, *Later Roman Empire*, pp. 446, 844 and Liebeschutz, *Antioch* for a discussion of the evidence. Julian fixed the price for wheat brought overland at ten *modii* per *solidus*, and for wheat brought later from Egypt at fifteen *modii* per *solidus*. Normal prices, in spite of Julian's claims, were substantially lower elsewhere.

[30] See n. 19 above.

[31] Jones, *Athenian democracy*, p. 14; *idem, Later Roman Empire*, pp. 834–835.

and cheek pieces. In general, then, provided there were local supplies of raw materials, goods could be made in small quantities for each local market as cheaply as they could be made in large quantities at a single centre of production, from which transport costs had also to be paid. In other words, there were no effective economies of scale. Conditions differed only when a particular town had better access to raw materials, or had a monopoly of skilled craftsmen or had a marketable reputation for certain goods (ropes from Capua, linen from Tarsus, women's clothes from Scythopolis).[32] These premium goods, like fine wines or other prized agricultural produce, fetched premium prices, and so were bought only by the elite; and therefore, since the elite was small, trade in premium goods involved only a low volume of transport.

This orthodoxy, which I have oversimplified, deserves some qualifications. First, the size of the cereal harvest varied each year, but the demand for food was relatively steady. Even in modern times, in spite of all the help from fertilizers and from mechanically pumped water, the mean interannual variation in the size of wheat crops in the fourteen nations which are the successor states to the Roman Empire was 28 per cent (unadjusted mean of means, 1921–30).[33] These are national figures. In Roman times, the interannual variation in crop size in small self-sufficient districts, in the rural areas around each town, must have been considerably larger. To some extent, one year's surplus could have been stored against the next year's deficit, particularly by rich men. But these stores were often not large enough. Local shortages, even famines, recurred. These local shortages and the complementary gluts elsewhere stimulated sizable flows of trade.

Bringing food from elsewhere cost money. In some towns, emergency supplies were paid for by regularly appointed local officials (*sitonai*) or by private benefactors (the central government usually concerned itself only with the city of Rome itself).[34] The volume of private or municipal help was usually small in each town in relation to the need, and, as we have seen, nothing much could be done to

[32] See Cato, *On agriculture*, 135; Diocletian, *Price edict* 26.

[33] The national figures on wheat harvests are taken from the *International Yearbook of Agricultural Statistics*, 1922–38. The median annual variation round the mean for a decade was 14 per cent.

[34] See Jones, *The Greek city*, p. 218; he cites two cases in which benefactors provided enough money or wheat to feed up to five thousand people for a month.

relieve famine in towns deep inland. But the aggregate volume of all such relief brought by trade or benefaction must have been large. The main difference between ancient and modern marketing systems lay in the absence of any regular routes of large-scale exchange between regions specializing in the production of an agricultural surplus and regions specializing in the production of manufactures. The lines of trade in staples produced by local gluts and shortages were unpredictable.

The second qualification relates to luxuries, which have always held considerable fascination for economic historians. Some Romans dressed in wool from Asia-Minor, in Egyptian linen or Chinese silks; women wore Indian pearls and diamonds, and beautified themselves with Arabian cosmetics; at table, they used Spanish silver ware and Syrian glass and ate eastern spices; they decorated their houses with African ivory and Greek marbles.[35] Yet there were very few such people.

Two questions arise: was the luxury trade important in its aggregate value, or was it only a small stream directed primarily at the Roman elite in Italy? As in other pre-industrial empires, the rich were very rich; Roman senators in the High Empire commonly had annual incomes 2,000 times higher than the levels of minimum subsistence of a peasant family.[36] But there were only six hundred senators and only a few thousand Roman knights. If the luxury trade was important, it must have penetrated well down the social scale and have concerned prosperous landowners in provincial towns throughout the empire. Luxuries allowed the elites, at metropolitan and provincial levels, to enhance their status and by ostentatious consumption to dramatize their differences from common folk. Even well-to-do peasants or prosperous merchants were sometimes involved. In a good year, some of them probably bought a trinket or a new cloak, or stored away some gold or a jewel for the family

[35] *Digest*, 39, 4, 16, 7.

[36] This ratio is given in an attempt to invest ancient money figures with some meaning and is based on the following co-ordinates. A senatorial fortune at 20 million *sesterces* yields an annual income of 1.2 million *sesterces* at a 6 per cent return on capital. The minimum subsistence for a family is taken as 1,000 kg wheat which would cost approximately 450 *sesterces* per year (wheat at 3 *sesterces* per *modius* of 6.5 kg). Several of these figures are disputable, but the suggested ratio of senatorial to poor peasant income seems of the right order of magnitude. On senatorial fortunes, see Duncan-Jones, *Economy of the Roman Empire*, pp. 17ff., 343–4.

chest or their daughter's dowry. Thus, in my view, although the elite at Rome constituted the single largest market for luxuries, the luxury trade was important both in economic and social terms, because it reflected stratification throughout the empire; in sum, it was widespread.

Two figures from ancient sources confirm this view. Pliny wrote that imports from China, India and Arabia cost the Romans a hundred million sesterces each year.[37] Of course such large round numbers in ancient sources make one sceptical (it equals 7 tonnes of gold), and there is only a remote chance that Pliny gleaned this figure from state records of customs dues. But it is reasonable to conclude that imports from the East were on a large scale. The geographer Strabo is more reliable, because he himself visited upper Egypt with its then governor in the reign of Augustus: he wrote that the trade with India had grown considerably and that in his time 120 ships set sail every year from the Red Sea port of Myos Hormos to India.[38] The trade in foreign luxuries was clearly substantial and probably grew in the first century AD. I am not refurbishing the old argument that foreign trade in luxuries ruined Rome; rather I am arguing that luxury trade on this scale helped provide a living for thousands of merchants, traders and other intermediaries, such as boat builders, and hauliers, most of them living in towns. Nor should we forget the luxuries, manufactured within the Mediterranean basin. If we interpret luxuries loosely to include such items as fine linens, papyri and unguents, then Roman luxuries probably exceeded eastern goods in value and volume.

Finally, we should take into account the huge variety of goods consumed in the ancient economy. No ancient source discusses this, except the encyclopaedist Pliny in his *Natural history*; but we are not concerned here with evidence for the existence of varied trade-goods but with their importance. Even the plentiful surviving Egyptian papyri do not help us, because they came from the country-side and so give only fragmentary information about trade. In the absence of data from the Roman period, we can perhaps legiti-mately use later evidence, such as the Geniza papyri from Cairo in the period AD 950–1250 to give us insights on classical trade.[39] It seems likely that the items traded, as distinct from the trading

[37] Pliny, *Natural history*, 12, 84.
[38] Strabo, 2, 5, 12.
[39] Goitein, *A Mediterranean society*; an exciting set of documents.

conditions, were very much the same as in Roman times. Even so, we still have to deal with fragments; we have no summary figures on trade.

Most of the items traded were natural products in the raw state, or at only a slight remove from the raw state (olive oil, wax, onyx), but some products such as chemicals were won from the earth only at the cost of considerable labour and were besides important for transforming natural produce elsewhere (alum and alkali for cloth, pitch for storing wine, dies for glazing pots). Few of the goods were manufactured in the sense of being the composites of several raw products; this reflects the underdeveloped state of manufactures and of the market. That said, the large total demand in the market, is reflected in the wide variety of and distance between provenances and destinations, and in the value and volume of throughput. The following list sets out the items traded by one large general merchant:

1. Flax (sent from Egypt to Tunisia and Sicily).
2. Silk (sent from Spain and Sicily); other fabrics, including cotton from Syria, felt from north Africa, and all types of garments, such as robes and bed-covers.
3. Olive oil, soap, wax (from Tunisia, Syria and Palestine).
4. Spices, such as pepper, cinnamon, cloves.
5. Dies and tanning materials, such as indigo, lacquer, sumac, gall-nuts and saffron.
6. Metals, such as copper, iron, lead, mercury, tin, silver (sent from the West).
7. Books.
8. Aromatics, perfumes and gums, such as aloe, ambergris, camphor, frankincense, musk and betel leaves.
9. Jewels and semiprecious stones, such as pearls, cornelians, turquoises, onyx.
10. Ornaments, such as coral, cowries, tortoiseshell.
11. Chemicals, such as alkali, alum, antimony, arsenic, borax, naphtha, sulphur, starch, vitriol.
12. Hides, leather including shoes.
13. Pitch.

This list by no means exhausts the items recorded in the Geniza documents, but that does not matter. The Geniza papyri reassure the classical historian by giving us a lively picture of the relationships between, on the one hand, small, fragmented units of production and mostly small-time traders and, on the other hand, the movement of large quantities of medium- and high-value goods along and across the Mediterranean, even when those lands were subjected to a diversity of competing rulers.

Textiles and Metals

Two products deserve special mention: textiles and metals. Any economic history of medieval Europe takes the cloth trade seriously; several towns in England, France, Flanders and Italy owed their prosperity in great measure to their capacity to make and sell large quantities of cloth. By contrast, few modern historians of the ancient world (A. H. M. Jones is an honourable exception)[40] have taken the ancient cloth trade seriously, partly because very little ancient cloth has survived, and partly because no surviving ancient source tells us much about it.

The cloth trade in classical times must have been important. Townspeople living in the cramped multi-storey blocks in the city of Rome or Ostia, or in the cramped two-storey houses in Pompeii, had no room for the complex process of scouring, combing, weaving, fulling and dyeing which turned raw wool into cloth. They may have spun at home, but spinning enough yarn for your clothes required more than casual labour. Moeller's recent study of wool-making at Pompeii shows that in a town with a population of about 20,000, there were at least forty establishments devoted to the manufacture of cloth or felt, some of them quite large, and employing perhaps twenty workers.[41] Even in Egyptian villages, there were professional weavers, organized in guilds, making cloth for local consumption, and apparently for delivery to army units in central Asia Minor and Palestine.[42]

A. H. M. Jones argued that army units in central Asia Minor or Palestine would not have ordered clothing in dribs and drabs (four cloaks and a tunic from one village, nineteen cloaks and five tunics for another) if single large suppliers had been available. Nor did the government help the development of large-scale production by levying tax in cloth and so opting out of the market. Later, in the fourth

---

[40] Jones, *Roman economy*, pp. 350ff.

[41] Moeller, *Wool trade*. Some of his conclusions seem speculative, but the double furnaces and large vats in some establishments can still be seen.

[42] The four papyri, cited by Jones (*Roman economy*) are BGU 1564 and 1572 and P. Ryl. 94 and 189. All date from the second century AD.

century, the central government did set up large wool- and linen-weaving establishments to supply the army. These were probably conglomerates of piece workers, all working together under a single roof; we know very little about them. And we know of only a handful of large or middling privately owned manufacturies engaged in making cloth. All their owners seem to have been primarily interested in other activities, as landowners or officials.[43] So far as I know, no fortunes in the ancient world were based on cloth-making, even if textiles contributed to some fortunes.

Too much is often made of the small scale of manufacturing units. Of course, most manufacturing units in a pre-industrial economy are small; so they were still in Germany and France at the beginning of the twentieth century.[44] What matters are the number and size of the exceptions and whether there was any system by which a host of small producers, each engaged in one stage of production, was integrated by the activities of capitalistic entrepreneurs, who took a share of the profits in return for their effort and capital risk. There is only slight evidence that such integration did take place in the Roman world, and it seems probable that in textiles, as in other handicrafts, the roles and institutions of integrating fragmented piece workers were never highly developed.[45]

The small scale of most weaving establishments and their obvious lack of capital, the general poverty of the populace, and the high

[43] The evidence for two of these largish units is discussed by Wipszycka, *L'industrie textile*, pp. 81ff. and in *Klio* (1961), pp. 185ff. The official Apollonius of the second century AD clearly had considerable landholdings, was personally involved in his textile business (choosing dyes, cut, etc.), and integrated the activities of outworkers. Another Egyptian was said to have employed 'many workmen in his workshop' making linen (P. Oxy. 2340). A municipal magistrate in a small north African town was a weaver who sat down to dinner with his workmen (Optatus, *On the schism of the Donatists*, app. 2). The house of L. Veranius Hypsaeus, a town magistrate at Pompeii, was equipped with large-scale fulling equipment (della Corte, *Case e abitanti*, p. 46).

[44] 95 per cent of all manufacturing and mining units in Germany and 98 per cent in France employed less than ten persons in 1906–7 (Gerschenkron, *Economic backwardness*, p. 64).

[45] See, for example, Wipszycka, *L'industrie textile*, p. 81. Of 328 tradesmen mentioned on tombstone inscriptions in the graveyard at Kōrykos in Rough Cilicia, four were *ergodotēs*, putters out. The existence of the word argues the frequency of the role. From Goitein's study of the Geniza papyri I should expect to find sleeping partners in small businesses in the Roman world, though the evidence is, I think, slight; but see, for example, the interesting papyrus P. Vindob. 19792 published in Casson, *Eos* (1965), p. 90, which shows active banking investment in trade.

cost of transport have all been used, in my opinion wrongly, to buttress the proposition that inter-regional trade in cloth was of low volume and of low aggregate value because only the elite could afford to buy. But the poverty of individual peasants should not be confused with their aggregate demand; even if fifty million people or even ten million people buy cloth or clothes once in a decade, their aggregate demand is still enormous. Even in the Egyptian villages mentioned above, there were several weavers (eight or twelve in one, seven in another); this suggests that many rustics bought rather than made their own clothes. The cloth trade did not serve only the elite. This is confirmed by Diocletian's Edict on Maximum Prices, which listed linens 'fit for the use of commoners or slaves' (*Edict* 26). The regular purchase of cloth even of the lowest quality by poor peasants or for slaves in local markets created a nexus of exchange. Consumers of cloth had to sell their produce on the market to get money to pay clothiers, just as clothiers paid a longish line of associates (fullers, spinners, dyers) for their help and peasants for their food. This is a process which medieval historians take for granted. But for the Roman world, especially for rural areas, the emergence, persistence and importance of a monetary exchange economy between peasants and artisans still has to be argued.

But was the inter-regional cloth trade exclusively concerned with the elite? The evidence of Diocletian's Edict on Maximum Prices shows decisively that it was not. The Edict was composed in the eastern capital of the empire (Nicomedeia in Asia Minor). Yet the provenances of the raw wool and of the woollen garments named were spread throughout the whole empire (from Britain, northern Gaul, Spain, Italy, Africa, Greece and the Balkans). This implies a far-reaching trade. And the value of raw wool, let alone of made-up cloth, was so high in relation to volume that long-distance transport, whether by road, river or sea, would have added only marginally to costs. Even the very cheapest wool was priced at seven and a half times the price of wheat (per unit of weight; *Edict* 1 and 25), so that a journey by mule of 300 kilometres would have added only 10 per cent to the cost price (*Edict* 17). Of course, the most costly cloths, wool, linen or silk, were for the very rich, but the Edict fixed a wide range of intermediate prices. We can see this best with linens, since that part of the inscription is best preserved: different prices were given for three distinct qualities of linen made in each of five towns, all of them in the eastern half of the empire. To be sure, linen was made elsewhere also; but these five towns were famous for linen and presumably were sizable centres of production, and not just for the elite. Prices for shirts, for example, ranged from 7,000 to 2,000 *denarii* in the named qualities, and then from 1,500 to 500 *denarii* in the qualities for soldiers, commoners and slaves (*Edict* 26). The wide range of price and provenance and the availability of knowledge about them all in the capital indicate a firm market pattern, in which cloth from different regions competed.

Perhaps one problem is that we split the population of the empire into only two strata: a tiny elite and the broad mass of peasants and proletarians, who lived near the level of minimum subsistence. But the aggregate demand from a middling stratum must have been quite large: best clothes for brides and grooms, or for rich peasants or prosperous traders to wear at festivals or in street parades, or ordinary clothes for respectable schoolteachers or doctors or for middling landlords; all these added up to a varied, significant and sophisticated market.

Metals

Two aspects of metal production in the ancient world deserve emphasis: first, the difficulty and cost of their extraction, which required a large labour force and, in some cases, huge capital investment; secondly, the importance of metals as items of trade, in the manufacture of implements (swords, saucepans, mirrors, water-pipes), and as money. The monetization of the Roman economy was possible only because the Romans mined vast quantities of precious metal, just as the effective defence of Roman frontiers by large armies, equipped with iron swords and breast plates, depended upon large-scale supplies from Roman iron mines.

Some idea of scale may be useful. A reliable source, the Greek historian Polybius, tells us that in the mid-second century BC, the silver mines near Cartagena in Spain were worked by 40,000 slaves and yielded 25,000 *drachmae* per day in government revenues.[46] If these figures are roughly right, government revenues from these mines alone equalled 35 tonnes of silver a year, to which we should add entrepreneurial profit. Let us consider what that meant. According to Patterson, the production of one tonne of silver in ancient

[46] In Strabo, 3, 2, 10.

conditions involved 500–1,000 man work years.[47] It involved digging up roughly 100,000 tonnes of rock with iron and stone picks, hammers, chisels and gads or by fire-setting; this rock had to be dragged to the surface in baskets by ropes and human muscle. In deep workings, and some Roman workings in the Spanish silver mines were 250 metres underground, this labour would involve the use of tonnes of illuminating oil. Once the ore was brought to the surface, it was broken up by hammers, picked over by hand, ground and washed. Ten thousand tonnes of trees provided enough charcoal (between 500 and 2,000 tonnes) to smelt the ore at the necessary temperature (1,000°C). The by-product was 400 tonnes of lead and lots of slag which had to be carted away. Often the silver was still impure and had to be washed and remelted to produce refined silver. All this was necessary to produce one tonne of silver. I thought it worthwhile going into such detail, in order to indicate the ramifications of large-scale silver production, in terms of investment, equipment, fuel and organization.

Other evidence from Spain shows the huge scale of Roman workings.[48] In southern Spain, the Rio Tinto and Tarsis mines each had an estimated volume of 20–30 million tonnes of slag. Tarin calculated that the ancient slag at Rio Tinto and Tarsis (neither of which was worked between late antiquity and the early modern period) would have involved 5,000 workmen for 300 years.[49] The workings go deep underground and there are several kilometres of underground galleries, usually only one metre high. This prevented the use of haulage animals, or animal-powered water wheels, which were apparently unknown in antiquity. Drainage was achieved by cutting long transverse channels and by banks of man-operated Archimedian screws or water-wheels, each of which painfully raised the water by only two metres. In the same region at Sotiel, there

[47] Patterson, Econ. Hist. Rev. (1972). Dr Patterson's article and figures are obviously speculative and as he himself emphasizes should be treated with some caution. They provide only rough orders of magnitude. I have no competence to judge the plausibility of most of them. Those I have checked with friendly metal-minded archaeologists were thought probable.

[48] The gold workings in north-western Spain, for example, are estimated to have involved moving more than seventy million tonnes of earth, some of it washed away by water brought in aqueducts, in one case some 50 km long. See Davies, Roman mines, pp. 100ff., Lewis and Jones, J. Rom. Stud. (1970), pp. 175–6 and Jones and Bird, J. Rom. Stud. (1972), pp. 59ff.

[49] Cited as an intelligent source by Nash, Rio Tinto, p. 19. See also Davies, Roman mines, pp. 102ff., Rickard, Man and metals, i, p. 428, and Avery, Not on Queen Victoria's birthday, a history of the Rio Tinto mine.

was an abortive exploratory mine which yielded nothing but 30,000 tonnes of rock. The scale of working, on exploration and on profitable and unprofitable exploitation, makes it clear that private entrepreneurs (for these were not state mines) spent very considerable sums on capital investment.

Silver- and gold-mining (together with salt-mining and tax-farming) were the four activities in which it was legal for Romans to form corporations with a collective legal persona.[50] The Romans did not develop a concept of limited liability nor a public market in shares; some corporations may have been broken up on the death of their president; but in spite of their transience and inflexibility, these corporations obviously provided an effective mechanism for raising private capital and for sharing risks in very large mining enterprises. Strabo tells us that Cadiz was a very prosperous town, and that in a census of his own time there were five hundred men from Cadiz registered as knights, a number equalled in Italy only by Rome and Padua.[51] Their presence reflected the agricultural wealth of the valley of the Guadalquivir, the mineral wealth nearby and the importance of long-distance trade.[52]

Up to now we have been dealing with the integration of the Roman economy and with the volume of trade. These are obviously germane to the function of towns in the economy, but they are no substitute for looking at the towns themselves and at the conditions under which they grew. However, before we do that, perhaps it would be sensible to review quickly two of the main arguments advanced and to enter some qualifications. I have argued (cf. figure 1) that the Roman economy was heavily monetized, and constituted a single entity in which sizable sums of money flowed between provinces. But most produce stood outside the money economy. Most produce

---

[50] *Digest*, 3, 4, 1. Iron was apparently worked at a much larger number of sites than silver or gold. Measurement of ancient slag at iron mines is often difficult because of subsequent working at the same site. But some idea of scale can be gained from local studies. From a careful study of the volume of slag and its metal content at six out of thirty sites in the east Weald in southern England, Cleere has conservatively estimated production at these six sites as averaging 550 tonnes per year from AD 120 to 240. The six sites would have kept about 500–700 men at work: Cleere, *Bull. Inst. Arch.* (1976), pp. 233ff. Production at the iron mines in Noricum was obviously greater.

[51] Strabo, 3, 5, 3.

[52] 'These are the men', wrote Strabo of the people of Cadiz, 'who fit out the most and the largest ships both for our sea and for the sea outside' (Strabo, 3, 5, 3).

was consumed by the peasants who produced it; each peasant and his family produced most of what he and his family consumed; the market was not involved. This was very important both at the economic and at the political level. The monetized economy was a thin veneer stretched over and at some remove from the subsistence economy; it was attached to that stable base by the tenons of tax, rent and exchange. At the political level, the prevalence of peasant self-sufficiency helps explain the stolidity of pre-industrial empires; they can survive crises, partly because the superstructure is only marginally relevant to the way most of the population live; the superstructure can be split asunder by civil wars and by regional fragmentation, as it was in the Roman Empire in the third century and repeatedly in Chinese history, and can then be swiftly reunited. The peasant base and the elite superstructure belonged to separate, encapsulated worlds.

The second main argument was that taxation can be considered as the prime mover, creating a high volume of interregional trade. This occurred because money taxes were typically spent at some distance from the taxpayers. The taxpayers then had to buy back their money by the export and sale of goods. This model posits that a large volume of goods, equal in value to the exported tax, were transformed in towns from simple natural produce into higher value, lower volume transportable exports. The main routes of this trade were from the rich core provinces of their empire on the one side, to Italy and the frontier provinces where the armies were stationed, on the other side. Distribution maps of durable exports, principally pottery tableware and wine jars, corroborate this model, if we can safely regard pots as proxy for perishable but economically more important exports, such as wooden barrels of wine, cloth and leather.[53] But no short list of 'important' items of trade can do justice to the variety of goods which passed often each in small quantities along the trade routes of the empire. Most of the inhabitants of the empire were poor, but even they bought something which they did not produce. The sum of their demands, and the demands from the prosperous non-gentry, and from the elite all added up to a significant trade in non-subsistence goods.

Three qualifications seem to be necessary. First, not all trade was

[53] I am very grateful to Dr M. J. Fulford for guidance on this point. There is no handy compendium of distribution maps, which archaeologists are just beginning to draw.

the reciprocal of taxation (although a significant part was similiarly the reciprocal of rents paid to absentee landowners resident in regional centres or in the metropolis). But some trade, and a significant part of the whole, represented the exchange of produce between town and country and between specialist producers and consumers. Secondly, this model takes the existence of taxation as given. But taxation was a result of conquest, an advance, for both parties, over piracy and plunder. The imposition of taxes helped increase the productivity of subject peoples. In order to pay their taxes, peasants had to grow a surplus which they previously had not grown and they had to sell this surplus on a market so that they could get money to pay taxes. This process occurred first in the eastern Mediterranean in the states and kingdoms which were formed before the Roman conquest (in the case of Egypt long before). It happened in the western Mediterranean and Balkans, largely under Roman influence. As Strabo wrote of the 'barbarians' in the back country behind Marseilles: 'they have become civilized, and instead of making war, they have turned to civic life and to settled agriculture, because of Roman rule'.[54] Thus taxation increased productivity, threw extra produce onto the market and helped the growth of towns, as this produce was transformed by urban artisans into goods exported in order to buy money to pay their taxes with. Thirdly, not all taxes were levied in money: those levied in kind obviously stood outside these market relationships. In the Later Empire, that is in the fourth century, most taxes were levied in kind, and there was apparently a downturn in trade and in the prosperity of many towns. This fits with, indeed it corroborates, our model.

Conquest and the Growth of Towns

The growth of towns was a function of conquest. We know most about this process in Italy during the last centuries before Christ, that is during the period of Rome's greatest expansion.[55] The Romans acquired their huge empire by a fanatical dedication to fighting wars. It is difficult to find a single index of their militarism; perhaps the award of triumphs can serve: Roman generals were

[54] Strabo, 4, 1, 5,

[55] This is a much shortened version of the discussion given in my forthcoming book, *Conquerors and slaves*. See below, figure 2, p. 62, where the interaction of several important factors is schematically portrayed.

awarded triumphs only if they had secured victories over 'worthy enemies' and if at least five thousand of the enemy had been killed in a single battle. The scale of Roman slaughter is reflected in the fact that in the two centuries to 50 BC over seventy triumphs were awarded. The profits of empire, booty, treasure, taxes and slaves poured into Italy. The privileged benefited most; that was one advantage of being privileged, at once a token of high status and a means of reinforcing it. Throughout the last two centuries BC, the rich grew steadily richer and their style of living became more luxuriously ostentatious. The grandest town house in the city of Rome in 78 BC was not even among the top hundred town houses a generation later;[56] this observation and the competition it implies reflect the growth of wealth inside the Roman elite.

For reasons of status and tradition, Roman aristocrats and knights invested most of their new wealth in Italian land. It was not only respectable and safe, it was almost the only large-scale form of long-term investment available. Poor peasants were bought out or forced off their land; their farms were amalgamated and were worked more efficiently by slaves, more efficiently in the sense that the surplus produced on the farms cultivated by slaves was (net of subsistence) considerably larger than the surplus produced on small family farms. An arable farm of 50 hectares could be cultivated, according to the Roman agricultural writer Columella, by eight male slaves with one supervisor and his wife (only the supervisor was allowed a wife).[57] In the second century BC, the same area (50 hectares) would have provided farms for between four and twenty colonists and their families.[58] The gain to the landowner from replacing free peasants with slaves was clear.

The dispossessed citizen peasants migrated to the city of Rome and to other Italian towns where they helped constitute a new market for the surplus grown on the estates of the rich, or they went to the newly formed colonies like Bologna and Piacenza in northern Italy, or they went into the army and so captured still more

[56] Pliny, *Natural history*, 36, 109.

[57] Columella, *On agriculture*, 2, 12.

[58] Details of colonial allotments are conveniently given in Frank, *Economic survey of ancient Rome*, i; pp. 122–3. Some of the colonial allotments at the beginning of the second century were so small that they could not have supported a family. To preserve the analogy, I have disregarded the smallest allotments, and have included only those of ten *iugera* (2.5 ha.) and above.

booty and slaves both for themselves and for their leaders. In this way, conquest materially, if indirectly, fed the growth of towns by stimulating migration from the countryside, and by providing a replacement agricultural labour force of slaves in the countryside. Some idea of scale may help; according to the ancient figures and by conservative estimates, it seems likely that in the last two centuries BC over two million slaves were imported into Italy; it is difficult to know, but it is possible to estimate that somewhat more than half these new slaves went into the countryside, and the rest went to work for their new masters in towns.[59] One consequence of their immigration was an acute and recurrent shortage of agricultural land in Italy; the crises were repeatedly 'solved' by allocating land to ex-soldiers but only at the cost of dispossessing a fresh set of peasants The final solution reached under Julius Caesar and the first Emperor Augustus was the settlement of over two hundred thousand adult male citizens overseas.[60] In all, I estimate, on Professor Brunt's figures, that nearly four hundred thousand adult male free Italians, that is a third of Italy's free population, were resettled by direct state intervention, in colonies sited in Italy or in the provinces during the second half of the last century BC. This removal of large numbers of free citizens from central Italy reduced the demand for Italian land and so formed one important economic foundation for the Augustan settlement.

We have then a nexus of interrelated factors: continuous wars, the import of booty, and of a massive number of slaves, the extrusion of free peasants, the growth of large estates, the creation of a large surplus, and the growth of towns both in Italy and in the provinces. The interaction of these factors is set out in figure 2. The growth of Italian towns was made possible, I think, by the very uneven distribution of profits from war, which in turn forced

[59] These figures are only very approximate. Their implications and the conclusions cited here are elaborated in my forthcoming book (see n. 55). I follow Beloch, *Bevölkerungsgeschichte*, pp. 418, 435–6 rather than Brunt, *Italian manpower*, p. 124, who thought in terms of three million slaves in Italy about the time of Christ. The difference between these careful scholarly estimates gives some idea of the inadequacy of the data. Of course, the sum of slave imports over two centuries far exceeded the number of slaves living at any one time.

[60] These figures are derived from those given by Brunt, *Italian manpower*, pp. 234ff. The gross figures for all migrations inside Italy and out of Italy are amazingly high; but even halved, for which there would be no justification, they would still be significant.

investment in land and increases in farm size and made possible economies of scale. The same forces simultaneously created a new surplus (grown on farms worked by slaves) and a new market, which consisted of imported urban slaves and the former peasants who had been extruded from their smallholdings and who had migrated to the city of Rome and to other Italian towns.

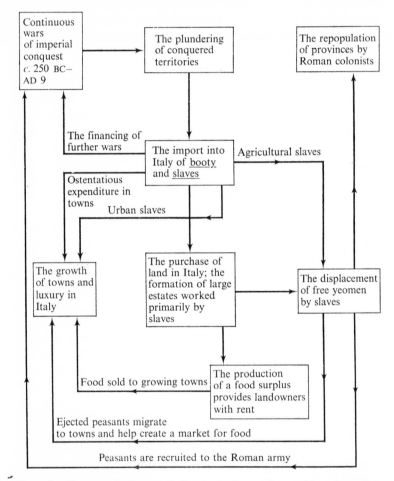

Figure 2.   The growth of towns in Roman Italy – a scheme of interdependence

Urbanization also depended upon an increase in inequality; the rich grew much richer and the poor became relatively poorer, and in many cases absolutely poorer, if they lost their farms and then became urban pensioners of the state. Let us discuss these developments. Much of the stored wealth of the Mediterranean basin was suddenly heaped into Italy. The wealth of the Roman elite grew commensurately with the growth of Rome's political power. Only a small part of this huge influx could be profitably invested in production; much of it was spent on importing slaves. Some of the provincial profits were lent back to provincial taxpayers at usurious rates of interest. Rich men also spent lavishly in the city of Rome. We know from dozens of references in our sources that the whole life style of the Roman elite was transformed by the wealth of conquest. Nobles ate from silver, instead of from wooden platters. Their wives bought jewellery and silks. Sumptuary laws which attempted to hold expenditure down at traditional levels were repeatedly passed and repeatedly ignored.

The stratification pyramid not only grew in height, but also thickened out at the top to incorporate new skills. Some were necessary for the administration of an increasingly complex empire, and some reflected the growing luxury of the elite. For example, advocates, consultant lawyers, doctors, architects, rhetoricians, poets, playwrights, school-teachers, secretaries, even bankers were all unknown as distinct occupations in Roman society before its imperial expansion overseas. Some of these new workers helped create and inculcate a new integrative culture common to the elite throughout the empire; others helped the elite govern; others simply helped the elite spend its money in ostentatious consumption.

Expenditure by the rich percolated through the economy. Nobles kept and fed slaves, built palaces, commandeered services; in short, they spent money, which by its multiplier effects gave lots of people living in the city of Rome enough, or nearly enough money to buy food, clothing and shelter. Without this expansion of the market and population in the city of Rome and a similar expansion in other Italian towns, nobles' investment in agriculture would have been fruitless.

The purchasing power of the urban proletariat must often have been in doubt. But its political power at Rome was strong enough to secure from state resources substantial distributions, at first (from 123/2 BC) of subsidized, and then (from 58 BC) of free wheat. The number of recipients (adult male citizens resident in the city of Rome) rose to 320,000 in 46 BC, and was 250,000 in 29 BC. These distributions of wheat must have encouraged urban immigration. They also underwrote with state funds the capacity of the poor to purchase the surplus food grown on the estates of the rich. A third function was to hold down the cost of services provided by the free poor to the rich. The economic cost of keeping a population of close on a million people in the city of Rome was disguised by transferring a substantial part of the cost to the state budget. Yet even if this helps explain away the huge size of Rome in a pre-industrial epoch, the size of Antioch, Carthage and Alexandria remains remarkable and unexplained.

One question seems outstanding and important: how significant was slavery in these developments? Slavery as a major productive force, mass slavery, has been extremely rare in human history. By mass slavery, I mean that about 20 per cent or more of the labour force were slaves.[61] Only five such slave societies are known in human history: three American societies (Brazil, the Caribbean islands and the southern states of the USA) and two from classical antiquity (Greece and Roman Italy). All these slave societies were closely associated with large-scale imperial conquests and with a shortage of easily exploitable labour. The rarity of known slave societies should take the edge out of the old Marxist contention that slavery was a universal stage in social development. Clearly it has not been. Even in the Roman Empire, slavery was concentrated in Italy, although significant pockets of slaves persisted in Greece and in Greek cities in western Asia Minor; but there too, the majority of both rural and urban workers was always free. In the rest of the Roman Empire, slavery was of little importance in production, although the ownership of domestic slaves was always a symbol of high status.

Slavery had three main economic functions. First, it secured the long-distance mobility of labour in a society in which there was no effective labour market. By defining humans as property at the disposal of the purchaser, slavery allowed conquering Romans to import an underclass of exploitable aliens. Without slaves, how could rich Romans have exploited their wealth? But slavery was

---

[61] The exact proportion of slaves is clearly arbitrary, but there does seem to be a real discontinuity. The number of slave societies would not be increased by changing the proportion to 15 per cent or even 10 per cent. And if slaves are a very small minority (less than 10 per cent) it is difficult to see how they can colour all exploitative relationships in a society.

not the only agent of migration; indeed in the process of conquest, slavery can be seen as the reciprocal of military movements and of colonization. Conquered slaves were brought from the provinces so that they could work for their new masters, while conquering soldiers, recruited from their farms and dispossessed of their lands by members of their own elite, eventually settled in huge numbers in colonies on the land of the conquered. Needless to say, the switch between imported slaves and exported peasant soldiers sounds neater than it was in reality. Moreover, imported slaves included large numbers of educated Greeks who upgraded the conquerors' administrative services; rather like the import of American technology into a modern underdeveloped economy, they partly deformed, partly improved the efficiency of the native culture.

Secondly, by the mass import of exploitable aliens, slavery made possible a rise in the height of the stratification pyramid, without forcing citizens into directly exploited roles, except in their traditional role as soldiers. In other words, slavery allowed the myth of notional equality among Roman citizens and of citizen rights to survive a tremendous increase in inequality. Indeed, slavery defined even poor free citizens as belonging to a superior stratum. And so in elite culture and sometimes in Roman law, certain relationships of exploitation, such as working long term for another free person, came to be regarded as slave-like. For example, free men resident as workers in the household of their employers were regarded in law as being like slaves (*in loco servorum*).[62] This degradation did not prevent some poor free men working in this way; presumably they had little choice. But, in general, the existence of mass slavery at the critical time of Roman economic expansion, precluded the use of wage labour as an alternative means of aggregating free men under the exploitation of single entrepreneurs.

This brings us to the third economic function of slavery. Slavery did allow the co-ordination of several workers under the domination of a single owner. Indeed slavery allowed, or even demanded, a greater degree of exploitation than free men were used to. Whereas free peasants on a largish subsistence plot could achieve more than minimum subsistence with only 100 man-work days per year, by my reckoning the normal price of an agricultural slave

---

[62] *Digest*, 43, 16, 1, 18 (Ulpian). See the commentary by de Robertis, *Lavoro*, pp. 101–42, and the corrective remarks by Nörr, *Zeitschrift der Savigny-Stiftung für Rechtsgeschichte* (1965), pp. 90ff.

implied a working year for slaves of at least 200 man days per year.[63] There is little surprising in that. Slaves were forced to work harder than free peasants. In this way slavery brought an increase in labour productivity in agriculture. Theoretically wage-labour might have been more efficient, but that was not a path open to Roman landowners in the Roman political culture.

Did slavery hold back economic development? Much debate on this problem has been doctrinaire.[64] We have seen that the massive import of slaves into Italy precipitated an increase in agricultural productivity, which in turn made possible an increase in the size of towns. Many of the imported slaves were skilled, and there is no evidence from the classical world, as there apparently is from the southern states of the USA, that slaves were entrusted only with unbreakable and therefore clumsily inefficient working tools. Slaves did cost a lot of money, and so perhaps diverted money away from more productive investment; but slavery expanded fastest when conquering Romans had at their disposal booty, unattached free-floating resources from an expanding empire, for which there was a shortage of potential investments. The rich in a sense wasted capital on the purchase of life-long labour, but it is difficult to think how else they could have used their capital more productively. Finally, it is argued that slavery restricted the size of the consumer market, because slaves were kept poor. But the majority of workers in town and countryside were always free. I cannot see that slavery was a critical factor in fixing consumer demand.

Up to now we have concentrated on the impact of conquest on economic development in Italy, with special reference to the import of slaves and the growth of the city of Rome. But the reciprocal flows of migration, the export of soldier colonists and some urban

---

[63] Such calculations are difficult and fraught with possible error. But if the normal price of an adult unskilled male slave was 500 *denarii* (see *Corpus inscriptionum latinarum*, viii, 23956 and Jones in Finley (ed.), *Slavery in classical antiquity*, pp. 9–10), and if that price were amortized over twenty years (a longish period) at 6 per cent per year (a minimum rate), and if maintenance including clothing and housing is reckoned at 400 kg wheat equivalent per year, then the annual cost of a slave equalled 750 kg per year. A free labourer according to Diocletian's Edict on Maximum Prices cost 2.5 kg wheat per day plus maintenance (a low price, but possible by the standards of underdeveloped economies; see Clark and Haswell, *Subsistence agriculture*, pp. 139ff.). Let us put the total cost as about 3.5 kg wheat equivalent per day. Then the slave would have to work 200 man days per year or more to rival free wage labour.

[64] Kiechle, *Sklavenarbeit*, reviews the varied views on this point.

proletarians from central Italy, contributed significantly to urban growth in the rest of Italy and in the provinces. Bologna, Genoa, Modena, Parma and Turin, for example, were all colonial foundations or refoundations. But the greatest impact of colonization was in the provinces: Julius Caesar and Augustus arranged for the foundation of over one hundred colonies scattered throughout the Mediterranean basin.[65] As we have seen, one of the main functions of these colonies was that they helped transfer some of the surplus free population out of Italy, so that more land was available there for occupation by the rich. In addition they allowed poor Romans some share in the fruits of conquest, without obliging the state to transfer extra taxes all the way from the provinces to Italy. In a low-level economy, it was more economical to move the conquerors out to occupy provincial land, where they created their own surplus on sequestrated farms, than to transport taxes and pay the conquerors a subsidy at home. Finally, of course, colonies overseas served as bastions of Romanization, and as garrison towns in the inner provinces. On the frontiers large towns grew up around legionary encampments, such as Cologne, Mainz and Strasbourg on the Rhine, Vienna and Belgrade on the Danube. Legionaries were paid twice as much as was necessary to maintain a peasant family at the level of minimum subsistence.[66] They therefore constituted new consumer markets, replete with cash, a situation rare in a pre-industrial economy.

Such urbanization (colonies and garrison towns) was a direct result of conquest. So too, perhaps, was the development of administrative towns, shaped by Roman strategies of government. Roman administration of the provinces depended upon the co-operation of town councillors (*decurions*) who were responsible probably for the allocation, and almost certainly for the collection, of taxes. Conquest by Rome seems therefore to have stimulated the development of tribal towns, especially in the western provinces;[67] the predominant pattern visible in the list of towns given, for example, in Ptolemy's *Geography* was that each tribe had just one town ('beyond them, the Parisii and the town Lucotecia, beyond

---

[65] Brunt, *Italian manpower*, pp. 589ff.

[66] Legionary pay in the first century AD was 900 *sesterces* per year; if wheat cost 3 *sesterces* per *modius* of 6.5 kg, this pay equalled almost two tonnes of wheat equivalent. I reckon minimum subsistence for an average peasant family of four persons at one tonne wheat equivalent per year.

[67] See, for example, Rivet, *Town and country*, pp. 72ff.

them the Tricasii and the town Augustobona and beyond them across the Loire, the Turonii and their town Caesorodunum').[68] In Gaul, Spain and Britain, some hill-top forts were dismantled and the population was resettled in a more accessible, less defensible site below.[69] We know of several cases, particularly in the eastern provinces in which towns vied with each other in the magnificence of their public buildings – temples, arcades, theatres, baths. Equipping towns with the appropriate urban adornments was an expensive business. In Italy itself, in the last century BC, village populations were sometimes synoecized, perhaps forcibly, into towns; and much money from provincial booty was spent on providing these towns with walls, forum, paved streets and fountains.[70] This was not just a question of aesthetics, but of political status; to have local autonomy, one's own magistrates, local laws (and tax-collectors), a place had to look like a real town. This was the prime stimulus to competitive expenditure.

Turning villages into agro-towns probably contributed little of itself to economic growth. Initially public building and municipal works may have offered temporary employment opportunities for rural workers, and even marginal gains made a difference to poor populations. But just as towns ostentatiously competed with other towns, so perhaps did local landowners compete with each other within towns. Towns gave them a stage: the forum, the porticoed arcades, the large town houses, in which they could show off their wealth. Perhaps competitive expenditure by local notables made them increase rents, just as conquest increased taxation. Certainly, the gradual integration of the Mediterranean economy, and the consequent growth of absentee landlordism (as large land-lords owned property in several townships), must have forced tenants to earn back exported rents, just as taxpayers had to earn back exported taxes. In this process, towns played a vital role as transformers of local produce into exportable items of trade.

The Level of Urbanization and the Functions of Towns

The level of urbanization in the Roman Empire was not equalled

---

[68] Ptolemy, *Geography*, 2, 8, 10–11.

[69] See, for example, Grenier in Déchelette (ed.). *Manuel d'archéologie*, vi, pp. 665ff.

[70] Gabba, *Studi classici e orientali* (1972), pp. 73ff.

or surpassed for at least a millennium.[71] That is a plausible claim and even probable; but how does one demonstrate that it is true? There are several indices which can be used: the size of the urban population, the inhabited area of towns, the area enclosed by walls, the sheer number of towns, the splendour of public monuments, the size of public benefactions, the sophistication of artefacts found by archaeologists, the known division of labour. Each index has its shortcomings, but all the indices seem to point in a similar direction, that is to a high level of urbanization.

Let us quickly review the evidence, and then discuss the functions of towns in the Roman economy. The size of the populations of the four or five largest Roman towns has already been mentioned. We have very little information on the size of other lesser towns. We have to rely on passing remarks and on stray bits of possibly inaccurate information. From these we gather, for example, that three cities in the eastern Mediterranean (Apamea, Ephesus, Pergamum) may have had free populations in excess of 100,000 – figures which by medieval or early modern European standards are substantial.[72] But the ancient figures may include the population of the rural area around the town.[73] Archaeological surveys have revealed the built-up area of Roman towns: for example, Leptis Magna covered an area of 120 hectares; Timgad 50 hectares; Thugga

---

[71] See M. I. Finley, 'The ancient city: from Fustel de Coulanges to Max Weber and beyond', *Comp. Stud. Soc. and Hist.* (1977). I am very grateful to Professor Finley for letting me see this article before its publication. I have been much influenced by it, without always agreeing with it.

[72] The evidence is found in *Inscriptiones latinae selectae*, 2683, a census figure of Augustan date; Keil, *J'hefte des öst. arch. Inst.*, *Beiblatt* (1930), p. 57; and a passing remark by Galen (*Opera omnia*, 5, 49) about a rich man, which I cite in full because it has been taken as concrete evidence: 'if our citizens number about four myriads, and if you add women and slaves, you will find yourself undoubtedly richer than twelve myriads of humans'. From this, having added children, Duncan-Jones deduces that the proportion of slaves in Italian towns was 22 per cent. I do not think it can properly bear that weight, but see his essay on 'Size of cities' in Duncan-Jones, *Economy of the Roman Empire*, which contains a careful review of all the ancient evidence, somewhat vitiated by misleading comparisons between Roman towns and modern populations (Italy 1951), large industrial cities (Berlin 1890), and the density of whole countries including large tracts of desert (Tunisia 1966).

[73] Even if these figures included the rural population, it seems that the urban population would have been sizeable. Most of Duncan-Jones' figures (Duncan-Jones, *Economy of the Roman Empire*, p. 273) are for citizens, that is for all adult males living in the area; one apparently urban figure, about 16,000 for Comum, is again large by post-medieval standards.

20 hectares; Ostia 69 hectares; Pompeii 65 hectares. As with the areas enclosed by walls, such figures mean little unless we also know the density of buildings, their height and their rate of occupancy. Yet compared with towns, for example, in the late medieval period, these ancient urban areas seem sizable and may indicate large urban populations.[74] The sheer number of Roman towns also seems large: nine hundred in the eastern provinces, over three hundrend along the north African littoral, excluding Egypt, and a similar number in the Iberian peninsula and in Italy.[75] Once again such an index is far from perfect; the distinction between large village and town is arbitrary and was sometimes unclear in the ancient world.[76] The frequency of towns in an area might reflect its past political fragmentation, as in central Greece, or the administrative policy of rulers, as in Britain, as much as economic prosperity.

The monumental ruins of classical towns, even of quite small towns, seem very impressive. Paved streets, life-size statues, shady colonnades, temples, gymnasia, public baths, fountains, theatres, amphitheatres and aqueducts all give the impression of urban prosperity. Yet once again interpretation of this evidence is ambiguous. First, if we cost a typical set of urban public buildings, and then spread this total cost over two or three centuries, the annual investment, even making allowances for maintenance, seems quite modest.[77] In any case, ostentatious expenditure on public buildings represents as much a cultural as an economic phenomenon; for example, it could have resulted from decisions to spend money on permanent public buildings rather than on transient rituals. Buildings may also reflect the degree to which the poor were exploited by rentiers as much as a general rise in prosperity. Of course, prosperity and exploitation are by no means mutually exclusive. Since we cannot be sure, I prefer to remain cautiously

[74] All these examples are given by Duncan-Jones (Duncan-Jones, *Economy of the Roman Empire*, p. 265). Data for Britain and Gaul are set out, rather more systematically than the evidence deserves I suspect, by Pounds, *Annals Am. Assoc. Geog.* (1969), pp. 148ff.: but enclosed area is not an accurate guide to relative importance. For later towns, see for example, but with caution, Russell, *Medieval regions*.

[75] A list of Roman towns in the eastern empire is given by Jones, *Cities of the eastern Roman provinces*. For the western empire the best list is by Ptolemy in his *Geography*, from which this count was made.

[76] Strabo, 3, 4, 13.

[77] This ingenious test was made by MacMullen, *Roman social relations*, pp. 142–5.

sceptical rather than to assume *a priori* that grand public buildings, from palaces to basilicas, reflected widespread increases in urban wealth.

Is there then any safe way of getting at general levels of prosperity in ancient towns? We do not know wage rates, we have no surviving census returns from towns.[78] The first temptation may be to give up in despair. But perhaps two indices hold out some hope.

The first is the stratified archaeological findings which in western provinces repeatedly show a higher concentration of artefacts at Roman compared to pre-Roman levels: more coins, pots, lamps, iron tools, carved stones, ornaments; in short a higher standard of living than was common in the pre-Roman population occupying the same sites.[79] The second index is the division of labour. Tombstones from the city of Rome show the existence of over two hundred named trades and occupations. An astrological handbook mentioned 264 occupations. This compares with about 350 trades listed in Campbell's *London tradesmen* published in the mid-eighteenth century.[80] Such lists obviously have to be used with caution (probably none is complete), but I think they reflect the fact that by the eighteenth century London and other large northern European towns had reached a level of economic sophistication such as classical Rome never reached.

Complete lists of trades from other classical towns are difficult to

[78] In about AD 300 the population of the city of Autun in Gaul was taxed at 25,000 heads as against 32,000 previously (*Panegyrici latini*, 5, 11), but that was the taxable population of the district, not specifically of the town. Besides, the government had little interest in an exact head count. They were interested in the relative capacity of towns to pay tax. I imagine that even if originally tax units related to heads, they were not regularly or efficiently re-examined, whatever the government intended.

[79] To an outsider, archaeological reports seem hopelessly fragmented. Archaeologists seem more interested in doing another dig and writing up last year's finds than in making sense of the last generation's advances. I can therefore cite only incidental studies of individual sites which make a passing reference to comparisons between Roman and pre-Roman levels: Clavel, *Bezières*, p. 332; Schulten, *Geschichte von Numantia*, pp. 154–5; Callu, *Thamusida*, pp. 187ff.; Kraeling, *Ptolemais*, pp. 270ff.

[80] *Corpus inscriptionum latinarum*, vi, pt 2, pp. vii–viii; Firmicus Maternus, *Ancient astrology*; Bücher, *Die Entstehung der Volkswirtschaft*, p. 286, stresses that the division of labour has different implications according to whether it implies division of production (spinner, fuller, weaver), specialization of trade (e.g. nailsmith, who turns raw product into finished article), or subdivision of labour (one man makes nail head, another the shaft). Each has different economic implications. The ancient division was obviously more of the first two types than the third.

get either because trades were not written on tombstones or because only few tombstones survive from each town. However, there is one set of tombstones, perhaps dating from the third to the sixth centuries AD, from Kōrykos, a small and insignificant town in Rough Cilicia in south-east Asia Minor.[81] Over half of the males commemorated (N=702) there had their occupations named, and these cover 110 different trades, probably not all present at one time. Extremely poor tradesmen were probably under-represented, but less than usual, since the tombs were reused and the inscriptions were both short and simple. Some of the trades mentioned were very humble, including wood-cutters, beggars, clothes menders and cooked-food sellers. Overall the distribution of tradesmen corroborates the view expressed above that luxury trades (13 per cent) and textiles (18 per cent) were important and it reinforces the idea that urban markets even in small towns met a complex of needs (pottery manufacturing 10 per cent, shipping 8 per cent, smithying 5 per cent, building 5 per cent, food-sales 15 per cent – N=328). The plausibility of this apparently large number of trades is confirmed by the eighty-five trades attested from Pompeii, a town with a population of about 20,000.[82]

What then was the function of ancient towns? One powerful view is that they were primarily centres of consumption; this is the definition given by Sombart: 'By a consumption city [Konsumptionsstadt] I mean one which pays for its maintenance. . .not with its own products, because it does not need to. It derives its maintenance rather on the basis of a legal claim [Rechtstitel] such as taxes or rents, without having to deliver return values.'[83] Now that is an ideal type; an ideal type according to Weber is formed by the one-sided accentuation of a particular point of view and by the

[81] These are to be found in the *Monumenta Asiae Minoris Antiqua*, iii, nos. 201–768. I have listed trades for males only, since females were markedly under-represented.

[82] The occupations from Pompeii are mostly attested in election posters daubed on stucco walls. They are to be found in the indices to *Corpus inscriptionum latinarum*, iv, and in della Corte, *Case e abitanti*. But when della Corte deduced an occupation without corroboration, it has not been included.

[83] In this and the following pages I am much indebted to, athough I diverge from, the stimulating article by M. I. Finley, 'The ancient city: from Fustel de Coulanges to Max Weber and beyond', *Comp. Stud. Soc. and Hist.* (1977). The quotation is from Sombart, *Der moderne Kapitalismus*, i, pp. 142–3, and is cited by Finley.

synthesis of several discrete and diffuse phenomena 'into a unified analytical construct (*Gedankenbild*)...this mental construct cannot be found empirically anywhere in reality. It is a *utopia*. Historical research faces the task of determining in each individual case, the extent to which this ideal-construct approximates to or diverges from reality.'[84]

The idea of a consumer city is brilliant. But it does not imply that only consumers lived in ancient towns; a considerable number of townsmen were obviously petty commodity producers. But in the 'consumer city', the producers were subsidiary to the consumers, and their 'existence was determined by the share of the consumption fund allowed to them by the consumption class'.[85]

The value of an ideal type does not lie in its precision, or in the exactness of its fit with 'historical reality', but in its isolation of a vital difference from alternative ideal types, such as the garrison town, the administrative city, and the village, and above all the manufacturing or commercial town of northern Europe in the post-medieval period. In the commercial city, the burghers were primarily interested in trade or manufacture, and they had some political independence from a rural aristocracy; they could set their own pace and could develop their own ethical and legal standards. By contrast, one of the prime strengths and limitations of the ancient city was that it coalesced the rural and urban population into a single autarchic autonomous unit, in which agricultural landowners set the tone. Roman conquest penetrated that autarchy but never separated the town from its countryside.

Were ancient cities consumer cities? The answer must be yes. Great landowners lived in towns. They drew the bulk of their income from their estates, whether by direct exploitation through bailiffs or from rents. Landowners were the wealthiest urban residents. The money they spent in towns was largely drawn from outside the towns. In that sense, ancient towns were parasitical on the surrounding countryside. Towns were centres of consumption in which landowners spent profits derived from rural property and from the hard work of dependent peasants.

From early times in the classical world, town and countryside had been integrated into single city-states. Landowners were citizens. This organization persisted even when city-states became the

---

[84] Weber, *Methodology of the social sciences*, p. 90.
[85] Sombart, *Der moderne Kapitalismus*, i, p. 143.

administrative units of empire. Therefore, there was no political organization specific to the town, which excluded the surrounding countryside. There were no institutions which fostered specifically urban, commercial or manufacturing activity and gave traders or manufacturers a status independent of, or parallel to, the traditional status of landowners. In this way, ancient towns differed, as I understand it, from those post-medieval European towns which grew up in the interstices of feudal baronies, and whose burghers had only very limited opportunities to become members of the landed aristocracy. Dutch or Hanseatic burghers concentrated therefore on the acquisition of commercial wealth and elaborated an ethos which morally elevated their own activities. In the ancient world, however, successful merchants sought respectability and safety by re-investing their commercial profits in the ownership of land. I suspect that this was only a difference of degree, since we find the same phenomenon of gentrification by the acquisition of land among English merchants. But Roman financiers, tax-farmers and public contractors were always required to give land as security for the performance of their duties. It was thus extremely rare in the Roman world for a man to be wealthy without being a landowner.

I do not mean by all this that Romans despised trade. Of course, some members of the literary elite, whose writings have survived, affected to despise trade, at least if it was on a small scale; philosophers despised trade because haggling over prices involved deception. Yet numerous monuments set up in the Greek and Roman world depict tradesmen and artisans at work; these monuments show in a convincing way that among the working classes, and even among the prosperous commercial classes, there was nothing demeaning about work.[86] But trade was less prestigious than owning land. And no prosperous, high-prestige stratum or corporation of urban merchants, as distinct from landowners, ever emerged in Roman society.

In the current orthodoxy, the contribution of manufactures to the urban economy in the Roman world is considered to have been negligible.[87] And it is true that most manufacturing and trading

---

[86] See numerous examples in Esperandieu, *Receuil général*, iii, esp. pp. 1881ff. The Pompeian wall paintings depict several manufacturing scenes; see Mau, *Pompeii*, pp. 376–7.
[87] 'In most of the cities of the empire trade and industry played a minor role...Trade and manufacture played a very minor role in the economy of

units were small; only a few can have employed slaves or apprentices or wage-labourers. Petty commodity production and a bazaar economy of fragmented services predominated. But the small scale of most units of production should not be taken as evidence of their aggregate unimportance. Indeed these small units of non-agricultural production elevated the average standard of living in the Roman empire above, even if only slightly above, the average standard of living in most preceding states.

The Roman Empire was borne on the backs of its peasants, and much of the taxes and rents which they paid were spent in towns, for the benefit of townsmen. But it is wrong to assume that peasants got nothing in return. They got law, protection, peace, rituals, ceremonies and medical advice, even surgery. Towns gave independent peasants and free tenants opportunty to buy extra food and services, necessities and luxuries (tools, pots, clothes, seeds, pastries). Moreover, the towns themselves generated economic activity. Urban artisans had to be serviced, housed; they bought goods. The list of tradesmen from Kōrykos, the small town in Rough Cilicia (see p. 72 above), shows that most tradesmen were engaged in making useful things. The very size of Roman towns indicates the volume of demand which they generated. Much of that demand required urban produce.

In sum, the ideal type of the consumer city has much to recommend it; it largely fits the towns of the ancient world, providing we realize that in reality, ancient towns also served other functions: they were administrative centres, they were garrison towns, they were centres of exchange both as between towns and regions, and between townsmen and the surrounding countryside. All these functions were important. The weakness of the ideal type, in spite of the intentions of its creators, is that it replaces complexity with oversimplification: all too easily, the 'consumer city' becomes the parasitical city, consisting exclusively of idle consumers, fed from the countryside and giving nothing in return.

In the ancient economy, agriculture was clearly pre-eminent; most adults in the Roman world worked in the fields; most wealth was based on landownership. This was because the institution of tenancy allowed rich Romans to aggregate the activities of tens, even hundreds of agricultural workers, with little managerial cost.

the Roman empire. The basic industry was agriculture' (Jones, *Roman economy*, pp. 29–30).

Land could therefore be the prime focus of rich men's investments. If we want to find economic growth in the ancient world, we should look for it in agriculture, not in towns. Average yields of cereals at four or more times seed in Italy and at ten times seed in Egypt were apparently well above early medieval levels. Conquest brought improved productivity and forced up yields through taxation. The Roman conquest of Britain, for example, induced the extension of settled agriculture and the introduction of new crops such as beans, cabbage, and peas which had a profound (and lasting) effect on British diets.[88] Further increases in peasants' productivity were limited partly by the technical inadequacy of agriculture, but even more by poor peasants' chronic underemployment. Their access to more land was restricted by the rich. Small farms kept peasants underworked, while their low consumption demands held down urban productivity, so that only about one family in ten lived away from the land.

The arena for strictly urban economic development was thus very limited. There was no urban institution which rivalled tenancy as a medium of exploitation. Slavery was expensive and important but as a form of production only a transient function of conquest. Tenancies of urban property were important only in the city of Rome. Partnerships in trade, both active and sleeping, were known but were usually on a small scale. Shared risks in sea-loans, on ships and their cargoes, helped investment in a risky branch of trade. But private corporations investing in tax-farming, in mining and in contracts for public works were probably the only productive non-agricultural outlet for large sums of capital.

These corporations are especially interesting because they seem to foreshadow developments which were of great importance in later European banking. In post-medieval Europe, kings borrowed from private bankers, who often protected their credit and their lives by living in other countries. Thus the fragmentation of Europe into rival nations and city-states afforded, even encouraged, developments which the overarching size of the Roman Empire precluded. Roman emperors never borrowed from private citizens; indeed, the emperors, in the interests of efficiency or good government, slowly

---

[88] See Applebaum in Finberg (ed.), *Agrarian history*, i, 2, pp. 108ff. Other imports under Roman influence include the turnip, cherry, mustard and radish. There was also a considerable and important improvement in the shape of the plough.

strangled the private tax-farming corporations. When they were in need of money, emperors either raised taxes, or confiscated the property of the rich or debased the currency. In some respects, Rome was a victim of its own success. In other societies, heavy state expenditure on war has stimulated economic growth; the competitive drive to win has promoted creative investment and the military has constituted a very large market for arms, supplies and ships. This also occurred in the Roman Empire, in that the exaction of taxes to pay troops was a major stimulus to long-distance trade. But Roman armies never faced an enemy which was significantly superior in equipment, so that war did not act as a spur to imitation or invention. Indeed, because of state power, military demands eventually restricted economic growth. In the Late Empire, military supplies and taxes were removed from the market; military supplies were demanded as taxes in kind; for a time, money taxes were virtually abolished. The response to increased external pressure from barbarians was thus not invention but a tightening of the screws of state repression. The standing army was doubled in size from about 300,000 to about 600,000 men; the army was already, by my reckoning, the largest occupational sub-set after the peasantry. This was both a reflection of the limits of economic and urban sophistication in the Roman Empire, and of the considerable resources that were used to preserve the safety of the state. Huge pre-industrial empires accumulate huge resources; they spend a large part of that accumulated surplus on self-preservation, not on economic growth.[89]

[89] I should like to thank Chester Starr, Mark Hassall and John North for advice and help.

3. Chinese Cities since the Sung Dynasty

MARK ELVIN

The medieval economic revolution in China, which may be dated between about 900 and 1200, was connected with two major changes in China's urban structure.[1]

Up to this time, the large centres had been predominantly cities of administrators and consumers, and the circulation of wealth and goods had depended primarily on the pumping mechanism provided by taxation. Now they also became commercial and industrial centres, in degrees varying from case to case. (Major religious centres seem mostly to have been rural, though sometimes modest towns grew up as the result of fairs held in conjunction with periodic religious celebrations.) Canton, previously the only coastal city of any importance, was joined by four or five other centres of maritime trade as commerce grew between China and the Indo-Islamic world. (There was a decline later, due to the Maritime Interdict imposed by the Ming until 1567.) These larger conurbations grew rapidly, often spilling out from their walls into suburbs. Internally, the old system of tightly controlled and segregated quarters broke down. Chinese population statistics, which do not usually distinguish between city and hinterland in an administrative area, do not permit any very exact measurement of the size of the most populous cities; but four or five were probably not far from a million inhabitants. The 1232 epidemic at K'ai-feng, when it was full of refugees just after the Mongols lifted the first siege of the city, carried off between 0.9 and 1.0 million people in from fifty to ninety days.[2]

[1] Twitchett, *Asia Major* (1966); Shiba, *Commerce and society*; Elvin, *The Chinese past*; Ma, *Commercial development and urban change*. Also of value are Balazs, *Annales, E.S.C.* (1957); Hartwell, *J. Asian Stud.* (1962); and *idem, J. Econ. and Soc. Hist. Orient* (1967). For general descriptions of Sung cities, see Gernet, *La vie quotidienne en Chine*; Latham, *Marco Polo*; and Balazs in Balazs (ed.), *Chinese civilization*.

[2] Imura Kōzen, *Chugāi iji shimpō* (1936–7), esp. pp. 272–4. The *Chin-shih* ('History of the Chin'), ch. 17, 14b, says that 'in the fifth moon [of 1232] there was a great epidemic in Pien-ching [K'ai-feng]. In the space of fifty days over 90,000 dead were taken out through the gates, those too poor to be buried not being included in this number.' Imura also quotes an account by Li Kao, a doctor, that fits with this *per diem* outflow of 1,500 per gate: 'Each day, from each of the twelve gates of the capital, between 1,000 and

The second trend was the appearance of a growing number of informal markets in empty sites, towns, and cities throughout the empire. This was part cause and part effect of the collapse of the earlier system of state-controlled walled urban markets. Concomitantly the state was obliged to levy both local and transit taxes on goods; and internal customs posts sprang up along the major routes. The informal, often periodic, markets increasingly became the focal points of peasant life, and standard marketing areas seem to have been the lowest unit of sub-cultural variation.[3] Other organizational systems, with different spatial patterns, crosscut this marketing system; we may instance water-control organizations as an obvious example.[4] We may note in passing that some parts of late traditional India, such as Bengal, had a system of periodic markets (*hāt*) not unlike its Chinese counterpart. The most obvious differences would seem to be that, in these parts of India, reciprocal status obligations to some extent supplied services that had to be bought in China, that barter was much commoner, that itinerant traders played a more significant role, and that the periodic religious fair (*mēla*), though not without Sung parallels, generated a relatively greater share of trade. In other regions of India (such as Broach, Pālanpur, and Mahikāntha in Bombay Presidency) permanent markets dominated.[5] An interesting topic for future research will be to specify the forces that produced the varying types of market

2.000 [corpses] were carried out.' But he gives the period as three months, which yields a death roll of over one million. Imura Kōzen, *Chūgai iji shimpō* (1936–7), p. 275.

[3] Skinner, *J. Asian Stud.* (1964). See also Crissman in Willmott (ed.), *Economic organization in Chinese society*, and Fei in Perkins (ed.), *China's modern economy*.

[4] Elvin, *Ch'ing-shih wen-t'i* (1975).

[5] Bengal District Gazetteers, by L. S. S. O'Malley and others (Calcutta, 1906–23), especially *Shahabad*, pp. 96–7; *Cuttack*, p. 143; *Darbhanga*, p. 90; *Balasore*, pp. 131, 134–41; *Patna*, p. 138; *Palamau*, pp. 117–18; *Champaran*, pp. 101, 106; *Angu*, pp. 109–10, 134–5; *Saran*, p. 99; *Puri*, p. 189; *Bankura*, pp. 116–17; *Khulna*, p. 125; *Sambalpur*, pp. 153, 156; *Monghyr*, p. 148; *Howrah*, p. 103; *Birbhum*, p. 77; *Singham, Saraikela and Kharsawan*, pp. 157, 232; *Feudatory States of Orissa*, pp. 81–3; *Santāl Parganas*, pp. 204–7; *Burdwan*, p. 126; *Manbhüm*, p. 168; *Rajshahi*, pp. 111–12; *Bhagalpur*, p. 123; *Midnapore*, p. 128; *Purnea*, p. 122; *Nadia*, p. 96; *Hooghly*, p. 192; *Jessore*, pp. 98, 101–2, 105; *24 Parganas*, p. 155; *Murshidabad*, p. 130; *Mymensingh*, pp. 87–8, 89–90; *Malda* pp. 61, 67; *Bakarganj*, p. 82; *Pabna*, pp. 68, 73; *Faridpur*, p. 80. Compare *Gazetteer of the Bombay Presidency* (Bombay, dates of publication of individual volumes given below), ii Gujarat (1877), pp. 181, 437; iii *Kaira* and *Panch Mahals* (1879), p. 251; v *Cutch, Palanpur, and Mahi Kantha* (1880), pp. 121, 300, 378–9. I am grateful to Wolf Mersch

system seen in these two pre-modern agrarian-urban civilizations. There was extensive serfdom and serflike tenancy in Sung and Yuan China. It involved mainly land-bondage and a depressed socio-legal status. So far as we can tell, the regional variations in this phenomenon bear no obvious positive or negative relation to the level of urbanization. Manor and market lived comfortably enough together. Chinese city air made nobody free. One of the most urbanized areas, the lower Yangtze delta, was one where serfdom (with some intermittent fluctuations due to state confiscation of lands) was common until the middle of the seventeenth century.

The underpinning of both trends of urban growth was an extension and intensification of irrigated rice agriculture, and the development of an efficient system of inland water transport. To some extent it is possible to speak from this time onwards of an 'economic dualism' in China: areas with access to water transport could and did support denser populations, more vigorous commerce, and a higher level of urbanization than those without. The mastery of large-scale hydraulic works also permitted the settlement of plains not previously easily accessible or secure. Map 1 shows the case of Ning-po on the south-east coast, little settled before mid-T'ang times, where locks were essential to stop the salinization of the paddy-fields and sea-walls to prevent flooding.[6]

In the Sung dynasty (960–1279), the first trend probably outran the second. The contrast between the great cities and the countryside and lesser centres must have been very marked. In the later Ming and the Ch'ing dynasty (roughly, the period after 1600) the second trend proved more powerful. The largest cities did not exceed their Sung maxima; and as total population tripled, their percentage share of the population fell. In some areas, at least, the lesser centres probably grew faster than the population. This was true, for example, of Shang-hai county as may be seen from figure 1.

In so far as this second trend in late traditional times reduced the contrast between cities and countryside, we may speak of a process of 'urban devolution'. Von Richtofen wrote of 'the Chinese type of town-like village', and observed that 'the difference of villages and

---

for drawing my attention to these gazetteers and to Mr S. Seidenberg and Dr T. Raychaudhuri for discussion though none of these friends should be held responsible for the views expressed here.
[6] Shiba, *Machikaneyama ronsō* (1969).

cities is generally more in size than in character, and the smallest hamlet has a tinge of the city'.[7] Most western discussions of the proportions of the Chinese 'urban' or 'rural' population thus have a certain air of unreality, arising from the precision of their terms.

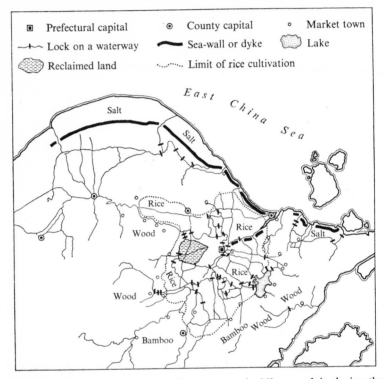

Map 1.   Urbanization and hydraulic works on the Ning-po plain during the Sung dynasty (after Shiba)

A substantial proportion occupied some sort of intermediate position; and map 2, which is a close-up of part of the Canton Delta around Fo-shan, is included here in the hope of conveying some sense of the type of settlement pattern here involved. Note that the area shown is only about 8 by 11 miles (13 by 18 kilometres).

On the other hand, there was also a process of 'urban concentration' during much the same period. After 1600, more and more landowners moved permanently into the cities, and their holdings

[7] Von Richtofen, *Baron Richtofen's letters*, p. 117.

became more fragmented. They became absentees, linked to their tenants by agents rather than personally and directly. In other words, power left the land. The old lower-level administrative system for tax-collection, hydraulic works, and security had been based on conscripting resident middle-level landowners to run it.

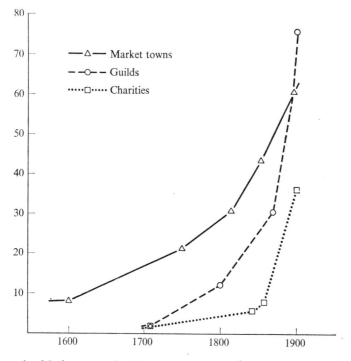

Figure 1. Market towns in Shang-hai county, and guilds and charities in Shanghai city, 1600–1900

Now it collapsed, and was replaced by a combination of government clerks and managerial 'gentry' (that is, holders of official titles and examination degrees), both mainly based in cities and towns. The financing of seasonal peasant deficits shifted from the manor lord or managerial landlord to the mainly urban pawnshop. Investment by the wealthy moved steadily away from farmland. Part consequence and part cause of these trends was a rise in peasant freedom and a virtual end to serflike tenancy.

Map 2. High-density rural settlement pattern: the countryside around Fo-shan, Kwangtung

Source. UK War Office, GSGS 4691, M8SW, M9NW, 1949

Another side to 'concentration' was the rise of certain characteristically urban institutions. Figure 1 shows how the late traditional
period witnessed a multiplication of gentry-run charities and
mercantile guilds in the city of Shanghai. There is also evidence
that higher educational institutions (the 'academies') became more
urban or at least suburban in location. Hydraulic works, often
important to inter-city water-borne commerce, were to some extent
financed by and managed from urban centres in the nineteenth
century. There is also some reason to suspect the emergence of a
fused gentry–merchant elite in the smaller centres, where the socio-
gravitational pull of the official world on the more wealthy and
ambitious gentry and merchants did not pull it apart.

Cities, as such, played a limited role in pre-modern Chinese political
history. The chief reason for this was the maintenance of a continuous centralized imperial authority, and the absence of political
fragmentation. The upper elite was geographically mobile; and
this inhibited the growth of a strong civic self-consciousness or
urban patriotism. The psychological implications of the 'rule of
avoidance', whereby an official was not permitted to serve in his
province of origin, are brought out in the comments of Lu Chi,
writing in the late Ming:

> There are two ways in which today's great officials behave when
> at home, and when holding an official post. Those who love a
> fine reputation show a firm purpose and self-control when they
> are in office, so everybody trusts them. When they come home
> they make exactions on the villages, extend invitations to the
> county magistrates and prefects and establish connections with
> them, the object being to enrich their families thereby. They take
> a delight in being loathed by the country folk, and show them no
> pity. *Per contra*, those who are greedy for profit put on a sly
> pretence of being uncorrupted while they are living at home;
> and they seek to make the village communities think well of them.
> When, however, they take up an official post, they seize excessive
> profits without a trace of restraint. Their delight is a life-time of
> destroying others, and it is this that they consider 'success'.[8]

Although this passage does not relate specifically to cities, the
distinction between an official's home and the place where he held
office is evident. There were exceptions to this separation, but these

[8] Fu I-ling, *Ming-tai*, p. 119.

were normally in a period of internal anarchy, such as Soochow under Chang Shih-ch'eng in the middle of the fourteenth century.[9] Our initial generalization is thus confirmed.

Below the upper elite, the leading members of urban communities were often outsiders and migrants. Many Chinese guilds in the late Ming and Ch'ing grew up as internal consulates, as it were, for traders of a common origin external to the locality where they traded. They often equalled in number, or even outnumbered Ming and Ch'ing guilds formed as associations of those of a similar trade. Since they were a phenomenon largely of the seventeenth century and later,[10] and rather different from the guilds of T'ang and Sung times (with no demonstrable historical continuity), the impression emerges of a period during which much inter-region trade altered from arbitrage, designed to remedy accidental shortages, to a more regularized and routinized form. These guilds were a response to this routinization. Thus arose such phenomena as the dominance of much of Shanghai's economy in the nineteenth century by merchants from Ning-po.[11]

Late Ch'ing guilds often co-operated. There were even a few cities run by confederations of guilds. But their existence as bodies drawn from different regions, worshipping different gods and sponsoring different festivals, though it enriched city life, also perpetuated a sense of separatism. Yet merchant families that had lived in an adopted city for several generations cannot have felt themselves entirely outsiders, and it is not always easy to know what weight to assign to these differences of origin.

At the lower end of the social scale, the part played by migration, permanent, temporary, and seasonal, in forming the late traditional city is a matter for conjecture until research has been done on it. It seems plausible that there was usually a preponderance of men over women, but it is impossible to be confident about this until we know more about the composition of the urban servant population.

The lesser burden of taxation and obligatory labour for the state in cities may have been an attraction to migrants. A late Ming gazetteer for Hsiao-kan county in Hupeh province observed, after listing abuses in the assessment and exaction of various levies, that 'people living in the villages have to provide twice as much as those

9 Mote, *The poet Kao Ch'i*, esp. chaps. 2 and 3.
10 Ho Ping-ti, *Hui-kuan*.
11 Mann Jones in Elvin and Skinner (eds.), *The Chinese city*.

who live in towns, and those in economically distressed circumstances provide twice as much again as the [ordinary] countryfolk'.[12] There is here an interesting subject for investigation.

What, then, did cities signify in the life of late-traditional China?
There was little civic awareness as such. Most county capitals
had walls for purposes of defence and police control, but they were
not formally distinguished from the administrative areas, the
counties in which they were embedded. The only exception to this
was at the religious level; the domain of the city god, with whom
every county capital was provided, appears not to have extended
beyond his moat. There were of course no municipal archives;
almost all Chinese archives seem in any case eventually to have
been abstracted and then destroyed. Little building was in stone;
and the inhabitants of no Chinese city lived surrounded by such
visible reminders of bygone urban splendours as linger to inspire
or haunt the Roman, the Venetian, and the Florentine. Apart from
a few millennial stone bridges and city walls, the past was incon-
spicuous, being preserved in objects of modest size such as bronze
vessels and stone inscriptions. There was almost no municipal art,
such as statues; and certainly no rivalry between cities in aesthetic
or religious projects.

The city was in some respects feared by peasants. One Ch'ing
official wrote that 'countryfolk are terrified to enter their county
capital, dreading the officials as if they were tigers'.[13] The city was
a place where taxes and rents were often paid, and where lawsuits
were tried. It was the haunt of criminals such as the 'market bullies'
who were experts at victimizing peasants. In times of famine, it was
in the city that farmers sold starving children whom they could no
longer feed,[14] and where they found it easiest to obtain relief from
public soup kitchens, or to buy grain at a reduced price from the
official granaries. It was where you went to find casual work, such
as hauling government boats along canals. And, as the proverb had
it, it was where you sought refuge during small disorders but a place
to flee from in a time of serious troubles.

Seen from within, the city was also a place of amenity and amuse-
ment. There were the specialized attractions that central places
characteristically provide according to their status: bookshops, bath

[12] Ku Yen-wu (ed.), *T'ien-hsia*, xxxvii, ts'e 25, Hu-kuang *hsia*.
[13] Chang Ying-ch'ang (ed.), *Ch'ing shih to*, p. 591.   [14] *Ibid.* p. 570.

houses, long-distance remittance banks (in the largest centres), letter-carriers, a succession of religious festivals and theatricals, flower shows, pleasure gardens, temples, bawdy houses, executions, and other delights. Living-time was slightly more structured than in the countryside, with gates ʰthat closed at sundown, and drum ·towers that sounded the watches of the night. There were also distinctive urban institutions such as fire brigades, and rudimentary organizations for cleaning and lighting streets, often linked to the gentry-run charities.

But there was one curious contrast with western Europe that deserves attention. Traditional Chinese cities were centres of political and economic power, as we have seen, but no rebellion ever originated in them apart from a few strikes by urban workers after the seventeenth century and occasional closures of the market by merchants as a form of political pressure. The sense of what one might call 'urban passivity' is inescapable.

One of the distinguishing features of 'modern' China is that this is no longer so. Since the later nineteenth century, the cities have been focal points of change, with the Maoist rural revolutionary detour of 1927–49 as a significant exception. The impact of the West, at least in its more positive aspects, was almost wholly urban. Modern education, modern business, modern communications, and modern politics were almost wholly confined to prefectural capitals and above, with a concentration in Shanghai, Tientsin, Wuchang, Canton, and Peking. There was an accompanying realignment of trade, which altered the pattern of relative city dominance away from inland routes and towards the coast.

While the concentration of development in the larger cities sharpened the differences between life there and in the rest of the country, or, put differently, between a modernized elite and every-body else, the telegraph revolution of 1880–1910 effected a change of a different sort. The five hundred or so most important centres were linked with each other, and with the world outside. Internal communications were speeded up by a factor of at least 100. The outcome was a national urban network whose component members were in some respects linked more tightly with each other than with their immediate hinterlands. Political interaction between Peking and the provinces was transformed. Already by the Boxer uprising of 1900 it had taken on that dizzying instantaneous quality that we recognize as 'modern'. The new pattern can be seen in the linked urban anti-American boycotts of 1905, in the interconnected bank failures of 1910, in the 1911 revolution when urban centres for the first time in Chinese history initiated a major political development, and in the movements of 4 May 1919 and 30 May 1925, which created mass urban political participation.[15]

The failure of this first 'urban period' of Chinese politics to create a durable new system was probably due to the cultural gap that had opened between the leading cities and the rest of the countryside. It has been one of the historic achievements of the Chinese Communist Party after 1949 to have bridged this gap and, to some extent, to have closed it.[16]

---

[15] Elvin and Skinner (eds.), *The Chinese city*. See also the map of cities participating in the 1911 revolution, with dates of entry into the Republican camp, in Elvin, *Modern China* (1976).

[16] Lewis (ed.), *The city in Communist China.*

4. The Origins of the Medieval Town Patriciate

A. B. HIBBERT

This article is concerned with the theory advanced by Henri Pirenne to explain the origins and early history of medieval towns. This theory may be summarized as follows.[1] During the ninth and much of the tenth centuries long-distance trade in Europe was at its lowest ebb, and during this period the only settlements which were not purely agricultural were the ecclesiastical, military and administrative centres which served the major needs of the feudal ruling classes: fortresses, monasteries, episcopal seats, royal residences and the like.[2] These had none of the characteristics of true towns and knew neither commercial nor industrial activity, but when long-distance trade revived in the tenth and eleventh centuries the merchants and artisans produced by changing economic conditions settled round them. The influx of such people made it possible for true town life to develop.

From the very beginning the incoming traders differed from the older inhabitants. They were set apart by their origins, for they were 'new men' and indeed outsiders to the feudal order itself, living on the margins of that society; they were set apart by their way of life for they lived exclusively by trade; they were set apart in a purely physical sense, for they lived outside the walls of the old feudal settlement or 'pre-urban nucleus' in a separate trading and manufacturing colony, the suburb.

The feudal 'core' of such double settlements remained static, inert, but the colony formed by the newcomers grew in numbers and in strength. Finally a time came when the traders and craftsmen felt themselves strong enough to challenge the control which the

---

[1] Pirenne's theory was first advanced in *Revue historique* (1895), and expanded in various later works. All these can be most conveniently consulted in the collection of his writings on urban history published in Pirenne, *Les villes.*

[2] The word 'feudal' will be used to refer to a kind of society in which economic and political power derive from large-scale landholding, and where there is direct and indirect exploitation of this land by means of dependent cultivators.

91

feudal element had hitherto exercised over them. They or their leaders struggled for independence, and by money or force of arms established a new regime which contrasted in all essentials with the old order. A distinctive social, economic and legal unit was brought into being, the medieval town, and this was the work of the merchants and artisans alone.

A group of the more important merchants commonly took the lead in the struggle to achieve these various changes, and after the town had thrown off or modified feudal control, this group developed into the characteristic medieval 'patriciate'. This patriciate was an increasingly narrow class which enjoyed social, political and economic control in the town and whose power and influence rested on the control of the wholesale and long-distance trades of the town. The changing relations between this dominant element and the rest of the townsmen were to determine a great deal of later town history.

This theory is certainly both powerful and fertile, and yet it may be questioned at many points. What follows is not an original or exhaustive examination of the hypothesis. I intend merely to probe some of its weak points in a preliminary way. I shall deal with one theme only in detail, that of the origin of the patriciate, and shall choose my facts and arguments from among those likely to be familiar to students of the subject.

We can most profitably criticize Pirenne's views in two ways: on theoretical grounds and by reference to fact. In the first instance we may ask whether he was right in his view of the role of the revival of long-distance trade in the tenth and eleventh centuries, and in his views on the relationship between trade and feudal society in general. In the second, we may ask whether a sharply contrasted feudal 'nucleus' and a trading suburb really occurred in the early stages of all towns and whether the patriciate really developed along the lines he suggested.

I shall make only the briefest reference to the effects and nature of the expansion of long-distance trade from the late tenth century onwards. Has long-distance trade as opposed to local trade any special virtue as a stimulant of town growth? Was long-distance trade before AD 1000 as unimportant as Pirenne's theory assumes? We may leave these questions aside, though Pirenne's answers to them may be, and have been, challenged. There are other grounds for disquiet. Pirenne treats a trade revival as though it were something which happens of itself, independent of surrounding circumstance.[3] Such treatment of historical fact is often justifiable, it is a useful piece of shorthand to prevent an infinite regress from cause to cause, but it loses its justification if instead of condensing argument to a convenient size, it involves the elimination of arguments vital to the discussion.

Just such a difficulty arises here. Pirenne's theory leans heavily on the idea that there is a natural incompatibility between arrangements of society suited to feudal lords and those suited to merchants and artisans, or between a 'feudal' settlement and one allowing the development of trade and industry. One cannot deny that such an antagonism between 'feudal' and 'burgess' interests did develop later in the Middle Ages. It may even be granted that it was potential or latent from the beginning. If, however, we consider how trade *must* originally have developed in the context of a feudal society, and how the earlier concentrations of merchants and artisans must equally have been the outcome of feudal circumstance, we may properly question any theory which assumes that the two were originally and inherently incompatible.

Both fact and theory suggest that in earlier medieval times trade was by no means a solvent of feudal society, but that it was a natural product of that society and that feudal rulers up to a point favoured its growth. There is the simple fact that whatever area and whatever century we may choose to take as being most typically 'feudal' there is still trade and there are still merchants. Feudalism could never dispense with merchants. The very structure, technical level and economic habits of society always made some local and long-distance trade necessary. It is possible to press this point further. It can be argued that the development of feudal lordships and of related changes in agricultural organization both increased total productivity and concentrated the wealth so produced. Ever greater and wealthier feudal establishments appeared and these acted as ever greater and more demanding consumers – thus directly stimulating trade and concentrating those who supplied the goods for them. Again, a substantial class of merchants and craftsmen had to be fed by the agricultural labours of the other groups; these therefore had to provide extra food. It may thus be suggested

---

[3] 'That the origin of medieval towns springs directly from the revival of commerce as cause and effect...is something which cannot be doubted' (Pirenne, *Les villes*, i, p. 376), 'The fundamental conception...which sees commerce as the essential cause of the growth of towns, is incontestably true' (*ibid.* ii, p. 259).

that growth of such a class depended essentially on changes in rural society which made either for increased productivity or lower consumption per head among the tillers, thus providing more food. Such changes must have been wrought *within* the 'feudal' structure and were a basic prerequisite of any town development.

The mass of evidence about what attitude feudal lords took in practice towards towns and trade adds weight to these arguments. They founded towns, encouraged merchant and artisan settlement, sketched out a staple policy in their attempts to direct trade through centres under their own control and, especially in southern Europe, took an active and direct part in town life. There were two obvious reasons why they should do this. They had to provision large private and public establishments, and they wished to gain profit from trade and industry, either by becoming traders themselves or by tapping the wealth produced by trade and industry through levies and charges upon goods or upon those who produced and distributed them.

Portions of Pirenne's theory can be tested by a more direct appeal to facts. Two questions seem particularly prominent: the nature and role of the 'pre-urban' or 'feudal' nucleus and the origins of the patriciate. For the sake of brevity I shall discuss only the second of these here. Pirenne's description of the social history of the burgess class and the rise among them of an urban patriciate, is of prime importance in his theory. For him the patricians were the main creators and moulders of urban life and institutions; they were the mainspring of town development. It is therefore of some consequence to establish who and what they were.

Pirenne answers this question in a fairly simple way. The more prosperous burgesses were the descendants of those newcomers who in the eleventh century and later had settled round fortresses, monasteries and similar centres for the sake of security. Each had originally been 'a little pedlar, a sailor, a boatman, a docker' or something of the sort.[4] Those who had prospered had become great merchants and from among the most notable of these was recruited, during the twelfth and thirteenth centuries, the ruling clique of the towns, a patriciate whose class dominance was based on their position as great wholesale traders.[5]

Any attempt to find out whether the patriciate really did originate

---

[4] Pirenne, *Economic and social history*, p. 48.
[5] *Ibid.* p. 201.

among merchants and 'new men' encounters very great difficulties, above all the sheer lack of documentary material. The obvious way to answer the question would be to sample the family histories of members of the early patriciate, but in practice this is almost impossible. Of course this difficulty cuts both ways and Pirenne himself has to rely more on inference than on direct evidence for his own theory. The career of St Godric of Finchale, which he uses as a picturesque illustration, is a rather shaky foundation on which to build a great theoretical edifice.[6]

The basic facts about many Italian towns are perhaps too well known to need much comment. There the petty nobility and the greater among the free landowners played a part which Pirenne himself admits to be different from that generally allotted to them in his theory.[7] They were favourably disposed towards the development of trade, they took a direct part in commercial activities and they were sometimes the most prominent subscribers of capital and the final controllers of commercial life.

At Genoa for example, where the first trading partnerships are found in the documents of the early eleventh century, the typical sleeping partner is a landowner who has some surplus capital to invest, presumably derived from land rents, loot from expeditions against the Moslems, or from feudal office. Later, during the course of the eleventh and twelfth centuries, it becomes even clearer that the greatest leaders of trade expansion were the men who already possessed influence and money because of their high position in a feudal society, men who received large revenues from rents or customs or market dues. In the very front rank, commercially as well as socially and politically, were great twelfth-century vice-comital families like the Burone, della Volta, Mallone and di Castro. They and people of the same general standing, such as the Embriaco family, dominated all aspects of Genoese life during this period. Then, in the later twelfth and thirteenth centuries, their position was challenged by new men who had risen from the lower ranks of society by the ladder of successful trade. Such newcomers were the Doria, Cigala and Lercari families who were to be so important in the period of Genoese maturity.[8]

This class of lesser nobles and landowners was equally important in the constitutional development of Italian towns. They took a

[6] *Ibid.* p. 47.   [7] *Ibid.* p. 48.
[8] Renouard, *Les hommes d'affaires italiens*, pp. 24, 47–54.

prominent part, and characteristically the lead, in the struggle against episcopal control. We find them to be the essential element of many of the earliest urban ruling groups; they provided the membership of the earliest Italian patriciates. From the earliest date Milan chose its consuls from the *capitanei, valvassores* and *cives*.[9] Elsewhere the *grandi* were typically recruited from the lesser nobility and great landlords, from the group which had usurped seignorial control. This group was so little composed of great merchants alone that these latter had subsequently to lead revolutions to secure a share of control with the earlier patriciate. Long after the towns had achieved a marked degree of independence, in the thirteenth century, great merchants combined against the old patriciate of semi-feudal nature in revolutionary movements at Florence and elsewhere. Few things could be more significant, for if the patriciate had already been composed simply of great merchants such struggles would have been superfluous. Hence A. Sapori, summing up the present state of investigations into Italian town history, sees town development as due to the formation of a group stronger and richer than the rest, which usurped the public and financial functions of the overlord and gave its personal and class unity a territorial basis. It was essentially formed, he holds, of petty vassals, great emphyteutic tenants and large-scale 'farmers', all of whom had developed a direct interest in trading matters.[10]

It therefore seems no exaggeration to say that in Italy the first stages of urban history in the Middle Ages were associated with the formation of a ruling group of largely aristocratic and feudal origin, which controlled town life and trading conditions. The later history of this patriciate would vary. Sometimes the original patriciate adapted itself to the changing volume and nature of trade by taking an interest in its development or by recruiting members from among the merchants themselves. In such cases an upper group, part feudal-aristocratic, part mercantile, would arise, a group of mixed nature like the 'magnates' of Bologna formed of nobles made bourgeois by business and bourgeois ennobled by city decree, both fused together in law.[11] In other towns the old patriciate would prove too unadaptable and powerful new groups would build up outside its ranks. Then the day would come when the controllers of

9 Pirenne, *Les villes*, i, p. 400.
10 Sapori in *IXe Congrès international, 1950.*
11 *Ibid.*

the great trades either overthrew the rule of the *grandi* or else forced them to share their powers. In the first case the history of the patriciate clearly consists, in various proportions, of the transformation of the old ruling group of feudal origin and the recruitment of new men into it. Even when events had the most revolutionary appearance, however, we have still to face two facts. An aristocratic patriciate held sway in the earlier and most formative period, and the supplanting group usually made little change in town organization and quickly formed itself into a body barely distinguishable from that which it had replaced.

Leaving aside the evidence of other southern regions, which is often so similar to the Italian, let us turn to northern Europe, for Pirenne in fact based his theory on the evidence of northern towns.

J. W. F. Hill has collected the information available about the families which dominated Lincoln immediately after it achieved some degree of self-government.[12] Take the three most prominent families of all, those which provided the first three mayors to be known by name. Adam, mayor between 1210 and 1216, had as grandfather a landowner and church benefactor, as uncles the holder of a fee and a bailiff of the lord; his father was a property owner, a man who leased houses to tradesmen, and supervisor of repairs to the castle gaol. His brothers-in-law were lords' bailiffs and considerable landowners within the city and in surrounding villages, his cousin another landowner. He himself possessed numerous lands, houses and rents, including land in the Bail, the area which remained under the feudal jurisdiction of the constable of the castle. His nephew, John Fleming de Holm, held a lordship at Langton as well as being an alderman of Lincoln, and John's son and grandson followed in his footsteps. The latter, Peter de Holm, held property within the Bail by homage and fealty to the Bishop of Durham, and his case is the first in which we *may* have evidence that the family engaged in trade: in 1268 he was granted life exemption from all tallages assessed in the city provided that he did not trade in the town. This seems very dubious and negative evidence on which to base a claim that the family was one of merchants. We must not make too much of an argument from silence, but it remains true that between 1150 and 1250 the family was one of important landowners, rentiers and feudal officials, on the fringe of the nobility.

[12] Hill, *Medieval Lincoln*, appendix v.

The second known mayor, William 'nephew of Warner', had relatives of the same generation who held the rectory of St Paul in the Bail, held half a knight's fee from the bishop, were owners of houses and market stalls, bailiffs and great landowners. William himself was bailiff to the lord on several occasions and a rich rentier into the bargain. There were trading interests in the family however; a certain Osbert, probably William's uncle, and owner of considerable landed property, was once fined for selling wine con- trary to the assize. Even so it is very arguable whether trade or land and office-holding ranked as the original and basic activity, and Osbert's sons and grandsons figured as prominently as bailiffs, landed proprietors and rent holders as they did as men with commercial interests. The third family, that of the mayor Peter de Ponte, conformed more closely to the pattern of the first. This family 'had its roots in the Bail', contained two bailiffs in Peter's father's generation, and was characteristically made up of large landholders and rentiers in the twelfth and early thirteenth centuries.

Naturally such evidence is not conclusive as to the origins of the thirteenth century patriciate of Lincoln. Somewhere in an unrecorded past these men *may* have first climbed to fortune by the profits of the Scandinavian trade. What the facts do tell us is that <u>at its very first documented appearance the patriciate has the character of a land-owning and rentier group, holding feudal office and then town office</u> without a break, merging with the smaller kind of feudal noble and landlord. If we can discriminate at all on such slender evidence we are shown that trading was at least as likely to be sometimes taken up as time went on, as something to be dropped as part of a shameful family past.

Evidence of varied nature comes from other places. In Poland Rutkowski derives the trading patriciate of those towns whose population remained on the whole Polish from the feudal nobles who settled in the towns while retaining their interests as great landholders.[13] In Norway the chief merchants in the twelfth and thirteenth centuries were great ecclesiastics and great landowners, while the ruling class of Bergen, and its dominant trading clique before the days of Hanseatic hegemony, was made up of important officials and the principal owners of *gaards* (*curtes*) within the town, to whom were joined, as more recent and less substantial elements,

13 Rutkowski, *Histoire économique de la Pologne*, p. 39.

some professional merchants and shipowners.[14] Pirenne himself goes so far as to agree that in the eleventh century there was at least some fusion between the knightly class and the upper rank of traders to form the patriciate in the northern towns, and he has also to admit that in some towns of his area, and especially in the episcopal cities of the Rhineland and the Liège region, the *ministeriales* of the lord entered into the patriciate.[15]

It is interesting that the evidence for his own theory is so very dubious in the one town on which Pirenne has published a detailed study – Dinant.[16] Here, under the presidency of the *villicus* of the Bishop of Liège, the chief officials were the *monetarii* who acted as judges in the town court and were the instruments of episcopal control. Pirenne describes this feudal group as 'gradually giving way before the slow but irresistible invasion of the bourgeoisie', the *échevinage* replacing the *monetarii* in the twelfth and thirteenth centuries. Pirenne's case would be firmer if the *monetarii-judices* survived by the side of the *échevins* as a contrasted group. As it is, their disappearance allows us to guess that both groups might in fact have been recruited from the same class of men and that one was transformed into the other. In fact, the evidence suggests just this. In 1227 when the four *monetarii* are mentioned for the last time, two of them *were échevins*, and another almost certainly belonged to a family which provided more than one *échevin* later in the century. In other words, three out of the four episcopal officials furnish direct proof of continuity and fusion with the *échevinage*. It should be noted that *échevins* were probably still elected by the bishop, that the law they administered was seigneurial, that they clung above all other things to competence in cases involving real estate. If the *échevinage* was the original form of the bourgeois patriciate as Pirenne says, then it must be conceded that it derived in great part, if not entirely from the same class as the original feudal officials. 'Their possession in the city and its surrounds of vineyards, curtileges, houses and land rents' was a primary basis of their economic power and their large-scale trading interests were probably derivative.

J. Lestocquoy's researches into the great patrician families of

[14] Gade, *Hanseatic control*, pp. 27–8.
[15] Pirenne, *Les villes*, i, pp. 54, 103–4, 216.
[16] 'Histoire de la constitution de la ville de Dinant au Moyen Age', in Pirenne, *Les villes*, ii, pp. 1–94.

Arras[17] provide most important direct evidence. He examines in detail five of the families who were in the top rank from the twelfth century onwards and in no case does he find their origins among landless newcomers or among a population of professional merchants some of whom gradually improved their position. Instead they seem to spring from a group who were feudal officials and moderately important landowners in the eleventh century. The Crespin family, which produced some of the greatest financiers of the Middle Ages and lent several times their annual income to most of the cities of Flanders, first appeared as modest landed proprietors and possessors of a mill in the mid-twelfth century. They took up money-lending on a moderate scale about the 1220s. The Huquedieu family started in the service of St Vaast monastery, as officials of the Count of Flanders and as cathedral canons about the same time. They may have had a military origin, and seem to have been high feudal officials; one of them was an *échevin* in 1111 when these officers receive their first mention.

Similar cases can be multiplied. At Cambridge we find that the alderman of the Gild Merchant and perhaps the first mayor of the town, Hervey Dunning, held land in a half-dozen villages, claimed the rank of knight and twice demanded wagers of battle in suits concerning landed property. His father, uncle and grandfather were all landowners.[18] At Brussels the patriciate dominated the Gild Merchant at the beginning of the fourteenth century and contained the most prominent merchant employers in the drapery industry; yet no thirteenth-century document shows the patrician *lignages* engaged in trade. Of course this is in part due to the chances of documentary survival, yet the further back patrician family histories are pushed, the more clearly the patricians appear as landholders and lesser feudatories. Families like the Clutines and Eggluys were farmers of tithes, tenants of castellanies, holders of ducal fiefs – they owed their wealth to lands, rents and the farming of feudal revenues.[19]

Perhaps there is much more similar evidence to be found. Who were the eleventh- and early twelfth-century aldermen of London? Who were the 'possessors' who lived near Ghent in the eleventh

[17] Lestocquoy, *Les dynasties bourgeoises*. See also *idem, Les villes de Flandre et d'Italie* which attacks the Pirenne thesis in greater detail along lines similar to those here indicated.

[18] Cam, *Liberties and communities*, pp. 23–4.

[19] Favresse, *Le régime démocratique*, pp. 32–3.

century and took their wool to the town to be woven? Who were the leading citizens of early Douai, two of whom can be found in the twelfth century selling their share in the town tolls to the Abbey of Andin?[20] The whole problem of patrician origins requires much more detailed investigation, but the evidence does seem to call for an interim revision of Pirenne's theory.

This revision must take account of two main facts: the evidence which shows that old-established families could adapt themselves to new economic conditions, and use their old power to achieve power in a new context; and the truth in Pirenne's contention that the more successful merchants among the newcomers to a town could make their way into the ruling class. Two processes are involved in the formation of the patriciate, the internal transformation of an old dominant class and the recruitment of new families from the more successful merchants and artisans, who were often immigrants or the descendants of immigrants. Let us take each process in turn.

In the earlier stages of town development there was often a class between the actual lords on the one hand, and agricultural workers, craftsmen, petty traders, porters, innkeepers and the like, on the other. This group comprised large freeholders and emphyteutic tenants, sometimes the lower grades of the nobility (especially in Italy), prominent officials in the service of a lay or ecclesiastical lord, like the more important among the *ministeriales* in Germany, and, possibly, such elements as burhthegns, cnihts, lawmen, or members of a witan, dimly discernible in early English towns. The economic position of the group was intimately associated with the possession of land and feudal office. At the same time its members were willing to take advantage of any opportunity to improve their position – by leasing their land or renting the buildings they had constructed on it, by letting out stalls in the market place, by farming mints, tolls or mills from the lord, by raising loans wherever required, and by engaging their capital in commercial and industrial enterprises beyond the scope of lesser men.

Two things would happen to such a group, made up of quite wealthy men, used to freedom and possessing initiative, men accustomed also to running the affairs of the town on the lord's behalf, or at least to being consulted by him. What more natural than that they should be in the lead of movements for freedom from seigneurial control? The new municipal powers created economic

[20] Pirenne, *Les villes*, i, p. 137 n.1; Espinas, *Douai*, i, p. 306.

and political opportunities of which they were in the best position to take advantage. Psychologically, socially and politically they were in the most suitable position to conduct a successful attack.

Secondly, these men would probably have had an interest in trade from the earliest times. As seigneurial officials many of them were well placed for controlling supplies to one of the best of the early markets, the feudal households, and the group as a whole possessed land and land rents, one of the greatest potential sources of liquid capital during the Middle Ages. They would therefore include the capitalization of trade among their varied activities, and where trade developed quickly they might be merchant capitalists among other things at a very early date. As M. Postan comments: 'It can well be doubted whether the conventional picture of a vagrant trader, travelling with his goods. . .ever represented the upper strata of the medieval merchant class.'[21] At first, however, trading, if present at all, would not normally be the greatest or most typical of their economic activities; but as economic change proceeded in Europe, trade and finance would come to rival, perhaps to overshadow, other means of gaining wealth. The leading families, or the more adaptable among them, invested proportionately more in the new activities, because men of their group characteristically seized all opportunities of advancement of any kind. They would retain, and even intensify their old landowning and office-holding interests by means of the new wealth, as methods of social and financial investment. By and large, however, the influence and power of the class increasingly depended on commerce and finance.

Thus the formation of the twelfth- and thirteenth-century patriciate involved *internal transformation* of a dominant class which already existed, and which was opportunist enough to shift the emphasis of its activities as conditions changed. Some of the leading townsfolk were, however, too conservative and rigid in outlook to adapt themselves. They were left as survivals of an older stage, like the *grandi* in Italy, opposing the great trades rather than merging with them; or like the *échevins* in some towns of the Liège group who refused to join their more progressive fellows in leadership of the new council of *jurés*; or like the Avvocato and Gavi families of twelfth-century Genoa who failed to join the rush of many of their social equals into trade. Sometimes the class as a whole failed in adaptability, especially when it was faced with fundamental economic

[21] Power and Postan, *Engish trade*, p. 146.

changes like those of the late thirteenth and fourteenth centuries. Then there were challenges of varying seriousness, and the ensuing battles filled much of town history in the later Middle Ages.

These problems cannot be treated here. Instead we must complete the explanation of patrician origins by looking at the recruitment of new men. Outsiders, and especially those merchants and artisans who had made more than a modest competence through their ability and good fortune, could and did enter the patriciate. Such recruitment could take two principal forms. There was the normal continuous inflow of rich *parvenus* into the ruling group, which was all the more easily assimilated when the patriciate itself had developed large trading interests. The rate of recruitment however would vary greatly and depended particularly on the attitude of the patricians themselves. This suggests the second form. If the ruling group proved unadaptable and exclusive, a class of *nouveaux riches* was likely to build up in opposition to them, particularly when economic conditions had opened up new ways of obtaining wealth. Recruitment was, so to speak, dammed back, and would therefore produce tensions and greater or lesser crises in which the new men would try to seize power or at least to share it with the old.

A satisfactory explanation of the origin of the medieval patriciate seems possible along these lines. Moreover, the explanation can be adjusted to suit the divergent circumstances of different towns and regions by allowing for variations in the relative importance of the two main processes, the internal transformation of a 'feudal' upper class and the recruitment of the new men.

Sometimes for instance the social constitution of an early town did not favour any large number of men of the 'feudal' type. This type seems to have been especially common in southern Europe, and particularly where there was substantial continuity of town life from late Roman times. It was fairly common in most of the episcopal centres and other large and old-established settlements in the north. But the old 'feudal' group might be weaker, and the association of the 'new' merchants coming up from below the stronger, for many social reasons. Then 'recruitment' would be a major factor and merchants rising from among the commons more important than an element of officials and landowners who had taken to trade. In the south such conditions may have obtained exceptionally, as in Venice, but in the non-episcopal towns of the north they were much more common, especially in England and 'new'

Germany, where they were often associated with the peculiar importance of the merchant guild. It is on such evidence that Pirenne founds his theory, on part of the evidence for part of Europe. We may freely admit that in certain cases his explanation seems close to the truth, but what matters is that an explanation, appropriate to cases at one end of the spectrum, is applied by him to the whole range. In fact even those examples best suited to Pirenne's theory usually show some small effects due to another type of development. Even in the north of Europe there are many important towns in which 'transformation' was at least as important as 'recruitment', and most towns in the south require a different approach altogether. Further, if there is a Pirennian extreme at one end of the scale, there seems to be an equally 'feudal' extreme at the other. This is constituted by such towns as those in northern Italy and especially in Piedmont where communes sprang from seigneurial families whose multiplying offspring formed themselves into an association, each the nucleus of a town commune.

We may in conclusion note a few auxiliary advantages of the foregoing explanation. Trade revival, and economic change generally, are retained as integral parts of the scheme of development, and merchant capitalists keep an important role though a different one from that postulated by Pirenne. The explanation tallies well with what we know of the forms of economic and political power actually exercised by established patriciates. It allows for a source of mercantile capital additional to or alternative to the windfalls of petty pedlars and porters. Finally it will allow for the idea that novel techniques or fresh markets might first be exploited by new men who in order to expand relied on association with wealthy men of older standing so that capital was gradually shifted from an older to a new use.

5. *Urban Growth and Family Structure in Medieval Genoa**

DIANE OWEN HUGHES

In assessing the impact of urbanization on the family structure of medieval Europe, we have been subtly influenced by sociological theories devised for a more modern industrial age, which saw capitalism, industrialization, urbanization and the nuclear family as associated developments in the modernization of the West. City air, according to these theories, fragmented the complex stem or joint families which were a regular feature of rural life in western Europe into individual nuclei and in so doing undermined the basis of that society's stability. If historians have recently begun to doubt that the family history of the West is one of progressive nuclearization, they have nevertheless been drawn to the notion that urban life encouraged the dissolution of larger family structures.[1]

It is now held that Europe's early urban growth came at a time when families had grown more complex. Herlihy has shown that Italian landowners moved in the eleventh century from the small family of the Carolingian period into larger groupings, towards great households. In part such a move towards larger family structures and group ownership reflects, as it does in the Mâconnais studied by Duby, a joining of forces for protection in an age that had lost governmental controls; in part it is an attempt to limit an excessive partitioning of the family patrimony, a practice which could threaten the social position and economic viability of the landed family in a period that increasingly placed more importance on wealth than on lingering memories of status. And as the minor nobility began to exploit the advantages that the city offered for securing and maintaining economic and political dominance, it did so initially in large

* I am grateful to the Canada Council for support of a project to which this is a prefatory study. For specific help and criticism I should like to thank Marvin Becker, David Herlihy and Brian Stock.

[1] Le Play's classic *L'organisation de la famille* and Goode's *World revolution and family patterns*, a qualified survey of such theories, come immediately to mind. Those like Laslett who have tried to refute theories of progressive nuclearization by denying the importance of the complex family at any stage of western development (Laslett and Wall (eds.), *Household and family*, pp. 1–81) must revise their argument in the light of Berkner's important article, *Am. Hist. Rev.* (1972).

family groupings. The ascendancy within the expanding cities of Italy of these corporate aristocratic families, which put their own concerns before those of their individual members or their city, was broken in the thirteenth century with the victory of the *popolo*, a group whose composition is difficult to define, but one that championed civic order, curtailed the activities of noble families within the city, and tried to break the cohesiveness of the great households, which had already been weakened in the previous century by the pressures of urban life.[2]

Recent analysis of the population of medieval and Renaissance Italy has been thought to lend demographic support to this assessment at the household level, showing the joint family of the Italian countryside in decline within city walls. Rural families were larger than their urban counterparts. The figures for Prato are typical: in 1298 the average rural household numbered 5.6 members; the average urban, 4.1; and after a century of demographic contraction, the figures were different but the proportion remained similar, 5 members in the rural household in 1427, 3.7 in the urban.[3] Furthermore, the rural population lived in households that were structurally more complex. Almost one-third of the households in the Pisan *contado* in 1427, for example, were enlarged or extended; and as the head of the family aged, he retained control and the household became correspondingly more complex. More than 35 per cent of households having a head aged sixty-five or older had a joint family structure, and over 12 per cent of the entire rural population lived in such 'great households' ruled by a head more than sixty-seven years of age. This was the common pattern for most of the Florentine countryside in the fifteenth century.[4]

In Florence itself, however, an analysis of the *Catasto* of 1427 has given us a different picture. Within the city an astonishingly high 43 per cent of all households deviated from even the nuclear norm of husband, wife and children and were headed instead by women or children or contained only a single person. Furthermore, instead of the joint pattern of rural life, where the ageing of the head produced an ever more complex structure as his sons married, within the city as the head of the household grew older, family members

[2] Herlihy in Herlihy, Lopez and Slessarev (eds.), *Economy, society and government*; Duby, *La société aux XIe et XIIe siècles*, pp. 263–81, and *idem*, *Annales, E.S.C.* (1972).

[3] Fiumi, *Demografia*, pp. 47–8 and 109–11.

[4] Klapisch and Demonet, *Annales, E.S.C.* (1972).

left and the structure became simpler. Although analysis of the fifteenth-century population suggests that greater wealth in the countryside supported larger families, within fifteenth-century Florence even the richest and most aristocratic families had lost solidarity and planned a more nuclear life in politics, in their business activities and in their domestic arrangements.[5]

But before this Tuscan model of the steady dissolution of the bonds of the complex family within the city is extended to the rest of communal Italy, we should take a closer look at other cities. It is instructive to turn to Genoa, whose initial period of great demographic growth and economic expansion in the twelfth century has been uniquely preserved in a series of notarial registers which add intimate family detail to the more usual laws and chronicles.[6] Genoa far more than Florence was a merchant city; as the saying went, *Genuensis ergo mercator* ('a Genoese, therefore a merchant'). Its aristocracy, drawn at first from the minor nobility of the surrounding Ligurian countryside and active in trade in partnership with lesser men from the very foundation of the medieval commune, by the mid-twelfth century controlled the city's overseas commerce. Although they retained and enlarged their holdings in the countryside, they centred their political and economic life within the city's walls, as did later most of the Ligurian nobles who were forced to submit to communal authority in the course of the thirteenth century.[7]

Far from loosening family bonds, urban association strengthened them. As the city's aristocracy rose to dominate Genoa's trade in the first half of the twelfth century, lineage ties became more clearly defined, more firmly patrilineal, and more frequently invoked; and the bonds of the domestic group, the joint patriarchal family, were tightened. The roots of this process can be traced to the first swearing in 1099 of the *campagna communis* by which all of the city's inhabitants bound themselves in a voluntary association, agreeing to reside in the city and comply with its customs. The *campagna* had a profoundly individualistic character in that both nobles and other citizens were associated through residence rather

---

[5] Herlihy, *Cath. Hist. Rev.* (1972); Goldthwaite, *Private wealth in Renaissance Florence*, pp. 234–75; and *idem, Am. Hist. Rev.* (1972). But see the qualifications of Kent, *J. Warburg and Courtauld Inst.* (1972).

[6] On the scope of Genoese and other medieval notarial archives and a method for their use, see Hughes, *Hist. Meth. Newsletter* (1974).

[7] Lopez, *Annales d'hist. éc. et soc.* (1937); Vitale, *Il comune*, pp. 60–120.

than through membership in a particular social or professional group.[8] But in a period of expanding economic opportunity its egalitarian nature emphasized the need for noble members of the *campagna* to safeguard the commercial and urban privileges on which their wealth and status had increasingly come to depend.

The division of Genoa into seven (later eight) districts called *campagne* bound the inhabitants of each district for military and commercial purposes in a temporary voluntary association. Each association received a roughly equivalent share of the geographic advantages and protection the city offered: the *campagne* ran in rectangles from the sea to the wall on the hills, each having its share of the urban fortification, each its outlet at the port.[9] Rapid economic development in the twelfth century, however, drove nobles to use the urban space in more self-serving ways, protecting themselves from the competition of urban growth which, in a revealing paradox, their own policies initiated and encouraged. To confirm their advantages, they tried to control important markets, gates and port areas, creating commercial districts whose markets they monopolized, whose land and buildings they owned, and whose residents were bound by ties of lineage, consorterial alliance or clientage.

A shortage of men and money may have encouraged the nobility to exploit at first the kind of consorterial alliance that we find in the contemporary tower-societies of Tuscany, where allied families held defensive towers together and jointly controlled particular areas of the city.[10] A survey of Genoa's three major markets in 1186 shows them surrounded by the houses, towers and shops of aristocratic families allied in politics and commerce, who often appear to have held neighbouring estates in the countryside.[11] Of the six families listed as holding property in the ancient Roman forum, one of Genoa's great commercial districts, which was destined to be transformed in the fifteenth century into its stock exchange, two, the della

[8] *Annali genovesi*, i, p. 5. I take these characteristics from the earliest extant oath of 1157, printed in *Codice diplomatica della Repubblica di Genova*, i, pp. 350–9. On the controversial nature of the *campagna*, see Vitale, *Breviario della storia*, ii, pp. 16–18.

[9] Formentini, *Genova*, p. 95; Heers in *Studi in onore di Amintore Fanfani*, i, pp. 373–7.

[10] Niccolai, *Rivista di storia del diritto italiano* (1940), pp. 116–47, 293–342 and 397–447.

[11] *Codice diplomatico della Repubblica di Genova*, ii, pp. 293–5.

Volta and Venti, were at once powerful and closely allied. They held neighbouring land in the Bisagno valley, acted together consistently in trade, were firmly allied in city politics, and seem even to have pursued a unified marriage policy.[12] But if consorterial bonds could be significant, they do not seem to have attained in Genoa the creative strength that they had in Tuscany in this period.

Within Genoa ties of lineage were the ones most frequently strengthened to bind aristocrats into common action groups. We should bear in mind, of course, that 'lineage ties may be recognized through more generations for some purposes than for others'.[13] For purposes of political alliance in the twelfth century these bonds could be extended effectively for five generations or more. A system of long-lasting alliance within lineages and enmity between them gave pattern to the seemingly pointless warfare played out on the streets of medieval Genoa and in its *contado*.

Most of these twelfth-century wars sprang from hostility between two opposed lineages, both perhaps of viscontal origin and hence of very early association with the city, which traced their descent from tenth-century founders, one from Obertus Vicecomes, son of Viscount Ydo, the other from a certain Obertus de Maneciano.[14] Allied to the second in the twelfth century was an equally important Genoese lineage, the della Volta, descendants of some now-forgotten tenth-century namesake. The battle in 1164 between Fulco di Castello and Rolando Advocato, both probably great-great-great-grandsons of the two original Oberti, pitted the heads of two segments of the opposed lineages against each other in a struggle that was only settled by the consuls of the city in 1170, after both sides had acknowledged through their elders that peace should be made.[15] The battle in 1179 between Amico Grillo and his kinsmen and the brothers of Ogerio Vento was a minor skirmish in the same hostilities involving consorterial allies; and the attack in the same year by the Doria on Rubaldo Porcello and Opizzo Lecavella set members of the della Volta lineage who traced their descent from a

---

[12] *Il registro*, p. 24; Bach, *La cité de Gênes*, pp. 109–12; and below pp. 114–15.

[13] Mair, *Br. J. Soc.* (1963), p. 22.

[14] For most early genealogical information, see Belgrano, *Tavole genealogiche*. In *Scritti di Mattia Moresco*, pp. 429–40, Moresco established the family base of these feuds without finding in them a patterned struggle between hostile lineages.

[15] *Annali genovesi*, i, pp. 160 and 231–2.

certain Oria de Volta against allies of the descendants of Obertus Vicecomes.[16] In 1183 Fulco di Castello joined with the della Volta's allies, the Venti, to battle against the party that had then come to be known as the Curia. These were the descendants of the same Obertus Vicecomes, who were now identified with the *curia* or courtyard before the house of their leader Lanfranco Pevere. The feud continued until 1190 when Fulco's sons and the son of his late brother murdered Lanfranco.[17] Three years later siege-warfare paralysed the western part of the city as the della Volta and their allies joined with the Spinola – whose leader Oberto was probably a great-great-grandson of Obertus de Maneciano – to attack the Curia's fortifications. This latter phase of the hostilities was resolved through a solemn swearing of the peace by both sides in 1203 after the della Volta had incited two servants of the murdered Lanfranco Pevere's son Sorleone to wound him in his house in the city.[18]

If these ancient lineage ties could still provoke the feud in twelfth-century Genoa, they were not much used for other purposes within the city and by the thirteenth century had begun to atrophy. For purposes of political alliance, economic advantage and urban settlement the unifying ties became those which bound certain segments of the lineage which adopted a common surname and began to emerge at the beginning of the twelfth century; just at the time, in other words, of the swearing of the *campagna*. Thus the descendants of Obertus Vicecomes organized themselves in families called Advocato, Pevere, de Mari, Serra and Usodimare; those of Obertus de Maneciano in families called Spinola, di Castello, Brusco, Embriaco, Alinerio, della Porta and de Marini, most tracing their descent from an ancestor born at the turn of the twelfth century. One sign of this appears in the larger lineage's abandonment of its earlier exogamous nature. At the beginning of the thirteenth century Doria for the first time married della Volta; Spinola for the first time married Embriaco or di Castello.[19]

If name came to identify an individual by family group in the twelfth century, so too did the district in which he lived. The family was physically defined by the commercial quarter in the city that it was building into a family enclave, sometimes, like the Richere,

---

[16] *Ibid.* ii, pp. 12, 14. 23 and 88; d'Oria, *La Chiesa*, p. 210.

[17] *Annali genovesi*, iii, pp. 19 and 37; Bach *La cité de Gênes*, pp. 154–5.

[18] *Annali genovesi*, ii, 44–5 and 87–8.

[19] Belgrano, *Tavole genealogiche, passim*; Ferretto, *Codice diplomatico*, ii, p. xiv.

turning public roads and markets into private property.[20] As Doria, della Volta and other noble families establised their family districts in the twelfth century, they gathered land, built houses and shops, bought out former neighbours, and settled the districts ever more densely with their kinsmen.[21] The Zaccaria, for example, drew together from their earlier scattered residences throughout the city to form the *contrata Jachariarum*, probably not very different from the della Volta settlement near the original Roman forum where Ingo della Volta had at least four houses (and his brothers several more) in 1161, when his cousin's grandson bought an adjoining house.[22] This private urban environment provided for the family's physical, economic and spiritual well-being. Houses, tower, family bath, and shops which they rented to merchants and artisans and which they used for their own business enterprises, surrounded the *curia* where the family could meet as a group. The Church of San Torpete, a tenth-century foundation that adjoined their property, was converted in 1180 into a family church for their private use.[23] By the beginning of the thirteenth century the number of della Volta in the area had increased markedly, and as the family's territory expanded, they constructed a second defensive tower.[24]

Both church and tower emphasize the essentially private and defensive character of these compounds, which were often enclosed behind barricades in times of prolonged factional strife.[25] As the remains of the old towers and the twelfth-century illustrations of the Genoese annals make clear, they were formidable structures built for the defence of the familial community. Usually placed between the interior square and its most vulnerable entrance, the towers rose far above the eighty-foot maximum that the consuls tried repeatedly to impose; and they became the corner-stone of the family's military (and to a large extent political) strength.[26]

Salvation may have been, as the church stressed, ultimately

---

[20] *Codice diplomatico della Repubblica di Genova*, ii, pp. 259–60.

[21] *Il cartolare di Giovanni Scriba*, nos. 342, 505, 713, 864 and 1093; and *Oberto Scriba (1190)*, nos. 48 and 206, for Doria and della Volta.

[22] Lopez, *Benedetto Zaccaria*, p. 16; *Il cartolare di Giovanni Scriba*, nos. 505 and 864.

[23] *Oberto Scriba (1190)*, no. 395; Moresco in *Scritti*, p. 5.

[24] *Oberto Scriba (1190)*, no. 206; Poleggi, *Urbanistica* (1965), p. 20.

[25] *Annali genovesi*, ii, p. 19, and iii, pp. 82–3.

[26] *Codice diplomatico della Repubblica di Genova*, i, pp. 159 and 165; *Annali genovesi*, ii, pp. 60–1, and fig. 33; Pastorino, *Dizionario*, i, pp. 463–4 and ii, p. 64.

individual, but in medieval Genoa the care of a noble soul could safely be tended only within the protected family quarter. When the head of the Camilla family petitioned the pope to hurry along his family's request for a private church next to their palace, a request opposed by the canons of the neighbouring Church of Santa Maria delle Vigne, he claimed that he and his family could not risk a trip to the nearby church. He was not overstating the danger: on the following Feast of Saint Peter, a kinsman was stabbed by the family's enemies while leaving church.[27] The private church not only cared for the souls of the living but also preserved the memory of the dead. A need to keep inviolate the family's graves and monuments also underlay and provoked such requests for a private church. In making their plea for a church protected by the family enclave the Spinola went beyond saying that the ancient and neighbouring Cathedral of San Siro was too public and hence too dangerous for them, and declared that they would not be buried there.[28]

Within its enclave and within the political life of the city, the aristocratic family behaved as a hierarchic unit. The head (or heads) of the family lived in the *domus magna* and controlled the adjoining tower. Although partible inheritance was almost universally practised, the central house and tower invariably went to one son, usually the eldest. When Nicola Embrone died in 1226, his property within the city was divided among his four sons, but his one-fifth share of the family's central tower was taken by what appears to be his eldest son.[29] In a division of paternal goods of the Stregghiaporco in 1269, the brothers received their respective portions of the goods, but the eldest was assigned the house and tower with authority over the *curia*.[30] With the possession of the house and tower went the governance of the great family. Although no private documents from Genoa show how these families were governed,

---

[27] Poleggi, *Urbanistica* (1965), p. 19: *Annali genovesi*, ii, p. 175.

[28] The archbishop said that he granted their request, 'seeing and learning from the consuls that the aforesaid men could not be secure at the aforesaid monastery [of San Siro]...Especially since Oberto Spinola with all his house and several and sundry others were prepared to swear that they would not be buried at that monastery' (*Guglielmo Cassinese*, no. 1492); and see Moresco in *Scritti*, pp. 397–411.

[29] The documents appear in Lopez in *Studi sull' economia genovese*, pp. 219–23.

[30] 'Domus et turris cum iure curiae'; cited by Poleggi, *Urbanistica* (1965), p. 18.

their political role in the city suggests that families worked out a leadership based on seniority, but flexible enough to recognize the possibility of shared leadership when circumstances demanded it.

How the city's consuls were elected remains unclear, but they were certainly chosen by men who understood the patterns of authority in these families. Let us take the case of the Advocato-Pevere family, all descendants of Lanfranco Advocato, himself a great-great-grandson of the original Viscount Ydo. Of his four known sons, only Guglielmo was consul, in 1125, 1128-9, 1131 and 1139. He prepared his son Lanfranco Pevere for similar service – or Lanfranco struggled for it, serving as consul in 1136 and 1138, then regularly in 1141, 1143, 1146, 1148, 1150, 1154, 1156, 1159, 1163 and 1167. It was probably Lanfranco's sons or nephews who next were consuls, Guglielmo Pevere in 1174 and 1186 and Lanfranco Pevere in 1183, 1185 and 1191, the year in which he was murdered by the sons of Fulco di Castello. Although the original Guglielmo's brother Lanfranco Advocato and his son Roland held land with the other branch of the family, acted with it in commerce, and were allied with it politically, they never held the consulship.[31]

In the della Volta family a similar pattern emerges. Guglielmo della Volta held the consulship frequently from 1123 to 1143. From 1148 until 1162 it was held in another branch of the family by two brothers who were Guglielmo's cousins, Guglielmo Burone and Ingo della Volta. It was then held during the 1170s by Ingo's son Ingo de Flessia, who occasionally shared it in the 1180s with his two brothers. Random selection of consuls from scattered branches of the family almost never occurs, and where it does it seems to indicate that something had gone seriously wrong with the family's internal organization. When shared consular power became suddenly apparent in the della Volta family in the 1190s, it was the sign of an internal struggle for family leadership which led to war in 1192.[32]

The solidarity of the lineage group is reflected in the marriages of its members. Usually contracted by the head of a particular household, marriages were nevertheless made only after consultation

---

[31] Olivieri, *Serie dei consoli, passim*; Belgrano, *Tavole genealogiche*, tables xxii–xxiii. The two Lanfranco Pevere may be one, as Belgrano assumes. If so, not only would he have died an extremely old man, he would have fathered children well into his sixties. Neither is impossible, of course; and both cases fit the argument.

[32] Olivieri, *Serie dei consoli, passim*; *Annali genovesi*, ii, p. 42.

within the lineage group, probably only after the permission of the heads had been secured. If in Genoa we find no documents showing that the matrimony of members had to be authorized by the governors of *consorteria*, as they were in some other Italian cities,[33] the nature of the marriages themselves indicates that the great aristocratic family in consultation and collaboration with its allies pursued a definite marriage policy.

The della Volta family is typical. Ingo della Volta married his daughter to Fulco di Castello, a tie that was maintained in the next generation when his son Rubeo married his daughter to Bellobruno di Castello, a kinsman but not a direct descendant of Fulco. And this match was mirrored in their ancient consorterial allies when Pietro Vento in 1190 married a daughter of Otto di Castello. Both the Venti and della Volta seem to have tried in concert to cement some kind of alliance with their enemies the Pevere when Guglielmo Vento married Lanfranco's daughter Comitissa and Rubeo della Volta her sister. We see a similar attempt to forge ties with the Piccamiglio when Guglielmo Burone (della Volta) married his daughter to Lanfranco Piccamiglio and the alliance was extended to the next generation by an agreement at the same time that his cousin's grandson would marry the daughter of Adrizzo Piccamiglio.[34]

The marriage bond could not compete with the lineage tie, and Genoese aristocrats rarely married their enemies. When they did, the marriage seldom had the desired effect. At best it simply neutralized the two partners, as in the case of Rubeo della Volta and Guglielmo Vento – married to two Pevere sisters – who abstained from the most active aggressions of their families against the Curia faction and who were elected to the consulship when compromise candidates were necessary.[35] At worst it provoked untold personal grief and intensified the feud. The wife of Sorleone Pevere left her husband soon after the di Castello had murdered his father. She then married one of his murderers, later excluding from her will the children of that first marriage, whom she had left behind in the Pevere enclave.[36] When marriage was used to

[33] Niccolai, *Rivista di storia del diritto italiano* (1940), p. 298.

[34] *Annali genovesi*, i, pp. 214–18; *Guglielmo Cassinese*, no. 399; *Oberto Scriba (1190)*, nos. 140 and 275; *Il cartolare di Giovanni Scriba*, nos. 139, 691, 1027–8 and 1145.

[35] Bach, *La cité de Gênes*, pp. 112–13 and 152–3.

[36] *Giovanni di Guiberto*, no. 390.

strengthen bonds between already allied families, however, it could be strikingly successful. The frequently renewed marriage ties between the di Castello and della Volta created an alliance between the two families that lasted for over a century. And the marriages seem to have entailed specific alliance obligations. When the consuls tried to end civil war in Genoa by calling men to swear the peace before the relics of John the Baptist, Fulco di Castello claimed that he could not swear without the permission of his father-in-law Ingo, the leader of the della Volta family.[37]

The tightening of lineage bonds in the eleventh century was undoubtedly accompanied in Liguria, as elsewhere in Europe, by the growing patrilineal nature of those bonds.[38] City life, far from upsetting this trend, continued and intensified it. In the twelfth century we find a few members of the aristocracy who identified themselves through their mother rather than their father, but by the thirteenth century there are none.[39] The links between political participation, residential strength and economic success within the city tended to diminish the rights of mothers, daughters and wives, who were excluded by custom from public office. One aspect of the transformation of their role is reflected in the history of the marriage gift.

Duing the formative years of urban development in the eleventh and early twelfth centuries, marriage in Liguria had involved three settlements, described in the sources as *dos, antefactum* and *tercia*. *Dos* and *antefactum* were closely linked. While *dos*, the traditional Roman marriage gift, was the portion of an estate settled on a daughter at marriage, *antefactum*, a donation that may have had both Roman and Frankish antecedents, was a marriage settlement, usually calculated as a percentage of the *dos*, of the husband or his family on the wife. Both passed under the trusteeship of the husband or his family for the duration of the marriage, but both were legally hers, and she reclaimed them at her husband's death.[40] *Tercia*, a settlement of Frankish origin, guaranteed to Ligurian women rights to one-third of their husbands' estates. They could

[37] 'nisi soceri mei Ingonis de Volta primitus data mihi licentia' (*Annali genovesi*, i, p. 218).
[38] Duby, *Revue hist.* (1961); *idem, Annales, E.S.C.* (1972), p. 23.
[39] *Il registro*, pp. 16, 23, 31, 57 and 58; Belgrano, *Tavole genealogiche*, table xxxv. Among other social groups in Genoa such identification is found more frequently.
[40] Forcheri, *Bolletino ligustico* (1970).

certainly claim this portion at the husband's death, but they may also have controlled it from the day of their marriage and thus have gained genuine economic leverage within the household.[41]

In 1143, however, by consular decree the women of Genoa lost their right to *tercia*.[42] This abolition, which has its counterparts throughout communal Italy in this period, should probably be seen as part of that larger attempt on the part of magnate families within the city to keep strategic urban property within the lineage group and thus preserve its political and military power.[43] If they were reluctant to consign property to daughters as dowry,[44] they were even less willing to give wives control through *tercia*. The absence of *tercia* from Genoa's notarial records, which begin in 1156, testifies to the decree's success.[45] It is a sign of how the married woman of every social group in Genoa suffered before the greater needs of the magnate families who ruled the city.

[41] For the long history of *tercia*, which resembles other Germanic marriage settlements of husband on wife, such as the *quarta* customary among the Lombards, see Vandenbossche, *La dos ex marito*; Ercole, *Archivio giuridico*, lxxx (1908), pp. 460–99, lxxxi (1908), pp. 92–116; Brandileone in Brandileone, *Scritti da storia*, i, pp. 229–319; and Bellomo in *Jus nostrum*, pp. 1–25. The earliest Genoese sources reveal little about the workings of the *tercia*. Two eleventh-century charters from Apulia, however, show married women exercising rights of donation over *tercia* while their husbands were still alive, rights also suggested by early Frankish sources, *Codice diplomatico...di Tremiti*, nos. 41 and 59. For evidence that Genoese women received both *tercia* and *antefactum* before 1143, see *Il registro*, p. 62.

[42] *Codice diplomatico della Repubblica di Genova*, i, p. 153. The consuls abolished all further donations of *tercia* and annulled all *tercia* that had already been granted, allowing only those in the possession of widows.

[43] Since the Genoese sources regarding *tercia* are so scarce, we must profit from scattered practices elsewhere in Italy. In almost all references to these one sees the link between the retention of strategic property within the male line of the family and the reduction of a woman's right to *tercia* and *quarta*. In the territory of Milan at the end of the eleventh century, for example, a priest, in donating all his goods, stipulated that in future no woman could have *quarta* from his fortress; and in a document from Vercelli in 1171 a husband guaranteed his wife *tercia* but excepted fortresses and churches from the grant: see Bellomo in *Jus nostrum*, pp. 6–7.

[44] When families were forced to alienate their central property for dowries, they often insisted on rights of repurchase within a specified time (usually from one to five years) at the same price: *Il cartolare di Giovanni Scriba*, no. 505; *Oberto Scriba (1190)*, no. 117; *Guglielmo Cassinese*, nos. 61, 618, 692, 796–7 and 826; Archivio di Stato Genoa, MS. 102 (Diversorum), fos. 197v.–198r. and 252v.–253r.

[45] The only notarial reference to *tercia* comes from the acts of the earlier extant notary and undoubtedly refers to a widow in possession before the 1143 legislation: *Il cartolare di Giovanni Scriba*, no. 376.

After 1143 the married woman of Genoa was entitled only to *antefactum*, and for the noblewoman it too was significantly reduced. Earlier, *antefactum* had often equalled or even exceeded the *dos*. In response to the latter's steady increase in the late twelfth century, however, *antefactum* was set at a fixed rate, as the city's magnate families became unwilling to contribute as *antefactum* ever increasing portions of money and land to wives who could remove them from the family's control at the husband's death. They therefore came legally to define *antefactum* as a sum representing one half the *dos*, but one that could in no case rise above 100 Genoese pounds (hereafter GL).[46] With the *dos* of the magnate class in some matches rising above 500 GL, the noblewoman's economic position within marriage came to be more and more dependent on her own family. The decline of the husband's gift and the rise of the dowry indicate that within this reorganized family men chose to endow the female members of their own descent group rather than their own wives, who were necessarily alien members; for families identified by a particular name were strictly exogamous. Property given as dowry to a daughter, they probably reasoned, remained closer to the newly strengthened family than property alienated to a wife. Genoese custom ensured this by requiring that the dowry of a woman who died childless revert to her own kin.[47]

Within this patrilineage, identified by common name and residence, the economic and domestic unit was the joint patriarchal family. Property was held in the city, as it was in the country, within the joint family and was transmitted through a system of partible inheritance. Although by law fathers could divert up to three quarters of their estate from their legal heirs,[48] the extant wills and inventories show that they almost never did so. At the father's death all property both movable and immovable was apportioned equally among his sons, while daughters received a smaller advance share as a dowry.

[46] *Codice diplomatico della Repubblica di Genova*, i, p. 153. Similar limits were later set in other cities: see Bellomo in *Jus nostrum*, pp. 27–59.

[47] *Il cartolare di Giovanni Scriba*, nos. 790 and 1047; *Oberto Scriba (1186)*, nos. 129–31; *Bonvillano*, no. 38; Forcheri, *Bolletino ligustico* (1970), pp. 14–18. Other communes required this by law: Bellomo in *Jus nostrum*, pp. 237–244.

[48] Genoa followed the provision of the *lex Falcidia* (*Dig.* 35, 2, 1ff.) that at least one quarter of an estate must be reserved for the legal heirs. When Genoese wished to cut off these heirs from a full share of the inheritance they took care to give them a small portion 'de falcidia'.

In a society where mortality was undoubtedly high, a network of familial relations was essential for the conduct of extensive commercial and financial transactions, particularly to ensure the continuity of business and the security of credit. This ego-centred network extended beyond the lineage to include affinal relatives and in-laws, but at its core stood the joint patriarchal family. Genoa did not create the permanent family companies that were a feature of commercial organization in some Italian cities. Its merchants dealt instead in a multiplicity of limited operations and investments, which have sometimes been thought to demonstrate their individualism and freedom from the restraints of kin.[49] But the economic enterprises of its merchant aristocracy rested in the security of the family. The Gontardi, for example, were extremely diverse in their commercial interests, active in the African, Levantine and northern cloth trade. In their dealings in all of these areas, however, they acted almost exclusively with family members, adding new personnel through marriage.[50] The business contracts of the di Pallo family show a similar multiplicity of interests, but they are based on a tight, specialized partnership among five brothers, some acting as investors, one concerning himself principally with shipping.[51] A similar specialization in a family that rose into the city's aristocracy through its successes in the eastern trade suggests that economic and social advancement in Genoa added to their family solidarity. Enrico Nepitella and Stregghiaporco – whose single and peculiar name was taken as a surname by his descendants – were brothers; and the glimpse we get of their business activities before 1191 shows them as solitary participants in commerce, lacking the network of family connections so clear in the contracts of the greatest Genoese families. Enrico's sons, however, act almost entirely with family members, with brothers, with aunts, with Stregghiaporco cousins. And the two branches of the family had

[49] Byrne, *Qu. J. Econ.* (1916–17); Vaccari, *Rivista di storia del diritto italiano* (1953–4); Lopez, *Annales, E.S.C.* (1958).

[50] *Giovanni di Guiberto*, nos. 165, 356, 360, 368, 389, 499, 508, 511, 519, 726, 727, 971, 994, 1090, 1098, 1114, 1134, 1135, 1150, 1151. A great deal of notarial evidence illustrating the joint family orientation of business life has been assembled in Buenger, 'Genoese enterprisers'.

[51] *Codice diplomatico della Repubblica di Genova*, ii, pp. 211 and 216; *Oberto Scriba (1186)*, nos. 3, 28 and 29; *Oberto Scriba (1190)*, nos. 207, 358 and 550; *Guglielmo Cassinese*, no. 1508; *Bonvillano*, nos. 129, 130 and 148; *Giovanni di Guiberto*, nos. 724, 725, 749, 750, 897, 1313, 1318, 1324 and 1411.

come to divide their responsibilities, the Stregghiaporco acting mainly as investors, the Nepitella as travelling partners in the family's business activities throughout the Mediterranean.[52]

Both within the business life and domestic arrangements of these families there was strong patriarchal control. Just as noble sons lived their lives within the shelter of family walls and towers, so too were they trained in the family business. Sons' first trips were taken with their fathers, uncles or older brothers. In 1163 two married brothers of the Vento family were being trained in the family business with their young half-brother, investing in the African trade on the authority of their father. Just over twenty years later the career of the young Fulco di Castello was launched in the presence and with the authority of his father, the head of one of Genoa's greatest families, as his maternal uncle Rubeo della Volta sent him as his agent to Constantinople.[53]

Traditionally sons could escape from this tutelage at the age of twenty-five through the formal act of emancipation from their fathers' *potestas*.[54] And yet by this age they were already husbands with growing families of their own. Their marriages had been arranged by their fathers, or in some cases by their grandfathers, as when Ingo della Volta in the presence of his son arranged his grandson's marriage.[55] Where those members were absent authority was passed on to the next senior member, such as an uncle or brother, who seems to have been willing to exercise it even over the minor's strong protests. Fulco di Castello arranged a marriage in 1160 for his brother, whose objections were expressed so strongly that Fulco was forced to pay the bride and her father 400 GL and accept responsibility for expenses that might arise for saving the marriage if his brother tried to have it dissolved.[56] Marriages were arranged and consummated while the participants were young. The few documents that we possess from the twelfth and early thirteenth century showing a marriage age for men indicate that they frequently married while still in their teens, marrying wives

[52] *Il cartolare di Giovanni Scriba*, nos. 497–500, 624, 934, 1011, 1125 and 1126; *Giovanni di Guiberto*, nos. 482, 484, 486, 617, 787, 803, 804, 806, 851, 923, 950, 951, 1140, 1215, 1266, 1268, 1342, 1721, 1731 and 1852–4.

[53] *Il Cartolare di Giovanni Scriba*, nos. 1047, 1102; *Oberto Scriba (1186)*, nos. 15 and 26.

[54] Bellomo, *Annali di storia del diritto* (1964).

[55] *Il cartolare di Giovanni Scriba*, nos. 1027, 1028, 1145.

[56] *Ibid.* no. 712.

who were anywhere from twelve to eighteen.[57] Thus for the formative years of their early married lives husband and wife were under the control of the husband's father.

Furthermore, though the ideal of emancipation at twenty-five carried with it the hope of receiving control of the wife's dowry, extant wills show that among the aristocratic classes this could be delayed until the father's death.[58] This is one sign of the reluctance of aristocratic fathers to relinquish control over their children. It is perhaps significant that of all the acts of emancipation recorded in the twelfth-century notarial registers almost none concern members of the city's consular nobility; and we have notice of at least one merchant active in the African trade who was still in his uncle's tutelage at the age of twenty-seven.[59] Those few cases that we do have of emancipation within the city's aristocratic or near-aristocratic classes are instructive; for emancipation is insisted upon by the bride's family as a condition of the marriage better to guarantee her rights. When Baldiziono Fornario married his son Ugo to the sister of Ansaldo di Brazile, he was forced to promise that although he received the dowry of Adalaxia from her brother, he would restore it to his son (with an additional 100 GL representing *ante-factum*) after Ugo had reached the age of twenty-five and demanded emancipation.[60] In the case of Buongiovanni Malfigliastro, an extremely active and rich merchant who pushed his family into the highest reaches of the city's consular nobility, he was forced to swear that he would emancipate his son Guglielmo with 400 GL in movables and 100 GL in lands in addition to his wife's dowry within fifteen days of the wedding. But this was exceptional; for Guglielmo was moving into the household of his future mother-in-law, where he swore to remain unless she gave him permission to leave.[61]

The government of Genoa, like the church, tried to emphasize individual responsibility in crime and contract. But they too met resistance. The consuls' attempt in 1130 to reduce to eighteen the age at which a man and wife could engage independently in property transactions was rescinded in 1147.[62] Although any such transac-

---

[57] *Oberto Scriba (1190)*, no. 6; *Guglielmo Cassinese*, nos. 96, 513, 514 and 618; Archivio di Stato Genoa, MS. 102 (Diversorum), fo. 233v.
[58] *Il cartolare di Giovanni Scriba*, nos. 408, 409 and 1047.
[59] Bach, *La cité de Gênes*, p. 124.
[60] *Il cartolare di Giovanni Scriba*, no. 1166.
[61] *Ibid.* nos. 989, 990 and 996.
[62] *Codice diplomatico della Repubblica di Genova*, i, pp. 62 and 219–20.

tions completed in the previous seventeen years were still valid, from 1147 both partners had to be twenty-five and act in the presence of kinsmen (or friends in their absence). Their attempt to penalize sons still in their fathers' *potestas* may have had more success, especially for small infringements, but it is worthwhile noting that the crimes of sons recorded in the chronicle were almost always punished by devastation of the father's property.[63]

The pressure that such patriarchal control created in these families is difficult to measure. But might not one of its signs be the frequent outbreaks of violence on the part of sons when their fathers had been elected consuls and were forced to be preoccupied with communal affairs rather than 'family control'?[64] And might not domestic pressures have made long-distance trade more attractive? The aristocratic participants in Genoa's overseas trade who appear in the earliest notarial records were investors who almost never travelled abroad.[65] By the thirteenth century, however, the agent son travelling to distant markets is a familiar figure.

All of the documents suggest that during the father's lifetime, in so far as the house was able to accommodate them, his unmarried children, married sons, and their families lived together under his control. This arrangement left room for diverse property arrangements which produced so complex a mixture of individual and joint ownership that division into simple 'private' and 'communal' categories would be misleading. Sometimes sons were given, with emancipation or without it, a share in the family estate. This could range from no more than an advance on their wives' dowries to grants of estates which brothers held in common; but it seems never to have consisted of central property or, as it did in some non-aristocratic, rich merchant families, of a large cash settlement.[66] At the father's death the estate was often divided. But again such division did not necessarily indicate a firm end to communal arrangements. At Nicola Embrone's death in 1227, for example, his sons divided his property within the city, some within the country,

---

[63] *Ibid.* pp. 157–60; *Annali genovesi*, ii, p. 37; and on the innovative nature of such legislation, see Niccolai, *Contributo allo studio.*

[64] *Annali genovesi*, i, pp. 160–1, ii, p. 12.

[65] Byrne, *Am. Hist. Rev.* (1919–20), pp. 208–9.

[66] Archivo di Stato Genoa, Cartolare 3(ii), fos. 123r. and 133v., MS. 102 (Diversorum) fos. 251r.–252v.; *Il cartolare di Giovanni Scriba*, nos. 278–9 and 325–6.

and some of his movable assets; but they left undivided an estate at Voltri and his commercial investments.[67] The records show that brothers often lived together long after their father's death, and even when they moved into separate (though usually neighbouring) accommodation, they remained business partners and held some property in common throughout their lives.

The joint patriarchal family whose household was contained in the fortified family compound was the preferred structure of the Genoese urban aristocracy. If many aristocrats deviated from this norm through premature death of the father or their inability to produce a male heir, the joint patriarchal family nevertheless shaped their economic lives and domestic expectations, just as the extending of patrilineal ties shaped the politics and topography of the city itself. When in 1188 one thousand Genoese came forward to swear the peace with Pisa, their names were affixed to the oath in a revealing way.[68] Roughly a third of the names are grouped in such lineage and residential blocs, composed first of the male leaders of the great family, followed by single individuals linked to them not by kinship but by economic (and undoubtedly political) clientage. In addition to the two della Volta who appear separately in their consular capacity, for example, ten others, whose relationship was as close as brothers and as distant as fourth cousins, swore the oath of peace together, followed by a group of twenty-four men who lived in the family district and with whom they had economic ties. Each lineage group is often surrounded by its political or consorterial allies. So the della Volta are preceded by the di Castello and followed by the Vento; Spinola are linked with Doria; and Pevere are followed by Advocato and Piccamiglio.

For the other citizens, the other two-thirds who swore the peace, we find single, apparently unrelated names. They are rarely described as sons, brothers, or cousins of the preceding oath-taker. These are the other Genoese. Substantial enough to be called on to swear the oath, they were nevertheless excluded from the city's political life. What is striking about members of this humbler social group in contrast to the city's aristocratic families is their independence, as oath-takers, citizens, and businessmen, from the ties of the larger family, the absence of kin. Their women, who were

---

[67] Lopez in *Studi sull' economia genovese*, pp. 219–23.
[68] The oath is printed in *Codice diplomatico della Repubblica di Genova*, ii, pp. 321–2.

required by law to act with counsel,[69] found neighbours to counsel them. The women of the city's magnate families almost never acted without the counsel of their kinsmen. From birth to death, the noblewoman was sheltered by them, and only exceptionally in widowhood or extreme old age could she escape or fail to find them. Only 9 per cent of those who stand as counsellors for noblewomen in the twelfth-century notarial records are not their kinsmen.

For humbler women, however, the move to the city had meant an abrupt loss of kin. In the acts of Oberto Scriba, a notary who dealt with a far less distinguished clientele than any of the other twelfth-century notaries whose acts are extant, 38 per cent of the counsellors of the women named were their neighbours (*vicini*) because, as the notaries felt compelled to explain, they had no kinsmen (*propinqui*) in Genoa.[70] If we isolate the artisan class both in this case, where it is most prominent, and in all the notarial documents of the twelfth century, we find that 60 per cent of counsellors of artisan women were not their kinsmen. What these statistics could mean in human terms is pathetically recorded in a number of acts of 1191.[71] A woman of some substance with four children and a servant to support had not heard from her husband for seven years. Since no kinsmen stood counsel to her in her distress, she seems to have had no one to appeal to but the consuls for permission to sell part of her husband's property to ward off the frightening threat of foreclosure. Clearly these newly arrived citizens acquired, as we all do, relatives of various kinds, who would later serve as counsellors to the women and companions to the men. But this social group does not seem to have developed extensive kin ties. Although immigration to the city may have loosened earlier ties of kinship, perhaps these humbler citizens had never really known them in the countryside. Many artisans had been (and often continued to be) property-owners in the countryside,[72] but we cannot easily assume that they shared in the movement towards great households that Herlihy has detected among the eleventh-century landholding classes in Italy. Patrilineal ties were, after all, extended largely to maintain political control

[69] *Ibid.* i, p. 222. This was the extension of a Lombard requirement: see Giardina, *Rivista di storia del diritto italiano* (1962).

[70] *Il cartolare di Giovanni Scriba*, nos. 26, 440, 584 and 939; *Guglielmo Cassinese*, no. 1877.

[71] *Ibid.* nos. 90, 91 and 104.

[72] Bach, *La cité de Gênes*, pp. 133–6.

and guarantee social status; and at a domestic level, the joint family seems to flourish best among the well-to-do.[73]

Among artisans, the lack of kin or the loss of it was, moreover, reinforced by the whole pattern of craft life. This may help to explain why, in the Pisan *contado* of the fifteenth century, artisan households supported noticeably simpler families than the households of their non-artisan neighbours.[74] Marriage for the Genoese artisan seems to have occurred later than for the aristocratic men and women of the city; for it was commonly delayed until the death of the couple's fathers. While this event is in itself only a suggestion of age, it is nevertheless striking that of the artisans whose parental situation at marriage is known in the twelfth century, 80 per cent of the men and 72 per cent of the women had no fathers living, in contrast to 32 per cent and 34 per cent respectively of their aristocratic counterparts.[75]

Postponement of marriage until the death of the father was frequently necessary to have enough to marry; for unlike the aristocrat, the artisan seldom lived in his father's house or under his father's authority after marriage. The couple were supported by inheritance, both directly and through dowry, and by their ability to earn a living. For aristocrats, dowry was an advance estate division for female heirs, but for artisans it was a burden parents often could not assume: many could not provide it except by dying. A certain Bonadonna who married a furrier in 1190, for example, might have been kinder to wait until her father's death. Her furrier uncle put up part of her 9 GL *dos*, but her father still had to contribute a third of his goods (excluding clothing) for the other 5 GL.[76] In order to marry sooner, children occasionally agreed to submit to parental control, particularly that of the woman's parents, as in the case of a blacksmith who in giving up half of his and his wife's goods to

[73] Herlihy in Herlihy *et al.* (eds.), *Economy, society and government*, pp. 173–8; Klapisch and Demonet, *Annales, E.S.C.* (1972), p. 884; Berkner, *Am. Hist. Rev.* (1972), p. 408.

[74] Klapisch and Demonet, *Annales, E.S.C.* (1972), p. 884.

[75] These figures are based on ninety-one artisan and ninety-two aristocratic marriage contracts contained in the twelfth-century notarial records catalogued in *Cartolari notarili genovesi*. Eighty-five artisan marriage contracts that appear in seven notarial chartularies of the thirteenth and early fourteenth centuries show a similar situation, 89 per cent of the men and 65 per cent of the women having no fathers alive at the time of their marriage: Archivio di Stato Genoa, Cartolari 8, 12, 50, 78, 82, Not. Bartolomeo Bracelli e Francesco di Silva, and Not. Tommaso Casanova, 10 (1343).

[76] *Oberto Scriba (1190)*, no. 563.

supply a 12 GL dowry for his (?last) daughter forced her and her
husband to live with them and serve them as long as he lived.[77]
But such commitments were uncommon. More common was the
act of emancipation accompanied by the gift of so generous a
portion of the father's estate – sometimes even by the whole of it –
that the father became dependent on his sons, a forced retirement
unthinkable among the city's aristocracy.[78]

Usually the small merchant or artisan waited to marry until such
emancipation or until he was firmly launched in business. For artisan
men (and sometimes for women as well) marriage was generally
delayed until the years of apprenticeship were over. These ranged in
the twelfth century from one to ten years, but were normally about
six. The few notarial indications of the age at entrance into apprenticeship seem to suggest that men began craft training in their late
adolescence or early adulthood. In one instance an apprentice of
eighteen was forbidden marriage until the end of his ten-year
apprenticeship; in two others, apprentices of seventeen could not
marry for nine and twelve years.[79] Although these cases may be
extreme, the years of apprenticeship, years of quite rigid restriction
and economic dependence, undoubtedly delayed artisan marriage
until at least the mid-twenties, one factor which may help to explain
the comparatively fewer children mentioned in artisan wills.[80]

Genoa's artisans seem, then, to have married later, after the man
was launched in his craft, usually after the death of both fathers.
This gave artisan marriage a different texture from aristocratic
unions. The two partners were far more independent, and that stern
patriarch and family head who was so familiar an aristocratic figure
was made rarer in the artisan class through death or early retirement.

The central bond in artisan life was the marriage bond, and artisan
marriage was a partnership. In economic terms, as a study of the
marriage gift shows, this was true from the outset. Artisan women,
along with all other Genoese women, had, of course, lost their right

[77] *Ibid.* nos. 502–3.

[78] *Il cartolare di Giovanni Scriba*, nos. 314–15, 633–6, 644–5, 710, 818–20
and 952; *Oberto Scriba (1190)*, nos. 5 and 141–4.

[79] *Lanfranco*, no. 1738; *Liber magistri Salmonis*, nos. 827, 857 and 1015.

[80] The artisan testators had an arithmetic average of 1.8 children, in
contrast to 3.5 for aristocratic testators. Given the small number of testators
(27 artisans, 25 aristocrats), their uncertain ages, and the practice of excluding
dowered daughters from their fathers' wills, these figures can be no more
than suggestions; but they are striking.

to *tercia* by the 1143 legislation; but often the *antefactum* that they received compensated for this loss. Indeed among this group, whose estates were far less valuable than those of the magnates, *tercia* and *antefactum* may have come to amount to the same thing. In any case, the artisan wife could expect, even after 1143, a proportionately more generous settlement from her husband than could the wife of a consular aristocrat.

The artisan *dos* in the twelfth century ranged from just over 2 GL to 140 GL, with an arithmetic average of 24 GL and a median of 20 GL. The *antefactum* fell into a similar pattern, ranging from just over 1 GL to 100 GL, with an arithmetic average of 19 GL and a median of 14 GL. Since the artisan *dos* never rose above 200 GL, the legislation that considerably reduced (by limiting to 100 GL) the traditional *antefactum* of the noblewoman, whose *dos* often exceeded this sum, did not touch the artisan woman. According to another condition of that law, of course, the *antefactum* was set for all citizens at no more than half the *dos*. But the *dos* and *antefactum* arrangements in the notarial documents shows that artisans ignored this legislation. Well over 70 per cent of the artisan women whose marriage settlements are extant for the twelfth century had an *antefactum* that was more than half the *dos*, but this was true in only 44 per cent of noble marriages.[81] Indeed almost 50 per cent of artisan *antefacta* equalled or exceeded the woman's *dos*. Thus, the artisan woman's support in widowhood came both from her kinsmen and from her husband.

The economic unit was frequently limited to the marriage partners alone, a condition that may have been encouraged by the absence of a fostering kin group as well as by the artisan's less pressing need for a network of kin to guarantee long-term credit. Evidence from twelfth-century Genoa is scarce. But business affairs of the weavers in the thirteenth century were nearly all husband–wife matters, and the activities of wives in the wool-working craft were also important.[82] The sense of partnership continued until death, whereupon it is reflected in wills. Among the city's magnates, a wife was never made heir to her husband's estate. If the marriage produced no children, other kinsmen were found. Among artisans, however, the wife was left heir to her husband's estate in 10 per cent of their extant

---

[81] Based on the marriage contracts cited in note 75.

[82] Reynolds, *J. Econ. Hist.* (1945), p. 6, n. 12; Lopez in *Studi sull' economia genovese*, pp. 114–15.

wills. Only once in these artisan wills where children were lacking was the wife excluded in favour of a kinsman. And conversely, artisan women sometimes left their estates to their husbands; noblewomen, tied by customary restrictions on their dowry, could not.[83]

The whole structure of artisan training may have cut deeply into close family bonds between parents and children, between brothers and sisters. The training of noble sons in the family business undoubtedly strengthened family ties. The training of the artisan, on the other hand, was often long, sending him away from the family into the control of men who formed no part of the kin group. This was, moreover, an arrangement that was used at times for the training of the smaller merchant.[84] The extent to which this kind of business training acted against kin ties to the advantage of the bond between husband and wife is difficult to measure in the twelfth-century sources. It is clear, however, that artisan families had a different character from their noble counterparts within the city. We see a hint of the difference in the importance that craft seems to have assumed over family when in document after document artisans identify themselves as furriers, cobblers, or cloth workers rather than as sons of this or that father. More substantially the difference is reflected in artisan living arrangements. In almost no instance did their property in the city border on that of their kin. And in the few twelfth-century documents that allow us a glimpse within artisan walls, we never find a family larger than parents and children living under one roof.

In Genoa, therefore, the impact of city life on the structure of the families within its walls depended largely on their economic and social role within the city. To maintain its wealth and privilege in an increasingly competitive urban world, the aristocracy intensified its family structure by further developing the patrilineal bonds of the descent group. The artisans, however, often lacking supportive kin within the city and effectively excluded from a political role, built their family life around the marriage bond. For both groups their economic life reinforced their family structures.

These patterns did not change markedly in Genoa in the following centuries. As smaller merchants and artisans grew rich they

[83] *Oberto Scriba (1190)*, nos. 300 and 514; *Giovanni di Guiberto*, nos. 1169 and 1912; *Lanfranco*, nos. 554, 681, 1319 and 1450. Sometimes even when a child was made heir, the wife showed genuine concern for her husband's welfare; *ibid.* no. 1351.

[84] *Oberto Scriba (1186)*, no. 47.

sometimes supported larger households and developed, often for purposes of inheritance, a network of ego-centred kin ties. While wealth and political ambition might encourage some of these families to ape aristocratic behaviour in family life, they rarely established the lineage structure so important among the city's aristocracy. For most, the marriage bond remained central. It is a sign both of the importance of the marriage bond and of the weakness of patriarchal authority in artisan families that the church's growing pressure for the consent of marriage partners made headway first among the artisans in Genoa. By the mid-thirteenth century, marriage contracts between artisans frequently record the consent of the parties, a custom which made its way much more slowly into the city's aristocracy.[85]

Some aristocratic families obviously grew more powerful while others declined or even died out, but among the group as a whole lineage ties for purposes of settlement, politics and self-definition remained strong and extended. The fortified Doria square, established in the twelfth century but largely rebuilt in the thirteenth and fourteenth, contains densely arranged houses for the use of the family and its clientele, houses that almost overwhelm the tiny square on which they face, turning in on themselves, away from the larger activities of the city. The central house and tower were passed down in the later Middle Ages as they had been earlier to the family's head. And the Doria Church of San Matteo called family members to private, protected worship in the presence of carved tributes to Doria ancestors and noble exploits.[86]

Enormously proud that the family could claim two hundred and fifty men of their name who fought together in the decisive Genoese victory over Pisa at Meloria in 1284, they identified them by name and descent.[87] And similar numbers could be summoned for factional war in the fourteenth century.[88] But this great lineage, like its other aristocratic counterparts in the city, remained a strictly exogamous unit. The ecclesiastical impediments to marriage of consanguinity and affinity were often circumvented in Genoa as they were elsewhere in Europe; but Genoese never married within

---

[85] Le Bras, *Cahiers de civilisation médiévale* (1968); sources cited in note 75; and Belgrano, *Della vita privata*, p. 413.

[86] di Sant'Angelo, *Jacopo d'Oria*, p. 345; d'Oria, *La Chiesa*; Ferretto, *Codice diplomatico*, ii, p. xxxiv.

[87] D'Oria, *La Chiesa*, pp. 250-8.

[88] Goria in *Miscellanea di storia*.

the lineage.[89] Doria never married Doria; Spinola, Spinola; nor Usodimare, Usodimare, no matter how distant the relation. Within the household the patriarchal nature of the family bond was maintained. Sons may have been more successful in securing emancipation with regularity, but in their business lives their attachment to their father's direction is noticeable; and they normally remained in his house until his death.[90] Furthermore, marriages may have been made at an even younger age in the thirteenth and fourteenth centuries than they had been in the twelfth. In 1255 Pasqualino Usodimare promised Luca Grimaldi that he would take the latter's daughter Alasina as his wife and would consummate the marriage when the girl was of marriageable age, that is, he said, 'when she is twelve'.[91] And towards the end of the century in the Zaccaria family a daughter was married off at thirteen, and obviously young sons witnessed the marriage transactions worked out for them by their fathers.[92]

In Tuscany, the victory of the *popolo*, it seems, so broke larger bonds of lineage among the aristocracy that when the economic and demographic crisis of the fourteenth century eroded the stability of the joint household, new attempts to extend lineage ties succeeded only in restoring some of the lineage's older social functions; for its larger economic unity had been lost for ever.[93] In Genoa neither the move into the city nor the legislation enacted against them by so-called popular governments significantly weakened the structure of these great aristocratic families.[94] They met the crisis of the fourteenth century in a way reminiscent of their original attempts to control the city. As economic uncertainty and death struck Genoa, its aristocratic families restrengthened consorterial ties with neighbours to form clan-like structures called *alberghi*. Each branch of a family entered separately, fathers enrolling themselves, their sons, grandsons, great-grandsons and their descendants. But the entrance of a single branch involved complex negotiations

[89] An impression formed in the notarial records and confirmed in genealogies such as Battilana, *Genealogia.*

[90] See, for example, the *résumé* of documents in Ferretto, *Codice diplomatico*, ii, pp. 181, 202–3, 230–1, 289 and 401–2.

[91] The document is printed in Belgrano, *Della vita privata*, p. 412.

[92] Lopez in *Miscellanea di storia.*

[93] Herlihy in Herlihy *et al.* (eds.), *Economy, society and government*, pp. 180–1.

[94] On the character of anti-magnate legislation in Liguria as a whole, see Fasoli, *Rivista di storia del diritto italiano* (1939), pp. 102–5.

throughout the lineage, and as the process progressed the entire lineage usually joined in one *albergo*.[95] The formally allied families jointly built and fortified their quarter of the city and assumed a common surname, usually that of the *albergo*'s most powerful lineage. By the fifteenth century to be noble one had to belong to one of the city's thirty or so *alberghi*, each of which contained from about five to fifteen separate lineage groups. Yet each *albergo* housed not only the rich and noble but also an attached clientele of the poor and middle class. Some *alberghi* became political and military powers while others assumed specialized economic functions within the state.[96]

Urban growth undoubtedly took a different course in Genoa and had a different effect on the family structures of its citizens from that proposed for Tuscany. Both politically and economically, of course, Genoa differed from Florence. It remained a merchant city throughout the Middle Ages, its trade controlled by the city's aristocracy; and its industry remained secondary. This is one reason why artisan-backed governments were not successful in curbing the power of Genoa's magnate families. The city's urban form gives us an indication of its *popolo*'s failure. A narrow strip of a city oriented towards a port, it never developed the public squares that were such a prominent feature of Tuscan urbanism, just as it never developed the civic humanism that was a feature of Tuscan culture. Genoa's squares, like its humanism, were instead private and noble, or they were small, popular gathering-places around a local church. The attempt, under pressure from popular demands, to create a proper civic square was, like so many public ventures in Genoa, a failure.[97] Such extensive social, physical and economic differences should prompt us to notice more than their comparative or negative aspects. Genoa was not only different from Florence; it was also, in its extended families and constricted enclaves, its private spaces and inchoate civic life, its noble clans and artisan couples, an urban reality of its own.

[95] See, for example, Ascheri, *Notizie intorno*, p. 74 and *passim*.
[96] Heers, *Gênes au XVe siècle*, pp. 564–76; Hughes, *Hist. Meth. Newsletter* (1974), pp. 66–8.
[97] Heers in *Studi in onore di Amintore Fanfani*, p. 380.

6. The Distribution of Wealth in a Renaissance Community: Florence 1427

DAVID HERLIHY

In what ways did the traditional European city contribute towards, and in what ways did it repress, economic growth and, ultimately, industrialization? In quest of answers to this difficult question it would seem essential to examine not the city alone, but the city as it interacted with the world around it, and, in particular, with its immediate region. In this paper, we shall consider only one city, or group of cities, set within one region, viewed during one year. The principal city which will occupy our attention is Florence, and the year is 1427. The commune or republic of Florence then held under its sway nearly the whole of the modern province of Tuscany; only Lucca and Siena, and their respective territories, escaped Florentine domination. Besides Florence itself, the territory of the commune contained several smaller cities – Pisa, Pistoia, Arezzo, Prato, Volterra and Cortona, to mention only those which contained 3,000 or more inhabitants. A study of Tuscany under Florentine rule should allow us to see how a regional capital – Florence itself – interacted with these secondary towns, and how all these urban communities stimulated or retarded regional economic growth.

We need also to explain the fascination of the year, 1427. The Florentine commune, locked at the time in a costly struggle with Milan, then undertook to register all persons, and all their possessions, in all areas, both urban and rural, under its authority. The survey, known as the _Catasto_, survives today, nearly intact, in the State Archives of Florence and of Pisa respectively.[1] The _Catasto_

[1] For some years I have worked in collaboration with Mme Christiane Klapisch, of the École des Hautes Études, Paris, on a computer-assisted analysis of the _Catasto_. The project has been supported by the National Science Foundation in the United States and the Centre National de la Recherche Scientifique in France, and to both institutions we wish to express our gratitude. The results will be published in a jointly authored volume. Until its appearance the reader may find a description of the project in Klapisch, _Annales_, _E.S.C._ (1969). The enabling legislation of May 1427, which established the office of the _Catasto_, is published in Karmin, _La legge del catasto_. For the history of methods of tax assessment in Florence the basic study is Conti, _I catasti agrari_. On the Florentine fiscal system in the fifteenth century, see also Molho, _Florentine public finances_.

is both a census and an inventory of properties, and its dimensions are imposing. As a census, it describes in its pages some 60,000 households, containing 260,000 persons, nearly all of whom are identified by name, sex and age. The inventory of the holdings of each household embraces most forms of property: in real estate, movables, loans, investments and shares in the public debt – with certain exceptions which we shall presently review. The Florentines themselves apparently did not anticipate the high costs in effort and in money which were needed to complete this thorough inquiry into their numbers and their wealth. Never afterwards, during the periods of the Middle Ages or the Renaissance, were they able to redact a survey of like comprehensiveness and detail.[2] But at least for the year 1427 the *Catasto* allows us to discern how both persons and wealth were distributed spatially across the Florentine domains, and up and down the levels of society.

In examining Florence in the year 1427 we take advantage of a happy accident – the survival of an extraordinarily rich and informative document. We are fortunate too in the city which this document illuminates. For Florence in the early fifteenth century represents very nearly the supreme achievement of medieval and Renaissance urbanism. In 1427 it ranked among the leading commercial, banking and manufacturing centres in Europe; it was already, or would soon become, a principal capital of western literature, art and thought. It possessed a reservoir of skilled hands and creative intellects which had few equals in Europe. If we dare to speculate, if we assume that any urban community in the fifteenth century could have reached a level of sustained economic growth, surely it was Florence. To inspect the characteristics of the Florentine economy and society may help us see why both this city, and lesser cities, could have then attained impressive wealth and manifested great ingenuity in managing their political and social affairs, and yet fall short of achieving an authentic breakthrough in the organization of economic production.

The population of the Florentine domains in 1427 was approximately 260,000 persons, and it included a large urban component. The city of Florence, with some 38,000 residents, contained 14 per

---

[2] Several partial surveys have survived from later years in the fifteenth century, separately for the city of Florence and for its own *contado* or county. But the region of the *distretto* (the area under Florentine rule beyond the historic county) was never later included in a survey together with these properly Florentine regions.

cent of the regional population. The six smaller towns (those with 3,000 or more inhabitants) possessed in all some 26,000 persons, or about 12 per cent of the regional total.[3] In 1427 slightly more than one out of four Tuscans was found in urban communities with a population greater than 3,000 persons. The same proportion of the population – some 26 per cent – had probably been residing in the Tuscan cities since at least the thirteenth century.[4] Tuscany in the fifteenth century remained, as it had been traditionally, one of the most urbanized regions of Europe. (25%)

Our chief interest here is not, however, the distribution of persons, but the distribution of the wealth they owned and the resources they commanded. If we are to identify the ownership of property in Tuscany from the declarations of the *Catasto*, we must first inquire what the statesmen and accountants who designed this great survey considered to be taxable wealth. The Florentine government in its fiscal policies hoped to meet the costs of the current war with Milan, but it also respected certain long-term goals of fiscal management. The most important of these goals was the protection of the community from the devastating effects of confiscatory taxation. The population of the Tuscan lands in 1427 was probably only one third of what it had been one hundred years before, and heavy fiscal exactions, in prompting the flight of taxpayers, threatened to reduce the population even further.[5] The rulers of Florence were aware of

[3] The exact figures for the respective towns are as follows: Pisa, 7,106; Pistoia, 4,292; Arezzo, 3,992; Prato, 3,488; Volterra, 3,329 and Cortona, 3,059. These and other figures from the *Catasto* will vary slightly, depending on who is included in the count (persons who died while the survey was being redacted, later additions, and so forth). The exact population of the city of Florence, excluding babies born in 1427–8 and additions made in 1428 and 1429, is 37,223.

[4] See Russell, *Medieval regions*, pp. 40–51, esp. p. 47 where he estimates that in the thirteenth century the population of the ten largest cities contained 26.3 per cent of the Tuscan population (he includes Lucca and Siena in the analysis). According to Russell, this percentage is 'a really stupendous one'.

[5] Pagolo Morelli, *Ricordi*, p. 102, lists taxes (*gravezze*) as one of the reasons, along with high mortalities (*mortalite*) and wars (*guerre*), for the marked decline in the population of the Mugello, the region of the upper valley of the Sieve river. Morelli composed his memoirs in the first decade of the fifteenth century. Cavalcanti, *Istorie fiorentine*, ii, p. 464, praises the Florentine statesman Maso degli Albizzi, who died in 1417, for reducing taxes in the countryside, which were provoking the flight of peasants. 'He retained consideration for the needs of the peasants, who, because of the insupportable taxes of the commune, were departing and emigrating, to work in lands outside our republic.'

this, and were too alert to strangle the goose from which they hoped to collect golden eggs for the indefinite future.

In order to protect the economy from its own needs and avarice, the Florentine government accordingly distinguished between two basic types of property: that which directly supported either production or the producing family; and surplus property, called 'valsente d'avanzo alla vita', in one source, assets not needed for survival.[6] This crucial distinction between property which served as means of production and property which was non-essential and expendable seems to anticipate later, mercantilistic conceptions of wealth; the *Catasto* itself represents an early effort to enlist fiscal policies in the pursuit of social goals.[7]

The possessions which kept the family alive and productive were, first of all, the domicile in which it resided. The Tuscan who owned a house in which he lived was not assessed for its value. If he rented a dwelling for himself and his family, he could deduct from his total assets the capitalized value of the rent he paid. Furnishings of all sorts within the house, intended for the private use of the family and appropriate for its station in life, went also unassessed. This policy seems to have encouraged the construction and embellishment of family dwellings, even palaces, in the fifteenth century. To the extent that the regulations of the *Catasto* were respected, the family's home and its furnishings offered a rare refuge, in which personal wealth could be sheltered from the insatiable hunger of governments.

Artisans within the city were also allowed to deduct the worth of the basic tools which kept them employed – a loom perhaps, spinning wheel, oven, and the like. The peasants enjoyed the exemption of one team of oxen and one donkey, which they needed to work the farm and to bring its produce to market.

Real property, both in the city and countryside, was usually assessed not on the basis of its market value but the returns it yielded. The return from the property was assumed to represent 7 per cent of its capital value. To assess agricultural land, the surveyors first registered the kinds and amounts of the harvests

---

[6] 'The *Catasto* was prepared. Its nature and method was this: those who possessed one hundred florins of wealth, beyond that needed for life, paid one half florin' (*ibid.* i, p. 197).

[7] On the efforts to secure an abundance of 'means of production' through mercantilistic policies, see Heckscher, *Mercantilism*, ii, p. 89.

the land rendered, converted the quantities into monetary terms according to a fixed schedule of prices, capitalized the resulting sum, and entered this on to the declaration as the value of the property. However, the peasant who worked his own property 'by his hand' or 'by his effort', in the language of the declarations, was charged with only one half the full capitalized value of the land he cultivated. This assured for the peasant and his family a basic supply of food; only rental returns – that is to say only the surplus of the harvest not needed for the support of the culitivator – were liable to assessment. The *mezzadro*, or sharecropper, for example, was not assessed or taxed for the half of the harvest he retained; the urban landlord supported, in other words, the entire burden of taxes for the lands he owned and leased to rural residents. The needs of the government, however pressing, ought not to reduce the peasant to starvation, or drive him to flight.

The law of the *Catasto* also includes a complex schedule of personal charges and personal exemptions, which need not detain us here. Nor are these personal charges or exemptions included in or deducted from the totals showing the distribution of wealth which we shall presently cite.

The *Catasto*, in sum, displays to us the distribution not of all forms of properties, but of those considered surplus, expendable, not needed for survival – and therefore taxable. Our picture of who owned what in Tuscany in 1427 is therefore incomplete. Still, the distribution of surplus and expendable wealth – possessions not rigorously committed to the maintenance of the taxpayer in his station in life – has its own interest. This was the wealth which supported all activities in Tuscany; beyond the basic operations of the subsistence economy. The pattern by which this wealth was distributed geographically and socially should help inform us what the economy was encouraged to produce, and to whose benefit.

The total of expendable wealth listed in the *Catasto*, for all areas of the Florentine domain, before allowable deductions, was approximately 15 million gold florins. Approximately 53 per cent of that sum – or 8 million florins – represented holdings in real property. Movable assets and private investments were assessed at 4.4 million florins, or 29 per cent of the total. Shares in the Florentine public debt, known as the *Monte*, added up to 2.6 million florins, or 17 per cent of all the taxable wealth in the region.[8]

[8] The exact totals are as follows: total wealth in the entire *Catasto*,

We shall first examine the spatial distribution of this taxable wealth. The categories we shall use are Florence itself; the six smaller towns with 3,000 or more inhabitants; fifteen villages; and the rural population. The fifteen villages contain on the average 1,650 persons, and the total number of their residents is sizable – some 25,000 inhabitants, or nearly 10 per cent of the total Tuscan population.[9] The defined size of a village as we use it here is somewhat arbitrary, and we could easily have adjusted the margins to include more or fewer rural communities. Still, it seems necessary to include as a separate category those communities which fall between the dispersed hamlets and homesteads of the peasants, and the true cities; while they cannot be regarded as towns, neither ought they to be counted among the authentically rural population.

Tuscans, as we have noted, show a pronounced tendency to gather into cities, but their wealth was even more intensely concentrated within the urban centres. The 176,000 Tuscans, peasants chiefly, who lived outside the Florentine metropolis, the six towns and fifteen villages, show, on a *per capita* basis, possessions assessed at less than 14 florins. The 25,000 Tuscans settled within the fifteen villages are more than twice as wealthy, with *per capita* possessions assessed at nearly 32 florins. Cortona, Volterra and Prato, the smaller of the six towns, surpass the villages, as their *per capita* wealth is approximately 45 florins. But they are themselves surpassed by the three still larger towns – Arezzo, Pistoia and Pisa – the *per capita* wealth of which ranges betwen 70 and 85 florins. The relationship between the size of the community and the *per capita* wealth of its residents is thus direct and unmistakable. Pisa, the second largest city of Tuscany, is also the second wealthiest, in spite of the fact that

15,085,331 florins; real property, 8,058,189; movables, 4,447,101; and shares in the public debt, 2,580,041. Allowable deductions, exclusive of personal exemptions in the city of Florence, were 3,293,350 florins. The net value of taxable property was 11,791,981 florins. Again, small variations will occur in these figures depending on which households are included in the count.

[9] Among the small villages are counted Empoli, Castel San Giovanni, Montevarchi, Carmignano, Cerreto Guidi, Borgo San Lorenzo, Dicomano, San Godenzo, Laterina, Terranuova, Bibbiena, Castiglione Fiorentino, Montepulciano, San Gimignano and Colle. It should be emphasized, however, that the administrative divisions of the *Catasto* are often vague, and do not allow a precise determination of what Tuscan communities were villages and what were hamlets. The above selection is in large part arbitrary, and intended only to provide a representative sample of the Tuscan population which inhabited large settlements which were not truly cities.

it does not appear to have been an especially flourishing community in the early fifteenth century.[10]

However, even the relative affluence of Pisa – 85 florins per resident, on the average – pales before the affluence of the Florentine metropolis. There, the average wealth per person was 273 florins, more than three times the Pisan average, and nearly 20 times the *per capita* wealth of the rural population outside the villages and towns.

As Florence was also a large city, so it claimed an overwhelming proportion of the wealth of Tuscany. The residents of Florence, who constituted some 14 per cent of the region's population, owned some 67 per cent of its total wealth.[11] The type of wealth which was most evenly distributed across the community was property in land. Florentines owned a comparatively modest 51 per cent of the taxable real estate in Tuscany. The six towns, with 12 per cent of the Tuscan population, owned 14 per cent of the assessed land. The numerous peasants, some two thirds of the population, held 27 per cent of the land; real property was the one form of wealth of which the rural residents possessed a significant part. Although many inhabitants of the countryside owned no property, still the peasant landlord had not entirely disappeared.

In contrast, the distribution of liquid assets was highly skewed in favour of the cities. The *per capita* holdings in liquid assets for the countryside, the fifteen villages, six towns and Florence itself are the following: 1.3 florins, 6.9 florins, 22.2 florins, and 93 florins, respectively.[12] Not only the countryside, but the villages and towns as well, were starved for liquid capital. The Florentines commanded an astonishing 78 per cent of all the movable property in Tuscany. Finally, the substantial public debt, assessed in 1427 at nearly 2.6 million florins, was owned almost exclusively by Florentine citizens.[13] In fifteenth-century Tuscany, movable capital tended inexorably to move to Florence.

[10] On Pisa and its economy in the fifteenth century, see Mallett in Rubinstein (ed.), *Florentine studies.*

[11] The total wealth of Florentine citizens is 10,169,109 florins. Their real property is valued at 4,128,024 florins; movables, 3,467,707; and public debt, 2,573,378.

[12] The totals of wealth for the four divisions of the Tuscan population, given in the same order, are as follows: 223,792; 170,245; 585,357; and 3,467,707 florins respectively.

[13] Only trivial amounts of the public debt were held by non-residents of the city, constituting only 0.25 per cent of the total (6.663 florins).

Florence was thus a blazing sun of affluence surrounded by dim planets of wealth in the small Tuscan cities and villages – all of them set within a dark, nearly destitute rural space. Still, it would clearly be an error to imply that this affluent metropolis contained only, or chiefly, or even many, affluent people. The richest one hundred Florentine households, which constituted less than 1 per cent of all the households, owned a fabulous 27 per cent of the city's already fabulous wealth. This mere one hundred households controlled more wealth than the 37,000 families which lived outside the towns and villages, and more even than the six towns of Tuscany apart from Florence taken together.[14] Favoured habitat of the rich, the Florentine metropolis was also crowded with paupers. The poorest 14 per cent of the Florentine households were absolutely destitute; some 31 per cent of households, nearly a third of the city, show more debts than assets. Going up the scale of urban wealth, we must pass through 85 per cent of the Florentine households before the total of their holdings equals that of the richest 1 per cent; in other words, the holdings of these approximately 8,500 urban households barely equal the possessions of the one hundred wealthiest families.

Of all forms of wealth, shares in the public debt were again the most concentrated. The richest one hundred Florentine households owned 43 per cent of the public debt. The majority of holdings in the *Monte* fell to a minuscule group of urban households comprising between 1 and 2 per cent of all households at Florence.

Statisticians sometimes use an 'index of concentration' to measure the distribution of wealth across a community.[15] The index ranges from a value of 1, which would indicate perfect equality in the distribution of wealth, to a value of 100. A score of 1 would mean that every household holds an equal share of the total social capital; a score of 100 shows, in our adaptation of the index here, that the richest 1 per cent of the households owns all the wealth.

[14] The wealth of the richest hundred households of Florence was 2,883,477 florins.
[15] The index is constructed as follows. The households are arranged in order of ascending wealth, divided into centiles, and the cumulative percentage held by each centile, and those below it, is calculated. On the basis of these results a Lorenz curve is drawn, which illustrates what percentage of the households controls what percentage of the wealth. The index represents the ratio of the areas under two curves: the one, theoretical, showing perfectly even distribution of wealth among all households; over the second, illustrating the results of the above calculations.

The index for the households of the city of Florence shows 70.5 in regard to the distribution of real property, a higher score of 80 for movables, and an extraordinary 90 for shares in the public debt. For all forms of property taken together, the index of concentration is 79. As these indices imply, the control of Florentine resources rested with a tiny number of the richest households.

Although the six small Tuscan towns look disadvantaged in comparison with Florence, nonetheless the distribution of the wealth they owned was almost as skewed as the Florentine in favour of the rich. The index of concentration in the six towns for all forms of wealth is 75, not much lower than the comparable figure of 79 within the city of Florence. In the towns the distribution of movable assets was 84 – even higher than the 80 registered at Florence. Perhaps this reflects the particular scarcity of liquid capital in the small urban communities. At all events, the mechanisms which kept wealth highly concentrated in the possession of a slim percentage of households operated not only at Florence but in all the Tuscan cities in the fifteenth century.

The Tuscan cities in the period of the *Catasto* were loci where the few with enormous possessions met and interacted with multitudes of the destitute. Perhaps the most surprising result of our inquiry is the scant importance, by measure of numbers or possessions, of the middle levels of urban society. Had the urban middle classes always been crushed between the rich, distinguished by their huge possessions, and the poor, distinguished by their numbers? We cannot give a firm answer to this question, but we do have indications that the highly skewed distribution of wealth in the fifteenth-century cities was a comparatively new development, and that wealth had been somewhat more evenly distributed across the population in the thirteenth century, before the onslaught of the great epidemics. A recent study of the city of Perugia in Umbria, which has preserved *estimi* or tax surveys from the middle thirteenth century, has shown a tendency for wealth to become concentrated in fewer hands as the fourteenth century progressed.[16] The growing importance of the richest families also corresponds with political changes in the north Italian cities. The latter half of the thirteenth

---

[16] See the study by S. R. Blanshei, 'Perugia'. On the distribution of wealth in the suburban community of Piuvica close to Pistoia, see Herlihy, *Medieval and Renaissance Pistoia*, pp. 181–3. Also for a rural village, *idem* in Rubinstein (ed.), *Florentine studies*.

century, at Perugia and in the Tuscan towns as well, witnessed the rise to power of the regime of the *Popolo*. The *Popolo* was a corporation of largely middle-class merchants and artisans, which successfully imposed political disabilities upon the so-called magnate families of the towns.[17] But by the fifteenth century the patrician households were once more exerting their dominance. The humanist historian Leonardo Bruni, who served as chancellor of Florence when the *Catasto* was redacted, offers this striking evaluation of the changes in the balance of classes experienced at Florence since the regime of the *Popolo* in the thirteenth century.

> In olden times [he states, in evident reference to the thirteenth century] the *Popolo* was accustomed to go to war in arms, and since the city was densely settled, it conquered almost all its neighbours. Therefore, in those days, the city's power depended principally upon numbers, and for this reason the *Popolo* held supremacy, so as virtually to exclude the nobles from government. As time passed, however, wars came to be fought rather by the mercenary soldier. Then the city's power was seen not to depend upon the masses, but upon the magnates and the wealthy, who supplied the government with money and utilized counsel rather than arms. The power of the *Popolo* gradually waned, and the régime took on the form it now possesses.[18]

Bruni maintains, and our limited sources suggest that he is right, that the middle classes at Florence were politically more powerful in the thirteenth century than they were to be in the period of the *Catasto*. His words should warn us against constructing simple and rigid models of the 'typical' traditional city. These cities, in their fundamental composition and the balance of classes, show considerable variations, not only across regions but also over time.

Bruni also offers an explanation for the change, from popular domination in the thirteenth century to the patrician preponderance in his own times. The paid mercenary, and no longer the armed citizen, had come to rule the battlefields. To say this is equally to affirm that money ruled the battlefields, and the governments showed a new dependence upon those affluent citizens who could supply it.

[17] The now classical interpretation of the struggle between the aristocratic and popular forces at Florence is Salvemini, *Magnati e popolani*. But on the difficulties of identifying magnates and *popolani* in another Tuscan city, see Cristiani, *Nobiltà e popolo*.

[18] 'Leonardo Arretini...', in *Philippi Villani*, ed. Galletti, pp. 94–6.

In the fifteenth century another eminent Tuscan humanist, Poggio Bracciolini, in a conversation he records on the subject of avarice, has given us the depiction with probably the most insight into the relationship among the great private fortunes, the needs of the community, and government. Poggio, or the character who seemingly represents his views in the discussion, flatly asserts that money had become 'the muscles by which the commonwealth is maintained'.[19] In helping both government and the community to meet their needs, the great fortunes served, in Poggio's effective image, as a 'barn of moneys' (*horreum pecuniarum*).[20] Just as the well-ordered commonwealth maintained public deposits of grain, which fed the populace in years of famine, so the great fortunes provided the government with the moneys it needed in moments of duress. Without the contributions of the rich, the governments of cities, and the lives of their citizens, would be a shambles.[21] The great fortunes, Poggio also states, further endowed cities with magnificent buildings and allowed the arts to flourish. Money not only assured the safety of cities but also supported their splendour.

The fiscal system of the Florentine government in the fifteenth century rested upon a kind of symbiosis between the public treasury and the private fortunes. In times of war the government tapped the wealth which the great households had conveniently assembled; in times of peace the 'barn of moneys' had to be replenished, and the government helped in the harvest.

How indeed were these huge concentrations of wealth accumulated, and how were they defended? The *Catasto* itself helps us identify some of the processes of capital accumulation. As the assessments of real property were based directly on rents, so the city of Florence, according to the *Catasto*, gathered in slightly more than one half the rents on real property paid throughout Tuscany. We can estimate the income from rents which flowed into Florence at 289,000 florins per year.[22] The residents of the six towns collected

---

[19] Bracciolini, *Opera omnia*, p. 15. The speaker is the papal secretary Antonio Loschi.

[20] 'For this reason, just as well-governed peoples and states maintain public granaries, to supply wheat during famines, so it would be advantageous that many [rich] misers be placed there, who would serve as a private barn of moneys, which could assist us' (*ibid.*).

[21] '...disruption of our life and public affairs will follow' (*ibid.* p. 13).

[22] This represents a return of 7 per cent on the value of the real property owned by Florentine citizens, assessed in the *Catasto* at 4,128,024 florins.

in the form of rents only 80,000 florins per year.[23] However, many of these rents, representing returns from agricultural holdings, were paid in kind; they could not alone generate the pools of liquid capital which the government primarily needed to carry on its wars.

Contemporaries laid particular emphasis upon commercial profits, which supplied both the government and the economy with abundant cash. 'Just as the wet nurse nourishes babies', Giovanni Cavalcanti once remarked, 'even so the merchants fed the people, and keep the commonwealth fat'.[24] If we can assume that movables, loans, business investments and the like returned 7 per cent of their capital value, so Florence reaped another 240,000 florins per year as the profits on its business and commercial ventures. And the assumed return of 7 per cent may well be too modest. The six towns, on the other hand, earned through comparable investments only an unimpressive 41,000 florins. We could estimate, in other words, that the income which came yearly into the city from all forms of private investments totalled slightly more than half a million florins. And two thirds of this income went to the richest 10 per cent of the Florentine households.[25]

In a description of Florence, Gregorio Dati, who appears in the *Catasto*, instructs a fellow Florentine, Bindo Altoviti, on the wonders of the city, and he dwells at length on its fiscal resources.[26] Between 1375 and 1405 the Florentine government allegedly spent on its major wars alone 11.5 million florins, an average of 380,000 florins a war. Bindo declares in response that there was not so much gold in all the world.[27] But Gregorio reassures him: although this huge amount could not be found at any one time in the city, still the continuous circulation of gold allowed the government to collect and spend the same florins over and over again. The Florentine merchants quickly retrieved, from within Florence and beyond its borders, the moneys spent in the waging of war. The *guadagni de' mercatanti* kept a constant stream of gold flowing back into the city, replenishing the pools of money available to the state. 'The

[23] This sum again represents a 7 per cent return on property assessed at 1,137,466 florins.

[24] Cavalcanti, *Istorie fiorentine*, i, p. 276.

[25] The poorest 90 per cent of Florentine urban households owned only 32.21 per cent of the total wealth of all kinds possessed by the citizens of the city.

[26] *L' 'Istoria di Firenze' di Gregorio Dati*, ed. Pratesi.

[27] *Ibid.* pp. 136–7.

florins which are spent in one year', Gregorio explains, 'return in large part the next or following year, as does the water which the sea scatters through clouds upon the earth by rain, and which by rivers returns to the sea.'[28] Moreover, the Florentine merchants who accomplished these marvels 'make together so large a number of valiant and rich men as has no equal in the world'.[29]

It is, however, also worth noting that cities such as Pisa and Pistoia, which had been major commercial centres in the thirteenth century, were earning only paltry amounts in comparison with Florence by the early fifteenth century.[30] These secondary urban centres of Tuscany clearly could no longer compete in international commerce and banking with the Florentine metropolis.

The *Catasto* and other sources give us a good picture of the capital owned by and the profits which accrued to the Florence patriciate, but they still do not entirely explain how the great urban families were able initially to accumulate and thereafter to preserve their enormous concentrations of wealth. Here a critical factor was the fiscal policies of the Florentine commune. Except in rare instances Florence in the fourteenth and fifteenth centuries did not impose a direct tax on property owned by the citizens and residents of the city. Rather, the payments which Florentine citizens made to the government – even those paid on the basis of the *Catasto* assessment – were counted as purchases of shares in the public debt.[31] These shares, until they were repaid, earned from the government a yearly interest of 5 per cent. Gregorio Dati claims that Florentines in the early fifteenth century were wealthier than ever before and one reason for this was the methods by which the public debt was serviced and repaid. 'Every year when the land is at peace', Gregorio explains, 'the commune makes great expenditures [in servicing its debt] and its citizens enjoy large revenue.'[32] 'The books of the *Monte*', he further states, 'contain what the citizens are to receive, and [their claims] are repaid little by little every year, when they are at peace, from the abundant revenues of

[28] *Ibid.* p. 137.
[29] *Ibid.* p. 59.
[30] On the assumption that they were earning 7 per cent on liquid investments, Pisans were gaining only 18,557 florins per year, and Pistoiesi only 6,054 florins, as distinct from the 240,000 florins which acrued to the Florentines.
[31] See especially Molho, *Florentine public finances*, pp. 81ff.
[32] *'Istoria di Firenze'*, ed. Pratesi, pp. 138 and 117.

the commune, and meanwhile. . .they have as profit five florins per hundred every year.'[33]

Dati does not tell us, as the *Catasto* does, that fewer than 200 Florentine households owned more than one half of the outstanding shares in the public debt. The payment of interest and the retirement of shares thus generated a flow of revenue from the heavily taxed countryside and the lower levels of society into the coffers of the few, stupendously wealthy Florentine families.

Another contemporary of the *Catasto*, Giovanni Cavalcanti, claims that the fiscal system not only protected, but at times created, great fortunes. Allegedly, the government sometimes paid interest only to the greatest shareholders in the public debt, ignoring the claims and rights of its humble creditors.[34] Cosimo de' Medici, Florence's second wealthiest citizen in 1427, may have profited from a special relationship with, and special treatment by, the tax office.[35] Cavalcanti describes the careers of two Florentines, who, he maintains, made fortunes by speculating in the shares of the *Monte*.[36] One method of amassing wealth at the public's expense was to buy up holdings in the *Monte* from churches and impoverished citizens, and then secure interest payments or reimbursements through special understandings with the tax officials. 'Thus', Cavalcanti concludes, 'the wealth of Florence passes from powerless to powerful citizens, under the name of taxes, with the favour of wars.'[37]

Cavalcanti's grim portrait of greed and fraud in the operations of the *Monte* may well be exaggerated and distorted. Still, there can be

---

[33] *Ibid.* p. 138.

[34] Cavalcanti, *Istorie fiorentine*, ii, p. 202.

[35] Rinaldo degli Albizzi, in a denunciation of Cosimo, alleges that he received unrecorded interest payments from the commune. 'One can guess the value of those shares, from which the profits go uncounted, because they are seen in public by everyone' (*ibid.* i, p. 504). Compare also the complaint that 'the coffers of the gates [i.e. the tariffs collected at the city gates] go to be emptied at the house of Cosimo' (*ibid.* ii, p. 211).

[36] See *ibid.* ii. p. 189 for the career of Giovanni Pucci. Pucci was at first an impoverished dry goods merchant (*merciaio*) who 'was found to have purchased for the meanest sums the shares of many men'. 'In seven years', Cavalcanti continues, 'he was found to have received from the commune through this highly shrewd way 54,000 florins.' On the similar career of Giovanni di Stefano Corsini, see *ibid.* ii, p. 195. Cavalcanti describes him thus: 'I saw this man absolutely impoverished; and if I had called him a beggar, the word would have been more accurate.' Later, however, 'he was appointed to administer the property of the commune. Of it he took for himself so large a part, that some say he took in value 20,000 florins.'

[37] *Ibid.* i, p. 24.

no doubt that the Florentine commune in its fiscal policies consciously favoured the great urban fortunes. To use Poggio's image once more, it eagerly sought to replenish the barn of moneys upon which its military and political power and its cultural splendour and prestige critically depended.

The flow of rents, the profits of merchants and investors, and the servicing of the public debt thus generated large pools of capital under the administration of the great urban houses but ultimately at the disposal of the state. Ideally, the primary producers – the peasants and artisans – would work energetically, and the rulers of society sought to guarantee for them the means and tools they needed in order to remain stable and productive. But through a variety of mechanisms – rents, interest payments, profits and taxes – the rich and powerful, pre-eminently Florentine, households rapidly siphoned off most if not all of the surplus output the peasants and the artisans were able to produce. How did this highly skewed distribution of wealth affect the Tuscan economy and its prospects for economic growth?

In terms of the regional economy, the concentration of wealth within the city greatly enlarged the importance of the Florentine market and the power of Florentine investors. The needs of the city of Florence, with 14 per cent of the region's population but with 67 per cent of its wealth, understandably influenced producers throughout Tuscany, who were eager to find cash payments for their outputs. A Florentine official, Giovanni Battista Tedaldi, has left us a description of Pistoia and its countryside in the sixteenth century, and he describes the produce of the region largely in terms of the money it earned on the Florentine market.[38] Moreover, the scant liquid capital available in the small towns gave to Florentine investors a dominant voice in the development of capital-intensive enterprises. The Florentine investors in the fifteenth century sent large sums abroad to finance the ventures of the travelling merchants (often their own sons), and they continued to place money in cloth manufactures, although, it would appear, chiefly at Florence. Outside the metropolis Florentines show an interest primarily in

---

[38] Minuti, *Archivio storico italiano* (1892). See his description of cereal production: 'One third [of the cereal harvest], or 112,000 *staia*, is turned entirely into gold. On market days it is sold in the Piazza, and it supplies Pistoia, Florence, Prato and other localities in the state. Through these sales the citizens of Pistoia. . .acquire cash for themselves.'

those products which commanded a good market at Florence: iron, mined at Elba and smelted in the Apennines; lumber and milling in the same regions; animals on the plain of Pisa; sheep, which moved in a system of transhumance between the mountains and the maritime plains; and animal products, such as leather and soap at Pisa.[39]

The importance of the Florentine market and the power of Florentine capital promoted what we would call the regional integration of the Tuscan economy. In the thirteenth century the numerous, independent and fiercely competitive communes which divided the Tuscan territory attempted to engage in many of the same economic activities and to undermine when they could the prosperity of their neighbours. But the subsequent political and, perhaps still more, the financial dominance of Florence suppressed the wasteful competition of this earlier period and stimulated the growth of a rational utilization of the area's resources.

The occupational structures of the Tuscan towns, evident from the *Catasto*, can help illustrate the development of local specializations, and regional integration, in the Tuscan economy. In 1427, in presenting their declarations, the household heads often declare an occupation; about 56 per cent of the family heads do so in the city of Florence, and the percentage is about the same in the other Tuscan cities. To be sure, it is difficult to analyse these declared occupations with any rigour. The richest citizens, for example, who often had many economic interests, rarely declare a profession. Artisans might exercise several trades simultaneously, or change from one to another; even the exact meaning of a declared profession, such as *faber* (smith), might vary subtly from region to region. We ought not, in other words, lay much stress upon the precise numbers found in the various occupations which the *Catasto* records, but in a rough way these figures illuminate for us the economic functions which the urban centres of Tuscany were fulfilling in 1427.

Table 1 gives, for the six largest Tuscan towns (excluding

---

[39] On the substantial investments of Florentine families, including the Medici, in Pisan lands, see Mallett in Rubinstein (ed.), *Florentine studies*. Lorenzo de'Medici had investments in iron foundries (*fabriche*) in the Pistoiese mountains: see de Roover, *Rise and decline of the Medici bank*, pp. 165–6. On the influence of the Florentine market upon the activities of one Pistoiese commercial house, the Partini, see Herlihy, *Medieval and Renaissance Pistoia*, pp. 168–71.

Cortona), the ten professions which appear most frequently in the declarations. The table also gives the absolute number of heads of households who declare a specific profession, and the ratio of that number to the size of the urban community, expressed in thousands.

The table allows us to distinguish two main types of functions which the Tuscan cities were fulfilling in 1427. Some functions were common to all the urban centres, and others represent specializations within the regional economy. All the towns served as markets and centres of distribution for the surrounding rural areas. Shoemakers (*calzolai*), who numbered 760 in Tuscany in 1427 and constituted the largest single profession, are important in all the towns. Wool merchants (*lanai*) are also numerous throughout Tuscany; they numbered 510 in 1427 – the third largest profession in the entire region after shoemakers and notaries. They are found even in Volterra, where there is no evidence of an important cloth manufacture. Many Tuscan *lanai* were certainly occupied in the sale of finished cloth rather than in its production. Spice merchants (269 in Tuscany in 1427) were also distributed throughout all the towns, although they do not appear among the ten largest professions at Florence (where they numbered 115) or at Volterra (where they were three). Another trade important in all the cities was that of carpenter (*legnaiolo*); they were 291 in the entire province. These urban centres also performed special services for the surrounding rural areas; notaries in particular were numerous everywhere, found in all the towns and even in many smaller villages. Their number – 750 – makes them the second largest of all the professions in the *Catasto*. The number of notaries per 1,000 of the population also seems remarkably constant from community to community; only Prato, perhaps because of its proximity to Florence, shows a ratio which drops below the common norm of 8 to 10 notaries per 1,000 of the population. The rural residents, in sum, came to the towns to market their produce; purchase condiments, clothing, shoes and other necessities; and have their important transactions redacted and recorded by a public notary.

Our list of occupations also gives evidence of specialized functions within the various towns. The large number of government employees in its population at once identifies Florence as the region's administrative capital. Florence, moreover, is the only Tuscan city which possessed a large industrial population. Four of its ten most

TABLE 1. The ten most common occupations of male household heads in six Tuscan cities in 1427

	Florence	Pisa	Pistoia	Arezzo	Prato	Volterra
1.	Notaries 307 (8.25)	Shoemakers 76 (10.38)	Shoemakers 50 (11.34)	Shoemakers 54 (13.11)	Peasant owners 43 (12.23)	Peasant tenants 116 (34.73)
2.	Civil Servants 261 (7.01)	Notaries 62 (8.47)	Peasant owners 48 (10.88)	Wool merchants 39 (9.47)	Wool merchants 36 (10.24)	Peasant owners 82 (24.55)
3.	Weavers 261 (7.01)	Peasant owners 44 (6.01)	Notaries 47 (10.66)	Notaries 29 (7.04)	Sharecroppers 34 (9.67)	Wool merchants 27 (8.08)
4.	Shoemakers 244 (6.56)	Tanners 41 (5.60)	Smiths 32 (7.25)	Smiths 21 (5.10)	Shoemakers 33 (9.38)	Notaries 25 (7.49)
5.	Wool merchants 222 (5.96)	Peasant tenants 39 (5.33)	Wool merchants 21 (4.76)	Doublet makers 17 (4.13)	Notaries 19 (5.40)	Sharecroppers 21 (6.2?)
6.	Carders 202 (5.43)	Wool merchants 33 (4.51)	Spice merchants 17 (3.85)	Labourers 16 (3.88)	Smiths 18 (5.12)	Civil servants 10 (2.99)
7.	Skinners 188 (5.05)	Spice merchants 31 (4.23)	Barbers 13 (2.95)	Spice merchants 12 (2.91)	Millers 15 (4.26)	Dry goods merchants 6 (1.80)
8.	Carpenters 169 (4.34)	Barbers 31 (4.23)	Carpenters 13 (2.95)	Carpenters 11 (2.67)	Spice merchants 13 (3.70)	Furnace owners 6 (1.80)
9.	Linen merchants 149 (4.00)	Brokers 25 (3.42)	Labourers 11 (2.49)	Food merchants 11 (2.67)	Carpenters 13 (3.70)	Carpenters 5 (1.50)
10.	Dyers 117 (3.14)	Goldsmiths 23 (3.14)	Coopers 10 (2.27)	Butchers 11 (2.67)	Peasant tenants 10 (2.84)	Millers 5 (1.50)

Figures show absolute numbers in the professional category and ratio per 1,000 of population. Brokers = *sensali*. Carders = *pettinatori*. Carpenters = *legnaioli*. Doublet makers = *farsettai*. Dry goods merchants = *merciai*. Food merchants = *pizzicagnoli*. Furnace owners = *fornaciai*. Linen merchants = *linaioli e rigattieri*. Skinners = *scardassieri*. Smiths = *fabri*. Tanners = *cuoai*. Wool merchants = *lanai*.

common occupations – weavers, carders, skinners and dyers – comprise industrial workers. It is difficult to determine whether the weavers and dyers were working in wool, silk or linen; Florentines were producing all three types of textile in 1427. In no other Tuscan town does even a single trade involved in the textile industry appear among the ten most common occupations. In the regionally integrated Tuscan economy, Florence had come to exercise a near monopoly in the manufacture of cloth.

Florence also appears as the centre of production and sale of luxury items, although here the second largest Tuscan town, Pisa, also retains prominence. Of the 123 Tuscan goldsmiths, 92 are found at Florence and 23 at Pisa; the two cities thus contain 94 per cent of all these craftsmen. Florence and Pisa further possess a majority of silk merchants (of whom there are 115 in all Tuscany, with 91 at Florence and 11 at Pisa); and of furriers (of 128 Tuscan furriers, 87 are Florentines and 17 Pisans). In sum, 88.7 per cent of Tuscan silk merchants and 81.3 per cent of furriers are residents of the two largest cities. Given Florence's wealth, its prominence as a centre of commerce in luxury articles is predictable, but Pisa's importance is somewhat surprising. Probably the proximity of the sea, the easy access to luxuries imported from abroad, and the presence of colonies of foreign merchants helped preserve Pisa's stature as a purveyor of luxury goods.

The presence at Pisa of a large number of brokers (*sensali*) further reflects the characteristic activities of a port city. Tanners are even more numerous at Pisa. The maritime pastures close to the city provided abundant fodder; large herds of cattle roamed the plain; and their presence supported a vigorous tanning industry in the city, and also favoured the manufacture of soap.[40] At Pistoia, smiths (*fabri*) were especially important. These were doubtless iron workers; abundant forests in the mountains above Pistoia supplied cheap charcoal for the smelting of iron ore, brought from Elba and elsewhere. Pistoia thus became a principal Tuscan centre of iron manufacture.[41] Smiths were numerous at Prato too, but there perhaps the more typical occupation was that of miller. The mills at Prato, driven by the rivers and streams coming down from the

[40] The importance of these industries at Pisa is examined by Mallett in Rubinstein (ed.), *Florentine studies*.
[41] On the iron industry at Pistoia, see Herlihy, *Medieval and Renaissance Pistoia*, pp. 175–6.

mountains above the city, were employed not only in grinding grain but in fulling cloth and sawing lumber. Finally, many residents of the smaller towns continued in 1427 to live from agricultural labours, At Volterra, for example, more than one half of the identifiable occupations in the city involve the cultivation of the land.

The Tuscan economy in 1427 thus shows these salient characteristics: a visible measure of local specialization and regional integration in economic production; and efficient means of recruiting capital; strong links with foreign markets; and a highly skilled and motivated community of merchants at Florence, who also exercised a powerful voice in the determination of public policy. Through exerting a near monopoly on the supplies of capital, the merchant rulers of Florence would seem to have had the capacity to control and redirect production in the ways they considered most advantageous. It might appear that Tuscany possessed all that was needed to assure continuing economic growth and prosperity. But this was not to be, and at least in relative measure Florence by the middle of the sixteenth century had clearly lost its position to more vigorous commercial and manufacturing centres – to Milan and Venice especially.[42] It is, of course, very difficult to explain why Florence was unable to maintain the pace of growth characteristic of these latter cities. The real wonder may be that Florence, set within a region poorly endowed with natural resources, could have maintained its leadership for so long. Still, the skewed distribution of wealth, and the fiscal and economic system which maintained it, did induce certain severe strains in the regional economy, which obstructed, if they did not entirely prevent, continuing economic expansion.

Let us first consider the agricultural sector of the economy. As the *Catasto* shows, rural areas generally were starved of liquid capital; they laboured under a constant and intense *carestia di danari*, a 'famine of money' which we might term a 'liquidity crisis'. Public taxes, private rents and commercial profits constantly drew money

---

[42] Florence, which was probably three quarters the size of Venice before the Great Pestilence of 1348, was not much more than one third its size by the middle of the sixteenth century. Although the extent of Florence's decline in the sixteenth century has often been exaggerated, there can still be no doubt that it was losing its relative position, in terms of size and commercial importance, among the cities of Italy and of Europe. See the recent comments of Cochrane, *Florence in the forgotten centuries*, pp. 112–15.

from the cultivators to the landlords, and from the countryside to the city, most especially to Florence. In spite of the usury prohibition, interest payments doubtless moved money in similar channels, stocking with still greater abundance the barns of the wealthy. To find money, residents of the countryside might contract usurious loans or sell their lands and possessions; they might join the ranks of the totally destitute, with whom Tuscany abounded in 1427. But indebtedness and proletarianization of the rural population did not permanently satisfy, but rather sharpened, the hunger for cash.

The Tuscan tenant often paid his rents in kind, but he needed cash for many reasons – to meet his tax assessments and to purchase at market the few necessities which he could not produce in his own household. Moreover, to work the land productively he frequently needed money for stock, seed, fertilizer, repairs, sometimes hired help, and a promise of security against the typically erratic Tuscan harvests. Mounting debts and unpaid taxes in rural areas might force peasants to flee the Florentine domains, leaving their creditors with increased possessions from their confiscated holdings, but with reduced returns. To strip the countryside of capital might eventually starve the cities of food. The huge concentrations of wealth in the hands of a few families visited Florence with the curse of Midas; the city risked deprivation amidst its accumulated gold.

The well-being of the agricultural economy required, in sum, that some liquid capital be constantly recycled from city to countryside. Arrangements for bringing capital back to the land accordingly became a characteristic part of the famous sharecropping contract, the *mezzadria*.[43] The *mezzadria* in what agrarian historians consider to be its classical form appears in Tuscan documents from the middle of the thirteenth century, but it does not become widespread in Tuscany until the fourteenth and fifteenth centuries. Under its terms, in return for one half of the harvest, the landlord provided to his tenant not only a *podere* or family farm, but also most or all of the stock and capital he needed to work it – seeds, fertilizer and

---

[43] The terms of numerous *mezzadria* contracts in the fifteenth century are summarized in Machiavelli, *Libro di ricordi*, as, for example, pp. 1–3, contract dated 16 October 1474. On the history of the *mezzadria*, with examples of earlier contracts, see Imberciadori, *Mezzadria classica toscana*. On the place of the *mezzadria* in the agricultural history of Tuscany, see Jones in Rubinstein (ed.), *Florentine studies*.

often even oxen. The classical *mezzadria* did not, however, create a recognizably modern economic relationship between landlord and tenant, based on cold calculation and the cash nexus. Rather, the landlord, the 'host' as he was called in the contemporary texts, was protector and patron of his tenants, his *lavoratori* or workers. He was expected to give advice to his workers and to aid them in times of need. In 1482, for example, in a typical incident the sharecropper of Bernardo Machiavelli appealed to his 'host', telling him that he was without food and could work the farm no longer, unless Bernardo supplied him with bread or grain.[44] In return for favours, the 'host' frequently received gifts from his 'workers', which gave visible recognition to his status as patron.[45]

The relationship of patron and client, embedded in the *mezzadria*, is especially manifest in the institution of the rural loan. In the fourteenth and fifteenth centuries, the 'host' seems almost always to have extended a loan to his worker when the latter took possession of the farm. These loans, given in close connection with the *mezzadria*, could amount to substantial sums. Palla di Nofri Strozzi, the richest citizen in the *Catasto* of 1427, lists in his declarations 122 such loans to his sharecroppers, amounting to 3,200 florins. At the end of the list of debtors, he notes that he had given many other loans to other peasants, who were now dead or 'gone with God'.[46] He does not bother to record the precise names and amounts, lest, as he says, he bore the tax assessors. The loans, he assures them, were all but worthless.

As shown through their domestic memoirs, Florentine landlords often tried to collect the loans they had extended to their share-

[44] Machiavelli, *Libro di recordi*, p. 164.

[45] Pagolo Morelli, *Ricordi*, p. 236, urges his descendants to avoid close ties with their workers (*lavoratori*), but his words imply that most 'hosts' expected gifts from their workers. 'Don't go seeking to receive presents from them, and don't wish to acquire them. And if they still give you presents, don't do anything special for them in return.' Even Morelli expects his descendants to help and counsel the sharecroppers and so to earn their love and respect. 'Aid them with advice and help and counsel them when a wrong or crime is done to them. . .Go quickly and do them these services. By doing this. . .you will be loved more than others, and they will be respectful to you, as far as they are able, and you will have from them that good which is possible to have.'

[46] 'I find that I have claims upon other dead labourers, and upon those who have gone with God. . .I do not give them, in order not to hold your minds in tedium, and they are of hardly any value' (Archivio de Stato di Firenze. Archivio del Catasto, reg. 76. fo. 169).

croppers, but they seem to have enjoyed only sporadic and partial success.[47] Perhaps more realistically, the officials of the *Catasto* refused to consider loans between host and labourer as taxable assets or deductible obligations. They were treated much as were loans between members of the same household.

The terms of tenancy under the system of *mezzadria* show close analogies to the policies which the communal government adopted in regard to the primary producers in the community. The 'host', like the government, tried to ensure that his tenants would possess the means they needed to work the land productively. But the 'host', like the government, was also eager to drain from his tenants most if not all of the surplus which the farm produced. Because the sharecroppers were almost always indebted to their landlords, their own poverty was their chief protection against demands for repayment.

Moreover, the system of flexible rents under the *mezzadria*, while it protected the peasant against failed harvests, did not encourage him to labour hard in order to increase the yields of the land. The *mezzadri*, to be sure, appear in the *Catasto* with relatively large families; and like peasants elsewhere, they seem to have expanded their efforts in relation to the number of mouths in their households.[48] But they had little incentive to strive after a higher standard of living, as their 'host' would claim one half of the increased abundance of the land, and often more, in repayment for outstanding debts. Understandably, the landlords accuse their sharecroppers of indifference and laziness, probably with reason. Bernardo Machiavelli, for example, once attributed the death of a valued ox to the 'malgoverno' of his sharecropper.[49]

Rampant indebtedness, and a structure of rents under the *mezzadria* system which gave little incentive to effort, left large

[47] Machiavelli, for example, frequently tried to retrieve loans given to his *lavoratori*. See Machiavelli, *Libro di ricordi*, p. 165, in which the *mezzadro* agrees to repay at the next harvest 'all that which he together with his father-in-law owes me or will owe me for oxen, loans, grain, fodder received. . . from me, without any exception'.

[48] See, for example, the study of Pisan peasant families by Klapisch and Demonet, *Annales, E.S.C.* (1972), esp. p. 883. More families of *mezzadri* fall into the category of large households of six to ten persons than the families of any other peasant group.

[49] 'I record that later, on 19 August, the best and the handsomest of the above-mentioned pair of oxen died. . .The said ox, which was mine, died through the negligence of the said Piero di Luca del Grosso, my share-cropper' (Machiavelli, *Libro di ricordi*, pp. 227–8).

numbers of the rural population in poverty and destitution. Nor could the rural areas develop or sustain a strong demand for urban manufactures.

An analogous set of financial and social relations was characteristic of the Tuscan cities. Indebtedness gripped the poorest levels of society. At Florence in 1427 debts outweighed assets in 31 per cent of the households. In the sixteenth century, Giovanni Battista Tedaldi described the urban proletariat, which he called the *plebei*, of Pistoia in the following terms: 'The plebeans are poor, as happens everywhere. For that reason, they daily support their lives with what little they can earn through their efforts, [but] they cannot much advance. When they might do so, nature and the quality of their life do not allow it; so they remain always victims of poverty.'[50] The desperation of the urban poor and the power of the wealthy invited the formation of systems of patronage and of factional alignments within urban society. Cosimo dei Medici allegedly cultivated support among the plebs by making loans to or paying the debts of impoverished citizens.[51] The formation of large and powerful factions and the outbursts of factional violence cast an almost feudal aura over Florence, this apparent bastion of early capitalism. But indebtedness also deprived the urban poor of much incentive to improve their lot, as increased earnings would largely benefit their creditors. In city as in countryside, the destitute found in their own poverty their chief protection against demands for repayment of debts. Crowded with paupers, the city was itself a poor consumer of its own manufactures.

The highly skewed distribution of wealth within the city, favouring the rich, had one other curious social effect, to which a contemporary of the *Catasto*, Giovanni Cavalcanti, calls attention. These comments on Florentine society he attributes to a patrician, Rinaldo degli Albizzi, who allegedly sought to warn his fellow magnates against the ambitions of the middle classes of the city. The small artisans and shopkeepers, according to Rinaldo, were desperate for capital, and they saw a convenient solution to their pressing needs in fomenting wars. Although they paid taxes continuously to the

---

[50] Minuti, *Archivio storico italiano* (1892), p. 324.

[51] See the denunciation of Cosimo attributed to Rinaldo degli Albizzi in Cavalcanti, *Istorie fiorentine*, i, p. 502: 'Don't you see, that he with his riches, enters on the road which may lead him to political domination? He lends the moneys they seek to family heads among the plebeans. . .' See also *ibid.* p. 497.

government, their few possessions and scant capital gave them relative immunity from extraordinary imposts. In times of war, the very rich – the *popolo grasso* – had to disgorge their accumulated wealth in the interest of the community. 'When there are wars', these lesser citizens allegedly reasoned, 'the city is always filled by a multitude of soldiers [who] must buy all their needs; artisans grow prosperous and well rewarded...'[52] 'War', Rinaldo instructed his fellow magnates, 'is the profit and the wealth [of these lesser citizens], and thus through your deprivation comes their abundance...Your ruin is their glory and exaltation. War among the wolves has always been and is today peace among the lambs: [the lesser citizens] say that they are the lambs, and you the wolves.'[53]

If Rinaldo's allegations are true, then the highly skewed distribution of wealth generated a will for war among the middle classes of the city, as war brought a forced redistribution of wealth. Paradoxically, if the fiscal system, largely designed as a preparation for war, stripped the lambs of the city, the waging of war fed them. At all events, the distribution of wealth introduced high social and political tensions in the city, and even, if we can believe Cavalcanti, encouraged the waging of useless wars, primarily to relieve the scarcity of money among the middle and lower levels of urban society.

The distribution of wealth in Tuscany in 1427 thus weakened incentives in both city and countryside, blocked the development of a strong local market for inexpensive manufactures, and introduced elements of instability into political and social life. The merchant rulers of Florence might still have been able to promote major changes in the economy in the direction of greater productivity, had they strong enough reasons for doing so. But the culminating obstacle to continuing economic growth at Florence in the fifteenth century was the lack of a strong market for inexpensive products even outside Tuscany. Europe in the first half of the fifteenth century contained a low population, apparently stable in numbers. The distribution of wealth across Europe, if probably less skewed than in Tuscany, surely also widely favoured small numbers of extremely rich households. The best European market was consequently for luxury commodities of high quality, produced in small volume. The Florentine merchants, according to one contemporary text, traded in

52 *Ibid*. i, p. 79.   53 *Ibid*.

France, England and Europe, not in 'cheap' but 'in noble and honest wares', and in this they took pride.[54] They understandably invested at home in the production of those commodities which they could most easily sell abroad. The thrust of their investment did not go towards increasing the production of inexpensive goods, but towards improving the quality of the luxury items from which they gained their principal profits.[55] The structures not only of Tuscan but of European society in the fifteenth century did not prepare or allow an industrial revolution.

This then is how the distribution of wealth in Tuscany, and Florence, in 1427 apparently affected regional economic growth. The fiscal and economic system gave to Florence – and to remarkably few patrician households within it – a near monopoly over the available supplies of capital. This concentration of money at Florence, the enhanced power of the Florentine market and of Florentine investors, helped overcome the intense, wasteful competition among the small Tuscan towns, which had been characteristic of the region in the thirteenth century. At least by 1427, Tuscans were making more rational use of local resources; we can mark the emergence of a regionally integrated, and presumably more productive economy. On the other hand, the primary producers in countryside and city were left in inescapable poverty, which deprived them of incentives to put forth greater effort in their labours. For them, poverty was protection against the demands of tax-collectors and of creditors, but poverty also limited the quantities of manufactured goods they could purchase and consume. And the fiscal system, in fomenting intense competition for capital among the social classes, also endangered social and political peace.

In spite of all this, access to a strong external market for inexpensive commodities might have stimulated changes in the organization of production and encouraged continuing economic growth. Tuscan artisans were surely among the most adroit and ingenious in Europe.

[54] See the depiction of the Florentine merchants by Lapo da Castiglionchio, cited by Petrucci, *Il libro di ricordanze*, p. ix: 'merchants, but of noble and honest merchandise, not mean'.

[55] Compare Dati's description of the fine wool and silk industries at Florence. 'Wool...more cloth and better cloth is made in Florence than in any other place in the world, and the masters of the art are great and honoured citizens, and they know how to get things done. Silk...silk damask is better made in Florence than in the Byzantine empire, or Venice, or Lucca, or Bologna, or other lands of the world. The silks of Florence surpass all others' (*'Istoria di Firenze'*, ed. Pratesi, p. 141).

The Florentine merchants were commercially alert, marvellously adept in their business practices, and able to direct social and political policies in their interests. But the state of the market at home and abroad gave them no reason to turn their skills and powers toward reorganizing production. They rather invested in the 'noble and honest' wares in which lay the chief expectation of profit. The fiscal and economic system which functioned in Tuscany in the fifteenth century helped Florence achieve splendour in its characteristic products, including, of course, its magnificent works of art. The revolutions of the fifteenth century in Tuscany were to be cultural and artistic, but not industrial.

7. *Urban Decay in Late Medieval England*

CHARLES PHYTHIAN-ADAMS

I

It is a curious fact that although early Tudor commentators both saw and even attempted to explain 'the desolatyon of cytes and tounes', recent historians have been reluctant to commit themselves on either matter.[1] A tendency amongst some economic historians to take the last decades of the fifteenth century as the end of the Middle Ages and for others to concentrate on 'Tawney's century', 1540–1640, has also led to a failure to link these two periods. Indeed, present opinion as to the condition of English towns in the later medieval period (which will be taken here to stretch into the third quarter of the sixteenth century) has been paralysed to some extent by attempts to compromise between the views of Professor Postan and Dr A. R. Bridbury.[2] Put over simply, we are now usually told that during the later Middle Ages, while most, if not all, towns experienced varying degrees of demographic attrition, and some towns – like Winchester and Lincoln – undoubtedly declined; nevertheless, others – like Exeter or Ipswich – unquestionably prospered. At a lower level, the period also witnessed the emergence of a number of palpably plump little towns, of which Lavenham is the most often quoted, in the context of a generally agreed trend towards rural industrialization.[3] The same handful of examples is frequently used to imply that points of urban decline and growth were roughly balanced.

It thus seems timely to review both the intensity and the chronology of the problem in broad terms, and to concentrate in particular on the most neglected period, the earlier sixteenth century. It will be necessary first, however, to examine briefly the major sources on which interpretation depends. An attempt will then be made to suggest a very approximate chronological framework of

[1] *England in the reign of King Henry the Eighth*, pt 1, p. lvii.
[2] Postan, *Econ. Hist. Rev.* (1938–9), pp. 163–4; Bridbury, *Economic growth.*
[3] E.g. Du Boulay, *Age of ambition*, pp. 44–8, and Baker in Darby (ed.), *New historical geography of England*, pp. 242–5.

urban decline, within which may be placed the changing fortunes of some seventy-five towns. Since not all of these can be discussed in the text, references are provided in the notes. The time has not yet come to provide a comprehensive gazetteer, but the reader is asked to remember that these examples provide the base on which the argument depends. From this, it will be suggested that as time went on during the later Middle Ages, those compensatory forces which made for urban replacement were decreasingly significant; that the period of urban decline may be traced down to the third quarter of the sixteenth century; and that the period 1520–70, during which even the leading towns of the provincial hierarchy were affected, may be fittingly described as one of urban crisis. The next section will seek to probe some symptoms and causes of urban weakness during this latter period. The last section looks both backwards and forwards to point a significant contrast between the changing fortunes of town and country.

II

The problem as a whole is beset with documentary pitfalls. Above all, recent work seems to show that it is extremely difficult, if not impossible, to measure the relative proportions of freemen in urban populations before and after the Black Death – a matter which raises something of an impediment to Dr Bridbury's espousal of economic growth. Since Dr Dobson exposed the analytical dangers involved in accepting freemen's registers at their face value, it has become a matter of some perplexity what reliance, if any, may be placed on the trends of burgess admissions which they reveal. There appears to have been, at least in the case of York (and a further complication will be suggested here for Norwich),[4] a host of administrative and other reasons that now help to distort the fluctuating annual totals even when, in some instance like Colchester and Leicester, they do betray unmistakable *later* downward trends.[5] This, it may be added, is quite apart from the insuperable difficulty of recovering what precisely were the respective *total* populations involved at the periods in question.

A second documentary problem concerns the weight that may be placed on the 1524 instalment of the lay subsidy. On this source essentially depends Dr Bridbury's case for the changing balance of

---

[4] Dobson, *Econ. Hist. Rev.* (1973); and p. 179 below.
[5] Bridbury, *Economic growth*, pp. 65, 68.

wealth between town and country in favour of the former since 1334. Yet it is extremely doubtful whether a comparison of urban and rural wealth in 1524 is even possible. The initiatory statute explains that a person with property in more than one place was to be taxed, and certified as having been so, where he 'at the tyme of the said certificates be made shall kepe his house or dwellyng, or where he then shallbe moost conversaunt abyding or resyaunt or shall have his moost resorte unto and shalbe best knowne'.[6] Now Professor Hoskins has taught us that, on the one hand, the merchants were unenthusiastic about investing much in urban property at this time, and, on the other, that urban wealth was commonly concentrated into the hands of a few individuals.[7] It is evident, moreover, that many of these merchants did own *rural* properties, the assessment of which, or of their movable appurtenances, consequently inflates the urban totals to an unknown degree, and correspondingly deflates those of the country. These individuals may have been few in number, but amongst them were some of the wealthiest people in the realm. There is thus no way of telling whether their assessment under towns, at a time when many were clearly investing in rural industries and often dealing directly with London, has consequently distorted the urban–rural comparison. Whatever the case, however, their disproportionate share of 'urban' wealth certainly does not imply that the benefits of 'economic growth' were widely shared.

If freeman's registers and the 1524 subsidy cannot safely be used as indices of urban prosperity, it might be suggested that other evidence from the localities should be reconsidered. Petitions for and grants of fee-farm and tax remissions seem to have taken on a quite unjustifiably leprous quality in the eyes of some historians. Pathologically exaggerated language, fiscal chicanery and local patronage have all been invoked in criticism and, it must be said, too often asserted rather than proved. Yet if Anglo-Saxon historians can detect fact from fiction in forged charters, and nineteenth-century scholars are learning how to exploit the Blue Books, it ill behoves late medievalists to cast aside a similarly important source of evidence. Not only do we have corroboratory case studies – Lincoln of course is the outstanding example[8] – but the evidence suggests that despite the rhetorical language in which the original

[6] *Statutes of the Realm*, 14 and 15 Henry VIII c. 16.
[7] Hoskins, *Provincial England*, pp. 73–4, 77–8.
[8] Hill, *Medieval Lincoln*, pp. 253–5, 278, 281, 285–8.

petitions were couched, such claims were investigated and usually confirmed by theoretically impartial commissioners drawn from the county not the town in question.[9] It is difficult to believe, moreover, that the monarchy was so feeble that between 1433 and 1482 inclusively, for example, it felt compelled to buy local civic support – often from unimportant places – at the substantial cost to itself of no less than £73,000 in lost revenue from remitted fee-farms and tax reliefs.[10] The evidence suggests that, on the contrary, remissions were often granted grudgingly and for limited terms of years, thus necessitating re-applications for grants when such terms expired.[11] It seems more appropriate consequently to accept that pleas of this kind enshrined truths which seemed self-evident to contemporaries, however inaccurate may have been their rounded sense of either retrospective chronology or the exact orders of magnitude involved when describing physical decay. At best – Richmond's is an outstanding example – such representations provide fascinating and valuable insights into contemporary modes of analysing current economic problems.[12]

Apart from the wealth of local variety found in these sources, however, two problems emerge as almost universal – so much so that the unanimity is impressive. In the first place we are told that such urban populations have drastically shrunk. *Local* estimates of this problem have been frequently dismissed as grossly exaggerated, yet no-one seems to deny that the later Middle Ages witnessed a calamitous demographic collapse in the country as a whole. Where documentation has survived, moreover, the scale of the problem by the end of the period is more than confirmed. When, for example, the citizens of Coventry (probably the sixth or seventh largest provincial city in the realm)[13] counted their population in 1523, they also checked on the numbers of houses vacant in each ward. The

---

[9] E.g. *Cal. Pat. Rolls, 1405–8*, p. 421; *Cal. Pat. Rolls, 1408–13*, pp. 201–2; *Cal. Pat. Rolls, 1436–41*, pp. 509–10.

[10] *Select cases before the King's Council*, ii, p. ciii and n.2.

[11] E.g. Great Yarmouth, see below, n.33.

[12] *Cal. Pat. Rolls, 1436–41*, pp. 509–10.

[13] Coventry with some 1,500 households and about 713 taxpayers in 1523–4 was exceeded in its number of taxpayers in 1524–5 by Norwich, Bristol, York, Exeter and Colchester, in that order. Newcastle, however, boasted a probable maximum of 1,545 families in 1563. Sheail, 'The regional distribution of wealth', *passim*; see my forthcoming book on Coventry and the problem of late medieval population to be published by the Cambridge University Press; Brit. Mus. Harleian MS. 594, fo. 191v.

resulting total came to 565 empty dwellings – a figure that represented some 25 per cent of the estimated housing stock, and which surpassed the total number of inhabited houses in the *county* town forty years later.[14] A petition from Leicester to the queen in 1587 is similarly instructive. There, a rounded total of 200 houses (once the property of the guilds and chantries) was claimed as 'in great ruyne and decay' as opposed to vacated. This figure in fact represented, not a rough estimate, but a rounded summary of the detailed findings reported by a commission, which had actually reported 235 tenements in decay, and that 406 bays of houses required wholly rebuilding.[15] For Thomas Starkey, indeed, 'the penury of pepul and lak of inhabytantys' was the self-evident cause of urban decline: 'other chiefe groundys I fynd not many'.[16]

Contemporary claims of serious population shrinkage, as opposed to precise figures, must then be taken seriously. For demographic contraction was inevitably accompanied by a marked decrease in those resources that customarily went to meet the payment of the fee-farm: from tolls at markets and fairs, the profits of justice and so on. The balance had to be made up in some way, and a number of towns thus earmarked the returns from certain properties or land to meet the burden – as at New Windsor (where the approval of the king was implicit), at Bedford, or, so it was proposed, at Bristol.[17] The deficit was consequently increased when such properties were in their turn vacated or when those who normally contributed to the fee-farm left the town. Both Oxford and Cambridge, for example, claimed that dwellings formerly contributory were abandoned, only to be replaced by colleges and halls for exempt scholars.[18]

If it is hard to question the seriousness of this first common problem – the local fiscal implications of demographic contraction, it is no less difficult to repudiate the evidence of the second. For if these palliatives failed, an insupportable strain was thrown on those

14 Phythian-Adams, forthcoming (see n.13).
15 Thompson, *Leicester*, pp. 282–4.
16 *England in the reign of King Henry the Eighth*, pt 1, p. lvii.
17 *Cal. Pat. Rolls, 1461–7*, p. 551; *Cal. Pat. Rolls, 1446–52*, p. 36; PRO, SP 1/236, fo. 355.
18 For Oxford see *Cal. Pat. Rolls, 1441–6*, p. 82; *Rotuli Parliamentorum*, v, p. 205; *Cal. Pat. Rolls, 1436–41*, p. 347; Salter, *Medieval Oxford*, pp. 87–8. For Cambridge see *Rotuli Parliamentorum*, v, p. 623; *ibid.* vi, pp. 40, 114; *Cal. Pat. Rolls, 1441–6*, p. 458; *Cal. Pat. Rolls, 1436–41*, p. 507; *VCH Cambridge and the Isle of Ely*, ii, pp. 12–14; Lobel, 'Cambridge', in Lobel (ed.), *Historic towns*, pp. 12–14.

responsible for paying the fee-farm into the Exchequer. There is thus no need to doubt the reluctance of substantial citizens to fill the relevant offices of bailiff or sheriff. The fifteenth century saw Lincoln[19] increase the number of its bailiffs from two to four in order to spread the load of financial liability; while both Gloucester[20] and Northampton[21] were clearly finding it difficult to elect suitable persons. In the following century, Bristol and Coventry both made the same complaint.[22] This situation, indeed, was recognized on a national scale in the statute of 1511–12, which stated that 'in many and the most partie of all the Cities, Bouroughes and Townes corporate wythin this realme of Englonde be fallen to ruyn and decaye, & not inhabited with Marchauntes and Men of such substaunce as they werre'. For this reason accordingly, precedents were broken, and henceforth, under certain safeguards, wealthy and hitherto mistrusted victuallers, who were 'contente to aunswere and paye unto the Kynge's grace his Fee Ferme wherwithe they be charged', were now permitted to hold civic offices.[23]

If then fee-farm and tax remissions may be accepted as implying official recognition of existing local problems, it should be possible, with the help of other evidence, to chart briefly a very approximate chronology of urban decay: to provide at least a possible framework both for discussion, and for detailed testing by the intensive regional research into this problem which is so badly needed.

III

On this basis, therefore, the declining fortunes of many towns may be traced to a time before the Black Death. Both then and during the succeeding period down perhaps to 1420, however, it is possible to detect a process of what might be called urban replacement: in very general terms what one town lost, another sometimes partly gained. But the casualties of this early period were often the worst, bearing all the signs of semi-desertion by the early sixteenth century; Ilchester, for example, could be described by Leland as 'yn wonder-

[19] See above n.8.
[20] *Calendar of...Gloucester*, no. 59.
[21] *Rotuli Parliamentorum*, ii, pp. 85, 86, 348; *Cal. Pat. Rolls, 1461–7*, p. 187; *The records of...Northampton*, ii, p. 98; *Materials for a history of... Henry VII*, ii, p. 349.
[22] PRO, SP 1/236, fos. 345–56; Phythian-Adams, forthcoming (see n.13).
[23] *Statutes of the Realm*, 3 Henry VIII c. 8.

ful decay, as a thing in a maner raisid with men of warre'.[24] Other notable victims were Wallingford,[25] which appears to have been overtaken by Reading, and Torksey[26] which decayed when the Foss dyke silted and Boston rose. Geographical factors were particularly acute on the coasts because of vulnerability both to enemy attack and to coastal erosion. The long-term decline of the Cinque Ports is, of course, well known, Winchelsea being one of the worst hit,[27] while other coastal towns like New Shoreham were similarly afflicted.[28] Further west, Wareham was superseded by Poole,[29] while the haven of Melcombe was eventually demoted from haven to creek in 1433.[30] In the north-east, Professor Beresford has made us familiar with the failure of the little Humber ports of Hedon and Ravenserod, the victims of Hull and the sea.[31] Erosion or silting also accelerated the decline of Dunwich[32] and especially Great Yarmouth;[33] while Chester came, increasingly, to depend on its downstream out-ports.[34]

Inland, there is no need to emphasize the early difficulties of the

[24] *The itinerary of John Leland*, i, p. 156; *Cal. Pat. Rolls, 1364–7*, p. 235; *Cal. Pat. Rolls, 1367–70*, p. 238; *Cal. Pat. Rolls, 1413–16*, p. 322.

[25] *VCH Berkshire*, iii, pp. 533–5; *Cal. Pat. Rolls, 1391–6*, p. 720; *Cal. Pat. Rolls, 1436–41*, pp. 317–18; *The itinerary of John Leland*, i, p. 118; *ibid.* v, p. 1.

[26] Cole, *Assoc. Architect. Soc.* (1905–6), pp. 496–7, 502; Hill, *Medieval Lincoln*, p. 312; *The itinerary of John Leland*, i, p. 32.

[27] Williamson, *History* (1926–7), pp. 97–115; and, for Dover, *Cal. Pat. Rolls, 1436–41*, pp. 392–3; *Cal. Pat. Rolls, 1446–52*, p. 427; for Folkestone, *The itinerary of John Leland*, iv, p. 64; for Hythe, *Cal. Pat. Rolls, 1399–1401*, p. 477; *The itinerary of John Leland*, iv, pp. 64–5; for Romney, *ibid.*, iv, p. 67; for Rye, *Cal. Pat. Rolls, 1446–52*, p. 276; for Sandwich, *The itinerary of John Leland*, iv, pp. 48, 62; for Winchelsea, Beresford, *New towns*, p. 498.

[28] *Rotuli Parliamentorum*, iv, p. 159.

[29] *The itinerary of John Leland*, i, p. 254.

[30] *Cal. Pat. Rolls, 1391–6*, p. 383; *Cal. Pat. Rolls, 1408–13*, pp. 201–2; *Cal. Pat. Rolls, 1429–36*, p. 298.

[31] Beresford, *History on the ground*, pp. 135–7, 139.

[32] *Cal. Pat. Rolls, 1408–13*, pp. 38, 105–6, 206; *The itinerary of John Leland*, ii, p. 28.

[33] See, for example, *Cal. Charter Rolls, 1341–1417*, p. 225; *Cal. Pat. Rolls, 1391–6*, p. 272; *Cal. Pat. Rolls, 1408–13*, pp. 96–7; *Cal. Pat. Rolls, 1461–7*, p. 262; *Cal. Pat. Rolls, 1467–77*, p. 250; Rowse, *The England of Elizabeth*, pp. 178–9; for reduced ranking, Hoskins, *Local history*, p. 176.

[34] Wilson, *Trans. Hist. Soc. Lancs and Cheshire* (1965), pp. 3, 6, and n.13. This circumstance, so fundamental to Chester's economic well-being, somewhat undermines Dr Wilson's rather optimistic view of the city's fortunes at this period. See also Morris, *Chester*, pp. 511–14, 516–24, for the later stagnation of trade with the Welsh and cut fee-farms.

leading textile centres, whose original misfortunes were identified in Professor Carus-Wilson's classic study.[35] Winchester[36] and Lincoln,[37] Northampton[38] and Oxford,[39] Leicester[40] and York[41] could trace the gradual demise of their staple industry back to the early fourteenth century and beyond. How immediate and how severe was their economic decline, however, is difficult to measure; in many such cases, it seems likely that the nadir was not reached until the fifteenth century. The same may well have been true of other inland centres: Nottingham, where the duration of the fifteen-day fair had to be cut by two thirds in 1378;[42] Warwick, which was in trouble by the mid-fourteenth century;[43] Bedford, which had apparently been overtaken by Dunstable as early as 1309;[44] and Huntingdon which traced its weaknesses back to the mid-fourteenth-century pestilences.[45]

In marked contrast to this broad picture of decay, and perhaps not unconnected with it, was the success of the largest centres in recovering from the impact of the mid-fourteenth-century malaise, especially during a fifty-year period between c. 1380 and 1430.[46] If York[47] revived, so too did other centres that had begun to show signs of strain like Norwich,[48] Boston and Lynn.[49] But if the latter

---

[35] Carus-Wilson, *Medieval merchant ventures*, pp. 204–6; cf. Miller, *Econ. Hist. Rev.* (1965), pp. 69–71.

[36] *Cal. Pat. Rolls, 1436–41*, p. 400; *Cal. Pat. Rolls, 1441–6*, p. 84; Atkinson, *Elizabethan Winchester*, p. 31.

[37] *Cal. Pat. Rolls, 1446–52*, p. 80; and n. 8 above.

[38] See n. 21 above.　　　[39] See n.18 above.

[40] *VCH Leicester*, iv, pp. 48–9, 53–4; *Materials for a history of... Henry VII*, ii, pp. 456–7; *Records of the borough of Leicester*, iii, pp. 43, 233–4.

[41] *Cal. Pat. Rolls, 1446–52*, p. 221; *Materials for a history of...Henry VII*, i, p. 462; Bartlett, *Econ. Hist. Rev.* (1959–60); *VCH City of York*, pp. 83–91. I am grateful to Dr D. M. Palliser for allowing me to see his draft chapter on the decline of York from his forthcoming book on Tudor York.

[42] Barley and Straw in Lobel (ed.), *Historic towns*; cf. *Rotuli Parliamentorum*, ii, p. 348.

[43] Cronne, *Borough of Warwick*, pp. 17–18; *VCH Warwickshire*, viii, p. 488.

[44] Godber, *Bedfordshire*, p. 117; *Cal. Pat. Rolls, 1446–52*, p. ₋o; *Cal. Pat. Rolls, 1494–1500*, p. 369.

[45] *Cal. Charter Rolls, 1341–1417*, p. 179; *Cal. Pat. Rolls, 1441–6*, p. 79; cf. *Rotuli Parliamentorum*, ii, p. 371.

[46] Postan, *Econ. Hist. Rev.* (1950), p. 254; McKisack, *The fourteenth century*, pp. 347–8.

[47] Bartlett, *Econ. Hist. Rev.* (1959–60), pp. 23–7.

[48] Green and Young, *Norwich*, pp. 16–17; Campbell in Lobel (ed.), *Historic towns*, where the 1377 population is clearly underestimated.

[49] Carus-Wilson, *Med. Arch.* (1962–3), pp. 198–200.

two were assisted, as Professor Carus-Wilson has shown, by
Coventry's new-found prosperity, there can be little doubt that that,
in its turn, was achieved partly at the expense of nearby Warwick.[50]
In a parallel way, Bristol appears to have absorbed the cloth trade
of Bath;[51] while Worcester and Hereford actually combined to force
the alteration of Leominster's profitable Saturday market to Fridays
because it was 'hindering their draping' – since when, sighed Leland,
'the town hath decayed'.[52] These then were golden years for those
towns which provide the predominant image of English medieval
urbanism like Salisbury, Reading, Southampton and Bristol. Even
Chester, Dr Wilson tells us, 'imported more wine in the decade
1410–20 than in any decade between 1350 and 1570', while its
'annual total of shipping arriving in the port in the 1420s was not
surpassed until the sixteenth century'.[53] It is thus surely these years
and such examples which provide, even when the evidence of the
freemen's registers is disallowed, unambiguous illustration of Dr
Bridbury's thesis of economic growth. But until we know a good
deal more about local prosperity or the lack of it, it looks as though
the major centres often recovered at the expense of their weaker
neighbours. Always in the background was the gradual decay of
scores of petty boroughs – like those whose fortunes have been
traced in Staffordshire by Dr Palliser[54] and the slow extinction of
even more numerous rural markets.[55]

Yet the story does not end there, for it would seem that the mid
to late fifteenth century witnessed the economic stagnation of a
number of more important towns – Canterbury[56] to the south-east;
and Gloucester,[57] Shrewsbury[58] and Bridgnorth[59] to the west. Above

[50] See above p. 166.
[51] *Rotuli Parliamentorum*, ii, p. 347; *The itinerary of John Leland*, i,
p. 143.   [52] *Ibid*. ii, p. 74.
[53] Wilson, *Trans. Hist. Soc. Lancs and Cheshire* (1965), p. 6.
[54] Palliser, *North Staffs. J. Field Stud.* (1972) pp. 66, 69, for the late
medieval decline of Tamworth and the lapse from borough status of six
petty towns out of the county's estimated total of twenty-two or twenty-three,
and also for an illuminating general comment by a contemporary, p. 71.
[55] Everitt, *English local history*, p. 10; *The itinerary of John Leland*, v,
pp. 110, 129; cf. Smith, *Land and politics*, p. 32; and Stephens (ed.), *History
of Congleton*, p. 36.
[56] *Cal. Pat. Rolls, 1408–13*, p. 104; *Cal. Charter Rolls, 1427–1516*, p. 139.
[57] *Cal. Pat. Rolls, 1446–52*, pp. 70–1; *Calendar of. . .Gloucester*, no. 59.
[58] *Cal. Pat. Rolls, 1441–6*, p. 411; *Cal. Pat. Rolls, 1485–94*, p. 118; *Select
cases before the King's Council*, i, pp. 179 and 182, n.5; Mendenhall, *The
Shrewsbury drapers*, p. 85.
[59] *The itinerary of John Leland*, ii, p. 85.

all, the period appears to have been distinguished by a marked deterioration in the relative importance of the towns on or near England's eastern seaboard, from Ripon,[60] Scarborough,[61] Beverley,[62] Hull,[63] and Grimsby,[64] via Stamford,[65] Boston and Lynn,[66] to Great Yarmouth.[67] In the south-west, the most serious case was undoubtedly that of Bridgwater, where Leland recorded, presumably in part from his own observations, that 'there hath fallen yn ruine and sore decay above 200 houses...in tyme of rememberaunce'.[68]

If there are therefore indications that the second tier of late medieval towns was under pressure by this period, it is perhaps notable that their experiences were soon to be echoed by most of the leading provincial centres. In the case of Norwich, it was possible to look back in 1495 (that is, even before the fire desolated some 718 houses in the early sixteenth century) at how 'many houses, habitacions and dwellynges stode onlaten and grue to ruyn' – no doubt a direct reflection of the difficulties increasingly being experienced by the city's textile industry.[69] The economic and demographic decay of York has been fully chronicled: the population falling from 'perhaps over 12,000 in the early fifteenth century to 8,000 in the mid-sixteenth'.[70] Rather less well-known is the case of Bristol; its fee-farm cut by nearly 60 per cent in 1486; its exports of cloths dramatically declining after 1500; the existence in 1518 of 'about

[60] *Ibid.* i, pp. 18, 82; Heaton, *Yorkshire woollen and worsted industries,* pp. xiv, 75.

[61] *Rotuli Parliamentorum,* v, p. 69; for lowered ranking, Hoskins, *Local history,* pp. 176–7; *The itinerary of John Leland,* i, p. 60; *Statutes of the Realm,* 37 Henry VIII c. 14.

[62] *The itinerary of John Leland,* i, p. 47; Heaton, *Yorkshire woollen and worsted industries,* p. 49.

[63] *VCH York, East Riding,* i, pp. 41–2, 56, 76.

[64] Gillett, *History of Grimsby,* pp. 21, 50–6, 63, 66–7.

[65] Rogers in Rogers (ed.), *The making of Stamford,* pp. 49–51; Thirsk in *ibid.,* pp. 58–60; *The itinerary of John Leland,* v, p. 5.

[66] Haward, *Reports and Papers of the Lincolnshire Architectural and Archaeological Societies* (1932–3), pp. 174–5; Carus-Wilson, *Med. Arch.* (1962–3), pp. 199–201.

[67] See above, n.33.

[68] *Cal. Charter Rolls, 1427–1516,* p. 226; *The itinerary of John Leland,* i, p. 163; Carus-Wilson, *The expansion of Exeter,* p. 20.

[69] *Records of the city of Norwich,* ii, pp. 105, 122; *Statutes of the Realm,* 11 Henry VII c. 11, 19 Henry VII c. 17, 26 Henry VIII c. 8; Green and Young, *Norwich,* pp. 18–20.

[70] See above n.41; Palliser in Clark and Slack (eds.), *Crisis and order.* p. 87.

viij^c howseholdes...desolate vacante and decayed' – an estimate that was raised to 900 in 1530; and its capping industry no longer competitive.[71] With respect to Coventry, the situation was more serious still. A population of possibly over 10,000 in 1440 dropped to *c.* 8,500 in 1500; to *c.* 7,500 in 1520, to *c.* 6,000 in 1523 and perhaps to between 4,000 and 5,000 by 1563 – a trend that was accompanied throughout by increasing economic strains, particularly in the textile and clothing industries.[72] At Southampton, the fragility of whose native economy was detected by Miss Coleman, 'the corporation was virtually insolvent' by 1531, a situation symptomatic of deeper strain still revealed in steep falls of customs receipts during the 1520s, and more especially the 1530s.[73] Indeed, of the provincial cities which were to lose their traditional preeminence, only Salisbury and Hereford[74] deferred their relative demotions to the mid-sixteenth century.

The first part of the sixteenth century therefore represents the last stages of an unparalleled period of urban contraction.[75] What is so conspicuous indeed is the status and geographical situation of the dwindling number of towns which appear to have remained or became prosperous. Most notable were those ports which could also boast and exploit expanding industrial *rural* hinterlands – New-

[71] Sherborne, *The port of Bristol*, pp. 28–30; *Select cases before the King's Council*, ii, p. ciii, 145, 146, 238, 268–9, 273; Carus-Wilson and Coleman, *England's export trade*, p. 143; PRO, SP 1/236.

[72] Phythian-Adams, forthcoming (see n. 13).

[73] Coleman, *Econ. Hist. Rev.* (1963–4), pp. 16–22; *Third book of... Southampton*, i, pp. xxix, xxviii–xxxi; *Statutes of the Realm*, 22 Henry VIII c. 20; Ruddock, *Italian merchants*, p. 262.

[74] *VCH Wiltshire*, iv, pp. 128–9; Lobel, 'Hereford', in Lobel (ed.), *Historic towns*, pp. 9–10.

[75] In addition to those declining towns already cited are: Appleby – see *Letters and papers of Henry VIII*, ii, p. 78; Holdgate, *Appleby*, pp. 32, 37–8; *The itinerary of John Leland*, v, p. 47; Truro – see *Cal. Pat. Rolls, 1401–5*, p. 3; *Cal. Pat. Rolls, 1408–13*, p. 215; New Windsor – see *Cal. Pat. Rolls, 1436–41*, p. 266; *Cal. Pat. Rolls, 1441–6*, p. 363; *Cal. Pat. Rolls, 1461–7*, p. 551; East Retford – see *Cal. Charter Rolls, 1427–1516*, p. 105; Wainfleet – see *ibid.* pp. 128–9; Bury St Edmunds – see Lobel, *Bury St. Edmunds*, p. 164; Thaxted – see Symonds, *The Reliquary* (1864–5), pp. 67–8; Cheltenham, Alresford, Andover and Headington – see *Rotuli Parliamentorum*, v, p. 69; Melton Mowbray – see Hoskins, *Provincial England*, pp. 65–7; Tickhill – see Hunter, *South Yorkshire*, i, p. 237 (I owe this reference to the kindness of Dr David Hey). Leland would add Bossiney, Fowey, Wilton and Prestbury, *The itinerary of John Leland*, i, p. 177; i, p. 323; i, p. 260; iv, p. 134. And for those towns just reviving, Lambourne, Thelwall and Thornbury, see *ibid.* v, pp. 109, 41, 100.

castle,[76] Colchester[77] and Ipswich[78] to the east; Exeter[79] to the south-west; and by this period, a renascent Chester[80] to the north-west. Pre-eminently there was London and its immediate localities. Inland, also with access to navigable rivers were Worcester,[81] Reading[82] and to a lesser extent Newbury.[83] Successful English towns apparently looked outwards.

In connection with this problem of urban replacement, it is instructive to make a rough comparison of thirty urban 'population' totals of markedly varying sizes, and taken from all parts of the country and in all cases where the exercise is possible, for the period 1524/5 to 1563 (see table 1). The comparison has to be between what was *not* meant to have been a full count of either households or heads – the lay subsidy returns – and what *was* meant to have been a full estimate of the numbers of families in 1563.[84] There are many problems in attempting such an analysis and there is too little space available to discuss them fully. Suffice it to say, firstly, that the 1523 census of Coventry indicates that the overwhelming majority of persons taxed in 1524 were household heads and that, therefore, the possible presence of large numbers of inmates over fifteen is not necessarily a complicatory factor.[85] Secondly, all authorities agree that a high proportion of households was omitted from the subsidy. At Coventry that proportion was between 50 and 55 per cent. At Lutterworth, a small market town in south-west Leicestershire, which contained only 116 dwellings in

[76] Carus-Wilson, *The expansion of Exeter*, pp. 4–5; Hoskins, *Provincial England*, p. 71 and see n.13 above. Northern towns, however, went through a bleak patch in the early fifteenth century: for Newcastle, see *Cal. Pat. Rolls, 1401–5*, p. 465, *Cal. Pat. Rolls, 1405–8*, p. 411, *Cal. Pat. Rolls, 1408–13*, p. 198, *Cal. Pat. Rolls, 1413–16*, pp. 273–4; for Berwick, see *Cal. Pat. Rolls, 1408–13*, p. 194; for Alnwick, *Cal. Pat. Rolls, 1429–36*, p. 345; for Bamburgh, *Cal. Pat. Rolls, 1441–6*, p. 403; for Carlisle, *Cal. Pat. Rolls, 1408–13*, p. 192.

[77] Martin, *Colchester*, pp. 28, 36, 41 and see n.13 above.

[78] Webb, *Great Tooley of Ipswich*, p. 9.

[79] Carus-Wilson, *The expansion of Exeter, passim.*

[80] Wilson, *Trans. Hist. Soc. Lancs and Cheshire* (1965), pp. 14–15.

[81] *The itinerary of John Leland*, ii, p. 91; Dyer, *Worcester*, pp. 93–4.

[82] Slade in Lobel (ed.), *Historic towns*, p. 6 and n.66; Bridbury, *Economic growth*, pp. 81–2.

[83] With 414 taxpayers in 1524/5, Newbury was one of the thirty largest towns in the land; Sheail, 'The regional distribution of wealth', gazetteer; cf. n.88 below.

[84] Since plague rarely killed off whole families, and in many places the then current visitation of it did not arrive until the following year, this factor should not have distorted these figures unduly.

[85] Phythian-Adams, forthcoming (see n.13).

TABLE 1.

A broad comparison of some urban 'population' totals, 1524/5–1563

The towns are ordered according to their numbers of taxpayers in 1524/5 except in those cases (small capitals) where the 1543–5 returns seem to indicate a higher position. Northern towns appear to have been more efficiently assessed in the 1540s, but the possibility of demographic growth during the intervening twenty years cannot be ignored. This is *not* intended to be an exact ranking. I have aimed for complete coverage (which is anyway limited by the dioceses included in 1563) for those towns with over 200 taxpayers (except for Spalding and Pinchbeck). Below this level I have excluded towns which are clearly distorted by the 1524–5 returns (e.g. Knaresborough with seventeen taxpayers).

1524/5 = The highest number of taxpayers recorded (when the choice is available) in one of the two years concerned.

1543–5 = Taxable populations for those towns with extant returns.

1563 = The numbers of families returned to the Privy Council.

( ) denotes the complication of a large encircling parish, and it should be added that local knowledge might well supplement a number of others in the table.

' ' denotes suspiciously rounded returns.

	1524/5	*1543–5*	*1563*
Over 700 taxpayers			
Canterbury	784	531	'700'
500–699 taxpayers			
Worcester	499+	507	1025
Lincoln	625	–	459 + 100
Cambridge	523	398	517
295–499 taxpayers			
Leicester	401	311	591
Lichfield	391	269	'400'
Ely	382	244	400 (max.)
200–294 taxpayers			
DERBY	232	281	507 (max.)
Wisbech	252?	271	292
(MANCHESTER	163	253	414)
Stamford	247 (with St Martin's)	246	213 (without St Martin's)
Glastonbury	209	–	246
100–199 taxpayers			
(PRESTON	56	197	243)
St Neots (Hunts.)	193	142	140
(RICHMOND	50	*c.* 171	340)
(Wolverhampton	168	111	323)
Leighton Buzzard	156	110	'140'
Birmingham	159	over 170	'200'
Luton	151	*c.* 168	129

(Bromsgrove	142	212	303)
Hitchin	131	117	245
St Ives	127	–	125
Grimsby	118	90	145
Stafford	117	–	342
Stratford-upon-Avon	116	110	320
Buckingham	111	122	351
(Walsall	108	102	290)

Below 100 taxpayers in 1524/5 but exceeding 200 families in 1563

Loughborough	c. 88	–	256
Pershore	82	–	216
(Uttoxeter	80 *cum*	–	240)
	membris		

Acknowledgements: I would like to record my gratitude to Dr John Sheail, who has most kindly allowed me to reproduce the 1524/5 figures from the remarkable gazetteer contained in his thesis 'The regional distribution of wealth', and who generously volunteered the figures for 1543–5. It is to be understood that in the nature of surveys of such magnitude, let alone the quality of the original evidence, the totals concerned represent size orders rather than absolutely precise figures. The 1563 figures are taken from Brit. Mus. Harleian MSS. 594, 595, 618. The addition to the Lincoln figures was suggested by Hill, *Tudor and Stuart Lincoln*, p. 88.

1509, it has been found from somewhat less firm evidence that there the proportion omitted may have been as high as 64 per cent.[86]

If therefore, simply for the sake of argument and to allow both for variation between town and town, and for the possibility that the 1563 figures although the best we have are too low, we assume the very low proportion of 33 per cent omitted in 1524/5, certain very interesting points emerge from this table. Even *before* adjustment, however, six towns, possibly Canterbury, and definitely Cambridge, Lichfield, Ely, Stamford and Glastonbury, all have 'populations' that are very broadly of the same magnitude in both years. In the case of Lincoln, even after inflating the 1563 figure, the trend is inescapably downward. To these examples may be added St Neots, Leighton Buzzard, Luton and St Ives. Unless the 1563 figures, which are taken from a number of different dioceses, were *consistently* inaccurate, the implication must be that many of these towns were contracting significantly. If we take the minimal 33 per cent omission rate in 1524/5 as a yardstick the trend is, of course, even more marked and to those already quoted would need to be

[86] I am grateful to Mr J. D. Goodacre for this information.

added Wisbech and Grimsby. In the upper reaches of this list, therefore, only Worcester, Derby and Leicester may have been holding their own on this over-generalized basis, although each could well have had an omitted proportion as high as Coventry's. An adjustment on these lines indeed would leave only Worcester, and (with its access to the Trent) Derby, as either reasonably stable or possibly increasing over this forty-year period.

The contrast between these well-established towns towards the upper half of the list, and those in the lower half, is thus most marked. In these latter cases, an omission rate of over 50 per cent would be required to indicate the decline of places like Manchester – 'the fairest, best buildid, quikkest, and most populus tounne in al Lancastreshire'; or Bromsgrove, with its 'metely good market' and its dependence 'somewhat by clothinge', or Stratford-upon-Avon, with its 'very great concourse of people' at the annual fair.[87] For this evidence does seem to reflect what was also true elsewhere: the relative buoyancy of the *upper levels* of the country market towns like Burford, Banbury and Petworth – many, but not necessarily all of which were benefiting from the various rural industries situated in their respective countrysides. Yet in the context of *urban* replacement, what is surely significant is their unimpressive size. Indeed, a number of those listed have populations that are disproportionately inflated by unknown numbers of people resident in their parochial hinterlands. At a time when the forty-two largest towns of England (many of which were betraying symptoms of decline) contained upwards of 294 taxpayers in 1524/5 or 450 families in 1563; even Totnes and Lavenham could only boast 220 and 199 taxpayers respectively.[88] Such towns hardly posed an economic threat to the upper levels of the urban hierarchy.

IV

In a period when the national population was at the very least stabilizing, and perhaps was even beginning to grow again, the failure of so many of the larger towns to respond is thus a matter of some significance. Yet the reasons for this state of affairs were

[87] *The itinerary of John Leland*, iv, p. 5; ii, pp. 95, 27.

[88] Sheail, 'The regional distribution of wealth', *passim*. In the second layer of the urban hierarchy some sixty towns contained less than 295 taxpayers in 1524/5 or 350 families in 1563, but over 200 taxpayers or 250 families and more.

frequently described by contemporaries. They saw and reported that the more substantial citizens were voluntarily *withdrawing* from many larger towns. It is surely difficult to dismiss such claims as special pleading by those towns which had no need to rest their cases on fiction, like Wallingford, Ilchester or Bridgwater; when this was specifically acknowledged by contemporary commissioners of inquiry elsewhere.

By the sixteenth century at least, the crux of the problem appears to have been not the old explanation of craft restrictionism, successfully dismissed by Dr Palliser in the case of York, and similarly irrelevant with regard to Coventry[89] – but the increasing expense of urban residence. The costs in question were associated not only with the growing burden of the fee-farms, but also with the over-elaborate structures of office-holding within urban communities, and the conspicuous expenditures associated with them. The situation was epitomized at Bristol from where, with some success, a youthful and financially over-stretched sheriff, one William Dale, brought a Star Chamber action in 1518. The detailed accounts connected with the proceedings indicate that Dale was correct in claiming that the traditional sources of income used to meet the cost of the fee-farm for example, had shrunk – in particular a reduction of from £80 to £50 of the income from certain properties, because of 'decay and ruine'; and (as a reflection of a decreased trading) a drop in the profits from tolls to be taken at the annual St James' fair. In addition, of the outgoings other than the fee-farm, no less than 30 per cent was accounted for by the costs of secular or religious ceremonies, obligatory drinkings, and entertainments like wrestling and bear-baiting; and a further 26 per cent by the cost of providing liveries in the form of scarlet cloth and fur for the permanent officials of the city – a percentage which, in monetary terms, was shown by Leadam to represent an increase of $2\frac{1}{2}$ times on the equivalent expenditure in 1479. It is noteworthy then that Wolsey was able to slash the total annual expenses of the sheriffs by almost £100 mainly by reducing conspicuous expenditures of this kind. Even so, the estimated sum of the *profits* to the sheriffs still left them out of pocket to the tune of £53 6s. 4d. – a total which was revealingly described in a related document as one 'which is not for any honest person called to any worshipful room in *any* town to

89 Palliser in Clark and Slack (eds.), *Crisis and order*, pp. 98, 111–12; Phythian-Adams, forthcoming (see n. 13).

complain of'. A petition from the corporation of Bristol a decade later, indeed, shows that such financial burdens remained a disincentive to office-holding.[90]

There can be little doubt that this represented a widespread urban problem. The situation was summarized by a Coventry citizen, Humfrey Reynolds – a self-confessed evader of office, who represented a local commonwealth group in the city, when he wrote to the king that

> the charges of the Citie be so great that euery man feareth theme, so that when a man haith goten eny good to find his lyvyng, for feirre of office which be so chargeable...he sueth to an abbey fore a Convent seall orelles goeth to farme in the Contre, and ther occupieth *boith* his occupacion *and* husbandry, to the great hynderaunce of the Citie and the undowyng of the poore husbondman.[91]

There can be no question of the accuracy of this statement: chamberlains, sheriffs and potential mayors frequently sought successfully to evade office, sometimes by procuring licences from the king. This, indeed, was the background to local legislation making election to civic statuses compulsory on pain of substantial fines in 1521;[92] while a similar by-law passed at Leicester eight years later and with regard to the Forty-Eight, may indicate a parallel situation there.[93]

But the Coventry example exposes wider problems still, because the fines threatened *also* encompassed refusals to accept election to be master of either of the two great city guilds. Here, as in so many other towns, civic and guild officers were inextricably intertwined. Some years after being sheriff, a man became master of the Corpus Christi Guild; then, after a short gap, mayor; and finally master of the Trinity Guild.[94] At Leicester, it is probable that the junior Guild of St George and the senior Guild of Corpus Christi and their masterships stood in a similar relation to the ruling body.[95] At

---

[90] *Select cases before the King's Council*, ii, pp. 142–65, cvii–cviii, cxvii; PRO, SP 1/236, fo. 349.

[91] PRO, SP 1/141, fo. 57r. (my italics); cf. York in Palliser, forthcoming (see n.41).

[92] Phythian-Adams, forthcoming (see n.13); *Coventry Leet Book*, pp. 676–7.

[93] *Records of the borough of Leicester*, iii, p. 27.

[94] Phythian-Adams in Clark and Slack (eds.), *Crisis and order*, pp. 60–1.

[95] This suggestion is based on a comparison of the known names of the

Norwich, Exeter and Salisbury other Guilds of St George seem likewise to have included the governing elite.[96] Parallel arrangements appear to have operated at Worcester, Hull and King's Lynn.[97] Membership of such bodies alone could cost as much as £5.[98]

Indeed, to ignore its ceremonial character is surely to under-estimate the essence of late medieval urbanism. Ceremony was a major *raison d'être* of civic guilds and was in general a further, and not inconsiderable financial burden on those responsible for up-holding what was widely described as the 'worship' of the com-munities concerned. At impoverished Leicester, the borough, not the guild, laid down in 1523 that the penalty to be exacted from the master for not riding the George (an obligation recently evaded) should be as much as £5 – perhaps an indication of the expenses normally to be incurred.[99] A year later, the same forfeit was threatened on the Master of St George's Guild Salisbury.[100] At Norwich, in 1532, the riding of the watch to the fair on 22 July and the wrestling diversions – then lately discontinued, but cus-tomarily financed by the mayor – were made incumbent on that dignitary on pain of £10.[101] At Bristol, the cost to the sheriffs of the midsummer watch was estimated to be £20 and a further £4 13s. 4d. on gallons of wine to the crafts.[102]

Yet guild and senior civic officers represented but the tip of an iceberg; less exalted, less wealthy, and above all, a shrinking number of people were similarly involved in subsidiary customary cere-monies, entertainments and drinkings. Detailed draconian restric-tions were necessarily imposed upon the scale of the over-elaborate feasts of the Norwich crafts in 1495, 1531 and 1543. For the implica-tions were serious: the main burden fell on the junior officers, the feast-makers, the costs being so great that many of them 'cowde nat after that recouer the gret losses that thei susteyned in makying of

relevant office-holders at various times, *Records of the borough of Leicester*, *passim*. I hope to examine this subject more closely on a later occasion.

[96] *Records of the city of Norwich*, i, pp. xcix–c; *Report on the records of. . .Exeter*, p. 45; Haskins, *The ancient trade guilds. . .of Salisbury*, pp. 28–9.

[97] Dyer, *Worcester*, pp. 189–90; *VCH York, East Riding*, i, p. 84; Parker, *King's Lynn*, p. 137.

[98] *Register of the Trinity Guild of Coventry*, p. 178; *Manuscripts. . .of Southampton and King's Lynn*, pp. 226–7.

[99] *Records of the borough of Leicester*, iii, pp. 24–5.

[100] Haskins, *The ancient trade guilds. . .of Salisbury*, p. 40.

[101] *Records of the city of Norwich*, ii, pp. 120–1.

[102] *Select cases before the King's Council*, i, p. 154, and for similar ex-penditures, pp. 155–6.

the same. By occasion whereoff many of them ffled and dayly went from the said citie and enhabited them selffe other where for pouertie. And many wold haue comen to the same citie iff it were nat for such costes and importune charges.'[103] The same pressures may well have been at work at Salisbury where the feasts of the craft guilds were discontinued in 1522.[104]

Exactly similar problems, which may be substantiated from other evidence, were privately reported to Thomas Cromwell from Coventry, where it was said,

at Corpus Christi-tide the poore comeners be at suche charges with ther playes and pageyonts that thei fare the worse all the yeire after; and on Midsomer even and on Seynt peter's even the maisters and kepers of craftes use suche excess in expenses in drynkyng that some suche as be not worthe v li. in goodes shalbe then at xls. charges to ther undoyng.[105]

The heavy cost of providing plays in particular was a widely experienced burden. Coventry was not alone in its attempts to spread the expense fairly amongst the crafts, particularly when the membership of fellowships, like the Tanners and Saddlers, had so shrunk that the costs became insupportable.[106] The weaver's craft spent over a third of its income on Corpus Christi and Midsummer celebrations in the early 1520s.[107] The wider ramifications of such obligations were explicitly recognized by the St Luke's Guild of Norwich, which prior to 1527 had alone supported pageants, disguisings, and tableaux there on Whit Monday and Tuesday. The 'coset and charge', it was said in that year, 'causeth many persons of substaunce and abilitie to withdrawe themself and also ther goode myndes from the said guylde, in suche manner that for lack of substanceall brethren and sustern and ther myghty helpyng handes for sustentacon of the premysses, the said gild is almost fully decayed'.[108] The guild's case was fully accepted by the city assembly, for the pageants were thenceforth divided amongst twelve groups of occupations.[109] Even so in 1544, it was felt that other financial burdens were so great that the crafts should be excused.[110]

---

[103] *Records of the city of Norwich*, ii, pp. 105, 111–15, 124, 162.
[104] Haskins, *The ancient trade guilds. . .of Salisbury*, p. 70 but cf. p. 73.
[105] PRO, SP 1/142, fo. 66.
[106] *Coventry Leet Book*, pp. 555–6, 558–9, 607, 707–10.
[107] Phythian-Adams, forthcoming (see n.13).
[108] Harrod, *Norfolk Archaeology* (1849), p. 7.
[109] *Records of the city of Norwich*, ii, p. liii.   [110] *Ibid.* p. 171.

Similar financial problems connected with pageants and plays may be illustrated from Leicester, where a group of wealthy citizens had to take responsibility,[111] or from Chester, where the declining fellowship of Cappers feared the burden would be too much.[112] Indeed, it was the expense of pageantry rather than 'progressive' economic motives, that often led to the amalgamation of many craft fellowships.[113] In all such cases, not only were craft officers affected, so too were their less prosperous colleagues.

It would seem true, therefore, that by the mid-sixteenth century, late medieval urban society and culture in the well-established towns had become too elaborate, too costly to be sustained by contracting economies and populations. Indeed it would be no exaggeration to describe these last years of medieval urbanism – roughly 1520 to 1570 and its first decade in particular – as years of acute urban crisis; when, in the context of the chronology already outlined, the widespread decline of so many towns continued (and was perhaps accelerated by the need to sustain such top-heavy structures). Not only was this the period when, as Professor Elton has recently suggested, town after town *applied* to be included in the series of statutes on urban re-edification in the decade after 1534,[114] but it was also a time when central government was showing a growing awareness of, and a sensitivity to, urban weakness in the face of rural exploitation. There is no need to repeat the situation described in the statute designed to protect the *urban* textile industry in, of all counties, Worcestershire; or the terms of the more general act of 1557–8, which recognized similar problems on a national scale.[115] Both statutes cited the depopulation of urban centres as a major

---

[111] Kelly, *Notices illustrative of the drama*, pp. 31, 34, 187–8.

[112] Morris, *Chester*, pp. 316–17.

[113] E.g. *York Memorandum Book*, pp. 297–8.

[114] Elton, *Reform and renewal*, pp. 108–9. It is worth adding that these statutes were concerned as much with the high streets as the back lanes. The changing retrospective coverage of the acts may also be significant. The first general act concerned repairs to houses and sites voided at *any* time in the past; but two acts of 1540 limited their application to the last twenty-five years; but the final two acts of the series extended the limit to forty-five years. The towns which appeared twice, and so had their retrospective time limits extended, were Canterbury, Rochester, Guildford, Buckingham, Shrewsbury, Ludlow and Maldon, *Statutes of the Realm.* 26 Henry VIII cs. 8 and 9; 27 Henry VII c. 1; 32 Henry VIII cs. 18 and 19; 33 Henry VIII c. 36; 35 Henry VIII c. 4.

[115] *Ibid.* 25 Henry VIII c. 18; 4 and 5 Philip and Mary c. 5 – amending 6 Edward VI c. 2.

cause; and both restricted cloth making to the towns; the latter with
some sweeping rural exceptions – to 'Cities, boroughes and towns
corporate' only. The statute of 1554–5, however, does not appear to
have received as much attention. Not only did it admit the shortage
of 'good able persons' traditionally chargeable for the fee-farms
and taxes, but it stated that the towns were being exploited by linen
drapers, woollen drapers and grocers resident in the countryside
who merely used the towns to sell their wares. With certain pro-
visos therefore, *retailing*, as opposed to the wholesale trade, was
restricted to the urban centres, countrymen being permitted to
retail only at the times of fairs.[116]

These measures reflected local realities; the two major economic
functions of English towns as traditional centres for industry and
marketing were openly threatened. At Norwich it emerges that,
before 1554, people had been coming to the city for just long enough
to qualify as freemen, and then, before they became liable to urban
charges, were departing thence – but now enfranchised to sell their
presumably manufactured products in Norwich markets.[117] How
many other freemen's registers, one wonders, reveal trends that are
misleadingly distorted in this way? Certainly Leicester was com-
plaining of outside exploitation in 1540, when it was claimed that,
within the previous forty years, the withdrawal of many persons
from the borough and hence the manifest decay of the high street,
was due to foreigners being allowed to sell by retail in the town.[118]
How far such pressures came from the senior market towns, it is
impossible to say; but local evidence from Coventry and Newcastle,
to name only two, suggests that these cities especially feared the
competition of their own rural hinterlands – the mileage of which
from the city is often indicated.[119] It would be a mistake to assume
that the problem of country competition was restricted to the newly
developing areas to the west and east of the Pennines, to the

[116] *Ibid.* 1 and 2 Philip and Mary c. 7.
[117] *Records of the city of Norwich*, ii, pp. 131–2.
[118] *Records of the borough of Leicester*, iii, p. 43.
[119] Coventry City Record Office, Weavers 2c.: draft recensions of the
Weaver's ordinances of the mid-sixteenth century. These enforce a 'trybute'
of four times the craft's usual quarterage payments on those weaving within
the liberties, and forbid the supply of yarn to those living within four miles
of the city. Newcastle ensured that all members of the Tailors' company
should be contributory to the craft when resident up to a distance of twelve
miles from the city. Welford (ed.), *History of Newcastle and Gateshead*,
p. 155.

Cotswolds or parts of East Anglia. Rather it had become a matter of contemporary realism that, while traditional urban facilities including entertainments were highly desirable, nevertheless many people were increasingly wishing to make use of those facilities without the costs and responsibilities involved in sustaining the traditional urban way of life.[120] The gradual weakening of the towns, in fact, might almost be described as a creeping process of de-urbanization.

This process was promoted by short-term factors which were particularly noticeable between 1520 and 1570. The graphs of cloth exports provided by Professor Carus-Wilson and Miss Coleman demonstrate (even with due allowance for evidential shortcomings) the years of economic crisis experienced even in the ports; steep falls during the early 1520s in the cases of Bristol, Hull, Southampton and even London, Ipswich and Exeter; with similar difficulties in the mid-1540s for Bristol, Exeter, Southampton – and again London.[121] Inland, Coventry was convulsed by various, basically economic forces between 1518 and 1525, the city being depopulated without much impetus from epidemics, by at least 20 per cent in the years 1520 to 1523 alone; while unemployment and a massive increase in mortality were both evident in 1547.[122] At Norwich similar factors were at work in 1549 and 1556.[123] The impact of the 1550s even on Worcester has been described by Dr Dyer. There, between 1556 and 1557 alone, there is reason to believe that those on poor relief increased from 700 to 1,000.[124]

A further exacerbatory factor was undoubtedly provided by the climate. Even Dr Harrison's smoothed account of harvest qualities reveals a contrast between the period 1470–1519, and that between 1520 and 1569; an increase in years of bad harvests and dearths of from two to six.[125] Professor Hoskins' original interpretation, however, which provides a more faithful reflection of *urban* fortunes, indicates a more dramatic increase in the incidence of 'bad' and dearth years from one in every eight years between 1480 and 1519,

[120] Registers of urban socio-religious fraternities frequently contain the names of numerous rural members.

[121] Carus-Wilson and Coleman, *England's export trade*, pp. 141–9, 153.

[122] Phythian-Adams, forthcoming (see n.13); *Coventry Leet Book*, pp. 783–4.

[123] Pound, *Past and Present* (1966), p. 59.

[124] Dyer, *Worcester*, pp. 109, 166–7.

[125] Harrison, *Ag. Hist. Rev.* (1971), pp. 151–3.

to one in only every three or four in the longer later period.[126] Confirmatory local evidence suggests that, in 1520, 'dearth' was the case at Exeter, Coventry, and Lincoln (and a little later at Newcastle and Bristol) even though this year is characterized by Dr Harrison as merely 'bad'.[127] The year 1527, likewise demoted to only a 'bad' rating, was specifically described as one of dearth at Shrewsbury,[128] while at Norwich, the harvest was so deficient that 'abowte Christemas, the comons of the cyttye, were redy to ryse upon the ryche men'.[129] There is no need to labour the later provision of permanent corn stocks at, for example, both Norwich and Great Yarmouth.[130] Even leaving aside the fact that the purchasing power of wage-earners was lagging badly behind inflation at this period, it seems clear that the spiralling problem of restricted cereal supplies was a major factor in the urban crises of an age when conversion to pasture had been the trend, and a probably increasing rural population had first access to what *was* available.

It was surely no coincidence, therefore, that it was these years, rather than the immediately succeeding period on which most emphasis is usually laid, that witnessed the emergence of a new urban problem – the poor. If Dr Graus found it difficult to find much evidence of pauperism in towns generally during the fifteenth century,[131] there can be no question of the scale of the problem in the early sixteenth. In the first instance, moreover, it was conspicuously a problem that had to be tackled by the towns themselves well in advance of central government thinking. Between 1514 and 1525, London, York, Coventry and Shrewsbury all appear to have instituted procedures for the licensing of beggars.[132] In the former three towns, there even appears at about this time a special official dubbed the master or the keeper of the beggars, a status

---

[126] Hoskins, *Ag. Hist. Rev.* (1964), pp. 44–5.
[127] *Ibid.* p. 3; Phythian-Adams, forthcoming (see n.13); Hill, *Tudor and Stuart Lincoln*, pp. 30, 222; Welford (ed.), *History of Newcastle and Gateshead*, ii, p. 5; *The Maire of Bristowe*, p. 49.
[128] Owen and Blakeway, *Shrewsbury*, i, p. 309.
[129] Blomefield, *Topographical history of...Norfolk*, iii, p. 198. In this year there was insufficient corn of all kinds to sustain the inhabitants of Staffordshire. *Select cases before the King's Council*, ii, pp. 165–7.
[130] Hoskins, *Ag. Hist. Rev.* (1964), p. 36.
[131] Graus in Thrupp (ed.), *Change in medieval society*, p. 317. Cf. Leonard, *English poor relief*, pp. 9–12.
[132] *Ibid.* p. 25; *VCH City of York*, p. 133; *Coventry Leet Book*, p. 677; Owen and Blakeway, *Shrewsbury*, i, p. 287.

which is echoed at Bristol and at Norwich in 1531–2.[133] This in itself indicates a pressing problem of some size: a point which is borne out by the growing need felt by some cities, to take censuses of their beggars – York in 1528, Norwich and Southampton in 1531, Chester in 1539, and of their unemployed or poor – at Coventry in 1547, and at Worcester both in 1556–7 and in 1563.[134]

But if these were years of increasing urban poverty, the period of urban crisis also witnessed turbulence and riot – a factor which has been frequently underestimated. Though a major treasonous conspiracy was successfully quashed at Coventry in 1523, two years later the same city was out of control for a fortnight; with its common box seized by the citizens; with threats of local reform in the air; and a major riot control operation necessarily mounted by the Marquis of Dorset with 2,000 men 'in a redynesse'.[135] In East Anglia, also in 1525, that oft-quoted example of urban replacement, Lavenham, was also near the centre of a notorious riotous protest against the Amicable Grant: and it is pertinent to ask rhetorically – whoever heard of Lavenham's urban significance after this?[136] In the later years of the same decade there were riots at Norwich and Great Yarmouth, and very nearly one at Bury St Edmunds.[137] Enclosure riots, although endemic – as at York during the early part of this period (and at Southampton in 1500 and 1517, as well as Cambridge in 1549) – often sparked off more serious trouble, as had been the case at Coventry in 1525, and was similarly to be so in 1549 at Bristol.[138] In the case of the latter, we learn, that having levelled the enclosures concerned, the rioters 'made insurrection against the mayor, who with the council and many armed men in

---

[133] Leonard, *English poor relief*, p. 25; *VCH City of York*, p. 133; Coventry Record Office, A 7 (a), p. 63; Latimer, *Bristol*, p. 26; *Records of the city of Norwich*, ii, p. xcviii. Cf. the 'Controller of Beggars' at Southampton (probably in 1524), *Third book of...Southampton*, i, p. 53 and n.3.

[134] *VCH City of York*, p. 133; *Records of the city of Norwich*, pp. 161–2; *Third book of...Southampton*, i, 52 and n.1; Morris, *Chester*, pp. 355–6, 257–8; *Coventry Leet Book*, pp. 783–5; Dyer, *Worcester*, pp. 166–7.

[135] Phythian-Adams, forthcoming (see n.13).

[136] *Letters and papers of Henry VIII*, iv, pt 1, nos. 1319, 1323, 1324; Scarfe, *Suffolk landscape*, pp. 189–90.

[137] Blomefield, *Topographical history of...Norfolk*, ii, p. 198; *Letters and papers of Henry VIII*, iv, pt 2, nos. 4012, 4309.

[138] Palliser, 'Social and economic history of York', p. 161. I am grateful to him for the opportunity to consult his thesis; Platt, *Medieval Southampton*, pp. 205, 218; *Manuscripts...of Southampton and King's Lynn*, p. 108; Lobel, 'Cambridge', in Lobel (ed.), *Historic towns*, ii, p. 17; Phythian-Adams, forthcoming (see n.13).

their defence went into the Marsh, where the matter was taken up, and within 4 days after the chief rebels were taken one after another and put into ward, but none of them were executed'.[139] It is perhaps hardly necessary to add the case of Norwich in the context of Ket's rebellion which, as Professor Bindoff has reminded us, was a rising of both 'the man in the street as well as the man in the field'.[140] Even feeble Lincoln may have summoned up at least one riot in connection with the Pilgrimage of Grace.[141] It does seem more than coincidence then that Exeter – one of the few *prosperous* provincial cities – managed to withstand the insidious temptations of the western rebellion of 1549.

v

The case that has been presented all too briefly in this paper, with its implicit emphasis on a connection between demographic contraction (with hence a shrinkage of demand) and economic decline, may be regarded as simplistic, but it may be appropriate to conclude by looking both backwards and forwards in order to point an important contrast. It has been suggested here that during the later Middle Ages, there were always some towns in decline, though in the fourteenth century particularly that process may have been broadly balanced by the emergence of newly prosperous centres or the revival of some older towns. Given the present limitations of the evidence we may properly use, only these, it might seem, when judged in a national context, would appear to merit the somewhat ambiguous accolade of 'economic growth', and then for only a limited period. With certain notable exceptions, by the *late* fifteenth and early sixteenth centuries even the more important towns and cities were under pressure; so much so indeed, that the period 1520–1570, the culminating years of that period, might well be regarded as a time of acute urban crisis. The two major elements in that crisis were, externally, the threatening growth of rural competition and, internally, the costly disincentives to urban residence. The result seems to have been a trend towards what might be described as de-urbanization from which, apart from the exceptions noted, the leading market towns appear to have been economically but not demographically the main beneficiaries.

---

[139] *Adam's chronicle*, p. 99.   [140] Bindoff, *Ket's rebellion*, p. 20.
[141] Hill, *Tudor and Stuart Lincoln*, p. 48.

For the paradox of the late medieval English town was that, while it retained its predominant image as the dynamic centre of contemporary culture (outside the court and the capital) – with its artistic workshops in stained glass, in wood, in alabaster and in stone, with its pageantry and drama, both sacred and secular, its triumphs of church and civic architecture, and its public music – at the same time it was tending to lose its essential *raison d'être* as a centre of industry and marketing. It can hardly be doubted that this was at least partly because of the financial strains placed on the shoulders of those who both had to uphold this splendid but costly fabric and, more relevantly, *had been* in the past the providers of urban capital: the vanishing clothiers of Bristol, the dying breed of great provincial merchants who made their penultimate public appearances in the subsidy rolls of 1524–5 at Coventry and Leicester; even, it may be added, the Springs of Lavenham.

The comparison that may thus be made between this and the succeeding period is surely significant. If the foregoing interpretation has any merit, then it is clear that much more attention needs to be focused on the impact of the Reformation which swept away both the religious guilds – with all that that meant for the slimming of civic office-holding structures – and also the extravagant public displays and processions which had cost all levels of the civic hierarchy so dear. Almost at a stroke, indeed, the towns lost their cultural predominance. Outside London and the court, the basic unit of the English Renaissance between 1540 and 1640 was the county; its vehicle the country house. The most we hear of towns in this connection are their libraries, with books often donated by the gentry; schools frequently patronized by the sons of the gentry; and drama provided by visiting players from aristocratic households.

At the same time, as population rose, demand increased, and rural surpluses migrated, the towns rediscovered their economic role. In particular, the years after 1570, which Professor Everitt has identified with a resurgence of inland trading,[142] were marked by a strengthened *urban* monopoly of marketing: the failure of medieval *rural* markets to resurrect themselves was signal. More or less the same period was characterized by the recovery of urban industry in places such as Norwich, Coventry and Shrewsbury. In short, the foundations of a new relationship between town and country were being laid although it was not to be fully recognizable until well after

142 Everitt in Thirsk (ed.), *Agrarian history*, pp. 502–6.

the Restoration. By then, a transition had occurred – from the age of the 'late medieval town' to that which most appropriately merits the label 'pre-industrial'. By then, not only was agriculture responding to urban needs down even to the minutiae of market gardening, but towns like Sheffield, Norwich, Exeter and even Leicester were wholly dominating and exploiting the village industries of their respective rural hinterlands. English provincial towns had recovered from a position of weakness *vis à vis* the country which has hardly been paralleled before or since.

8. Capitalism, Mobility and Class Formation in the Early Modern German City

CHRISTOPHER R. FRIEDRICHS

One of the most significant developments in German urban history of the early modern era was the emergence of a lower middle class – a class of *Kleinbürger*, who were socially and economically as distinct from the capitalist bourgeoisie as they were from the propertyless proletariat. The existence of this urban lower middle class by the end of the *ancien régime* is clear, yet its historical development has not been closely examined.[1] An inquiry into the origins of this class is certainly called for – not only because of the subsequent importance of the lower middle class in German history but, even more so, because the formation of this class was a crucial process in the transition from the medieval to the modern city in Germany.

First, however, we must establish clearly what is meant by the term 'lower middle class' in the German urban context. For it must be emphasized that this class was fundamentally different in character both from the 'upper' middle class – the bourgeoisie – and from the proletariat of the early modern German city. The term 'bourgeoisie' is taken in this paper to refer to a class which tends both to control the means of production – especially non-agricultural production – and to enjoy a concentration of political power and prestige in urban society. 'Lower middle class' refers to an urban class which has lost control of the means of production and is economically subordinate to the bourgeoisie – while at the same time its members continue to own property and enjoy specific social and

[1] There is a considerable literature on German crafts and craftsmen and a small but growing body of work on the broadly defined 'middle stratum' of German cities, notably in the collection of essays edited by Maschke and Sydow, *Städtische Mittelschichten*. But only one major work deals with the *Kleinbürgertum* as such: Möller, *Die kleinbürgerliche Familie* (Möller, however, accepts the existence of *Kleinbürger* in the eighteenth century as given and attempts no discussion of the origins of this class). East German historians appear to be even less interested in the *Kleinbürgertum*; their concern is almost exclusively with the origins of the bourgeoisie. See for example Hoffman and Mittenzwei, *Z'tschr. f. Geschichtswissenschaft* (1974), pp. 190–207.

political advantages which prevent their deterioration into a fully-fledged proletariat. The term 'proletariat' denotes a propertyless and politically powerless working class – in the case of a pre-industrial city, a class of day-labourers, menials, servants and journeymen with no prospects of advancement.

The bourgeoisie and the lower middle class were clearly differentiated from one another in German cities by the end of the eighteenth century. Merchants, entrepreneurs, professionals and municipal officials formed the core of the urban bourgeoisie – to use one historian's recent phrase, they were the 'movers and doers' of German society, men whose economic and political horizons extended beyond the limits of their local milieu.[2] The lower middle class – the *Kleinbürger* – were predominantly craftsmen but also shopkeepers, petty traders and minor office-holders, men with that narrow, particularistic outlook on life which has often (and mistakenly) been attributed to the German city as a whole.[3] Yet both of these classes, clearly articulated as they were by the end of the *ancien régime*, had their origins in a single source: the citizenry, or *Bürgerschaft*, of the traditional German city. The division into an upper and a lower middle class did not take place all over Germany at the same time; it was a process which could occur centuries apart in different cities. In fact, only by a minute examination of each city's history would it be possible to determine the overall chronology of this process. The aim of this paper, then, is not so much to establish 'when' the lower middle class emerged into German urban society as to suggest a general model of the way in which this occurred, and to suggest why it occurred in different places at such different times.

One element in this model is the process by which craftsmen became economically dependent on capitalist merchants. The social importance of this process in late medieval or early modern cities has long been recognized by historians, but not usually in connection with the formation of a lower middle class. Years ago George

---

[2] This term is borrowed from Walker, *German home towns*, pp. 119ff., although I am using it here in a slightly narrower sense than Walker himself does.

[3] I have selected 'lower middle class' as the best available translation of *Kleinbürger*. An alternative translation would be 'petty bourgeoisie', but that term is not always understood to include skilled craft masters, who formed the core of the *Kleinbürgertum*. Indeed, one historian refers to the 'contempt of the petty bourgeoisie for the craftsmen': Liebel, *Internat. Rev. Soc. Hist.* (1965), p. 299.

Unwin linked this type of economic differentiation to 'class formation', but he posited such a multiplicity of classes as to render the term almost meaningless – a problem that recurs among some more recent historians.[4] Others, by contrast – especially Marxists – tend to reduce the number of urban classes to a minimum. Drawing chiefly on the English experience, Maurice Dobb maintains that craftsmen either escaped economic subordination and became capitalists or else succumbed to it and became 'semi-proletarians'; there is no room in his model for a distinct urban lower middle class.[5] Whatever the merits of this argument for England, however, it does not apply to Germany – for there the decay of the economic position of the craftsmen took place in a political and social environment which protected them from proletarianization and made them instead into the core of the emerging lower middle class.

For this reason the German case deserves careful examination. Fortunately, the German town also offers particularly promising materials for investigating social change in the early modern era – above all, the remarkably detailed tax records which have survived in many German communities. Such records can be used to illustrate the relationship between economic structure, distribution of wealth, and social mobility in the overall process of class formation.

In describing this process I shall draw heavily on data collected in one such community: the town of Nördlingen, a north Swabian centre of commerce and textile production whose population – between seven and eight thousand in the late sixteenth century[6] –

---

[4] Unwin, *Industrial organization*, pp. 10–14 and *passim*. Cf. Pierre Goubert's comment, 'it is the basic concept of economic independence which provides the best criterion for the formation of urban "classes"' – but Goubert also posits a multiplicity of classes: 'urban proletariats', 'bourgeoisies', etc. (*The ancien régime*, pp. 217, 232–52).

[5] Dobb, *Development of capitalism*, esp. pp. 123–61, 229–30. In a brief discussion of the Low Countries (pp. 151–6), Dobb draws primarily on Pirenne's findings. Pirenne was acutely conscious of the economic subordination of some medieval craftsmen (especially those in the export trades) to capitalist merchants, but he saw in this development not so much the origins of a lower middle class as the creation of a virtual proletariat of industrial wage-earners: Pirenne, *Belgian democracy*, pp. 90–9, 170–1.

[6] In 1597 there were 1,659 citizen households in Nördlingen: Stadtarchiv Nördlingen (hereafter StAN), 'Steuerbuch' 1597. Assuming a ratio of 1:4.5 between citizen households and the total population (the coefficient must account not only for citizens, but for non-citizens as well), the total population of Nördlingen in 1597 would have been 7,465. Population estimates for Nördlingen are discussed in greater detail in Friedrichs, 'Nördlingen', pp. 88–91, 108–9.

placed it among the forty or fifty largest communities in the Empire. There is no implication, of course, that the sequence of events in Nördlingen can be taken as universal. But the experiences of this community will illustrate effectively both the factors involved in class formation and the materials available for studying this process in German towns of the early modern era.

I

'Clearly the first step is to discuss the social structure of the 'traditional' German city, before the emergence of a modern class structure. And to do so we must start with the most fundamental aspect of social organization in the late medieval German community: the division of its inhabitants into citizens and non-citizens. The citizens, or *Bürger*, were the permanent, protected members of the community – in juridical terms, the heirs of members of the original commune.[7] Non-citizens were merely tolerated outsiders, who participated in the social and economic life of the community only by permission of the magistrates. Membership in the citizenry was normally an inherited right – the son of a citizen could generally count on his admission to the *Bürgerschaft* as soon as he was prepared to marry, establish a household, and begin practising a trade. A non-citizen, however, had to apply for admission, and would only be accepted if he met stringent financial and moral standards – and if the trade he practised happened to be in demand. Above all, however, the distinction was economic: the citizens were property-owning and economically independent merchants, shopkeepers, professionals and artisans. The non-citizens were propertyless and powerless – day-labourers, journeymen, apprentices, servants and transients.

Not every 'non-citizen' of a given community was excluded from power and privilege. Many towns granted residence permits to a few wealthy merchants or professionals who retained their citizenship in other communities. Nor could all apprentices or journeymen really be classified as non-citizens: some, after all, were the sons of local citizens and were simply waiting until their fathers were ready to set them up on their own. But the term non-citizen as used in this paper does not pertain to these groups; it refers, instead, to persons who were the citizens of *no* city – people whose right to work and

[7] Mauersberg, *Sozial- und Wirtschaftsgeschichte*, pp. 80–92.

live in any community depended on the needs or whims of the citizens of that town. Certainly there were some economic variations within this non-citizen group, but overall its members formed a clearly defined, legally and economically dependent *Unterschicht* – the lower class of the traditional German city.

But what of the *Bürgerschaft*? Was it a single class? Certainly we cannot call the citizenry of the traditional German city a unitary class in any modern sense of the term, for it was characterized by extreme variations in wealth, political power and standards of living. One need only consider the distribution of wealth in the traditional city. In 1460, for example, there were 1,040 taxpaying citizens of Schwäbisch Hall; a mere thirteen of them owned fully 28 per cent of the community's wealth, while the poorest 600 possessed only 6 per cent of the total.[8] Similarly uneven distributions can be demonstrated for numerous other German cities of the fifteenth and sixteenth centuries.[9] As for Nördlingen, in 1579 just 2 per cent of the citizens owned about 25 per cent of the wealth, while the bottom half of the citizenry controlled less than 5 per cent of the community's assets.[10] Normally, of course, income distributions are not as highly skewed as wealth distributions, but even so there is little doubt that in all but the smallest towns very great economic inequality was to be found.

Nor was political power evenly distributed among the citizens. Only a tiny handful of cities had developed a closed ruling caste – a true patriciate – by the late Middle Ages, but in almost every German community access to political power, in the form of membership of city councils, was limited to citizens above a certain threshold of wealth. This even applies to those cities in which the so-called 'guild wars' of the fourteenth century had resulted in revised constitutions in which the craft guilds were guaranteed a certain number of places on the city councils; generally, as Erich Maschke has shown, the guilds' representatives in city government tended to be wealthy men engaged in trade, scarcely different in fact from the patricians they supplanted or shared power with.[11]

[8] Wunder in Mayer (ed.), *Untersuchungen*, pp. 27–9.

[9] For example, see: Eitel, *Die oberschwäbischen Reichsstädte*, pp. 117–23; Schildhauer, *Auseinandersetzungen*, pp. 42–8; Kirchgässner in Maschke and Sydow, *Gesellschaftliche Unterschichten*, p. 83.

[10] StAN, 'Steuerbuch', 1579, provides the basis for this calculation. See Friedrichs, 'Nördlingen', p. 118.

[11] Maschke, *Vierteljahrschr. f. Soz.- u. Wirtschaftsgesch.* (1959), pp. 289–349, 433–76. See also Maschke's remarks in *Annales, E.S.C.* (1960).

Clearly it would be difficult to describe the *Bürgerschaft* of the late medieval city as a single class. Yet it would be equally difficult to divide the citizenry neatly into two or more classes. For there is one thing which all citizens had in common: all of them – merchants and craftsmen alike – were economically independent. Each craftsman, however poor, was an independent producer, whose right to buy raw materials and sell finished goods on the open market was stoutly protected both by his guild and by the government of his city. Indeed, I take this to be the defining characteristic of the 'traditional' German city – the fact that virtually all citizens still enjoyed some degree of control over the means of production. For as long as this was the case, class differences within the *Bürgerschaft* remained ambiguous and blurred.

Nothing makes this clearer than the tremendous variations in wealth to be found among members of the same occupation in 'traditional' urban society. Modern social theorists almost always see occupation as the principal determinant of class,[12] but this concept, however valid it may be for the highly differentiated occupational structure of modern industrial society, scarcely applies to the pre-modern community. One can see this, for example, by taking another look at the data for Nördlingen in 1579. We have already drawn attention to the highly unequal distribution of wealth among the citizenry as a whole in that year, but, as table 1 indicates, the distribution of wealth within individual craft groups could also be very widely spread out.[13] The wool weavers, for example, were predominantly poor men, yet 14 per cent of them belonged to the richest quarter of the citizenry. In one craft, in fact – fine-cloth weaving – the distribution of wealth was strongly bimodal. Facts like these suggest how misleading it would be to regard any citizen of such a community as the member of a certain 'class' on the basis of his occupation alone.

But if not occupation, then perhaps wealth levels might be used to determine 'class' differences within the citizenry of the traditional German city. Yet wealth is a notoriously unsatisfactory indicator of class, because of the enormous variations that are often experienced

[12] As Thernstrom notes, 'virtually every significant theorist of class sees occupation as the central determinant' (*Poverty and progress*, p. 255).
[13] These calculations are based on an analysis of StAN, 'Steuerbuch', 1579; cf. Friedrichs, 'Nördlingen', pp. 121–3. Laube, *Z'tschr. f. Geschichtswissenschaft* (1957), presents some similar evidence for Rostock in the 1380s, although his overall line of argument is rather different from mine.

during the course of an ordinary life-cycle, even among individuals who cannot possibly be said to have changed class. This was certainly true – indeed, I would argue, particularly true – for the German community in its traditional form, when economic opportunity remained relatively widespread because each citizen retained a certain degree of economic independence. Statistical evidence

TABLE 1. Distribution of wealth in Nördlingen 1579 (%)
(adult male citizens)

	All male citizens	All crafts-men	Wool weavers	Fine-cloth weavers	Butchers	Tanners	Shoe-makers
Up to 100 fl.	49	52	68	70	24	38	53
101–400 fl.	26	25	19	6	35	27	22
401–1,600 fl.	19	19	13	13	33	23	22
Over 1,600 fl.	7	4	1	11	7	12	2
Numbers	1,266	1,003	269	62	54	108	60

about the degree of wealth mobility in medieval German cities is hard to come by, but here again data from Nördlingen – from a post-medieval but still 'traditional' phase of the city's history – can serve to illustrate the possible dimensions of wealth mobility in such a community. Table A of the appendix records the wealth mobility of one cohort of the citizenry of Nördlingen – the men who began paying taxes as adult citizens in 1580–5. Over half of these men – 187 of them – were still alive a quarter of a century later. As the table shows, wealth mobility was overwhelmingly the norm in their lives: only 12 per cent of these men showed no substantial change in their level of wealth over twenty-four years. Many of them – 31 per cent to be exact – were unable to sustain the wealth they had inherited and were poorer, in real terms, as middle-aged men than they had been when they began their careers. But 57 per cent of this cohort at least doubled their wealth between 1585 and 1609; and, more interestingly, fully 26 per cent of them increased their wealth fivefold or more. Those who started out poor shared fully in this upward trend; in fact, of those who started out in the bottom category, 31 per cent quintupled their wealth. The exact degree of mobility evident here may reflect a particularly prosperous phase in the city's economic history, but it is clear in any case that upward wealth mobility could form part of the normal career expectations among all segments of the citizenry in traditional Nördlingen.

At the same time, it should be emphasized that occupational mobility was not nearly so extensive as wealth mobility.[14] Once a citizen had gone through the years of training required for admission to one craft, it was highly unlikely that he would ever switch to another; whereas modern sociologists normally look for movement from one occupation to another as a sign of social mobility, in the traditional city mobility was more likely to take place *within* the context of a single occupation. A poor artisan might work, inherit or marry his way upward to became a well-to-do and financially secure member of his craft. But only if he were very rich would he dare to abandon the security of a loom or shop to undertake a riskier (though potentially more remunerative) career as a merchant.

In his recent analysis of German 'home towns' after 1648 Mack Walker suggested that 'guilds were conscious and recognized instruments for maintaining a satisfactory degree of equality' among their members.[15] Yet it could be argued that in the traditional city, guilds and other craft organizations had actually functioned in the opposite direction – as conscious and recognized instruments to promote or make possible a satisfactory degree of mobility. If so, they served this function by insisting on the right of each craftsman to operate as an independent producer and distributor of his own goods. For as long as craftsmen retained this degree of economic independence, opportunities for upward mobility remained very open – and a community retained its 'traditional' character.

II

As long as this situation lasted – as long as municipal institutions protected the economic independence of the individual artisan, which in turn guaranteed him access to upward wealth mobility and created a wide range of levels of wealth within each craft – it would have been difficult to divide the citizenry into clearly defined classes.

---

[14] Of 3,608 men who became adult citizens of Nördlingen between 1580 and 1670, only 550 experienced any change of occupation during their careers. 288 of these men were craftsmen, of whom 18 per cent switched over to other crafts, 30 per cent entered the victualling or distributive trades, 28 per cent assumed city office and 24 per cent entered other, mostly unskilled, occupations. See Friedrichs, 'Nördlingen', pp. 207–13.

[15] Walker, *German home towns*, p. 134.

When, however, this situation began to break down – when crafts-men began to lose control of production, when upward mobility was blocked, when the range of wealth within each craft was more narrowly constricted towards the bottom of the scale, leaving the merchants and professionals more exclusively in possession of the upper wealth ranges – then the formation of a clearly defined lower middle class can be said to have begun. But what exactly were the circumstances under which this process was likely to begin in any given community?

On the one hand, the institutional framework which had protected the craftsmen's economic independence might begin to decay. Wherever craft guilds shared in the municipal government – and after the guild wars of the fourteenth century this was very widely the case – there existed institutional guarantees to uphold the interests of the craftsmen. But these guarantees were only valid as long as the guild representatives on the city councils were willing or able to function on behalf of their fellow-citizens. In some communities, the guild representatives began to be alienated from their poorer fellow masters and tended to adopt the interests and outlook of the merchant patricians whom they joined in ruling the city.[16] In other cases, the patricians themselves aggressively asserted their primacy in city government and strove to put their *Obrigkeitsgedanke* ('concept of authority') into practice by chipping away at the autonomy of the guilds.[17]

Communal institutions, then, might offer the craftsmen less and less protection from threats to their economic autonomy. But from where exactly did these threats come? The answer is to be found, essentially, in the *Verlagssystem* – the putting-out system, under which an artisan who was engaged in a production craft continued to work in his own shop as his own master, but received his raw materials from, and rendered the finished products to, a capitalist entrepreneur, the *Verleger*. While the *Verlagssystem* is most commonly associated with the textile industry, it could in fact arise in connection with almost any type of production. In Nuremberg by the early sixteenth century the *Verlagssystem* had been introduced into numerous branches of the metal industry and in the manu-facture of purses, gloves, brushes, paper and books as well as linen

---

[16] Maschke, *Vierteljahrschr. f. Soz.- u. Wirtschaftsgesch.* (1959), esp. pp. 454–67.
[17] See Naujoks, *Obrigkeitsgedanke*.

and fustian. In late seventeenth-century Nuremberg even the production of pencils was organized on the basis of *Verlag*.[18]

In some cases, the *Verleger* emerged as the organizer of a production process in which many different crafts were involved; but even if the production process were relatively simple, a *Verleger* might emerge when local sources of supply dried up, or when local demand diminished and craftsmen had to depend on someone with access to distant markets beyond their own reach. In principle, of course, the system could work to the benefit of the craftsmen, by guaranteeing them a steady market for their goods. Where a guild was strong, in fact, the relationship between *Verleger* and artisan was often carefully regulated by contract, and the guild could terminate the arrangement when the relationship proved detrimental to its members.[19] Where the guild was weak, however, in times of economic distress craftsmen might turn to the *Verleger* on an individual basis for advances of cash or raw materials – and under these circumstances, especially if unprotected by municipal institutions, artisans might easily fall into permanent economic dependence.

It is the element of *permanent* dependence that is so crucial here. It was perfectly normal, after all, for a craftsman to fall into debt to a merchant or even to a wealthier member of his own craft. An astute *Verleger*, however, would build systematically on an initial debt-relationship, exploiting his position as creditor to make craftsmen permanently dependent on him and him alone. The *Verleger* supplied all the raw materials; in return he received all the finished goods and marketed them at his own profit. The more completely he could corner the supply of raw materials or the access to markets, the more effectively he could exert his control over the craftsmen in his debt – and the more unlikely that they would ever escape their indebtedness.

When craftsmen fell permanently and inescapably into debt, however, their opportunities for upward mobility began to contract. Eventually, in fact, aspirations for mobility gave way to more immediate concerns: a consciousness of their exploitation, and a growing determination to resist it. Their interests, in other words,

---

[18] Aubin, *Beiträge zur Wirtschaftsgeschichte Nürnbergs* (1967), Hoffman, *Tradition* (1967). For the development of the putting-out system in the textile industry in general, see Furger, *Verlagssystem*.

[19] See the discussion in Furger, *Verlagssystem*, pp. 61–3, 68. Cf. Endres, *J'buch f. fränk. Landesforschung* (1962).

became increasingly antagonistic to those of the capitalist bourgeoisie.

Yet at the same time, as *Bürger*, as heads of households, and as skilled craft masters who continued to work in their own shops, the artisans still felt sharply differentiated from the propertyless noncitizens. Indeed, the differences between them and the non-citizens often became increasingly acute. The more economic pressure the craft masters were subjected to from above, the more they tried to defend themselves from further competition by blocking off the admission of new masters from below. Some journeymen, especially the sons of local citizens, could still expect to be promoted to masterships in the course of time. But the craftsmen's willingness to extend admission to non-citizen journeymen generally diminished in times of economic stress.

In other words, at the same time as a sharper distinction was being drawn between the craftsmen and the emerging bourgeoisie, the loopholes through which non-citizens had risen into the ranks of the craft masters were also being tightened. As their chances of becoming masters diminished, these journeymen lost their sense of solidarity with the values and traditions of the guild as a whole, and began to take on the mentality of wage-labourers, which they were becoming. Both above and below the master craftsmen, therefore, class lines were being drawn more clearly than ever before. Inevitably, the men between these two lines themselves began to form the nucleus of what became a new class: the urban lower middle class, the *Kleinbürgertum* of late pre-industrial Germany.

III

The preceding, of course, must be regarded primarily as a model, an analytical framework to help us interpret the obscure and glacial changes which took place in the society of the early modern German town. It must always be borne in mind not only that this process began at different times in different communities, but also that it developed in very different ways. Economic and constitutional differences betwen various communities – even those within the same geographical region – were often very substantial. In the first place, the rate of economic change was highly variable; the moment at which entrepreneurial capitalism penetrated two communities might differ by centuries. In the second place, constitutional factors could have a profound impact on the process of class formation. A constitution which, for example, gave artisans continued access to political power even as they experienced the loss of economic independence could retard the process by which a lower middle class was distilled from the *Bürgerschaft* as a whole. By the same token, a constitution which excluded artisans from political power could serve to accelerate the process by which their identity and interests became alienated from those of the upper middle class.

How these different factors interacted can best be illustrated by looking, however briefly, at the example of a single community. For the case of Nördlingen suggests clearly how important both economic and political factors are in understanding the process of class formation – especially in its early stages – in the early modern German town.

The formal, institutional structure which guaranteed the craftsmen of Nördlingen representation for their interests had been destroyed in 1552. Until that time, each of the city's twelve guilds had selected one council member, thus filling half the places on the twenty-four-man city council. In 1552, however, Charles V revoked the constitution of Nördlingen, along with those of dozens of other imperial cities, and reorganized the council as a self-perpetuating fifteen-member magistracy. The guilds, in fact, were not merely stripped of political power; they were also dissolved as autonomous economic organizations, to be succeeded by craft organizations under the direct supervision of the city council.[20]

For a number of decades, craftsmen continued to be appointed to the council as individuals. But there were no institutional guarantees to protect the artisans' participation in city government, and during the Thirty Years War, when the council was under financial pressure to fill vacancies with particularly wealthy men, the proportion of craftsmen appointed to the council began to decline. After the war, this trend persisted: in the last four decades of the seventeenth century, of twenty-six council vacancies, only one was filled by a craftsman. Council membership became restricted to merchants, professionals and municipal bureaucrats – in fact, to the group which would eventually form the emerging bourgeoisie.[21]

For a long time, however, despite its changing character, the

[20] Kammerer, *J'buch hist. Ver. Nördlingen* (1930).
[21] See Friedrichs, 'Nördlingen', ch. 7, for evidence concerning the changing composition of the city council between 1580 and 1700.

council of Nördlingen remained responsive to the interests of craftsmen. The artisans persistently feared, for example, that their crafts would be *übersetzt* – that too many new masters would be admitted and thus that too many men would be competing within a static or declining market. The council shared this concern, and co-operated with craftsmen in raising the standards for admission to specific crafts or to citizenship in general when reductions in the number of new masters seemed necessary.[22] In doing so, the council may have been motivated in part by a concern that craftsmen should not become destitute, and thus dependent on the institutions of civic welfare. Yet their concern went deeper than this. For throughout the seventeenth century the council of Nördlingen remained faithful in more general terms to the ideology of *Bürgerschaft* – to the concept that all citizens, despite the economic and social differences among them, were bound together by a common interest and a common purpose. A particularly vivid expression of this attitude came in 1667, when the council forbade the citizens of Nördlingen to patronize cabinet-makers outside the city because the citizens, 'who should stand by one another through thick and thin, and must partake of each other's joys and sorrows', should not 'cause any further diminution of each other's livelihoods, which are already far too difficult to obtain, by granting a foreigner their money'.[23]

Thus it is not surprising that the magistrates observed the development of the putting-out system in Nördlingen with considerable reservations. Their concern can only have been intensified by the fact that the introduction of the *Verlagssystem* in Nördlingen was predominantly the work of a single family: that of Daniel Wörner (1621–99) and his sons. When he began his adult career as a wool weaver in 1652 Daniel Wörner was only about the hundredth richest among Nördlingen's 887 citizen taxpayers. But by 1697, shortly before his death, he was by far the richest man in the city – for he had built up an entrepreneurial empire in which scores of Nördlingen wool weavers depended on him or his son for advances of cash or raw materials as the source of their livelihoods.[24]

---

[22] For some explicit examples of this, see StAN, 'Ordnungsbücher', 1567–1587, fo. 230b; 1641–88, fos. 359b–361a.

[23] *Ibid.* fos. 252a–b.

[24] The principal sources for the story of Daniel Wörner and his relationship with the weavers of Nördlingen, as presented here and in the following passages, are StAN, 'Ratsprotokolle', 1660–1700; and 'Lodweberakten:

In building up this empire Wörner had displayed all of the personal characteristics of the textbook entrepreneur – vision, tenacity and a streak of ruthlessness. But his success was also made possible by a severe deterioration in the economic position of the city's poorer craftsmen, particularly after 1670. The huge burden of taxation associated with the Thirty Years War (1618–48) had already undermined the position of the city's poorer citizens. Although a period of economic recovery following the war had brought about some redistribution of wealth, the revival of heavy wartime taxation from the 1670s onward, which affected the poor with particular severity, reversed this trend.[25] The wool weavers were especially vulnerable, moreover, since the local demand for their product had declined in the seventeenth century; by the end of the century, in fact, the principal market for their products was in distant Switzerland. Under such circumstances it was easy for an enterprising capitalist like Wörner to convert many a weaver's temporary indebtedness into permanent dependence.

Concerned about this challenge to traditional economic relationships – and also, perhaps, jealous of Wörner's economic success – the magistrates of Nördlingen repeatedly attempted to restrain Wörner from exploiting his power over the weavers. But he, in turn, could reply with a potent counter-threat: if pushed too hard, he would simply stop buying cloth, thus plunging the weavers into even greater desperation. The result was an uneasy stalemate between magistrates and entrepreneur which lasted until 1698 – when the weavers themselves rebelled. Squeezed between excessively high prices for the wool Wörner sold them and low prices for the cloth he bought back, some sixty wool-weaving masters – about half of the city's total – protested to the council and demanded redress. After months of agitation by the weavers and painstaking investigation by the magistrates, the council decided against the Wörners and required them to distribute 4,000 fl. in compensation among sixty-three aggrieved weavers.

In the following years the magistrates went even further in attempting to liberate the artisans from their bondage to the city's leading entrepreneurs. In 1700 they established a civic co-operative

Loder contra Daniel Wörner, Lodenhandel 1696–1715'. Complete references will be found in Friedrichs, 'Nördlingen', ch. 10.

[25] This can be demonstrated from an analysis of the tax registers (StAN, 'Steuerbücher') for 1615–1700. See Friedrichs, 'Nördlingen', pp. 149–56.

to conduct business with distant markets, primarily in Switzerland, on behalf of any interested weaver. Within a few years, however, it became obvious that this venture was not economically viable, and in 1712 the council re-established 'free trading' – another term for the Wörners' exploitation of the city's weaving community.[26]

Even more interesting, however, than the magistrates' lingering attempts to resist the emergence of a new economic system is the weavers' own perception of their position. The rhetoric employed by the weavers during the agitation of 1698 is, of course, the best available expression of this perception. On the one hand, the weavers accused the Wörners of causing the 'ruin of the craft', of wanting, as one master put it, 'forcibly to ruin me, with my wife and children and my fellow masters'. At the same time, the weavers complained that if current practices were permitted to continue, they would be turned into the 'slaves and serfs of the Wörners'.[27] This mixture of vocabulary aptly suggests the emerging mentality of an urban lower middle class: the mentality of men who continue to emphasize that they are masters of their craft, yet who fear their reduction to economic slavery – and who blame their troubles on a member of the capitalist bourgeoisie.

The emergence of a lower middle class, however, is evident not only in the mentality of a particularly aggrieved group of craftsmen. For in addition, the initial stages of this development are evident in the changing economic and social structure of the community – in changes which both contributed to the growth of the *Verlagssystem* and then, in turn, were reinforced and made irreversible by it. The three decades before 1700 were a period of economic stagnation in Nördlingen, reflected both in a decline in wealth *per capita* and in a decrease in wealth mobility. In the quarter-century between 1670 and 1694, the wealth *per capita* of Nördlingen's citizens declined by 9 per cent in nominal terms, or by fully 39 per cent in real terms.[28] Equally striking is the decline in wealth mobility evident during the same years. Table B of the appendix records the wealth mobility of

[26] The establishment and failure of this civic co-operative are described in Ebert, *Die Lodweberei*, pp. 41–4.

[27] StAN, 'Lodweberakten: Loder c. Daniel Wörner: Supplicationes', no. 1 (p. 3); 'Confrontations-Protokoll', pp. 7, 157.

[28] The wealth *per capita* of all citizens (i.e. heads of citizen households) in 1670 was 860 fl.; in 1694 it was 780 fl. (calculations based on StAN, 'Steuerbücher', 1670, 1694). The adjustment for real wealth is made on the basis of the price index discussed below in the appendix.

the generation of citizens who began paying taxes in 1665–70 and who were still alive in 1694. The contrast between this group and the 1585-to-1609 generation discussed earlier is striking indeed: between 1670 and 1694 less than a quarter of these men (instead of 57 per cent) had even doubled their wealth in real terms and only two of them had succeeded in quintupling it. Wealth mobility, then, was much less likely to form part of the life expectations of a poor Nördlingen citizen in the late seventeenth century than it had a century before.

This decline in wealth mobility also left its mark on the pattern of wealth distribution among the citizens. The distribution of wealth in 1700, as shown in table 2,[29] merits close comparison with the data for 1579 presented in table 1 above. (In table 2, the interval represented by each wealth category has been doubled in size, to counterbalance a decline of almost 50 per cent in the value of the gulden between 1579 and 1700.[30] Once this adjustment has been made, the distribution of wealth in these two years can meaningfully be compared.) This comparison shows that the distribution of wealth among the citizenry *as a whole* closely resembled that of 1579. But the distribution of wealth *within* the craft occupations shows some marked differences, for the proportion of craftsmen to be found in the highest wealth registers has sharply contracted; the crafts were beginning to lose their character as groups that comprehended a wide variety of wealth levels. What we can see here, in fact, are the beginnings of a development that is essential to the process of class formation: a growing correlation between wealth levels and occupation.

It is in this context that both the Wörners' activities and the weavers' agitation can best be understood. For the Wörners had exploited and thereby also aggravated the economic weaknesses of a very vulnerable group of their fellow-citizens. By the end of the century more and more weavers were clustered in the bottom wealth categories – and fewer and fewer of them perceived any likelihood of liberating themselves from the *Verlagssystem* and climbing up the

---

[29] These calculations are based on an analysis of StAN, 'Steuerbücher', 1700. (The occupations selected are the same as those considered in 1579, except for linen weaving, which had replaced fine-cloth weaving as the city's second largest textile craft.)

[30] On the basis of the price index described in the appendix, it can be estimated that the purchasing power of the gulden in 1700 was only about 55 per cent of what it had been in 1579.

social ladder. Under such circumstances *Bürger* solidarity would begin to break down, and direct antagonisms between members of a lower and an upper middle class could emerge.

TABLE 2. Distribution of wealth in Nördlingen 1700 (%)
(adult male citizens)

	All male citizens	All crafts-men	Wool weavers	Linen weavers	Butchers	Tanners	Shoe-makers
Up to 200 fl.	47	54	79	76	52	40	61
201–800 fl.	30	32	14	19	36	34	31
801–3,200 fl.	16	13	7	5	10	20	9
Over 3,200 fl.	6	2	0	0	1	5	0
Numbers	952	698	138	38	75	75	35

In 1700, to be sure, these antagonisms continued to affect only a small part of the community; most citizens of Nördlingen were still caught in the middle. The magistracy itself, as we have seen, continued for a while to uphold the interests of the city's craft masters. But by the end of the seventeenth century the ruling elite of Nördlingen had come to consist of a close-knit, intermarried coterie of merchants, professionals and bureaucrats – in short, a bourgeoisie. It was not long before the civic idealism of these men began to give way to the recognition that they had more in common with the city's dominant economic figures than with the poorest of their fellow-citizens. In 1712 the civic co-operative was abandoned; in 1716 David Wörner – Daniel's son – was appointed to the city council; and from then on the interests of entrepreneurial capitalism and municipal rule ceased to be in conflict.

Nothing makes this clearer than the career of Georg Christian von Troeltsch in the second half of the eighteenth century. Troeltsch was another ruthless entrepreneur, who brought the linen weavers of Nördlingen under his control by obtaining monopolies over the regional supply of flax and the local facilities for bleaching. But Troeltsch was not only a *Verleger* in the classic mould; he was also a member of the city council and for years the mayor of Nördlingen. Under these circumstances persistent efforts by the city's linen weavers to destroy Troeltsch's monopoly position – including appeals to the imperial court and, in 1796, an outbreak of violence – proved completely ineffective.[31]

No doubt even at the end of the eighteenth century there were still citizens of Nördlingen whose class identity and interests remained ambiguous; although statistical evidence for the late eighteenth century is unavailable, it seems unlikely that social mobility had come to be completely cut off or that occupations had become totally uniform in terms of wealth. But on the other hand there is no doubt that the *Bürgerschaft* by then was essentially divided into two classes: on the one side, a small bourgeoisie which controlled both the means of production and the organs of government which protected that economic control; and, on the other, a large lower middle class, a *Kleinbürgertum* consisting predominantly of artisans who took pride in their status as craft masters and citizens but who in fact were excluded from all political influence and remained helpless against the power of capital. And it was the *Verlagssystem*, which was capable of transforming temporary artisanal hardships into permanent economic dependence, which had set into motion the formation of this lower middle class.

IV

Nördlingen was only one of countless German cities which experienced the process of class formation in the early modern era. In each city the process began and developed somewhat differently. Yet the case of Nördlingen does illustrate the kinds of evidence we must look for in trying to answer the two main questions posed in this paper: first, what caused this process of class formation to get under way? And secondly, how can we tell, in looking at the historical record for any given community, when this process began?

In answer to the first question, the importance of the *Verlagssystem* has already been sufficiently emphasized. But it in turn could only be introduced on a large scale under specific economic conditions. Any economic climate in which craftsmen were unable to function effectively in the open market was likely to favour the penetration of the *Verlagssystem*. But this was particularly so when a period of economic growth and expansion of credit was followed by a sudden contraction of demand or increases in overheads which

[31] Dannenbauer, *Z'tschr. f. bay. Landesgesch.* (1930), pp. 305–15.

left artisans at the mercy of their creditors. Ingomar Bog has shown how such conditions caused the *Verlagssystem* to flourish in six-teenth-century Nuremberg.[32] In Nördlingen, however, such a pattern can be detected most clearly in the second half of the seventeenth century, and the key factor seems to have been the financial demands imposed in connection with the imperial wars against the French and the Turks. The crushing tax burdens of the Thirty Years War did not have this impact, for they affected all citizens so severely that rich families were probably in no position to make loans to poor ones. But the second half of the century presented a different pattern. The city's striking recovery from the Thirty Years War was suddenly interrupted in the 1670s by the onset of renewed warfare which dragged on until 1714. This cycle of warfare, however, proved less uniformly catastrophic in Nördlingen than the Thirty Years War; the financial squeeze was severe enough to cripple the weavers but not so great as to wipe out the resources of a family like the Wörners. Under such circumstances the *Verlagssystem* thrived.

Of almost equal importance in the process of class formation, however, was a political climate in which the magistrates ceased to regulate a city's economy with the artisans' benefit in mind, and thus abandoned the craftsmen to the forces of the market. In sixteenth-century Ulm, according to Eberhard Naujoks, 'the abolition of the guilds' share in ruling opened the door to "free trading" of an early-capitalist type, since the importance of the broad stratum of poorer craftsmen receded while the richer merchants, retailers and shop-keepers were preferred for election to the council'.[33] In Nördlingen, by contrast, the exclusion of craftsmen from the council was not completed until the mid-seventeenth century, and the whole-hearted adoption of a 'free-trading' attitude sympathetic to entrepreneurial capitalism did not occur until the eighteenth. Only when this had happened could the *Verlagssystem* operate with full effectiveness, and would the process of class formation occur without impediment.

These, then, are the characteristic economic and political pre-conditions for the formation of an urban lower middle class. As for the second question, our hypothesis has also already been outlined: that there are two key indicators which suggest that the process of class formation was under way. One is a downward constriction in

[32] Bog in Lütge (ed.), *Wirtschaftliche und soziale Probleme*, pp. 66–75, 79–84.
[33] Naujoks, *Obrigkeitsgedanke*, pp. 189–90.

the range of wealth among members of the craft occupations; the other is a decline in the rate of upward mobility – or, more specifically, of upward mobility among members of the crafts.

It can hardly be emphasized ⸗nough that an inequality of wealth .distribution is not, as such, an indicator of the existence or the formation of classes, for a grossly uneven distribution of wealth among the *Bürgerschaft* was a normal feature of the traditional German city. Discussing the social structure of Hanseatic cities, Ernst Pitz warns historians to avoid the formulation: 'He is poor who seems on the basis of city tax registers to be without property.' For one thing, he points out, the amount of property (*Vermögen*) a man owned was not always precisely correlated to his level of income. But in addition, Pitz suggests, we should recognize more clearly that 'above all, he is poor who perceives himself as such'.[34] And in the traditional German city a poor craftsman might well be unwilling to recognize himself as such; as long as he was economically independent and could thus realistically aspire to upward mobility, his sense of solidarity with the citizenry as a whole would prevent his adoption of a separate 'class' mentality. On the other hand, nothing is more certain to make a man regard himself as poor than the fact that his chances of moving upward have sharply diminished. A journeyman who has lost all hope of becoming a master will adopt the mentality of the proletariat. But a citizen and craft master who has lost hope of escaping his dependence on a bourgeois entrepreneur will adopt the mentality of the lower middle class.

For a long time, of course, some members of the *Bürgerschaft* continued to be situated between the capitalist bourgeoisie and the dependent artisanry. Small retailers, members of victualling and transport trades, petty officials, teachers and clerics – these men belonged to neither end of the *Verlag* relationship. But the antagonism between *Verleger* and craftsmen created a polarity within the *Bürgerschaft*, and gradually members of this middle group of citizens came to be drawn in one direction or the other. The economically and politically powerful bourgeoisie of large-scale merchants and civic magistrates drew into its ranks a third group: university-trained lawyers and (in Protestant cities) clergymen, whose sense of acquired status was manifested in a determined effort

[34] Pitz in Lütge (ed.), *Wirtschaftliche und soziale Probleme*, pp. 26–8, 42–3.

to create social distance between themselves and the uneducated craftsmen.[35] Most of the middle group, however, was drawn in the other direction – for the more economic and political power the bourgeoisie acquired, the more dependent upon it most members of this middle group became. Retailers depended on bourgeois wholesalers for merchandise, transporters depended on bourgeois merchants for commissions, petty officials depended on the bourgeois elite for appointments to office. Inevitably, then, members of this middle group coalesced with the dependent craftsmen to form the urban lower middle class in its fully articulated form. By the eighteenth century, as Helmut Möller has shown, a distinctly *kleinbürgerliches* way of life and value system had emerged. Craftsmen still formed the core of this class, but much more than economic activity defined the *Kleinbürger* as such: 'In the late seventeenth and early eighteenth century', Möller writes, 'the "great" and "small" citizens were distinguished from one another not only by their material opportunities, but also by educational goals, or at least educational chances' – education (*Bildung*) is here used in the broadest sense of the term.[36]

Yet although there were differences in values and life-style between the upper and the lower middle classes, the differences between the lower middle class and the proletariat were even more sharply drawn. In fact, in much of what Möller describes as the characteristic behaviour of the eighteenth-century *Kleinbürger* – in his regular work habits, his emphasis on conformity and piety, his deep respect for authority, and his tenacious insistence on preserving the purity of his caste through the ideology of *Ehrbarkeit*[37] – we can detect a relentless effort to distinguish himself from what he considered the shiftless, irresponsible and propertyless lower orders. The *Kleinbürger* had lost his economic autonomy and political significance; status became his last line of defence against proletarianization.[38]

---

[35] Liebel, *Internat. Rev. Soc. Hist.* (1965), esp. pp. 301–3.

[36] Möller, *Die kleinbürgerliche Familie*, p. 5. Cf. Eitel's observation about the upper Swabian cities, 'The sixteenth and seventeenth centuries give the impression of an increasing polarization of urban society into a patrician-academic upper stratum and a *kleinbürgerliches* and politically insignificant [lower] stratum of craftsmen and tradesmen, between which two groups the connections and common characteristics became ever scarcer': Eitel in Maschke and Sydow (eds.), *Städtische Mittelschichten*, p. 93.

[37] Möller, *Die kleinbürgerliche Familie*, esp. pp. 36–66, 89–94, 203–14.

[38] This attitude persisted well into the nineteenth century. Commenting on

V

Only by looking at a community in detail, of course, can one establish when the process of class formation began in that particular environment. This paper has only attempted to suggest what preconditions and what indicators the historian should look for when he tries to trace the origins of this process in whatever community he studies – or, to put it another way, to suggest a general model against which one can weigh the evidence for any particular case. It is possible, however, to hazard some very general observations about what historians will find when they do so.

In the first place, they may find that the larger a city was, the sooner the process of class formation got under way. For, as a rule, the techniques of entrepreneurial capitalism were first developed in the larger cities, and only gradually penetrated the smaller ones. A city like Strassburg, for example, can provide evidence for the *Verlagssystem* in wool production from the mid-1400s,[39] whereas a smaller city like Nördlingen might show no signs of it for another two centuries.

Yet a distinction based on size alone can only serve as the coarsest rule of thumb. For the crucial distinctions between cities will be found not in their respective sizes but in their different economic structures. Thus, from the point of view of class formation, the critical difference appears to have been between cities in which craftsmen produced primarily for a local market and those in which they produced chiefly or largely for export.[40] Discussing north German cities of the fifteenth and sixteenth centuries, Pitz observes that 'in the Hansa cities, the *Verlagssystem*, which led to sharp social differentiation, was not able to establish itself. Even the term itself is unknown in the Hanseatic sources'. For there, he explains, craft masters were oriented to providing goods and services which

a proposed reform which would, in effect, have eliminated the *Bürgerrecht* in Prussian cities, the *Conversations-Lexicon* of F. A. Brockhaus observed, 'Whoever realizes how much it means to people to be known as *Bürger* – the only distinction which separates the independent practitioner of a trade from the journeymen and wage-labourers – will realize that unless these paragraphs are revised the *Städteordnung* of 1831 will be very difficult to impose' (*Conversations-Lexicon der Gegenwart*, ix (Leipzig, 1841), p. 713, cited in Koselleck, *Preussen*, p. 576).

[39] Furger, *Verlagssystem*, pp. 41–3.
[40] Cf. the classic paper by Jecht, *Vierteljahrschr. f. Soz.- u. Wirtschaftsgesch.* (1926).

were immediately required in the commercial port-cities in which they lived.[41] By contrast, as is well known, the *Verlagssystem* got an early start in the cities of southern Germany – in some cases it was already fully evident by the fifteenth century.[42] Not only did craftsmen in the south German cities produce a significant proportion of their wages for alpine or transalpine markets, but in times of war or hardship, when local demand was reduced, dependence on these distant markets increased. The wars of the seventeenth century, which generally imposed heavier strains on southern Germany than on the cities of the north, promoted in the former a much faster development of the *Verlagssystem* – and of its accompanying phenomenon of economic dependence.

It is also clear that both the very largest and the very smallest cities provide important variations on the basic theme of class formation. To start with, the very largest cities, such as Frankfurt, Hamburg and Nuremberg, experienced not a two-way but instead a three-way division of the *Bürgerschaft*, for there the ruling elites strove with some success to establish themselves as patriciates in the true sense – as socially exclusive, hereditary castes with a monopoly of political power. The classic example of patriciate formation is provided by the Nuremberg 'dance statute' of 1521, which codified the list of families whose members were eligible for all the leading positions in the magistracy.[43] A true patriciate generally exhibited pronounced aristocratic pretensions – if not in the direct pursuit of noble titles, at least in a turning away from commerce towards dependence on income from investments and rents. Only the largest cities could support such a patriciate – a group as different from the emerging bourgeoisie of merchants and professionals as this bourgeoisie, in turn, was from the emerging class of *Kleinbürger*.

In many of the largest cities, merchants who resented their exclusion from participation in the government spearheaded revolts against patrician rule – revolts in which they were often able to rally large segments of the *Bürgerschaft* to their support.[44] Conflicts of

[41] Pitz in Lütge (ed.), *Wirtschaftliche und soziale Probleme*, p. 41.
[42] See, for example, the evidence from Constance in Furger, *Verlagssystem*, pp. 58–60. In the case of Nuremberg, Aubin finds some evidence of *Verlag* as early as the beginning of the fourteenth century, although a really capitalistic *Verlagssystem* did not emerge until later: Aubin, *Beiträge zur Wirtschaftsgeschichte Nürnbergs* (1967), pp. 623ff.
[43] Hirschmann in Rössler (ed.), *Deutsches Patriziat*, pp. 265–6.
[44] The great constitutional conflict between *Rat* and *Bürgerschaft* in

this kind, taking as they did the customary form of *Rat contra Bürgerschaft*, could serve to obscure temporarily the process of class division taking place within the citizenry at the same time. But the long-term separation of the *Bürgerschaft* into an upper and a lower middle class could not be prevented by any temporary alliance against an unpopular patriciate. Indeed, nothing suggests more clearly the eventual breakdown of *Bürger* solidarity in such large cities as Frankfurt, Hamburg or Munich than the fact that by the eighteenth century fewer and fewer immigrants bothered to seek admission to the citizenry – for the status of *Bürger* had ceased to confer any special advantages.[45]

In the largest cities, then, the historian may find that the *Bürgerschaft* dissolved not into two but into three classes – a tiny patriciate caste; a somewhat larger bourgeoisie; and a much larger lower middle class. At the other end of the spectrum, however, in the smallest towns of Germany, he may be confronted with a very different variation on the basic model we have presented. For in the smallest towns there was often nobody with sufficient capital to form the basis for the development of a bourgeoisie. In such communities – the small towns which form the basis for Walker's description of the German 'home town' – the *Bürgerschaft* never divided into classes; craftsmen continued to enjoy economic and political opportunities, and the sense of communal solidarity within the *Bürgerschaft* remained relatively strong.[46]

In a sense, however, the citizens of these small communities also came to develop a class identity by the end of the old regime – for

Frankfurt am Main between 1705 and 1732 conforms essentially to this pattern, especially in its later years; although merchants came increasingly to dominate this anti-patrician movement, there was always support from a wide spectrum in the citizenry. See Soliday, *Community in conflict*, esp. ch. 5. For a more general assessment of such conflicts in large imperial cities, see Brunner, *Vierteljahrschr. f. Soz.- u. Wirtschaftsgesch.* (1963). By contrast, in small imperial cities without patriciates, where merchants controlled the political machinery, opposition movements were normally led by craft masters and small retailers: Hildebrandt, *Z'tschr. f. Stadtgesch., Stadtsoz. u. Denkmalpflege* (1974).

[45] Mauersberg, *Sozial- und Wirtschaftsgeschichte*, pp. 134–51.

[46] Walker, *German home towns*, esp. chaps. 3 and 4. I find Walker's description of the 'home town' entirely convincing, but only for a somewhat narrower range of communities than he himself suggests. For middle-sized communities (such as Nördlingen, despite the fact that Walker himself describes it as a 'home town', pp. 42–3), his model does not seem as fully applicable as it does for smaller communities.

they too can be identified as *Kleinbürger*, as members of the urban lower middle class. After all, we have seen that in a city like Nördlingen the aims of the emerging lower middle class were in many ways an attempt to enforce or revive communal values formerly shared by the community as a whole – values which promoted a certain degree of economic autonomy and opportunity for each citizen. In medium or larger cities, these values became identified with a specific and increasingly powerless class within the *Bürgerschaft*; in small towns they continued to be shared by the citizenry as a whole – but the values were, in fact, the same. These values were challenged and undermined by the emergence of entrepreneurial capitalism. In the larger communities the threat was more obvious and immediate. But by the eighteenth century the citizenry of the smaller 'home towns' also felt challenged by the emerging mercantile and administrative bourgeoisie – to use Walker's phrase again, by the 'movers and doers' whose activities threatened, even from afar, to upset the delicate equilibrium of small-town life.

Thus the urban lower middle class emerged via two different routes. But either way, it evolved out of the *Bürgerschaft* of the traditional German city. In middle or larger cities, as we have seen, it was formed out of only part of the traditional citizenry. In smaller towns, where the professional and merchant group was negligible and where the craftsmen and guilds were correspondingly more important, the *Bürgerschaft* as a whole began to adopt the mentality and policies of *Kleinbürgertum*. In the long run, however, and in the overall German context, these variant origins made little difference, for by the end of the eighteenth century these two groups had come to represent a single, clearly identifiable class. Many labels can be attached to this group, but some of them – *Handwerkerstand*, for example, or Walker's 'hometownsmen' – are somewhat too narrow. The term *Kleinbürger* or, better yet, the term 'lower middle class' will suggest more clearly the character of this distinctive sector of German urban society.

APPENDIX
WEALTH MOBILITY IN NÖRDLINGEN 1585–1609 AND 1670–94

Table A establishes the wealth mobility of all male citizens who had begun paying taxes in 1580–5 and were still alive in 1609 (out of

353 men, 187 survived). The table compares the wealth of each man in 1609 with his wealth in 1585.

The category 'Same' refers to all those whose wealth in 1609 equalled 1.0–1.99 of their wealth in 1585; the category '2x–4x' includes those whose wealth in 1609 was 2.0–4.99 of their wealth in 1585; and so on.

TABLE A.   Wealth mobility of 187 citizens of Nördlingen between 1585 and 1609

Wealth level in 1585	Total number in 1585	Number of men whose wealth in 1609 was:				
		Lower	Same	2x–4x	5x–9x	10x or more
Under 100 fl.	128	39	10	39	18	22
		(14)	(31)	(29)	(21)	(33)
101–400 fl.	41	13	8	11	6	3
		(13)	(6)	(11)	(7)	(4)
Over 400 fl.	18	6	5	6	1	–
		(5)	(5)	(4)	(3)	(1)
Totals	187	58	23	56	25	25
		(32)	(42)	(44)	(31)	(38)

Note: Calculations have been made after adjustment for changes in the real value of money between 1585 and 1609; figures in brackets indicate the results before such adjustment is made.
Source: See table B.

The real value of money changed between 1585 and 1609. On the basis of the data cited below from Augsburg, about fifty miles south of Nördlingen, it can be estimated that the purchasing power of the gulden (fl.) in 1609 was about 80 per cent of what it had been in 1585. The first line of figures in each row indicates the number of individuals in each category when adjustment has been made for this decline in the real value of the gulden. The second line provides the number of individuals in each category when nominal wealth in 1585 and 1609 is compared.

Table B carries out the identical procedure for citizens who began paying taxes in 1665–70 and who were still alive in 1694 (out of 187 men, 100 survived). For this period it is estimated that the value of the gulden in 1694 was 67 per cent of what it had been in 1670.

TABLE B. Wealth mobility of 100 citizens of Nördlingen between 1670 and 1694

Wealth level in 1670	Total number in 1670	Number of men whose wealth in 1694 was:				
		Lower	Same	2x–4x	5x–9x	10x or more
Under 100 fl.	26	13	8	4	1	–
		(8)	(11)	(6)	(–)	(1)
101–400 fl.	42	25	9	8	–	–
		(17)	(11)	(12)	(2)	(–)
Over 400 fl.	32	15	7	9	1	–
		(9)	(10)	(8)	(4)	(1)
Totals	100	53	24	21	2	–
		(34)	(32)	(26)	(6)	(2)

Note: Calculations have been made after adjustment for changes in the real value of money between 1670 and 1694; figures in brackets indicate the results before such adjustment is made.

Sources for tables A and B

Data: StAN, 'Steuerbücher', 1585, 1609, 1670 and 1694. Continuity of individual careers was established from the intervening 'Steuerbücher'.

Value of fl.: Phelps Brown and Hopkins, *Economica* (1959), provide an annual price index of consumables in Augsburg, based on data from Elsas, *Umriss einer Geschichte*. I have estimated changes in the purchasing power of the gulden on the basis of nine-year averages for 1585, 1609, 1670 and 1694.

9. A Simple Model of London's Importance in Changing English Society and Economy 1650–1750*

E. A. WRIGLEY

'Soon London will be all England': James I

Towards the end of the seventeenth century London became the largest city in Europe. The population of Paris had reached about 400,000 by the beginning of the seventeenth century and was nearing 500,000 towards its end, but thereafter grew very little for a further century. At the time of the 1801 census its population was still just less than 550,000. London, on the other hand, grew rapidly throughout the seventeenth and eighteenth centuries. Its exact population at any time before the first census is a matter for argument but in round figures it appears to have grown from about 200,000 in 1600 to perhaps 400,000 in 1650, 575,000 by the end of the century, 675,000 in 1750 and 900,000 in 1800.[1] London and Paris were much larger than other cities in Europe during these two centuries and each was very much larger than any rival in the same country. The contrast between the size and rates of growth of the two cities is

* I am greatly indebted to Dr P. Abrams, Professor T. C. Barker, Mr P. Laslett and Dr R. S. Schofield for their comments on an earlier draft of this paper.

[1] There is a very useful compilation of estimates of the size of towns and cities in western Europe chiefly for the period 1500–1800 in Hélin, *La démographie de Liège*, pp. 238–52. Brett-James summarizes the calculations of contemporaries and later scholars in *The growth of Stuart London*, esp. pp. 496–512. He himself suggests figures of 250,000 in 1603 and 320,000 in 1625 (p. 512). John Gaunt estimated the population of the capital to be 460,000 in about 1660, *Natural and political observations*, ii, p. 371. Petty concluded that in 1682 London's population was already 670,000, *The growth of the city of London*, ii, p. 460. Gregory King made a calculation of London's population in 1695 from the number of households, arriving at a figure of 527,560, *Two tracts by Gregory King*, p. 18. Creighton's estimates of London's population for 1603, 1625 and 1665 agree very closely with those of Brett-James and Graunt for the same periods: Creighton, *History of epidemics*, i, p. 660. Mrs George accepts figures of 674,500 for 1700 and 676,750 for 1750 based on the number of baptisms in the London parish registers: George, *London life*, pp. 24, 329–30. See also Jones and Judges, *Econ. Hist. Rev.* (1935–6). The figures used in this text are rounded for convenience and are probably of the right order of magnitude, but nothing more can be claimed for them.

particularly striking when it is borne in mind that until the last half of the eighteenth cntury, when the rate of growth of population in England increased sharply, the total population of France was about four times as large as that of England. In 1650 about $2\frac{1}{2}$ per cent of the population of France lived in Paris; in 1750 the figure was little changed. London, on the other hand, housed about 7 per cent of England's total population in 1650 and about 11 per cent in 1750. Only in Holland does any one city appear to have contained such a high percentage of the total national population. Amsterdam in 1650 was already a city of about 150,000 people and contained 8 per cent of the Dutch total. But Amsterdam by this time had ceased to grow quickly and a century later had increased only to about 200,000, or 9 per cent of the total.[2]

These rough facts suggest immediately that it may be valuable to look more closely at the rapid growth of London between 1650 and 1750. Anything which distinguished England from other parts of Europe during the century preceding the industrial revolution is necessarily a subject of particular interest since it may help to throw light on the origins of that extraordinary and momentous period of rapid change which has transformed country after country across the face of the globe.

I

It is convenient to begin by examining first some demographic aspects of the rapid growth of population which took place in London. The implications of London's growth can be seen from a very simple model. The rates and quantities embodied in the model are at best approximations, and it is probable that within the next five years work already in train will make it possible to give much more precise estimates than can be made as yet; but it would require

[2] See Hélin, *La démographie de Liège*, p. 242, and Faber *et al. A.A.G. Bijdragen*, xii (1965), pp. 58, 110. It should perhaps be said that only in countries like England, France and the Netherlands, if anywhere, does it make sense to relate city and national population totals. In areas like Germany, Italy or Spain, political or economic fragmentation makes this a pointless exercise. The only cities in Europe with populations of 100,000 or more *c.* 1650 apart from London, Paris and Amsterdam were Naples which was a very large city (250,000–300,000), and Palermo, Venice, Rome and Lisbon (all 100,000–125,000); none of these grew much in the following century. By the mid-eighteenth century Vienna and Berlin were in this size class (*c.* 175,000 and 110,000 respectively), and perhaps Lyons. See Hélin, *La démographie de Liège*, pp. 244, 247, 249. 251.

a radical revision of the assumptions used here to upset the general argument.

We may note first that since the population of London rose by about 275,000 between 1650 and 1750 it will on an average have been increasing annually by 2,750. Secondly, it seems clear that the crude death rate in London was substantially higher than the crude birth rate over the period as a whole. The gap between the two rates is difficult to estimate accurately and varied considerably during the hundred years in question, being apparently much higher in the last three or four decades of the period than earlier. The difference between the two rates is most unlikely to have been less than 10 per 1,000 per annum over the century as a whole, however, and may well have been considerably larger.[3] For the purpose of illustrating the implications of the model we may assume that this figure held throughout. Thus at the time when the population of London was, say, 500,000 the shortfall of births each year is assumed to be 5,000. At that time to make good this shortfall and to permit an annual increase of the total population of 2,750, the net immigration into London must have been about 8,000 per annum.

---

[3] The uncertainty arises because of the problem of under-registration. Jones and Judges underlined this heavily in their examination of London's population at the end of the seventeenth century. They were able to show wide discrepancies between totals of baptisms and burials drawn from the three available sources: the returns made under the Marriage Duty Act of 1694, the Bills of Mortality, and the counts made in parish registers at Rickman's behest in 1801. See Jones and Judges, *Econ. Hist. Rev.* (1935–6). Glass has made estimates of the degree of under-registration of baptisms and burials in the parish registers and the collectors' returns under the 1694 act for two city parishes: Glass, *London Rec. Soc. Pub.* ii (1966), pp. xxxv–xxxvii. There is a convenient summary of some of the available data in George, *London life*, pp. 405–10. Gregory King made estimates based on a notional time of peace which imply only a rather small burial surplus in the capital (about 4 per 1,000); however, elsewhere he produced figures for the year 1695 which suggest a much larger shortfall of baptisms: *Two tracts by Gregory King*, esp. pp. 27, 43. It is worth noting that Deane and Cole suggest a rate of natural increase for London in the period 1701–50 of −10.8 per cent per annum and envisage an annual average net immigration into London of 10–12,000 (it should be added that they regard London's population as stationary in number during this half century): Deane and Cole, *British economic growth*, table 26, p. 115 and p. 11. William Farr thought the London death rate in the later seventeenth century was 80 per 1,000 declining to 50 per 1,000 in the eighteenth century: Farr, *Vital statistics*, p. 131. Buer estimated that between 1700 and 1750 London needed an average immigration of 10,200 a year to maintain her population, and that during this period the ratio of deaths to births was 3 to 2: Buer, *Health, wealth and population*, p. 33.

Towards the end of the period when the population of London was well above half a million and the gap between birth and death rates was at its greatest, the net figure must have been considerably larger than this. At other times it may have been rather less.

In any population it is normally the young and single who migrate most readily. There is a growing volume of evidence that in England in the seventeenth and eighteenth centuries mobility before marriage was very high but was reduced once marriage had taken place.[4] In view of this, let us assume, as a part of the demographic model of London's growth, that the mean age of those migrating into London was twenty years. Given the mortality conditions of the day any large group of twenty-year-olds coming into London would represent the survivors of a birth population at least half as large again. Some 12,000 births, therefore, in the rest of England and elsewhere were earmarked, as it were, each year to make it possible for London's population to grow as it did during this period. Once again this is a very rough figure, too high for a part of the century, too low for the later decades, but useful as a means of illustrating the nature of the general demographic relationship between London and the rest of the country.

One further assumption will make the significance of this relationship clearer. If the average surplus of births over deaths in provincial England was 5 per 1,000 per annum (and assuming for the moment that London grew by immigration from England alone), then it follows that London's growth was absorbing the natural increase of a population of some two-and-a-half millions.[5] The total population of England excluding London was only about five million (varying, of course, a little over the century in question), and there were some areas, especially in the west and north, in which for much of this century there was either no natural increase, or even a natural decrease of population.

---

[4] This appears very clearly in family reconstitution work based on parish registers. The analysis of successive nominal listings of inhabitants supports the same conclusion. See Laslett and Harrison in Bell and Ollard (eds.), *Historical essays*.

[5] A rate of increase of 5 per 1,000 is a generous estimate for this period. Gregory King supposed that the annual number of births in England excluding London was 170,000 and of deaths 148,000. Assuming the population of England without London to have been 4.9 million, this suggests a difference between the two rates of about 4.5 per 1,000. But King uses different assumptions elsewhere and presents material which implies a rate of increase less than half as high: *Two tracts by Gregory King*, pp. 25, 27.

In view of the general demographic history of England at this time London's demographic characteristics assume a singular importance. For there are some surprising features in English demographic history in the century 1650–1750. Family reconstitution studies show that in some parts of the country at least this was a time of very late first marriage for women. And the reduced fertility which is usually associated with a rise in the average age of women at first marriage appears to have been still further diminished in places by the practice of family limitation. Moreover, there is some evidence that age-specific mortality rates, especially of young children, were higher at this time than either earlier or later, so that natural increase was much reduced or was replaced by a surplus of deaths over births.[6]

The preliminary results of a large-scale survey of parish register material using straightforward aggregative methods[7] suggest that these trends were least evident in the home counties and the Midlands, the areas from which access to London was easiest; and it may prove to be the case that a substantial surplus of births continued to be characteristic of these counties throughout the century 1650–1750 but that, instead of building up local populations, the surplus was siphoned off into London to counterbalance the burial surplus there, and to enable it to continue to grow quickly at a time when the rest of the country was barely holding its own.[8] The absence of any great upward press of numbers in England as a whole in this century meant that population growth did not frustrate a slow rise in real incomes, in contrast with the preceding hundred years.[9] Yet this did not prevent a very marked growth in the country's largest city.

One further implication of the demography of London's growth

[6] On these points see Wrigley, *Econ. Hist. Rev.* (1966) and *Daedalus* (1968).

[7] The survey has been carried out by the Cambridge Group for the History of Population and Social Structure. More than two hundred local historians have been kind enough to help in this work.

8 The London apprenticeship records show that the proportion of apprentices coming from the north and west fell dramatically during the seventeenth century, while the proportion from the home counties rose. One reason for this may well have been the disappearance of a surplus of births in the north and west and its continuance near London. See Stone, *Past and Present* (1966), pp. 31–2. Marshall noted that the great bulk of the inter-county migration from Bedfordshire was to London: Marshall, *Beds. Hist. Rec. Soc.* (1934), p. 45.

9 See Wrigley, *Econ. Hist. Rev.* (1966), pp. 106–8.

is worth stressing. Let us assume that there was a time when the population of London was 500,000 and the population of the rest of the kingdom was 5,000,000. Let it further be assumed that the birth rate was uniformly at a rate of 34 per 1,000 (this is an arbitrary assumption but too little is known of the age and sex structure of these populations and of the prevailing age-specific fertility rates to provide substantially more accurate figures; and in any case the main line of the argument would be unaffected except by radical adjustments). If this were so, then the number of births taking place annually in London would be 17,000 and in the rest of the country 170,000. If we assume that all the children born in London remained in London, and if to the figure of 17,000 children born each year in London is added the 12,000 born in the provinces and needed to maintain London's growth, then it is apparent that the survivors to adult years of almost one sixth of all the births taking place in the country (29,000 out of a total of 187,000) would be living in London twenty years or so after the arrival of the birth cohort used as an illustration.

It does not, of course, follow from this that a sixth of the national total of adults lived in London. The infant and child mortality rates of those born in London were far higher than elsewhere so that many fewer of these children survived to adult years. Indeed the fact that this was so is one of the main reasons for the large inflow of migrants from outside London. The calculation assumes, moreover, that immigrants to London came only from England, whereas there was also, of course, a steady stream of young Scots, Welsh and Irish into the capital. Nor should it be forgotten that London was a great international centre with substantial Dutch, French and German communities.

On the other hand, all the calculations made above are based on figures of *net* immigration into London. The gross figures must certainly have been considerably higher since there was at all times a flow of migrants out of London as well as a heavier flow inward. If therefore one were attempting to estimate the proportion of the total adult population of England who had at some stage in their lives had direct experience of life in the great city, a sixth or an even higher fraction is as plausible a guess as any other.[10]

[10] See George, *London life*, pp. 109–10, for an interesting discussion of the chief types of migrants into and out of London. She suggests that the settlement laws tended to encourage rather than prevent migration and that

II

If it is fair to assume that one adult in six in England in this period had had direct experience of London life, it is probably also fair to assume that this must have acted as a powerful solvent of the customs, prejudices and modes of action of traditional, rural England. The leaven of change would have a much better chance of transforming the lump than in, say, France even if living in Paris produced the same change of attitude and action as living in London, since there were proportionately four or five times fewer Frenchmen caught up in Parisian life than Englishmen in London life. Possibly there is a threshold level in a situation of this type, beneath which the values and attitudes of a traditional, rural society are very little affected by the existence of a large city, but above which a sufficiently large proportion of the population is exposed to a different way of life to effect a slow transformation in rural society. Too little is known of the sociological differences between life in London and life in provincial England to afford a clear perception of the impact of London's growth upon the country as a whole. Some things, however, are already known, and other points can be adumbrated in the hope that more research will resolve present uncertainties.

London was so very much bigger than any other town in the country that the lives of the inhabitants of London were inevitably very different from the lives of men living in the middle rank of towns, such as Leicester or Derby, where local landed society could continue to dominate many aspects of town life and the ties with the surrounding countryside were ancient and intimate. Family life in London, at least for the very large number who had come to London from elsewhere, was necessarily different from the family life of those who lived within five or ten miles of their birthplace all their lives. Near relatives were less likely to live close at hand. Households in the central parts of London were larger on

London exercised a strong attraction upon those dislodged from their original settlement. She also quotes a contemporary, Burrington, writing in 1757, who thought that two-thirds of London's adult population came from 'distant parts'. The records of the Westminster General Dispensary between 1774 and 1781 reveal that only a quarter (824 out of 3,236) of the married people served were London born. Of the rest, 209 were born in Scotland, 280 in Ireland and 53 abroad, a total of 542 in the three categories, or 17 per cent. The balance were born elsewhere in England or Wales: *ibid.* p. 111.

average than those in provincial England. And this was not because the conjugal families contained more children but because other members of the households were more numerous. There were many more lodgers than in the countryside, as well as servants, apprentices and other kin in varying proportions according to the social type of the parish.[11]

Outside the household, moreover, a far higher proportion of day-to-day contacts was inevitably casual. Urban sociologists describe the characteristic tendency of modern city life to cause individuals in these circumstances to be treated not as occupying an invariable status position in the community, but in terms of the role associated with the particular transaction which gave rise to the fleeting contact. They stress the encouragement which city life gives to what Weber called 'rational' as opposed to 'traditional' patterns of action and the tendency for contract to replace custom. The ' "aping" of one's betters' which often attracted unfavourable comment at the time, and which has sometimes been seen as a powerful influence in establishing new patterns of consumption, is a common product of social situations like that in which the inhabitants of London found themselves at this period. Coleman has recently suggested that in the seventeenth century there was probably a backward-sloping supply curve for labour.[12] It would be fascinating to know how far the new patterns of consumption behaviour established in London may have helped to reduce any preference for leisure rather than high earnings. There is much literary evidence of the shiftless and disorderly behaviour of many members of London's population at this time, but there were important countervailing influences at work upon the bulk of the population. The shop, a most important, new influence upon consumer behaviour, was a normal feature of the London scene by the latter half of the seventeenth century.[13] Sugar, tea and tobacco had become articles of mass consumption by the early eighteenth century. Life in London probably encouraged educational achievement in a wider spectrum of the population than might be expected. In 1838–9 fewer men and women were unable to sign their names on marriage than anywhere else in the country (marks were made as a substitute for signatures by only 12 per cent of

[11] Glass's analysis of some of these London parish listings, though only a first survey of the material, provides much valuable information about the city: Glass, *London Rec. Soc. Pub.* ii (1966).

[12] Coleman in Carus-Wilson (ed.), *Essays in economic history*, ii, p. 303.

[13] John in Carus-Wilson (ed.), *Essays in economic history*, ii, pp. 366, 369.

grooms and 24 per cent of brides, whereas the national averages were 33 per cent and 49 per cent respectively). How long this differential had existed is not yet known but if it proves to have been true of earlier periods in London's history also, it suggests that the London environment put a high premium on at least a minimum degree of literacy.[14]

There were many ways in which seventeenth-century London differed from a modern city. Glass, for example, notes that in 1695 the proportion of wealthy and substantial households was highest near the centre of London and tended to fall with distance from the centre, being very low outside the city walls (apart from St Dunstan in the west). 'This kind of gradient is in contrast to that found in the modern city, in which the centrifugal movement of population has occurred particularly among the middle classes.'[15] In this respect London was still in 1695 a pre-industrial city, but in general London was far removed from the classical type of pre-industrial city. Sjoberg's account of the typical pre-industrial city may serve as a means of underlining the 'modernity' of London at this point. He draws illustrative material not only from the cities of Asia today, from ancient Mesopotamia and the Near East, and from the classical cultures of the Mediterranean, but also from medieval Europe.

Sjoberg's pre-industrial city is fed because the city houses the ruling elite. The elite 'induces the peasantry to increase its production and relinquish some of its harvest to the urban community'. It 'must persuade many persons subsisting, relative to industrial standards, on the very margins of existence, under conditions of near starvation or malnutrition, to surrender food and other items that they themselves could readily use'.[16] The farmer 'brings his produce to the urban centers at irregular intervals and in varying amounts'.[17] Within the city the merchants, those responsible for the organization of much of its economic life, are 'ideally excluded from membership of the elite'. A few manage to achieve high status under sufferance, but 'most are unequivocally in the lower class or outcaste groups'.[18]

---

[14] Registrar-General, *First Annual Report*, pp. 8–9. The materials assembled by Dr R. S. Schofield at the Cambridge Group show that exceptionally few Londoners were illiterate (in the sense of being unable to sign their names in marriage registers) during the hundred years preceding the inception of civil registration.

[15] Glass, *London Rec. Soc. Pub.* ii, p. xxi.

[16] Sjoberg, *Preindustrial city*, p. 118.

[17] *Ibid.* p. 207.   [18] *Ibid.* pp. 120, 121.

The chief reason for excluding merchants is that they necessarily meet all types of people, making casual contacts with men in all positions, and are therefore a menace to the stability of the existing societal arrangements.[19] Men are largely indifferent to the discipline of the clock and only half attentive to the passage of time. Almost all transactions, however trivial, are concluded only after long haggling.[20] There is little specialization of function in craft industrial production, though a good deal of product specialization.[21]

In the pre-industrial city the dominant type of family is the extended family, though necessity may prevent it developing so fully in the lower classes as in the elite.[22] Marriage takes place early, and before marriage a man does not reach full adult status.[23] On marriage the bride normally expects to move into the household of her husband's family.[24] 'However, as industrial-urbanization becomes firmly entrenched, the large extended household is no longer the ideal toward which people strive. The conjugal family system now becomes the accepted, and often the preferred norm.' This occurs because 'a fluid, flexible, small family unit is necessarily the dominant form in a social order characterized by extensive social and spatial mobility'.[25]

In his anxiety to correct the naive assumptions of some sociologists about cities in the past and in the developing world today, Sjoberg may well have been tempted to straitjacket his material at times in a way which does violence to history. At all events, not only London but all England had moved far from his archetypal pre-industrial society by the seventeenth century. The conjugal family system was firmly established in England at that time. On marriage a man and his wife set up a new household.[26] And both sexes married late, later than in England today, and far later than in extra-European societies in which marriage, for women at least, almost invariably occurred at or even before puberty.[27] Where three generations did live together in the same household this was not usually because a son on marriage brought his wife to his parents' home, but because a grandparent came to live in the household of a

[19] *Ibid.* p. 136.   [20] *Ibid.* pp. 204–5, 209–10.
[21] *Ibid.* p. 197.   [22] *Ibid.* pp. 157–9.
[23] *Ibid.* pp. 145–6.   [24] *Ibid.* p. 157.   [25] *Ibid.* p. 162.
[26] Laslett, *The world we have lost*, pp. 90–2.
[27] Hajnal in Glass and Eversley (eds.), *Population in history*. Also Wrigley, *Econ. Hist. Rev.* (1966), and, more generally, Goode, *World revolution and family patterns.*

married son or daughter when no longer able to look after himself or herself, for example on the death of a spouse.

London shared these sociological and demographic characteristics with the rest of the country. Three-generational households were possibly rather commoner in the wealthier parts of London than was usual elsewhere,[28] but everywhere the conjugal family appears to have been the dominant form. The status of merchants in London varied with their wealth but it would be difficult to argue that they were largely excluded from the ruling elite. The provisioning of London was secured by an elaborate and sophisticated set of economic institutions and activities, and many of the farmers who sent their produce to the London market geared their land to commodity production in a thoroughly 'modern' fashion. In short, whereas pre-industrial cities might grow large and powerful without in any way undermining the structure of traditional society, a city like London in the later seventeenth century was so constituted sociologically, demographically and economically that it could well reinforce and accelerate incipient change.

What might be called the demonstration effect of London's wealth and growth, for instance, played an important part in engendering changes elsewhere. London contained many men of great wealth and power whose sources of wealth did not lie in the land and who found it possible to maintain power and status without acquiring large landed estates.[29] Indeed in as much as it was the backing of London which assured the Parliamentary armies of success in their struggle with the king, London could be said at the beginning of the century 1650–1750 to have shown that it possessed the power necessary to sway the rest of the country to its will. In the provinces in the later seventeenth and early eighteenth centuries there were increasingly large numbers of men of wealth and position who stood outside the traditional landed system. These were the group whom Everitt has recently termed the 'pseudo-

---

[28] Glass, *London Rec. Soc. Pub.* ii, pp. xxxii–xxxiv.

[29] Stone discussing the wealth generated by the great commercial expansion of the late seventeenth century remarks, 'The closing down of the land market suggests that, however it was distributed, less of this wealth than before was being converted into social status by the purchase of an estate, and more of it was being reinvested in long-term mortgages, commerce and banking.' One reason for less money being invested in land was perhaps simply that rich Londoners no longer felt moved to use money in this way if their status did not suffer by refraining from acquiring land. See Stone, *Past and Present* (1966), p. 34.

gentry'. They formed 'that class of leisured and predominantly urban families who, by their manner of life, were commonly regarded as gentry, though they were not supported by a landed estate'.[30] Their links with London were close and their journeys thither frequent. They were urban in their habit of life but would have been powerless to protect their position in society if London had not existed. London both provided them with a pattern of behaviour, and, because of its immense economic strength and prestige, protected them from any hostility on the part of the traditional elements in society. London was, as it were, both their normative reference group[31] and their guarantee against the withdrawal of status respect.

III

The social and economic changes of the seventeenth and eighteenth centuries reached their culmination in the industrial revolution. Although this was far more than simply an economic phenomenon, economic change was what defined it. It is natural, therefore, to consider the strictly economic effects of London's rapid growth as well as the demographic and sociological changes which accompanied it.

The importance of the London food market in promoting change in the agriculture of Kent and East Anglia from an early date has long been recognized. Fisher showed how even during the century before 1650 London was large enough to exercise a great influence upon the agriculture of the surrounding counties, causing a rapid spread of market gardening, increasing local specialization, and encouraging the wholesalers to move back up the chain of production and exchange to engage directly in the production of food, or to sink capital in the improvement of productive facilities. The influence of the London food market was 'not merely in the direction of increased production but also in that of specialization, and in that direction lay agricultural progress' – 'Poulterers made loans to warreners and themselves bred poultry. Fruiterers helped to establish orchards and leased them when established. Butchers themselves became graziers.' Between 1650 and 1750 it is reasonable to suppose

---

30 Everitt, *Past and Present* (1966), p. 71.
31 To use the term employed by Runciman in a very lucid exposition of the concept of the reference group generally: Runciman, *Relative deprivation*, ch. 2.

that the demand for food in the London market must have increased by about three-quarters since population increased roughly in that proportion. The increased demand was met from home sources rather than by import, and it follows that all those changes which Fisher observed in the preceding century were spread over a larger area and intensified.[32]

Once more it is interesting to work initially in terms of a very crude model and review its implications, though in this case the orders of magnitude assumed are even more open to question than those embodied in the demographic model used earlier. Suppose, firstly, that in 1650 the population of London was 400,000 and the population of the rest of the country 5,100,000 and that in the country outside the metropolis the proportion of the male labour force engaged in agriculture was 60 per cent.[33] This would imply that 3,060,000 were dependent on agriculture (those directly employed plus their families), and that every 100 farming families supported a total of 80 families who earned their living in other ways. If in the next century the population of London rose to 675,000 and that of the whole country to 6,140,000[34] but the pro-

---

[32] Fisher, *Econ. Hist. Rev.* (1934–5), pp. 56, 63. The steady spread of the influence of London is well illustrated by the remark of a contemporary, John Houghton, who wrote *à propos* meat production for the London market, 'The bigness and greatness of London doth not only encourage the breeders of provisions and higglers thirty miles off but even to four score miles. Wherefore I think it will necessarily follow. . .that if London should consume as much again country for eighty miles around would have greater employment or else those that are further off would have some of it' (Houghton, *A collection of letters*, pp. 165–6). I owe this reference to the kindness of Dr J. Thirsk.

[33] This is once more rather an arbitrary figure. Different assumptions about its size produce slightly higher or lower estimates of increase in agricultural production per head. A higher percentage engaged in agriculture will result in a lower figure of increased productivity and *vice versa*. The Tawneys' analysis of the Gloucestershire Muster Roll of 1608 suggests that a rather lower figure might have been appropriate: Tawney and Tawney, *Econ. Hist. Rev.* (1934–5), esp. p. 39. Gregory King's work does not lend itself to a breakdown along these lines but is consistent with a figure of 60 per cent or slightly higher. This is true also of the analyses of listings of inhabitants surviving from the period. Stone's assumption, based partly on King, that 90 per cent of the population (presumptively in the mid-seventeenth century) were manual workers on the land is very difficult to accept. Even at the peak of the harvest period when men normally engaged in other pursuits might work on the land this would be an extraordinarily high figure. See Stone. *Past and Present* (1966), p. 20.

[34] Brownlee's estimate, supported by Deane and Cole: Deane and Cole, *British economic growth*, pp. 5–6.

portion engaged in agriculture outside the capital remained the same, then the agricultural population in 1750 would have numbered 3,279,000 and every 100 farming families would have supported 87 other families.[35] This in turn would imply a rise in agricultural productivity per head of about 4 per cent. This figure is certainly too low, however, since this was a century of rising exports of grain, especially after 1700. By 1750 exports formed about 6 per cent of total grain production; at the beginning of the century they were only a little over 1 per cent.[36] Grain was not, of course, the only product of agriculture, but there were parallel movements in some other _agricultural_ products. Imports of wool, for example, fell markedly in the early eighteenth century, while domestic production rose. There was a sharp rise in the production of mutton, though not of beef, and some minor agricultural products, notably hops, were grown in greater quantities.[37] All in all it is reasonable to suppose that these changes represent a rise of not less than 5 per cent in agricultural productivity per head. This, in combination with the rise which must have occurred in meeting London's demands, suggests a rise of about 10 per cent in agricultural productivity per head.

A rise of 10 per cent in productivity is far from trivial. It could have released a substantial amount of purchasing power into other channels as the price of foodstuffs fell and at the same time have made it possible for a substantially higher proportion of the population to be drawn into secondary and tertiary employment. The rise, however, is almost certainly understated at 10 per cent, since the percentage of the total labour force outside the capital engaged in agriculture probably fell somewhat, implying a still steeper rise in agricultural productivity per head. It has been suggested, indeed, that the numbers engaged in agriculture actually fell in the first half of the eighteenth century.[38] This is an extreme hypothesis. Suppose, however, that the population dependent on agriculture rose only

---

[35] This assumes that farming and non-farming families were of the same average size, but could be rephrased without damaging the sense of the passage if this assumption were denied.

[36] Deane and Cole, _British economic growth_, table 17, p. 65.

[37] For wool see Deane and Cole, _British economic growth_, p. 68 and Mitchell and Deane, _British historical statistics_, pp. 190–1. For mutton and beef, see Deane and Cole, pp. 68–71. For hops see Ashton, _An economic history of England_, p. 240.

[38] Deane and Cole, _British economic growth_, p. 75.

from 3,060,000 to 3,150,000 between 1650 and 1750, and not to 3,279,000 as in the first variant of the model (that is the proportion engaged in agriculture fell over the century from 60 to $57\frac{1}{2}$ per cent of the total population outside London). If this were the case, and making the suggested allowance also for growing exports and declining imports, then the rise in agricultural productivity per head would be about 13 per cent during the century. This is not an extreme figure. Indeed it is very probably too low. Deane and Cole suggest that the rise may have been as high as 25 per cent in the first half of the eighteenth century alone.[39] But a rise in agricultural productivity even of this magnitude is a formidable achievement and goes far to suggesting how a pre-industrial economy can slowly lever itself up by its own bootstraps to the point where a rapid growth of secondary industry can occur. The fact that income elasticity of demand for food is substantially less than unity makes it easy to understand how grain prices might sag in these circumstances and how considerable the diversion of purchasing power into the products of secondary industry may have been.

It does not follow from the above, of course, that the considerable rise in agricultural productivity per head which appears to have taken place was due to London's growth in its entirety. What can be said is that the steady growth in demand for food in London as population there increased, necessarily caused great changes in the methods used on farms over a wider and wider area, in the commercial organization of the food market, and in the transport of food. It must also have tended to increase the proportion of people living outside London who were not engaged directly in agriculture since tertiary employment was sure to increase in these circumstances. Drovers, carters, badgers, brokers, cattle dealers, corn chandlers, hostlers, innkeepers and the like grew more and more numerous as larger and larger fractions of the year's flocks and crops were consumed at a distance from the areas in which they were produced. As yet it is difficult to quantify the changes in employment structure satisfactorily, but many parish registers began regularly to record occupations from the later seventeenth or early eighteenth centuries onwards,[40] and it is therefore a fairly straight-

[39] *Ibid.* p. 75.
[40] In the case of marriages the occupation of the groom was given; in baptism and burial entries the occupation of the head of the household in which the birth or death had occurred. Frequently occupations were noted in only one or two of the series rather than in all three.

forward matter to produce a picture of changing employment structure for this period for many parts of the country, given sufficient time and effort. Such an exercise may well reveal not only a slow fall in the proportion of men directly employed on the land, but also differences in the timing and speed of change related to the accessibility of the market.

There were other ways in which the immense demands of the London market helped to promote economic and technological changes in the structure of English production during this period. The inhabitants of London needed fuel as well as food, and before the end of the sixteenth century they were beginning to abandon wood for coal as the chief source of domestic fuel. The annual shipment of coal south along the coast from Tyneside and Wearside had reached about 650,000 tons by 1750, having doubled in the preceding hundred years.[41] This represented a very substantial fraction of the total production of coal in the north-east, and perhaps as much as a sixth of the total national production. Coal production in England was on a much larger scale during these years than in any other country in Europe, and the coal industry was the forcing house for many of the technical improvements which were to come to a fuller fruition during the classical years of the industrial revolution. Newcomen's engine was developed largely to meet the drainage problem in coal mines and found its largest sale among mine-owners. And it was in the Newcastle area that the first railways were constructed to enable horses to pull much heavier loads from the pitheads to the coal staithes. The first beginnings of the new technology of the steam engine and the railway lay in the eighteenth-century coal-mining industry, and one of its chief supports in turn was the large and steadily growing demand for coal afforded by the London coal market.[42]

Furthermore, the increased shipment of coal down the east coast to the Thames required a major expansion in shipping capacity. Nef estimated that during this period about half the total tonnage of the English merchant marine was engaged in the Newcastle coal trade.

When we add, to the ships employed by the coal trade from Durham and Northumberland, the ships employed by that from

---

[41] Nef, *Rise of the British coal industry*, ii, pp. 381–2.
[42] I have discussed these changes from a different viewpoint and at greater length elsewhere: Wrigley, *Econ. Hist. Rev.* (1962).

Scottish and west-coast ports, it seems likely that, at the time of the Restoration, the tonnage of colliers had come to exceed the tonnage of all other British merchantmen. The coal trade from Newcastle to London was relatively no less important in the late seventeenth century than in the late eighteenth century, when, Adam Smith observes, it 'Employs more shipping than all the carrying trades of England'.[43]

Apart from serving as an important reservoir of trained seamen in time of war, the growth of the coal trade played a notable part in the expansion of the English shipbuilding industry and the development of vessels which could be worked by far fewer hands per ton of cargo.[44]

The crude quantification of the importance of the London coal trade can be approached in a different way. If output per man-year of coalminers at this time was about 200 tons in favourable circumstances,[45] then by 1750 some 3,500 men must have been engaged in digging London's coal. Gregory King supposed that about 50,000 men were employed in his day as common seamen[46] and it is therefore probable that at least a further 10,000 men[47] were employed on the colliers easing their way up and down the east coast (though the ships were laid up in the winter so that the employment was heavily seasonal). In addition the movement of coal to the staithes must have been the livelihood of hundreds of carters, waggoners and coal heavers.[48] In all the total employment afforded by the London coal trade outside London (except in as much as the sailors were Londoners) may well have risen from about 8,000 in

[43] Nef, *Rise of the British coal industry*, i, pp. 239–40.

[44] It is interesting to remember John's comment on the growth of the export trade in corn at this time: 'Grain became a major bulk cargo and between 1730 and 1763 about 110,000–130,000 tons were, on an average, carried annually from English ports in ships which only occasionally exceeded a hundred tons burthen. This had its effect upon the more efficient use of shipping, upon investment in shipbuilding and upon the employment of dock-side labour.' Coal shipments along the coast at this time were running at about five times the level of corn shipments by tonnage. John in Carus-Wilson (ed.), *Essays in economic history*, ii, p. 364.

[45] Nef, *Rise of the British coal industry*, ii, p. 138.

[46] *Two tracts by Gregory King*, p. 31.

[47] The problem of moving coal in bulk by sea brought about a substantial saving in men employed per ton of cargo moved during the seventeenth century. For this reason it is likely that fewer men were employed on colliers than might be expected in view of their large share in the tonnage of the English merchant marine. Nef, *Rise of the British coal industry*, i, pp. 390–2.

[48] *Ibid.* ii, p. 142.

the mid-seventeenth century to 15,000 a century later. Including their families increases the numbers directly dependent on the coal trade to about 25,000 and 50,000 people respectively. The multiplier effect of the presence and growth of London is well illustrated by this example. Secondary and tertiary employment increased considerably at a distance as well as in London itself.[49] No doubt the flourishing state of the mines round Newcastle and the consequent local demand for food produced in miniature in that area the sort of changes in agriculture which London had already produced in the home counties at an earlier date.

London's importance as a centre of consumption, which prompted Defoe in 1724 to write of the 'general dependence of the whole country upon the city of London...for the consumption of its produce',[50] sprang not only from its size but also from the relatively high level of wages prevailing there. Gilboy's work on eighteenth-century wage rates provides evidence of this. 'The London laborer had the highest wages of any group we have examined. In the first part of the century, at least, he had surplus income to spend and there is every indication that real wages improved as the century progressed.'[51] When George remarked that 'as early as 1751 it was said that the shoes sold in London were chiefly made in the country where labour was cheaper',[52] she was touching upon a general phenomenon. Men and women were put in work over much of the home counties and Midlands because their labour was much cheaper than the labour of London artisans and journeymen. The existence of a mass of relatively well paid labour in London played a major part in creating new levels of real wages and new standards of consumption in the century after the Restoration, when 'there was a rise in internal demand which permanently affected the level of expectation of most classes in English society'.[53]

Access to the London market was the making of many a manufacturer and a forcing house of change in methods of manufacture,

[49] This is true of a wide range of manufacturing and service industries. Fisher, for example, noted that London had no malting facilities and few corn mills, 'Consequently, a number of country towns found their major employment in the processing of the city's corn, and their inhabitants a regular occupation as middlemen' (Fisher, *Econ. Hist. Rev.* (1934–5), p. 60).

[50] *Ibid.* p. 51.

[51] Gilboy, *Wages in eighteenth century England*, p. 241. See also chaps. 1 and 2.

[52] George, *London life*, p. 198.

[53] John in Carus-Wilson (ed.), *Essays in economic history*, ii, p. 373.

in marketing techniques and in systems of distribution. Josiah Wedgwood was drawn thither.

[He] was quick to realize the value of a warehouse in London. For high quality goods he needed a market accustomed to 'fine prices'. He was not likely to find it in the annual market fairs of Staffordshire – the time-honoured *entrepôt* of their county's pots – nor among the country folk who haggled over their wares straight from the crateman's back or the hawker's basket, and to whom expense was the controlling factor in deciding their custom.[54]

But this did not isolate him from mass markets. Once having secured the custom of the London elite he was able to sell his less expensive lines to the middle and lower classes. He studied closely the idiosyncrasies of each group at home and abroad and produced goods designed to appeal peculiarly to each of them. 'By these means Wedgwood had created an enormous demand for his ware both ornamental and useful. The upper classes bought both, but mainly the expensive ornamental wares, and in imitation of their social superiors the lower classes bought the useful.'[55] Moreover, his efforts to command a countrywide market drew him into canal construction and the promotion of turnpike trusts.[56]

Wedgwood was one of the most original and successful entrepreneurs of his age. The actions of his fellows seldom show the same appreciation of the opportunities for new methods. And his product may have lent itself more than most to illustrating the sense in which a triumph in London opened up the markets of the whole country. Yet it is reasonable to quote his example, for his success hinged upon an economic and social fact of importance before Wedgwood's time – through the London market the whole country might be won.

For a fashionable appeal in London had a vital influence even in the depths of the provinces. The woman in Newcastle upon Tyne who insisted on a dinner service of 'Arabesque Border' before her local shopkeeper had even heard of it, wanted it because it was 'much used in London at present', and she steadfastly 'declin'd taking any till she had seen that pattern'.[57]

The London market, of course, supported many industries within the city itself. Silk weaving at Spitalfields, brewing, gin manufacture,

[54] McKendrick, *Econ. Hist. Rev.* (1959–60), pp. 418–19.
[55] *Ibid.* p. 429.   [56] *Ibid.* p. 429.   [57] *Ibid.* p. 420.

watch and clock making, cabinet making, the manufacture of soap, glass and furniture, and a wide range of luxury industries have all received notice. They all added to the economic weight of London, and furthered its growth, though few of them produced striking technological advances or were transformed into path-breaking industries during the industrial revolution. They were impressive in their range but were not for the most part greatly different in kind from the industries to be found in large cities elsewhere in Europe. London's prime economic foundation, however, had long been her trade rather than her industry. English trade expanded greatly during the century and London enjoyed the lion's share of it. It has been estimated that a quarter of the population depended directly on employment in port trades in 1700 and, allowing for the multiplier effect of this employment, 'it is clear that the greatness of London depended, before everything else, on the activity in the port of London'.[58] London's merchants, not her manufacturers, dominated her activities economically and politically, and it has long been a momentous question how best to conceive the mechanism by which the large fortunes made in London from commerce helped to transform the national economy.

Many London merchants bought land in the country. Some in doing so hastened agricultural change. The banking and general commercial facilities of London were available to men throughout England and played some part in financing the agricultural and industrial changes which occurred in many parts of the country. The success of the London merchants fostered a change of attitude towards trade. It helped to fulfil one of the necessary conditions of rapid economic growth in Leibenstein's analysis – that 'the rate of growth of the new entrepreneurial class must be sufficiently rapid and its success, power and importance sufficiently evident so that entrepreneurship, in some form or other, becomes an "honorific" mode of life in men's minds'.[59] But it is doubtful whether the prime connection between the growth of London and the great changes going forward outside London is to be sought in points of this type. London's trading pre-eminence is perhaps better conceived as acting more powerfully at one remove. It was the fact that the

---

[58] Davis, *Rise of the English shipping industry*, p. 390. See also pp. 34–5 on the rapid growth of English commerce and London's predominance among English ports.

[59] Leibenstein, *Economic backwardness*, p. 129.

growth of her trading wealth enabled London herself to grow, to develop as a centre of consumption, and to dominate English society, which formed her greatest contribution to the total process of change in the country as a whole. The relationship between rising trading wealth and economic and social change outside London was primarily, as it were, indirect, springing from the changes which the steady growth of London provoked elsewhere in ways already discussed. While other big European cities during this century could do little more than maintain their population size, London almost doubled her population. Already as large as any other European city in 1650, it was much larger than any rival a century later. In order to meet the food and fuel requirements of a city of this size old methods in many cases were simply inadequate. And the new methods developed often produced those substantial increases in productivity per head which form the most promising base for a continuing beneficent spiral of economic activity.

IV

It is always well to be chary of accepting explanations which explain too much. The industrial revolution in England was a vastly complex congerie of changes so diverse that it would be absurd to suppose that any one development of earlier times can serve to explain more than a part of it. It will not do to pyramid everything upon changes in the supply of capital, or the burgeoning of Nonconformist entrepreneurship, or an increase in upward social mobility. Complicated results had, in this case at least, complicated origins. It is therefore no part of this argument that the growth of London in the century before 1750 was the sole engine of change in the country, to which all the chief preconditions of the industrial revolution can be traced. But London's growth is a fine vantage point from which to review much that was happening. The period between the rapid rise in population and economic activity which ended early in the seventeenth century and the onset of renewed rapid growth of population and production in the last third of the eighteenth century has remained something of an enigma in economic history. It was a period in which population grew little if at all over the country as a whole. In some areas for long periods it was probably falling. Many of the chief indices of production, when estimates of them are possible, show comparatively little change and certainly grew much less spectacularly than either before or after.[60] There was a slow, if cumulatively important, improvement in agricultural productivity because of the introduction of new crops like roots and clover, and because there was both a slow drift of land into enclosure and increasing flexibility of land use in the champion areas. Trade and industry expanded but in general at a modest rate.

How then should this period be understood? It was immediately followed by a period which saw the birth of a radically new economic system, the transition from the pre-industrial to the industrial world. Was England in 1750 greatly improved when compared with the England of the Commonwealth as a springboard for rapid economic and social change? Was the triggering off of the period of rapid growth connected, as it were, in great depth with the preceding period, or could it have occurred almost equally readily at a considerably earlier period? It is against a background of questions of this type that the growth of London appears so strategically important.

There were a number of developments tending to promote economic change and growth in the hundred years 1650–1750. Apart from the growth of London, for example, there were the agricultural advances which improved animal husbandry and lay behind the secular tendency of grain prices to fall (thus helping real wages to rise where money wages were unchanged or improved). Or again there is the probability that because of stable numbers and a modest increase in production the national product/population ratio rose significantly. The idea of critical mass has been invoked recently as a concept of value in conveying the nature of the importance of cumulative slow change in the period immediately preceding rapid industrialization.[61] It could be used appropriately of any of these progressive changes, but is particularly telling when related to London's growth. It is not so much that London's growth was independently more important than the other major changes which modified English economy and society during the century, as that it is a most convenient point of entry into the study of the whole range of changes which took place, especially since some aspects of

---

[60] For the second half of the period there is a good summary of available quantitative evidence in Deane and Cole, *British economic growth*, pp. 50–82.

[61] See Landes, *Bull. soc. d'hist. mod.*, 12th ser. no. 18. This concept is discussed also in an article by Crouzet which clearly owes much to the idea: Crouzet, *Annales, E.S.C.* (1966), esp. pp. 290–1.

London's growth can be quantified fairly satisfactorily. Both the changes in agriculture which took place and the failure of national population to increase are closely intertwined with the growth of London, but not with each other. Demographically the existence of London counterbalanced any 'natural' growth of population in much of the rest of the country, and the necessity of feeding London created market conditions over great tracts of England which fostered agricultural improvement and reduced economic regionalism. The absence or slightness of population growth overall, had it not been for London's expansion, might well have inhibited agricultural change.

V

It is possible to write out a check-list of changes which by their occurrence in a traditional and predominantly agricultural society tend to promote social and economic change and may succeed in engendering the magic 'take-off'. On any such list the following items are likely to appear (the list is far from being exhaustive).

A. Economic changes

1. The creation of a single national market (or at least very much larger regional markets) for a wide range of goods and services, so that specialization of function may be developed and economies of scale exploited.

2. The fostering of changes in agricultural methods which increase the productivity of those engaged in agriculture so that the cost of foodstuffs will fall and real wages rise; so that a rising proportion of the workforce can find employment in secondary and tertiary activities without prejudicing the supply of food or raising its price inordinately; and possibly so that a larger export income can be derived from the sale of surplus food supplies abroad.

3. The development of new sources of raw material supply which are not subject to the problem of rising marginal costs of production in the manner characteristic of raw materials in pre-industrial economies.[62] This occurs when mineral raw materials are substituted for animal or vegetable products (for example, coal for wood) and

---

[62] For a fuller discussion of the point see Wrigley, *Econ. Hist. Rev.* (1962), esp. pp. 1–6.

may well be accompanied by important technological changes contrived to overcome novel production problems (for example, the Newcomen engine or the coke-fired blast furnace).

4. The provision of a wider range of commercial and credit facilities so that the latent strengths of the company can be more expertly, quickly and cheaply mobilized. Under this head might fall, for example, the cluster of changes accompanying and reflected in the establishment and development of the Bank of England.

5. The creation of a better transport network to reduce the cost of moving goods from place to place; to make it possible for goods to move freely at all seasons of the year in spite of inclement weather; to shorten the time involved and so to economize in the capital locked up in goods in transit; and more generally to foster all the changes of the type mentioned in (1) above.

6. The securing of a steady rise in real incomes so that the volume of effective demand rises *in toto* and its composition changes with the diversion of an increased fraction of the total purchasing power into the market for the products of industry. This is closely connected with (2) above.

B.   Demographic changes

7. The interplay between fertility, mortality and nuptiality must be such that population does not expand too rapidly and this must hold true for some time after real incomes per head have begun to trend upwards. If this is not so, the cycle of events which is often termed Malthusian can hardly be avoided – there is a great danger that real incomes will be depressed and economic growth will peter out. This happened often enough before the industrial revolution. Leibenstein remarks with justice that 'historical evidence would seem to suggest...[that] it was the rate of population growth, whether or not induced by economic expansion, that ate up the fruits of expansion and resulted in expansion in the aggregate sense without much improvement per head'.[63] Too rapid population growth can, of course, be avoided by the existence of areas of surplus mortality which counterbalance those of surplus fertility as well as by the existence of a rough balance of births and deaths in each area throughout the country.

---

[63] Leibenstein in Rostow (ed.), *The economics of take-off*, p. 173.

C. Sociological changes

8. The steady spread of environments in which the socialization process produces individuals 'rationally' rather than 'traditionally' oriented in their values and patterns of action.

9. The establishment of conditions in which upward social mobility need not necessarily lead to what might be called the recirculation of ability within traditional society but can also produce a steady strengthening of new groups who do not subscribe to the same priorities or use their wealth and status in the same ways as the upper levels of traditional society.

10. The spread of the practice of aping one's betters. When consumption habits become more fluid and the new style and wants of the upper ranks are rapidly suffused throughout the lower ranks of society, men experience a stronger spur to improve their incomes, and the first steps are taken towards the era of uniform, mass consumption. To be aware that a change in one's pattern of life is possible and to consider it desirable is a vital first step to the securing of the change itself. No doubt this awareness is never wholly absent, but it may be present in widely varying intensities and its increase is an important stimulant to economic change.[64]

This check-list is, of course, also a catalogue of the ways in which the growth of London may have promoted social and economic change in England in the period between the dying away of the economic upthrust of Elizabethan and early Stuart times and the sharp acceleration at the end of the eighteenth century. It may also be represented diagrammatically in a form which enables the interconnection between some of the items on the list to be appreciated more concisely.

Many of the changes are connected with the growth of London in two directions, at once produced or emphasized by London's growth and serving in turn to reinforce the growth process, a typical positive

---

[64] George quotes Defoe's description of the 'topping workmen' to be found in England, 'who only by their handy labour as journeymen can earn from fifteen to fifty shillings per week wages as thousands of artisans in England can...'Tis plain the dearness of wages forms our people into more classes than other nations can show. These men live better in England than the masters and employers in foreign countries can, and you have a class of your topping workmen in England, who, being only journeymen under manufacturers, are yet very substantial fellows, maintain their families very well...' (George, *London life*, p. 157).

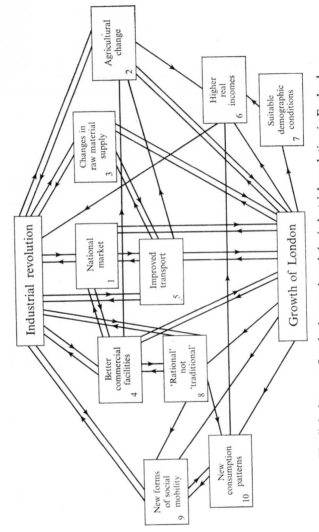

The links between London's growth and the industrial revolution in England

feedback situation, to borrow a term from communication engineering. In some cases growth was possible only because of this mutual relationship. For example, the growth of London could not have gone very far if it had not produced substantial change in agriculture over large areas and brought about sufficient improvements in the transport system to make it feasible to maintain a reliable and moderately cheap movement of food surpluses from the home counties and East Anglia into London. In other cases there is no return connection between London and one of the aspects of social and economic change promoted by its growth. For example, the continued growth of London had much to do with the slightness of population growth over the country as a whole, but it would be difficult to argue that the reverse was also true. And in still other cases, even though no arrow is drawn in on the diagram, it is obvious that some degree of connection must have existed. A link may be presumed, for instance, between higher real incomes (6) and improved transport (5), or between new consumption patterns (10) and agricultural change (2). Only those connections which appear more direct and more important have been shown – though of course a connection between any two boxes can be shown by moving round the network: for example, there is no direct link shown between improved transport (5) and higher real incomes (6), but an indirect link exists via agricultural change (2) and by other more circuitous routes.

Sometimes, where a connection is shown only in one direction, the absence of a return arrow may seem arbitrary: for example in the case of new forms of social mobility (9) and 'rational' not 'traditional' behaviour (8). In several of these cases there was certainly some return effect, and with equal propriety but on different assumptions a return arrow might have been drawn. The act of judgement involved here demands careful scrutiny because the relationships which are expressed by a single arrow are of particular interest. Where there are arrows in both directions this implies an interconnection so intimate that in some ways it will prove pointless to distinguish between them. They are jointly parts of a larger situation which it is convenient to record separately for clarity's sake and for some analytic purposes. Where an arrow in only one direction exists, however, a clearer distinction, a lack of interdependence and in some cases a causal sequence is implied. For example, the diagram suggests that the growth of London stimulated the development of 'rational' modes of behaviour (8), but that this in turn did not have any important direct return effect on London's growth (though very soon an indirect path is opened up via (4), better commercial facilities). This is a different type of relationship from that between London and improved land and water communication (5) which is represented as facilitating the growth of London directly. The latter is shown as a chicken and egg situation, as it were; the former is not. In the one case the positive feedback is direct; in the other this is not so.

A special interest attaches to boxes (6) higher real incomes, (2) agricultural change, and (8) 'rational' rather than 'traditional' behaviour. They are key nodes in the system connected to more boxes than others, and tied into the system by single as well as double arrows. If the relationships are correctly stated it is these aspects of the total social and economic situation which should prove most repaying to future analyses (and possibly also (5) improved transport). Unhappily the system embodies far too many subjective judgements to justify any but conditional statements about it in its present form.

The diagram underlines the poverty of our knowledge of many things which it is important to know. Sometimes the absence of an arrow betrays simple ignorance as much as an act of judgement. For example, it is impossible to feel sure as yet about the nature of the relationship between the demographic situation in the period 1650–1750 and economic and social change. Some points seem clear. It is reasonable to suppose that the relationship indicated in the diagram between population balance and higher real incomes is accurate. But other points are far from clear. It is very uncertain whether the reverse relationship holds good – that is to say whether higher real incomes tended to retard population growth, and in what ways this effect, if it existed (and it would certainly be premature to rule out this possibility), was produced.

This model is, like all models, intended as an aid to further thought. It is not more than this. It may be noted, incidentally, that some lines leading to the industrial revolution box, and more particularly those leading back from the industrial revolution box, should be viewed in a different light from other connections. The industrial revolution did not get fully into its stride until after the period discussed in this essay. Arrows pointing to it, therefore, show circumstances tending to promote its occurrence. Those in the opposite direction, on the other hand, cannot have existed before the event itself, if its place in time is strictly defined. In a more general sense, however, they simply underline the positive feedback elements in the situation which grew stronger as time passed but were present from an early date. In contrast with this, the period of economic growth in the sixteenth and early seventeenth centuries produced relationships between major variables which might be termed typically those of negative feedback. The very growth of industry and population, by increasing the demand for food and industrial raw materials in circumstances where there were increasing marginal costs of production, and by oversupplying the labour market, drove up food prices, forced wages down, and increased the difficulties of industrial production, thus throttling back the growth process.

VI

The comparative neglect of London as a potent engine working towards change in England in the century 1650–1750[65] is the more paradoxical in that the dominance of Paris within France has long been a familiar notion in political history. Yet London was larger than Paris, was growing much faster, and contained a far higher fraction of the national population. All leavens do not, of course, work equally effectively in their lumps; and political dominance connotes different issues from economic and social change, but the irony remains.[66] A just appreciation of London's importance must await a fuller knowledge of many points which are still obscure. Meanwhile this short sketch of a possible model of London's relationship with the rest of the country will have served its purpose if it helps to promote further interest in the complexities of the changes to which no doubt it does only the roughest of justice.

[65] See Laslett in Wrigley (ed.), *English historical demography*, pp. 11–12, for a brief discussion of much the same point.

[66] It is symptomatic of the neglect of this topic that a work as perceptive and authoritative as Deane and Cole's analysis of British economic growth from the late seventeenth century onwards passes over the growth of London almost completely. Where London is mentioned at all it is incidental to some other main line of argument.

10. *Towns and Economic Growth in Eighteenth-Century England*

M. J. DAUNTON

I

What is at issue is growth in the economy of the *ancien régime*. The towns there were an example of deep-seated disequilibrium, asymmetrical growth, and irrational and unproductive investment on a nation-wide scale. Was luxury – the appetite of these enormous parasites – responsible for it?. . .Suppose that a historian at the end of the eighteenth century, better informed than we are about the contemporary scene, had indulged in long-term forecasts. He would have asked himself whether these urban monsters in the west were not proof of a kind of seizing-up process analogous to what happened to the Roman Empire with the dead-weight of Rome, and China with the enormous inert mass of Peking in the far north; that is to say, he would have asked if they were not ends of evolution instead of promises for the future, the forces they unleashed resulting in nothing more than themselves. . .In any case, it has been proved that these enormous urban formations are more linked to the past, to accomplished evolutions, faults and weaknesses of the societies and economies of the *ancien régime* than to preparations for the future. Werner Sombart saw the luxury of the large towns and states as an accelerator of capitalism. But what capitalism? Capitalism is protean, a hydra with a hundred heads. The obvious fact was that the capital cities would be present at the forthcoming industrial revolution in the role of spectators. Not London, but Manchester, Birmingham, Leeds, Glasgow and innumerable small proletarian towns launched the new era. It was not even the capital accumulated by eighteenth-century patricians that was to be invested in the new venture.[1]

Certainly, eighteenth-century London was seen by contemporaries as a destroyer, of men, of social order, of rural prosperity. The death rate was considerably above the birth rate until the 1790s, so the continued growth of London was seen as a drain on the rest of

[1] Braudel, *Capitalism and material life*, pp. 439–40.

the country. According to one writer in 1754, 'London has grown, and continues still to grow, out of compass, at the expense of, and to the sensible diminution of the other towns and boroughs.' The countryside, it was believed, was being depopulated by the growth of luxury. Trade and consumption were increasing, but this – so it was argued – was because wealth and luxury were being concentrated, particularly in London, and to the detriment of the rest of the country. London was a luxury for which others had to pay, its needs only balanced by resources from outside. 'The increase of buildings in London', it was claimed in 1779, 'is derived from the increase of luxury, an evil which, while it flatters, never fails to destroy.' Mr Solicitor Winnington would agree: 'Nothing decays rents in the country like new buildings in London.' And London was undermining social order. 'In London amongst the lower class all is anarchy, drunkenness and thievery, in the country, good order, sobriety and honesty.' Contemporaries, then, thought firmly on the lines of Braudel and tried – albeit with little success – to make their analysis a policy prescription. Throughout the seventeenth century, government had tried to check the growth of London by forbidding new buildings and the subdivision of old property. In the eighteenth century, the inevitable was accepted, but without equanimity. 'London, the Metropolis of Great Britain', it was said in 1783, was 'a kind of monster, with a head enormously large, and out of all proportion to its body. . ., no better than a wen or excrescence upon the body politic'.[2]

The old urban hierarchy was indeed overturned during the eighteenth century, after relative stability for a century. The five towns at the head of the urban hierarchy after London in 1700 were the same as in 1600.[3] But by 1801, only Bristol remained among the largest five provincial towns. Braudel seems to be right. It *was* Manchester, Birmingham and Leeds emerging to the top of the urban scale as the creatures and creators of the future, driving out the erstwhile leaders as representatives of the past. This is shown in table 1. Before the eighteenth century, the towns which were already at the head of the hierarchy – with the exception of York – had

---

[2] This account is based on George, *London life*, pp. 22–5, 63–107. See also the restatement by Kiernan, *New Left Review* (1972), p. 77, 'all through history the town has been largely parasitic on the countryside, and the metropolis has carried this further by concentrating in itself the parasitism of state and ruling class'.

[3] Darby in Darby (ed.), *New historical geography of England*, p. 381.

been able to expand in step with the newer industrial communities. During the eighteenth century, this was no longer true and the industrial centres which had been emerging in the period 1500 to 1700 took over.[4] Certainly, the industrial revolution did not occur in London. If anything, the 'industrial revolution in England *accentuated* "pre-industrial characteristics" in London'. There was obviously a geographical separation between the new industrial areas

TABLE 1. The changing urban hierarchy of England, 1600–1801

1600		1750		1801	
Rank	Popu-lation	Rank	Popu-lation	Rank	Popu-lation
1 London	250,000	1 London	675,000	1 London	960,000
2 Norwich	15,000	2 Bristol	50,000	2 Manchester	84,000
3 York	12,000	3 Norwich	36,000	3 Liverpool	78,000
4 Bristol	12,000	4 Newcastle	29,000	4 Birmingham	74,000
5 Newcastle	10,000	5 Birmingham	23,700	5 Bristol	64,000
6 Exeter	9,000	6 Liverpool	22,000	6 Leeds	53,000
		7 Exeter	16,000	8 Norwich	37,000
		16 York	11,400	14 Newcastle	28,000
				15 Exeter	17,000
				17 York	16,000

Sources:
1600: Emery in Darby (ed.), *New historical geography of England*, pp. 294–6.
1750: Law, *Local Historian* (1972), pp. 22–6.
1801: Prince in Darby (ed.), *New historical geography of England*.

and the industrial bourgeoisie and proletariat on the one hand, and London, 'the headquarters of all this *ancien régime*', on the other. Professor Kiernan is surely right to point to the consequences of this separation of industrial power and the industrial proletariat from the centre of state power. In some cases such as Germany, the two – industry and the capital – were combined, 'the State requiring technology for power politics, the factories requiring tariffs, subsidies, orders'. Where they were close together, a working-class

[4] A general discussion of these changes is found in the editors' introduction to Clark and Slack (eds.), *Crisis and order*, pp. 1–56; Law, *Local Historian* (1972); Chalklin, *The provincial towns*, chaps. 1 and 2.

movement could be a direct threat to the state. In England, the capital lacked modern industry and a strong working-class movement, whilst movements in the industrial north because of their distance from the capital lacked a 'hegemonic impulse'.[5]

So the old towns at the head of the urban hierarchy – including London whose supremacy was never challenged – appear as spectators in the process of industrialization. This point can in fact be extended to a more general proposition about the relationship between the processes of industrialization and urbanization. Perhaps the percentage of the population which was urban had doubled in the course of the eighteenth century. Deane and Cole have estimated that around 1700, 13 per cent of the British population lived in towns with a population of 5,000 and above. By mid-century this had risen to 15 or 16 per cent, by 1801 to about 25 per cent.[6] The alternative estimate of C. M. Law places 24.1 per cent of the population of England and Wales in towns of 2,500 plus in the middle of the eighteenth century, which had risen by 1801 to 33.8 per cent.[7] Certainly, by 1801 England was more urbanized than any country except the Netherlands. Around 1800, the percentage of the population living in towns of 10,000+ was 21.3 in England and Wales, 29.5 in the Netherlands, 13.5 in Belgium, 10.9 in Denmark, 9.5 in France, 8.9 in Saxony and 7.2 in Prussia.[8] England was also, of course, the pioneer of industrialization. The crucial question is the relationship between the two processes.

It could well be that industrial growth was proceeding ahead of urban growth during the eighteenth century, and that the vital point was what was happening in agriculture. With population not growing rapidly in the years up to 1750, improved agricultural productivity in certain locations might have led to tighter profit margins for those in less favoured areas in the north and west and on the Midland clays. In these areas, the population had to seek supplementary income from industrial by-employment. Industry had left the towns for the countryside in the late Middle Ages, when a division emerged between cereal surplus areas and pastoral areas with rural domestic industry. It could be that the new techniques of the late seventeenth and first half of the eighteenth centuries made

[5] Kiernan, *New Left Review* (1972), pp. 75, 78–81.
[6] Deane and Cole, *British economic growth*, p. 7.
[7] Law, *Local Historian* (1972), p. 18.
[8] Weber, *The growth of cities*, pp. 144–5.

this contrast even more marked, with the south concentrating on improved agricultural techniques while rural domestic industry spread in the north, west and Midlands. For areas which had become relatively poorer as food producers, 'rural industry was their recourse and retreat'.[9]

Is this to say that rural industry increased relative to urban, that industrialization proceeded ahead of urbanization? Probably it is. According to Deane and Cole, the proportion of the population living in towns doubled over the century, whilst the order of increase in industrial output was three to fourfold.[10] There was probably overall no *absolute* decline in urban industry. London probably remained the most important industrial centre, based upon traditional forms of production, and locations such as Liverpool and Bristol had at least in the earlier decades of the century been developing industry. But almost certainly there was relative decline in urban industry. Heavy industry migrated from the commercial centres towards the end of the century. Textiles expanded in the countryside, based upon outwork by agriculturalists. Towns like Manchester were as yet not so much industrial centres as co-ordinators of production by rural outworkers. The same applies to metal production around Birmingham and Sheffield. The growth of iron output for the bulk of the eighteenth century was by an increase in the number of dispersed rural furnaces rather than by agglomeration in urban settings. It was in the nineteenth century with the development of factories and steam power – a development which was less rapid than is often assumed – that the economies of urban location increased. It seems likely, therefore, granted the obvious weaknesses in the statistics, that industrialization led urbanization in eighteenth-century England.[11]

Further, it could be argued that by the eighteenth century the

[9] Thirsk in Fisher (ed.), *Essays in the economic and social history of Tudor and Stuart England*; Jones, *Past and Present* (1968).

[10] Deane and Cole, *British economic growth*, pp. 78, 103. Real output in home and export industries rose from 100 in 1700 to 148 in 1750 and 387 in 1800.

[11] Gill, *History of Birmingham*; Wise, *Univ. Birmingham Hist. J.* (1949–1950); Chaloner, *Bulletin of John Rylands Library* (1959–60); Court, *Rise of the Midland industries*; Hey, *Rural metalworkers of the Sheffield region*; Flinn, *Men of iron*, pp. 3–4. See Thompson, *Making of the English working class*, pp. 211, 259–60, 288, on the untypicality of factory production: 'In 1830 the characteristic industrial worker worked not in a mill or factory but (as an artisan or "mechanic") in a small workshop or in his own home, or

established towns had become a conservative influence which had to be by-passed. The town in the West in the Middle Ages had certainly been a crucial element in change. 'Capitalism and the towns', says Braudel, 'were basically the same thing in the west.'[12] They achieved at least in some areas complete autonomy and had the freedom to pursue new lines of development. But in time, he says, the towns were captured, were subjected to the state. And to quote Pizzorno:

> at a certain point not only did urban institutions cease to develop in their role as centres fostering development, but they actually constituted a barrier in some respects. The cities' economic system, founded on the gilds and corporations, becomes an obstacle when economic life begins to structure itself in inter-urban combinations. ...The situation has reversed itself, and the cities which had formerly fought for the establishment of a new progressive economic system now become a nucleus of interests fighting against the new type of development.[13]

The opinion of contemporaries, the overthrow of the urban hierarchy, the lag of urbanization behind industrialization, the move to subject towns with inflexible institutions, all make for a strong case for denying the towns any role – or rather any positive role – in the build-up to the industrial revolution. But the proponents of towns as key agents of change can put up a reasonable case for the contrary point of view.

II

The view that the town was an essential element in economic growth largely rests upon its role as the locus of a new attitude to life, as the centre for cultural change. It is not of great relevance whether or not industry is located in the city; what *is* relevant is the city's function as creator of new patterns of consumption without which industrial growth wherever located would be impossible. The case of the proponents of the cities as crucial components of the process of economic growth rests upon the cities as the location of non-traditional consumption patterns and as the vital market inducing change in agriculture and other industries. This is the nub of

(as a labourer) on more or less casual employment in the streets, on building sites, on the docks.'

[12] Braudel, *Capitalism and material life*, p. 400.

[13] Pizzorno in Germani (ed.), *Modernisation, urbanisation and the urban crisis*, p. 125.

E. A. Wrigley's argument that far from being 'a kind of monster', an 'excrescence upon the body politic', the very size of London played a crucial role in the process of industrialization; it was in fact a preparation for the future, the growth of the small proletarian towns being at least partially a product of its existence. Wrigley points not to the growth of anarchy and disorder, but to the break-ing down of traditional patterns of behaviour based on custom, to the creation of more rational outlooks, and to the emergence of new patterns of consumption. The existence of a mass of relatively well-paid labour in London played a major part in creating new stan-dards of consumption. The London market, argues Wrigley, was a forcing house of change in manufacturing and marketing. It had a key role in creating a national market. The luxury, the wealth of London helped engender change elsewhere rather than leading to decay. Braudel similarly argues that the capitals 'produced the national markets without which the modern state would be a pure fiction'. But, he says, 'the price demanded was very high' for 'their economy was only balanced by outside resources; others had to pay for their luxury'. Wrigley's analysis differs: he sees other areas not being exploited by London so much as responding positively to the opportunities it provided. The building of houses in London did not so much depress the countryside, as the demands of the London market promoted changes in agriculture, in distribution, in the coal industry, in transport.[14]

The approach of Wrigley is related to a popular concept in development economics, that of dualism, which sees an economy containing both a peasant, subsistence sector and a market sector, with urbanization occurring by movement from one to the other.[15] Essentially, it is seen as a rural–urban difference. As Hoselitz has put it, 'the economic organisation of the city represented the predominant form of capitalist economy; that of the countryside still contained many elements of pre-capitalist economic forms'.[16] The towns, he says,

> exhibit a spirit different from that of the countryside. They are the main force and the chief locus for the introduction of new ideas and new ways of doing things. One may look therefore to

[14] Braudel, *Capitalism and material life*, p. 414, Wrigley, *Past and Present* (1967).

[15] See, for example, Higgins, *Econ. Dev. and Cult. Change* (1956); Boeke, *Economics and economic policy of dual societies*.

[16] Hoselitz, *J. Pol. Econ.* (1953), p. 204.

the cities as the crucial places in underdeveloped countries in which the adaptation to new ways, new techniques, new consumption and production patterns, and new social institutions is achieved. The main problem remaining is the nature of this adaptation in the various underdeveloped countries and the degree to which the changed culture of the urban centers affects the surrounding 'sea' of traditional folk-like ways of life.[17]

This is very different from Braudel's view of the city, and on balance it is more closely in accord with the facts. However, while the towns were the locus of *some* change, this must be kept very clearly in perspective. For the striking thing about eighteenth-century England is how less dual it was than many societies at the time and since when about to embark on the process of economic development.

The concept of dualism makes the city an island of modernity in a sea of tradition, an enclave of capitalism in a pre-capitalist countryside. This is less applicable to eighteenth-century England than other countries at the time or since, with the exception of the United States. English towns were not islands in a sea of traditionalism, for agriculture was capitalist rather than peasant organized. Professor Saville is surely right to place emphasis on

the uniqueness of British history in the eighteenth century. In no other country did pre-industrial society attain the pervasiveness of the market economy, the widespread acceptance of the profit motive, or the levels of commercial and financial sophistication that existed in Britain in the second half of the eighteenth century. Nowhere save in Britain was the peasantry virtually eliminated *before* the acceleration of economic growth that is associated with the development of industrial capitalism. . .The striking characteristic of English farming, and its distinctive feature compared with the greater part of continental Europe, was the large farm using hired labour and working wholly for the market. . .It was a society in which the penetration of the capitalist ethos has reached into all important sectors of economic life.[18]

In France, there was 'a small class of luxury consumers and a large mass of consumption-resisting peasants'.[19] Peasants tended not to spend but to hoard any surplus. In England, however, the largest social group in the countryside by the middle of the century was wage-earners, and the economy does not appear particularly

[17] *Ibid.* p. 197.   [18] Saville, *Socialist Register* (1969), pp. 250, 258, 269.
[19] Perkin, *Origins of modern English society*, p. 91.

dualistic.[20] This is also in striking contrast with the situation in currently developing economies in the third world. The most important reason for the rapid growth of the urban population there is the 'push' from an over-populated countryside. But secondarily, and reflecting the dualism of these economies, there is a very wide differential between wages in the town and the country, of between 100 and 200 per cent.[21] In eighteenth-century England the differential was certainly narrower: an unskilled agricultural labourer in Oxfordshire earned 1s. 2d. a day at the beginning of the century, 1s. 4d. at the end; in London daily wage rates were between 1s. 10d. and 2s. throughout the century.[22] In real terms the difference was probably narrower. Much less in eighteenth-century England than in other contexts did a move from the country to the town seem necessary in order to increase *per capita* incomes and to move from a pre-capitalist to a capitalist environment.

So it can be argued that eighteenth-century England was less a dual economy than most at the time and since when the process of development commenced. The role of the town must be severely curtailed, but it should not be completely denied. There was *some* differential in the wages of the unskilled, and the towns did have more artisans earning higher wages. There is also the matter of patterns of consumption which underwent fundamental change in the eighteenth century. The writers of the time complained that workers tended to be idle in times of high wages, preferring leisure to an increased income. There was a conventionally defined standard of life and largely fixed patterns of expenditure. Once income reached the necessary level the labourer simply ceased to work. Alternatively, any surplus income above the conventional level of life would be spent on wild excesses of drink and gambling. As Defoe put it, 'there's nothing more frequent than for an Englishman to work until he has got his pocket full of money, and then go and be idle, or *perhaps drunk*, till 't's all gone'. This led to a belief in the utility of low wages. 'Every one but an idiot knows', said Arthur Young, 'that the lower classes must be kept poor or they will never be industrious.' At a lower wage, it was necessary to work longer to reach the conventional standard of life, and the labourer would also be more stable and reliable. 'When the framework knitters or

[20] Saville, *Socialist Register* (1969), p. 262.
[21] Bairoch, *Urban unemployment in developing countries*, pp. 30–3.
[22] Mathias, *First industrial nation*, p. 217.

makers of silk stockings had a great price for their work, they have
been observed seldom to work on Mondays and Tuesdays but to
spend most of their time at the ale-house or nine-pins. . .The
weavers, 't is common with them to be drunk on Monday, have
their head-ache on Tuesday, and their tools out of order on Wednes-
day.'[23]

The vital change was when higher wages were taken in increased
earnings rather than in leisure, and when increased earnings were
spent on new types of consumption.[24] The first change was eventually imposed from outside by the new work discipline of factories
which removed the freedom to choose hours of work, as well as
being internalized by workers through education and religion.[25] But
also of relevance, and of more importance in the second change of
the establishment of new patterns of consumption, was the move to
an urban environment. In part this was a reflection of the distributive system, for there were obviously greater opportunities to buy
new commodities as a matter of course in the towns than in the
countryside.[26] It was also a reflection of the social emulation found
in towns (and especially London) which some historians see as the
key to consumers' demand and hence to the industrial revolution.
Defoe, for example, remarked on the 'flourishing pride' of London
which 'has dictated new methods of living to the people; and while
the poorest citizens live like the rich, the rich like the gentry, the
gentry like the nobility, and the nobility striving to outshine one
another'.[27] It is in respect to leisure preference that dualism has
some relevance and the towns have a role: the knowledge of new
goods increased and the hold of convention lessened in an urban
environment. But it is important to refine the argument, for there
was not a black and white contrast between old attitudes in the
towns. 'There was a time lag following the attainment of more
regular, higher wages until the patterns of expenditure and a new
social discipline were built up in response to industrial employment
and urban living.'[28] The huge expenditure on gin in London in the

[23] These comments and quotations are drawn from Furniss, *Position of
the labourer*, pp. 99–159.
[24] Furniss, *Position of the labourer*, pp. 234–5; Lewis, *Theory of economic
growth*, pp. 30–1; Mathias, *Hist. J.* (1958), pp. 109–10.
[25] Thompson, *Past and Present* (1967), pp. 81–90.
[26] Alexander, *Retailing in England*.
[27] Quoted in Perkin, *Origins of modern English society*, p. 92.
[28] Mathias, *Hist. J.* (1958), pp. 109–10.

early eighteenth century is a clear indication that at first increased income in the towns could be taken in drink.[29] It can be argued that the move into the towns meant the translation of rural patterns of spending of occasional surpluses after, say, the harvest into an urban context where money wages came every week. There was a time lag before higher wage rates adjusted from old patterns of spending to new ways of disposing of increased purchasing power. But towns were the chief locus of change. Rural attitudes continued for a while, lingering into the nineteenth century (as is clear from the activities of the temperance movement),[30] but eventually new attitudes to consumption did emerge in the towns along the lines suggested by Defoe.

The other argument of the proponents of the towns as agents of change relates to demography. Again, Wrigley has presented this point of view in the case of London. During the eighteenth century, it was an area of natural decrease of population. Its continued growth depended upon heavy migration, taking a large part of the population growth of the rest of England. This acted as a safety-valve, preventing too rapid an increase in population which might have led to a fall in real incomes and an aborting of economic growth. London as an area of surplus mortality counterbalanced areas of surplus fertility and so regulated the national level of population growth. But by concentrating population – and London doubled its population where other European capitals were static – it provided the necessary market conditions as well, reducing economic regionalism and fostering agricultural improvement.[31] This analysis can be extended from London in particular to towns in general. As Eversley has put it, 'population growth at this time was "right" – neither so small as to cause shortages of labour, or of demand for goods and services, nor so large as to reduce real wages, create labour surpluses and destroy the basis of demand'.[32] London in particular and the towns in general acted as regulators in this achievement of the 'right' level. Urban mortality was well above that for rural regions, and urban fertility also exceeded rural fertility. But the difference was far greater in mortality rates than in fertility

[29] George, *London life*, pp. 27–42.
[30] Harrison, *Drink and the Victorians*, pp. 305–6, 322–34.
[31] Wrigley, *Past and Present* (1967), pp. 45–9.
[32] Eversley in Jones and Mingay (eds.), *Land, labour and population*, p. 249.

rates and this made the towns an area of natural decrease of population until the end of the century in the case of London, at least to mid-century in the case of the provinces. Thereafter, they were areas of lower natural increase than the countryside. Their role was indeed very different from the current experience, where cities in the third world have a lower death rate and higher birth rate than the countryside, and so exacerbate the growth of population.[33] Of course, much more important is the great difference between the overall rate of population growth in the two experiences. Nevertheless, the towns did have a part to play in creating the demographic context for development in eighteenth-century England. They siphoned off the growth of the population from rural areas and checked the aggregate national increase. But because the population was being concentrated, the towns were also bolstering the market, increasing demand more than proportionately to the growth in population.

TABLE 2.   Crude urban and rural birth and death rates per 1,000

	1600	1750	1780
Birth rate			
urban	39.0	40.8	40.1
rural	29.1	30.4	30.0
Death rate			
urban	40.2	41.2	38.8
rural	20.5	21.0	19.8

Source: Loschky, *J. Eur. Econ. Hist.* (1972), p. 705.

Towns were the location of new consumption patterns; they were concentrating population and so increasing demand more than proportionately to the growth in population. The towns had to be fed and provided with fuel, and they were important centres of demand for the products of industry wherever the actual production was located. It was the urban population which provided, it could be argued, much of the rationale for the greater specialization between the agricultural south and the industrial by-employment in the north, west and Midlands. The surplus of the south went to feed the urban population. The existence of urban markets for food kept up profits at a reasonable level, and enabled the agricultural sector to

[33] Lampard in Dyos and Wolff (eds.), *The Victorian city.*

purchase the products of rural industry. And it could be argued that towns were markets in their own right for industrial goods, being the <u>centre of a new sort of attitude towards consumption</u>. This was crucial if it is accepted that the major demand behind industrialization came from the home market rather than from exports.[34] Further, the need to fuel the towns put pressure on the coal industry, requiring improvements both in the methods of production and of transport.[35] <u>But the crucial point is the role of urban demand in inducing agricultural change.</u>

Certainly, the urban market had a wide influence on agriculture – Bristol was drawing from west and south Wales, the Midlands and West Country, London from the south-east, East Anglia and even farther afield.[36] In 1724 Defoe could write of the 'general dependence of the whole country upon the city of London for the consumption of its produce'.[37] As F. J. Fisher has said, the 'stimulus was not merely in the direction of increased production but also in that of specialisation, and in that direction lay agricultural progress'.[38] Such indeed was the outcome, but surely it is wrong to stress the level of urban demand *per se*. <u>The crucial point is</u> not so much the undeniable fact that towns provided the demands for the produce of agriculture; it was <u>the way in which agricultural interests met these demands. In England, the demands involved the removal of the peasantry, the introduction of new techniques, and the institution of commercial capitalist agriculture</u> (with those areas which were less competitive switching to rural outwork). In France, the impulse to commercial agriculture was weak, and demands were met by using the existing social and political framework to squeeze more out of the peasants. Agriculture remained traditional, in techniques and in the continuance of feudal controls.[39] It might be that 'cities are formed through the geographic concentration of a social surplus product',[40] but the social surplus can be created in different ways in various societies. Even if Paris had been as big as London, with 11 rather than 2.5 per cent of the French population, would it have

---

[34] Eversley in Jones and Mingay (eds.), *Land, labour and population.*

[35] Wrigley, *Past and Present* (1967), pp. 58–60, and *idem, Econ. Hist. Rev.* (1962).

[36] Wrigley, *Past and Present* (1967), pp. 55–8; Minchinton, *Trans. Roy. Hist. Soc.* (1954).

[37] Quoted by Fisher, *Econ. Hist. Rev.* (1934–5), p. 51.

[38] Fisher, *Econ. Hist. Rev.* (1934–5), p. 56.

[39] Moore, *Social origins of dictatorship and democracy*, pp. 45–56.

[40] Harvey, *Social justice and the city*, p. 216.

produced the same effect upon the agricultural sector? It could be argued that the difference between the agricultural sectors is in fact dependent upon the size of urban demand which at a certain point creates bottlenecks and warrants specialization. There is, however, nothing inevitable about this. Such might be the outcome, but there were other possibilities. Bottlenecks might lead to technical progress to overcome them, but might as well lead to an aborting of urban growth or the wider or more intensive use of old procedures. It was, after all, only at the time of Gregory King that London became the largest city in western Europe. During the period analysed by Fisher (1540–1640) London was eclipsed by Paris and Naples.[41] The contrast in the method of provisioning had by then already arisen. London was unlike the continental capitals whose bread was assured whatever the circumstances by forces other than the market. Commercial processes were adequate. The English government might look askance at the developing middlemen, but if the state was concerned by the development of new techniques of provisioning, neither was there a need for it to take responsibility for supplies. The way in which the supply side responds becomes the major variable, and it cannot be assumed that a given level of urbanization will necessarily produce the same response. The nature of the response will largely be determined by the internal development and dynamic of the agricultural sector over time. Urban demand is important; but more important is the way in which supply is increased. One exaggeration deserves another: if the demands of London for food contributed to the agricultural revolution, the demands of Paris for food contributed to the French revolution.[42]

What of the view that the characteristic institutions of the towns had become barriers to change which had to be by-passed? There were two arguments here: the move from autonomy to subjection by a superior authority; and the development of inflexibility from within. On balance, neither factor was of much weight as far as eighteenth-century England was concerned.

The city in medieval Europe was unique in being autonomous. This is to deny Sjoberg's theory that the pre-industrial city is

---

[41] Helleiner in Rich and Wilson (eds.), *Cambridge Economic History of Europe*, iv, pp. 81–2.

[42] For an account of the hostilities between Paris and the surrounding area, see Cobb, *Paris and its provinces*. For an earlier period, see the comments on the problems of provisioning towns in Braudel, *The Mediterranean and the Mediterranean world*, i, pp. 328–32, 346–7, 350–2.

essentially the same across time and between cultures,[43] for the pre-industrial cities in the West had unparalleled freedom, having 'developed as autonomous worlds and according to their own propensities'.[44] The towns in the West became centres of change, whereas elsewhere in the world they were shut in periods of immobility. 'The towns caused the west to advance.'[45] As Braudel says,

> the town won entirely, at least in Italy, Flanders and Germany. It was able to try the experiment of leading a completely separate life for quite a long time. This was a colossal event...[They] built an original civilization on the basis of this freedom...They were able to follow fairly rare political, social and economic experiments right through to the end...A new state of mind was established, broadly that of an early, still faltering, western capitalism.[46]

In the East, the towns did not win independence and continued to be under the princes and mandarins. English towns had never achieved such independence as in Germany, Italy and Flanders. However, at the end of the Middle Ages towns in these latter countries were subjected and lost their capacity for change; the English towns had won less but kept more. An important variable was the manner in which the towns were integrated into the developing states.

In the period from about the fourteenth to the eighteenth century, there was a move from the autonomous city closed in on itself, to the subject city, disciplined by the state. In the medieval period, the towns won independence from their immediate feudal lord. In certain areas, they also pre-empted the power of the emperor or monarch. But the period of autonomy was limited. In Germany, from about 1400 the princes increased their relative power and the towns were controlled, coming under the influence of new territorial national units. The towns in Italy had similarly won independence. Unlike in Germany, the towns *themselves* became the territorial states. They grew at the expense of feudal power areas, becoming city-states, ending by being disciplined through internal dynamics rather than external constraints.[47]

[43] Sjoberg, *Preindustrial city*, pp. 4–5.
[44] Braudel, *Capitalism and material life*, p. 396; Weber, *The city*, pp. 80–1.
[45] Braudel, *Capitalism and material life*, p. 411.
[46] *Ibid.* pp. 398–400.
[47] These comments are based on Rörig, *Medieval city*.

In England, the monarchy beyond the immediate feudal lords was much stronger. London might at one time have tried to make the full progression to the 'commune of London' in an Italian sense. The claim could not be made good. The London commune could survive as a commune only by compromise with the established order. That is, it won from the kings recognition of a commune in the sense of a sworn, self-governing community under an elected head who embodied its legal personality, coupled with a refusal to permit this commune to break free from the general royal surveillance.[48] Limits were set to communal independence, but in the end it retained under the king more freedom than the fully fledged continental communes, and much more than Paris under the French kings. 'The City Corporation [had] an extraordinary degree of independence, unknown to the administrators of other capitals... actually adjoining the seat of government, it could yet shut its gates against the King and his officers.'[49] The towns and the king had combined against feudalism. The king wanted to subdue and control the lords; the towns which had prevailed over their lords wanted a guarantee of independence. The king confirmed the legal position they had achieved by their own efforts, thus subjecting them to a supreme royal sovereignty. But the subjection was unlike that in Germany where there was a revival of feudal territorial power over the towns. Rather the feudal system was overcome in return for acceptance of ultimate royal power. There was not to be any room for urban autonomy dangerous to the crown. The towns had freedom from the lords, but never the degree of autonomy found in Italy or Germany. However, the more limited freedom they achieved was never surrendered. They never had their own foreign policy or coinage or legal system, but the king dared not meddle in their internal affairs. The English towns arrived at – and maintained – a position of independence dependent upon the king's grace. This was unlike the other country – France – with a strong monarchy. As in England, the towns did not escape from royal control, but it was in France much more immediately present. 'Paris did not offer the protection of a town free to do what it wanted and accountable to

[48] Williams, *Medieval London.*
[49] Webb and Webb, *English local government*, pp. 570–1. See also Miller in Tillott (ed.), *VCH City of York*, pp. 30–40. Miller shows how York achieved autonomy by the mid-thirteenth century, dependent on the king's grace.

no one.'[50] In France, the king could meddle in the internal affairs of Paris, in England, the king dared not meddle in the internal affairs of London. The towns in England were integrated into the developing state: the towns did not become the state as in Italy; neither were they subjected to an inadequate state system as in Germany; rather were they integrated into a larger unity which gave new opportunities.

Towns in England, then, had a continuing opportunity to experiment, to establish new forms. Their trade was not subjected to tolls and taxes, their economy and government were not controlled from above. But if inflexibilities were not enforced from outside, they could emerge from within. The freedom was not inevitably going to make the towns progressive. Indeed, urban institutions by the eighteenth century might have become inflexible and hostile to the forces of change as Pizzorno suggested. The way in which towns had been integrated into the state did not impose external constraints upon them. But the constraints might have emerged internally as the self-elective corporations and the restrictive guilds developed rigid controls, opposing new techniques which threatened traditional skills and social structures.

It is an easy matter to find examples of conservatism and inflexibility. In 1736 it was complained at York that

Our magistrates have been too tenacious of their privileges, and have for many years last past, by virtue of their charters, as it were locked themselves up from the world, and wholly prevented any foreigner from settling any manufacture amongst them; unless under such restrictions as they are unlikely to accept of. The paying a large sum of money for their freedoms, with the troublesome and chargeable offices they must often undertake, would deter any person of an enterprising genius in regard of manufacture, from coming to reside at York.[51]

Enforcement of freedom regulations continued at York throughout the eighteenth century, although admittedly with declining effectiveness. The corporation even in the eighteenth century added to the ordinances and created new companies. There was in the 1720s, indeed, a concerted effort by the corporation to strengthen guild control. The corporation appointed a series of committees during

---

[50] Braudel, *Capitalism and material life*, p. 401; Sagnac, *La formation de la société française moderne*, pp. 46, 63.
[51] Quoted in Allison and Tillott in Tillot (ed.), *VCH City of York*, p. 215.

the eighteenth century to pursue offenders, but were finding it difficult to enforce the regulations. The committee of 1775 found 239 defaulters, but admitted that 'as it always has been, so it will ever continue impossible to find out, or if found to compel, every individual who may be liable, to purchase his or her freedom, from the various causes of poverty, contrivance, secretion, connivance and deceit'.[52]

The continued attempt to maintain controls was rarely, then, entirely successful. During the eighteenth century some practical compromise had to be worked out between the full rigour of the enactments and their complete demise. London is a good example of the process. In London by the early eighteenth century, guild and corporation control over trade seemed to have been effectively undermined by the growth of suburban production and by a series of legal decisions questioning the powers of the companies. The corporation had retreated and left enforcement to the companies, which had also retreated, so that by the early eighteenth century the enforcing of regulations was largely left to individuals. Although in 1712 an attempt was made to reverse the process of decay, it was largely unsuccessful and the companies continued to lose ground in the early eighteenth century. The economic benefits of joining a company were by then minimal, and some compromise had to be found which kept the principle of guild regulation whilst accepting that membership could not be enforced. The solution of 1750 was a system of controlled licensing of non-freemen. This kept some control over trades which would otherwise have been completely unregulated. The entire collapse of guild control was postponed. In theory, the whole system remained to the early nineteenth century and was only finally abandoned in 1856. In practice, it was rapidly disintegrating, although guild functions did persist for a long time, propped up by the compromise of 1750.[53]

The political systems of towns up to 1835 remained firmly wedded to past forms. The corporations with a few exceptions – notably the 'ratepayers democracy' of the City of London – were closed and self-perpetuating bodies, often excluding the new interest groups emerging within towns. As the Webbs said, they were 'Close Corporations, "self-creative and self-creating", and nevertheless exercising compulsive powers over the citizens'.[54] At New-

---

[52] *Ibid.* pp. 215–16.   [53] Kellett, *Econ. Hist. Rev.* (1957–8).
[54] Webb and Webb, *English local government*, pp. 702–3.

castle, for example, the election of the council was still the work of the twelve mysteries or leading trade guilds and the fifteen companies in the by-trades.[55] But it is difficult to generalize about the consequences of such archaic bodies. Liverpool and Bristol had similar political forms, differently utilized. Liverpool corporation was 'ambitious and capable', constructing a dock system; Bristol corporation was marked by a 'supine neglect of all the public interests of the city', in particular over harbour improvements.[56] There is no denying that political forms were archaic and could be frustrating, but perhaps more on the level of petty annoyances than as crippling barriers to development. In London, which did have an open democratic government, the leading merchants and shipowners nevertheless did not choose to seek representation. They left the corporation to small retailers, and preferred to provide docks on the joint-stock principle.[57] Nonconformists and Whigs might feel aggrieved by their exclusion from closed corporations, but this was scarcely central to economic development.

There are some indications, therefore, that Pizzorno might be right and that the old institutions had become stultifying. However, his remarks have less weight for the eighteenth century than for earlier periods when there was more vitality in the old forms and less vigour in the new forces of change. The migration of industry from the towns at the end of the Middle Ages was certainly in part a response to the disadvantages of urban control. It has indeed been argued that 'the disincentive of existing urban controls was a more important factor than the positive incentives of the rural economy'.[58] By the eighteenth century the urban controls whilst certainly nuisances were not of such central importance. They had perhaps lost their major significance in the sixteenth century,[59] so that by the eighteenth, while certainly archaic, they did not form barriers of any great magnitude.

Nevertheless, after all reservations have been made, there was in

[55] *Municipal Corporation Enquiry.*
[56] Webb and Webb, *English local government*, pp. 470, 481.
[57] *Ibid.* pp. 687–92.
[58] Clark and Slack (eds.), *Crisis and order*, p. 11.
[59] Phythian-Adams in Clark and Slack (eds.), *Crisis and order*, outlines the ceremonies and rituals found in the city in the late Middle Ages, and suggests their functions in the society. With their demise in the sixteenth century, the remaining guild controls were removed from their previous context. They became private rather than public, at the margin and not an integral part of a total pattern.

the eighteenth century more freedom in towns which had persisted under manorial control and so avoided the companies and guilds and corporation controls of the medieval towns. As one commentator put it, 'a town without a charter is a town without a shackle'.[60] Manchester and Birmingham, for example, were new settlements growing in the eighteenth century under the aegis of manorial controls and the court leet.[61] These controls were little of a hindrance. J. T. Bunce wrote in 1878 that 'the great glory of Birmingham, the source of its strength and the cause of its rapid advance in ·prosperity and population was that it was a free town. Neither personal or corporate hindrances existed in it'.[62] To a large extent, the towns which expanded most rapidly in the eighteenth century were post-medieval, outside the traditional controls of the urban community. Even where they had achieved corporate status, they remained comparatively free communities. Leeds obtained a charter, but the attempt to erect a system of guilds never succeeded. A contrast could be drawn between open and closed towns as well as between open and closed villages. The closed towns by 1700 were those which had been free in the Middle Ages. York had achieved its autonomy by the mid-thirteenth century, but by 1700 was closed and exclusive. It was defeated by the open towns on either side – Leeds and Hull – which emerged in the place of York as the industrial and commercial centres of the woollen trade.[63] If older towns grew it was outside the scope of the old institutions. In London, industrial growth was in the suburbs, commercial developments in such bodies as the East India Company rather than the old guilds. At Norwich, company regulations lapsed in the late seventeenth century; at Exeter the monopoly organization of merchants in the French trade was replaced by free commerce with the Netherlands. The point made by Clark and Slack on the years before 1700 could in fact be extended to cover the eighteenth century:

> growth appears to have been encouraged by the absence of stringent community control...it tended to occur either in the absence of some of those political, economic and social structures which we identify with medieval urban communities (the case with the new urban centres) or through economic initiative

[60] Quoted in Gill, *History of Birmingham*, i, p. 59.
[61] Redford and Russell, *Local government in Manchester*, i, pt 1; Gill, *History of Birmingham*, pp. 59–60.
[62] Bunce, *Corporation of Birmingham*, i, p. 36.
[63] Jackson, *Hull in the eighteenth century*; Wilson, *Gentlemen merchants*.

external to the traditional community (as with the expanding old towns).[64]

A good example of the way in which the process could work is the coal trade of the north-east.

By the charter of 1600, the Newcastle-based Company of Hostmen, the coal merchants, won control over the municipality and the economy of Tyneside. They had the exclusive right to trade in coal on Tyneside, whilst they had a virtual monopoly of municipal offices. During the seventeenth century they represented the town in Parliament, sat on the river conservancy, and owned the collieries along the Tyne. By the eighteenth century, however, it was becoming more difficult to prevent dealers who were not hostmen from trading, and the monopoly of the company was weakened. The major developments in the eighteenth century were not made by hostmen but by newcomers 'away from the islands of corporate or ecclesiastical privilege'. William Cotesworth, for example, one of the leading owners of the early eighteenth century, based himself across the river at Gateshead, fulminating against the 'oppressions' of the Newcastle corporation. Power in fact shifted away from the Newcastle hostmen to the owners south of the Tyne and on the Wear. Sunderland in particular had no chartered hostmen or powerful corporation to 'oppress' traders.[65]

It is, however, probably wrong to stress these barriers to change, the inflexibilities of past forms. If the town was growing, they were overcome – as they eventually were at Newcastle. They persisted where the town was in any case declining – as at York. This is to move the analysis away from the general to the study of particular towns. Indeed, an inspection of a range of specific areas suggests the complexities of the relationship between the towns and industrial development, a complexity which is masked by the general point that industrialization proceeded ahead of urbanization. The leading towns of the first half of the eighteenth century were in their own right important industrial centres, but as industrialization proceeded they suffered a relative decline as industrial locations. However, in some cases the growth of industry outside the towns was actually

[64] Clark and Slack (eds.), *Crisis and order*, pp. 33–4.
[65] These comments are based on *Extracts from the records of the Hostmen*; Ashton and Sykes, *The coal industry*; Nef, *Rise of the British coal industry*; Middlebrook, *Newcastle-upon-Tyne*; and Hughes, *North country life*.

financed by urban interests. The relative decline of urban industry does not mean that towns were necessarily passive spectators. Some, it is true, simply declined because of processes in which they did not share, but in other cases it could be argued that the relative decline was aided by participation of interests from within the town. A closer analysis of individual cases shows that the lead of industrialization and the relative decline of established centres within the urban hierarchy should not result in the simple conclusion that the towns were spectators of a process in which they did not participate.

The way in which urban interests could encourage industry in non-urban locations and themselves decline as industrial centres is exemplified by Bristol and Liverpool. These towns were primarily commercial centres which developed industry internally both to service shipping and ancillaries, and to provide commodities for trade. Liverpool traded in Cheshire salt, Lancashire coal, glass from St Helens, pottery from Staffordshire. But the majority of cargoes were in fact supplied by Liverpool's growing internal industrial base, which increased rapidly after about 1715, in salt, sugar, metal products, leather goods, glass, and later in the century in pottery, china, clocks and watches. 'Liverpool itself was a centre not merely of commerce and its associated service industries, but of manufacturing ones.'[66] Similarly at Bristol. In the early eighteenth century it became the second city in the country, the 'metropolis of the west'. It acted as an agricultural market for the Midlands, West Country, and south and west Wales. It was a market for industrial raw materials, the distribution centre for the western cloth trade, Birmingham metal goods, Irish commodities, and for iron between south Wales, the Black Country and overseas suppliers. It was a major entrepôt, a convenient point of trans-shipment and of collection of small consignments to complete a cargo. But on top of all this it was an important industrial centre. Brass and copper works used Cornish tin and Anglesey copper. There were soap works and glass factories, sugar refineries and distilleries, and a wide range of finishing trades.[67]

In both towns, the demands of commerce created industry internally. Carrying this process further, they encouraged industrial

[66] Hyde, *Liverpool and the Mersey*, pp. 10–12. Harris in Centre National de la Recherche Scientifique, *L'industrialisation en Europe*, p. 60.
[67] Minchinton, *Trans. Roy. Hist. Soc.* (1954), pp. 69–89.

development in areas outside themselves, and this led certainly to relative and possibly to absolute decline in their internal industrial base. In other words, their industrial decay was, in part at least, an outcome of their own efforts. The Liverpool merchants provided the backing and capital for the necessary transport links with the hinterland – the dock of 1709, the Sankey navigation, the Grand Trunk Canal – and this led to the decline and disappearance of Liverpool's industries during the early nineteenth century. The Liverpool merchants themselves invested heavily in the industries of the hinterland. To some extent, the needs of Liverpool as a port, its demands for cargo, sponsored the industrial development of the hinterland and in this way Liverpool's own demands as a port turned the town into a commercial rather than an industrial centre. The industrial decline of Liverpool from about 1800 was, therefore, largely self-induced, and interests from the town played an active role in the process of industrialization. It continued, however, to act as the commercial centre for the industrial area in its hinterland.[68] Bristol was not able to adapt so readily. In part this was because opportunities were missed. Whilst Liverpool was providing dock accommodation, at Bristol there was considerable delay. Although it was clear that port improvement was necessary by the end of the seventeenth century, nothing was achieved until 1802. Since 1661 this had been the responsibility of the Society of Merchant Adventurers which did not cope with the demands put upon it. Neither were adequate communications constructed with the Midlands, which instead turned to Liverpool. The more important consideration, however, is that while Liverpool was investing in industry in its own immediate hinterland, and could continue to act as the commercial centre, Bristol was investing in a geographically distinct area which eventually supplied its own commercial services. Bristol invested heavily in south Wales from the early eighteenth century. The town had itself become a high-cost location for heavy industry, and Bristol merchants developed the iron, coal, and copper industries in south Wales. As output in these increased, Bristol ceased not only to be a producing centre, but also ceased to be a centre of the entrepôt trade. Unlike Liverpool, it could not adjust and continue expansion, because the industrial development was outside its

[68] Hyde, *Liverpool and the Mersey*; Harris in Centre National de la Recherche Scientifique, *L'industrialisation en Europe*, pp. 64, 67; Barker, *Trans. Hist. Soc. Lancs and Cheshire* (1951).

immediate hinterland. Bristol's quasi-metropolitan function in the West was thus transitional, 'when trade was comparatively small in volume, communication as yet imperfect, industry not fully developed and capital investment personal and specific. The improvement of communications and the growth of institutions and methods of organisation appropriate for the expanding industrialism were responsible for the decline in Bristol's position.'[69] The outcome in the two towns was different, but the process was the same. Liverpool and Bristol had developed industry internally to serve commerce and the local market. Then at a certain point heavy industry was relocated and these towns ceased to be industrial, or at least declined relatively as industrial centres, keeping mainly own-use industry of a handicraft variety. The process of relocation was actively sponsored by interests from within Liverpool and Bristol: the capital accumulated by eighteenth-century patricians *did* indeed play a role, although it was of course not the only source of investment.[70] The misfortune of Bristol was that the area of relocation was outside its immediate physical hinterland. The switch from an industrial to a commercial role is not necessarily evidence of a loss of momentum in economic growth but of a change in the type of growth. In Bristol, however, industry escaped from the commercial

---

[69] Minchinton, *Trans. Roy. Hist. Soc.* (1954), and *idem* in McGrath (ed.), *Bristol in the eighteenth century.*

[70] The major source of long-term capital was ploughed-back profits from within industry. So far as merchant capital is concerned, the interesting point is how much went into the land rather than into industry. In the case of Liverpool, Hyde, *Liverpool and the Mersey*, p. 25, argues that while some went into land, more was ploughed back into trade and industry. Bristol was almost certainly the same in this respect. Looking outwards from south Wales, the capital came almost entirely from London and Bristol merchants, even if they were also investing in land. See John, *Industrial development of south Wales*, p. 166; Namier, *J. Econ. and Business Hist.* (1929); Evans, *Nat. Lib. of Wales J.* (1951). South Wales was probably uniquely dependent upon mercantile capital, and throughout the nineteenth century it remained a capital importing area. There was no prior industrial base to permit a ploughing back of profits, and investment in the iron industry was in any case more 'lumpy' than in textiles. West Riding textiles, for example, would more readily expand by reinvesting profits made in the industry. Wilson, *Gentlemen merchants*, pp. 1–4, suggests that the merchants of Leeds were trying to adapt their life-style to that of the landowners; their role was certainly less than that of the Bristol merchants in south Wales. The importance of mercantile capital varied but it cannot be denied. In any case, circulating capital was more important than fixed capital in the eighteenth century, and merchants had a role in this quantitatively more significant sector by, for example, providing credit on the purchase of materials.

orbit of the town whereas in Liverpool it did not. Bristol was eclipsed both as a commercial and as an industrial centre.

Other towns declined as industrial centres and were demoted in the urban hierarchy through the impact of processes in which they played no part. They were passively acted upon by forces beyond their control, were indeed present at the industrial revolution 'in the role of spectators'. This was so successively of <u>York, Exeter and Norwich.</u> In each case, a town which was primarily industrial <u>surrendered to forces of economic change in which it had no part, being left simply as the regional centre of an agricultural hinterland and with no continuing role in the process of industrialization</u>. They succumbed to changes which they did nothing to encourage.

York had already by 1700 ceased to be either a producing or commercial centre for the woollen textile industry. In the Middle Ages, the town had been an important centre of cloth manufacture, but had declined in the late fifteenth century as industry migrated to such locations as Halifax, Leeds, Wakefield. For a time, York remained an important trading centre to the North Sea and the Baltic, but it also surrendered this function to Hull. By 1700 York was simply the regional capital of an agricultural hinterland, the social capital and centre of consumption for the local gentry, a cathedral and county town. It had ceased to play any role in the industrialization of the West Riding.[71]

During the eighteenth century, Exeter followed the path of development traced by York between 1500 and 1700. Exeter in 1700 was the finishing and market centre for the local serge industry. It was not a major centre of weaving, but concentrated upon the finishing, dyeing and exporting of goods manufactured in its hinterland. These processes were closely regulated by the Company of Weavers, Fullers and Shearmen which had been incorporated in 1490 and which continued to enforce apprenticeship, to limit entry to freemen, to fix rates and prices. Membership became virtually a hereditary class, the company becoming inbred and inflexible. This was more a response to than a cause of the decline in the serge industry, which occurred in two stages, from about 1714 to 1748 and then in the mid 1790s. By 1800 the industry was insignificant in the economy of the town, and with the industry went Exeter's commercial function. The town experienced severe relative decline,

[71] Bartlett, *Econ. Hist. Rev.* (1959); Foster in Tillott (ed.), *VCH City of York*.

and by 1800 it was what York had become by 1700 – a centre for shopkeeping and services, a social and regional capital, and market for an agricultural hinterland. By 1800 the commercial and industrial town of 1700 had gone. 'The town which had once extended its entrepôt trade from Holland to Newfoundland, and from Norway to the Canaries, was now a small market town collecting and distributing for only twenty miles around.'[72]

Norwich in 1800 was still like Exeter in 1700. Its decline came in the nineteenth century, placed by Clapham between 1818 and 1850, although it has recently been pushed even further into the century. Certainly, it is unlikely that any actual or even relative decline started in the eighteenth century. Norwich was itself a major weaving centre, specializing in luxury production using cheap, plentiful labour, and by the eighteenth century relatively free of control by the Weavers' Company. The new techniques used in the north were simply not applicable to luxury production or necessary with cheap labour. Norwich was essentially a survival, a persistence of old forms of production. Mass production by steam power and factories did not immediately triumph over high quality production on handicraft lines. Norwich kept its niche as long as this was so. What is also true is that Norwich did not foster the development of these new forms. It survived for some time, but it was being acted upon by a process in which it did not participate. Sooner or later its niche would disappear before the assault of the new forces at work in the economy. Once again, the town was left with the residual function of social and regional capital of an agricultural hinterland. Like York and Exeter before it, Norwich was adjusting to changes elsewhere in a negative fashion and not making any positive contribution itself.[73]

It is, of course, also true that towns *expanded* because of processes outside themselves. This raises a conceptual problem which is discussed in the next section. For the moment, it is simply being pointed out that a case can be made in contradiction of those who deny that the towns could have played any role in creating the preconditions of the industrial revolution. The towns can indeed be portrayed as the vital markets inducing change, as the locations

[72] Hoskins, *Industry, trade and people in Exeter.*
[73] Clapham, *Econ. J.* (1910); Lloyd-Pritchard, *Econ. Hist. Rev.* (1950–1); Edwards, *Yorks Bull. Econ. and Soc. Res.* (1964); Corfield in Clark and Slack (eds.), *Crisis and order.*

of non-traditional consumption patterns, and as demographic regulators. Certainly, there is a danger of exaggeration and the significance must be played down, perhaps with the emphasis placed rather upon the manner in which agriculture responded and the fact that English society was much less 'dual' than usual at the onset of industrialization. Against this it can be argued that the actual location of industry is of less relevance than the demand for its products, and that in any case the relative decline of urban industry was in some cases encouraged by interests from within the towns. And while some urban institutions had become anachronistic, if the trend was in any case set in the direction of growth they could be by-passed. This all amounts to saying that the towns were on balance factors assisting and not hindering development – but not of the importance suggested by some authors.

What is clear is that the claim that 'the presence of an overly large city in a pre-industrial society may act as a curb rather than a stimulus to wider economic growth'[74] cannot be applied to London – although if any European city was 'overly large' in the eighteenth century it was London, in terms both of the gap between it and the next largest city, and the proportion of total population it contained. The hostility of contemporaries to the size of London in the eighteenth century has been echoed more recently by those who see large or 'primate' cities in developing countries as 'somewhat parasitical in the sense that profits of trade, capital accumulated in agricultural and other primary pursuits have been dissipated in grandiose urban construction, servicing and consuming'.[75] Wrigley denies this for eighteenth-century London, and it must be agreed that London was on balance not 'parasitical' even if its role as a positive agent of change is played down – it was more than a symbol of the past. Some writers on currently developing countries are taking a similar line. Analysts of the third world have – like

[74] Lampard, *Econ. Dev. and Cult. Change* (1955), p. 131.

[75] As a general phenomenon, it has been suggested that the second city in the urban hierarchy will be half the size of the first, the next will have a population one-third that of the largest, and so on. When this rule is broken, the largest city is referred to as a 'primate' city. London's population was about thirty times that of the second city. The concept is from Zipf, *National unity*. There has since been a large literature on the subject, primarily by geographers. The idea has had practical importance in the attempts of planners to guide the process of development: see Berry, *The human consequences of urbanisation*, pp. 99–114. The quotation is from Lampard, *Econ. Dev. and Cult. Change*, p. 131.

commentators on London – seen the large cities as non-productive, as centres of conspicuous consumption, of luxury. But S. K. Mehta's rigorous statistical analysis of the effects upon economic development have led him to suggest that 'the results do not warrant a clear negative judgement of primacy'.[76] B. J. L. Berry goes further and argues that at least in the West during its development, primacy is a positive feature. In the third world, only the primate city is the centre of modernization. This city has been the seat of the colonial power and of the commercial interests exploiting the hinterland. The countryside and the small towns remain traditional. On this argument, London as a primate city was of less significance, for it was not the only centre of modernization. As Berry points out, in the West the pattern was one of 'development filtering down the urban hierarchy and spreading its effects outwards within urban fields'.[77] Each town, he argues, was a centre of modernization, the process not being solely concentrated upon the primate city at the head of the urban hierarchy. Neither for that matter was it concentrated entirely upon the towns. London, then, was a force for change but not the only one, the other towns having a role as well, whilst the changes in the countryside must also be given independent weight.

The historian looking forward at the end of the eighteenth century could have been Adam Smith – familiar with British towns – rather than Braudel's suggested Rousseau, who was more familiar with French towns:

> the increase and riches of commercial and manufacturing towns contributed to the improvement and cultivation of the countries to which they belonged...through the greater part of Europe the commerce and manufactures of cities, instead of being the effect, have been the cause and occasion of the improvement and cultivation of the country.[78]

Perhaps this is to err too far in the opposite direction – the greater part of Europe? – but at least for England the direction *is* right.

III

The word used by Braudel to describe the capitals of the *ancien*

[76] Mehta, *Demography* (1964).
[77] Berry, *The human consequences of urbanisation*, pp. 98–9.
[78] Smith, *Wealth of nations*, pp. 507, 515.

régime is 'parasites'. But Hoselitz has suggested that a town may be parasitic in one sense while generative in another. According to his typology, there are four categories: towns which foster economic growth and cultural change; towns which foster cultural change but with an unfavourable impact upon economic development; towns which foster economic growth but are resistant to cultural change; towns which induce economic stagnation and impede cultural change.[79] It might be queried to what extent these are really independent variables. If by cultural change is meant the development of non-traditional consumption patterns, it seems likely that there can be only a limited degree of economic growth in the absence of cultural change (and, as the reverse, little cultural change in the absence of economic growth). The two variables are not, then, fully independent and the intermediate cases can only be of short duration. Braudel's interpretation utilizes the two extremes – the towns of medieval Europe had been in the first category, but had by the eighteenth century moved into the fourth category. They had broken with feudal society but then their institutions had become barriers to further cultural change, whilst they drew surpluses away from the country for non-productive uses. This is to neglect the albeit shortlived intermediate cases. Some English towns in the eighteenth century might have become parasitic in one sense, with their guilds, corporations and charters, but not in both senses. Much more were they generative in both senses, acting as solvents of cultural traditionalism and as centres of demand helping to induce economic growth.

It could, however, be objected that both sides in the debate have missed the crucial point – that towns are social products, simply the containers of interests, and have no independent significance in their own right. It is more than thirty years since William Diamond warned of the 'dangers of an urban interpretation of history' – a warning which is now perhaps even more necessary.[80] The towns, it can be argued, could be neither agents of nor barriers to change, because they are themselves dependent variables; the historian should concentrate not on differences in the internal characteristics of towns but rather upon the wider forces at work more generally. The town in itself – so the argument runs – has no independent causal significance but is simply a product of various social and

---

[79] Hoselitz, *Econ. Dev. and Cult. Change* (1954–5).
[80] Diamond in Goldman (ed.), *Historiography and urbanization*.

economic processes, a real understanding of which is obscured by concentration on the town in isolation. The town is simply not a useful heuristic device.

Two levels of analysis should be distinguished. The first (or micro) level of analysis concentrates on the variation in the experience of towns in relation to the changes occurring in the society and economy as a whole. Why, for example, did Liverpool corporation build a dock system and seize new opportunities, whereas Bristol corporation did not, although both had a closed membership, largely dominated by merchants? Certainly, an urban interpretation of history must be guarded against, but such an analysis of urban rivalry is of interest in its own right, and helps to locate the precise 'mix' needed for growth. It is analogous to asking on the national level why Britain grew faster than France. The town – or nation – is not being given causal significance; the concern is simply with the exact nature of the interests which enable one area to experience more rapid development than another. This is to inquire into what causes urban growth, why one town has greater success than another within the general growth process. In part it helps locate the exact causes of that general growth, but the main consideration is whether towns can affect their own destiny or not. The analysis of 'urban rivalry' – the way in which merchants of one city compete with the merchants of another city for as large a share of trade and as wide a hinterland, as possible – is a low-level but useful exercise. It was a phenomenon which was often repeated. But of course it is not the town itself which is the independent factor – it is the merchants and others whose investments happen to be in that particular location. At most, the urban institutions and forms which have grown up over time might be more or less flexible, but even this is marginal, for if growth was taking place inflexible forms could be by-passed. It was only if decline was occurring in any case that the old institutions would persist. In any case, for the general process of growth it matters very little if town (A) grows quicker than town (B) or *vice versa*.[81]

The analysis must also be on a second (or macro) level, asking if the degree of urbanization has any independent effect upon industrialization. This is to move from explaining differences between towns in response to a society-wide process, to asking whether towns *en masse* could shape that process as independent agents.

[81] Glaab in Hauser and Schnore (eds.), *Study of urbanisation*, pp. 67–9.

Development economists have certainly argued that the level of urbanization in a society is of independent significance – an area might be 'overurbanised' which acts as a barrier to development.[82] It could, however, be argued that the level of urban population at any time is simply a function of population growth and the capacity to absorb that population, so that to argue that the towns are a barrier to development is a tautology. Development economists who try to define a level of urbanization which is somehow 'correct' are surely missing the point, for the relative level of urbanization is a dependent variable reflecting the respective rates of growth of population and industrial employment. The 'correct' level of urbanization relative to industrialization has been defined in two ways. One is to define the relationship on the basis of all countries at one point in time.[83] This is obviously unhistorical, confusing societies at very different stages of development. The second approach takes the experience of the United States, Germany, Britain as the 'correct' relationship to be followed. So if one in twelve live in cities in Asia, the proportion of the work force in non-agricultural activities should be 55 per cent as it was in western countries at such a level of urbanization. In fact, the Asian figure is 30 per cent, so the area is said to be 'overurbanised'.[84] But there is in fact no reason why the relationship should be the same, for the level of urbanization is a dependent variable, and the other items in the two experiences are different. The population in currently developing countries has been increasing at well above twice the rate found in eighteenth-century England. This completely changed the whole problem of the shifting pattern of labour supply and demand, particularly because, as a result of industrialization in the West,

[82] See Sovani, *Econ. Dev. and Cult. Change* (1964).
[83] Davis and Golden, *Econ. Dev. and Cult. Change* (1954–5).
[84] *Urbanisation in Asia*, p. 133. This approach has led development economists to suggest 'urban developments in the west as a model by means of which the interaction between urbanisation and economic growth can best be studied' and to urge 'the comparative study of urbanisation processes in currently underdeveloped countries and similar processes in the history of advanced countries, especially in western Europe' (Hoselitz, *J. Pol. Econ.* (1953), pp. 198, 207). See also the critical remarks of McGee, *Urbanization process in the third world*, pp. 13–34. To economists there seems an attraction in exchanging a complex present for a more tractable past which has a spurious simplicity, because the 'result' of the processes seems obvious. In fact, as Law has said, 'very little is known about urban growth and urban economics in the eighteenth century' (Law, *Local Historian* (1972), p. 13).

there was actually a fall in the percentage of population in developing countries engaged in manufacturing, from perhaps 10 per cent in the mid-nineteenth century to about 7.6 per cent in 1950. In eighteenth-century England, the growth of the population was low enough to be absorbed fairly easily by the growing industrial employment, whether in country or town. But in the third world between 1950 and 1960 industry has been able to absorb only about 10 per cent of the surplus active rural population. Manufacturing employment has been increasing in absolute terms as rapidly as it did in the West; the crucial difference is the much faster rate of population growth. The rural areas simply have not been able to handle the increased population, and optimum densities were reached in most areas by the early years of this century. In eighteenth-century England, the relatively slow growth of population made possible a relatively smooth absorption of labour in outwork in the countryside and a manageable increase in the urban population from 13 to 25 per cent over the century. In the third world, the population increase cannot be absorbed in industry wherever located and has simply been pushed into the towns which increased between 1920 and 1960 at an annual rate of about 4 per cent. The whole situation is thus completely different, and it is difficult to see why the exact relationship between the percentage of population living in towns and working in non-agricultural occupations should be taken as a constant when everything else has changed. The level of urbanization also appears much more as a reflection of other variables than as an independent factor.[85]

This is to minimize the role of towns as an independent variable but it cannot be entirely denied. For after all, one of the determinants (if not the most significant) of the lower population growth in England was that the high urban death rate acted as a regulator, whereas in the third world today, urban death rates are above the rural because of the presence of western medicine, and so population growth is exacerbated. The towns do also act as a solvent of social norms and traditional consumption patterns. To the extent that the towns did have an independent role, it was on the side of modernization. But it would on the whole be wiser simply to take the level of urban population as given and concentrate on a different range of questions which do not raise these conceptual problems. How were cities provisioned? What were the processes by which the

[85] Bairoch, *Urban unemployment in developing countries*, pp. 7–24.

cities were built – who erected the houses, who provided the land and capital? Dr Chalklin has recently studied this aspect.[86] And how did men adjust to life in this new environment, how was the society controlled and governed? On this level, it is certainly important that industrialization proceeded ahead of urbanization, for the process of adjustment was thereby eased.[87] Certainly, the towns of the eighteenth century merit study – but perhaps not as useful analytical tools in explaining economic growth.

[86] Chalklin, *The provincial towns.*
[87] Reissman, *Urban process*, pp. 212–34.

11. *Aspects of Urbanization and Economic Development in Germany 1815-1914*

J. J. LEE

The population of Germany rose from about 15 million in 1750 to 35 million in 1850 and to 67 million in 1914.[1] The urban proportion of this population, defined to include those living in settlements of more than 2,000 people, remained fairly stable, at about 25 per cent, between 1750 and 1850. The pace of urbanization accelerated dramatically in the 1850s, when the urban population grew about two and a half times as fast as the rural population, reflecting the industrial spurt that began about mid-century.[2] The urban proportion reached 36 per cent in 1871 and 60 per cent in 1914.[3] The number of urban places may have doubled during the nineteenth century from about 1,500 to 3,000.[4] About 600 of these had between 10,000 and 25,000 inhabitants on the eve of the First World War, 100 had between 25,000 and 50,000, about 50 had from 50,000 to 100,000, and nearly another 50 had over 100,000. Two-thirds of the increase in total urban population after 1870, however, was concentrated in the cities with more than 100,000 inhabitants in 1914. Only Berlin and Hamburg had reached this size in 1830. Eight cities reached it by 1870, and forty-eight by 1910.[5] The number of German cities in this category surpassed Britain's thirty-nine in 1905, when Russia had nineteen, France fifteen and Italy eleven.[6]

[1] 1914 frontiers.   [2] Weber, *The growth of cities*, p. 85.
[3] *Ibid.* pp. 82-3. See also Köllman, *Bevölkerung in der industriellen Revolution*, and especially, *J. Contemp. Hist.* (1969). This article by a leading German authority provides an admirable survey of the subject. I have generally taken it as a point of departure for this essay, and have tried to avoid duplication except for the barest essentials.
[4] Calculated - on crude assumptions - from Weber, *The growth of cities*, pp. 83, 90.
[5] Calculated from Dawson, *Municipal life*, p. 156 and from *Statistisches Jahrbuch für das Deutsche Reich*, 1921-2, p. 6. Note that city in the text without further qualification henceforth refers to centres with populations exceeding 100,000.
[6] Schott, *Die grossstädtischen Agglomerationen*, pp. 1, 4; Most in Kaiser Wilhelm Dank (ed.), *Deutschland*, p. 168, n.2. The precision in these comparisons is inevitably misleading. Some suburbs of Berlin with populations

Five types can be loosely distinguished among German cities. Firstly, the old maritime ports. Their fortunes diverged. Hamburg, Altona, and Bremen flourished by virtue of the growing North Sea–Atlantic orientation of German foreign trade in the nineteenth century while their Baltic Sea sisters, Lübeck, Danzig and Königsberg, grew much more slowly. Bremen, it is true, fell from tenth to seventeenth place in the urban league table, but the Baltic Sea cities fell further – Königsberg from third to eighteenth, Lübeck from ninth to thirty-seventh, Danzig from eleventh to twenty-fourth. Stettin, which retained twentieth place in the rankings, proved the sole exception to the retarded rate of growth among the Baltic cities.[7]

The textile towns expanded particularly rapidly between 1750 and 1850. The growth of Aachen, Crefeld, Elberfeld, Barmen and Plauen, which remained primarily textile towns, lagged somewhat later in the nineteenth century as other growth sectors superseded textiles. Chemnitz maintained its ranking by diversifying into mechanical engineering.

Nine cities in the Ruhr and Saar owed their initial growth to their favourable location in relation to natural resources. The spectacular development of these cities, which as a type grew more rapidly than any other, has tended to divert attention from the growth of the other twenty inland cities. These can be loosely sub-divided into eleven commercial cities, whose importance depended primarily on their command of strategic internal trade routes, and nine court cities, who derived their initial importance, by definition, from the presence of the court. The division remains loose because these types inevitably overlapped to some extent. But the distinction retains some analytical use.

Kiel and Ludwigshafen defy convenient categorization. Kiel owed its spectacular growth after 1880 to naval expansion, and Ludwig-

exceeding 1,000,000 were still classified as separate cities in 1905, thus exaggerating the German number. Nevertheless, the general point stands.

[7] The 'urban league table' of the text has been compiled in rough and ready fashion. Where administrative and economic criteria jostle each other confusedly in the statistics it would be foolhardy to claim finality for the precise rankings in the table. However, the direction of movement seems to survive suspicion. The population data for c. 1800 are drawn from Bruford, *Germany in the eighteenth century*, appendix 2, pp. 333–6, supplemented by several incidental references and spot checks on data for contiguous dates. The early twentieth-century figures come mainly from statistical yearbooks and from Schott, *Die grossstädtischen Agglomerationen*, whose appendices contain a mass of useful data.

shafen, which began from virtually nothing in 1850, grew up around the great chemical enterprise, the Badische Analin- und Sodafabrik. This typology is obviously a very elementary one indeed. It does, however, serve to emphasize the fact that except for the cities based on natural resources, and a couple of residual mavericks, the remainder were 'old' cities. Three quarters of the German cities of 1914 were already leading urban centres, by the then standards of urbanization, a century previously. This may seem somewhat surprising in view of the disruptive consequences frequently attributed to the speed of German industrialization.

The most important influence on this pattern of urbanization appears to be the manner in which the railway came to Germany. The impact of the railway helped differentiate the growth rates of Stettin and its sister cities on the Baltic coast. The change in the relative fortunes of the Baltic ports can be traced to the fifteen years between 1840 and 1855, when Danzig's population rose only 9 per cent, and Königsberg's 18 per cent, compared with Stettin's 48 per cent.[8] Stettin had the good fortune to be the Prussian port closest to Berlin, which helped it acquire a railway link with the capital in 1843, whereas Danzig and Königsberg had both to wait until the following decade.[9] Improved communications were a prerequisite for the urbanization of the Ruhr. It was through the railway that the inland communication centres generally consolidated their position, while the apparently more vulnerable court cities transformed themselves into major industrial centres. The court cities had not featured conspicuously in the first stage – the textile stage – of German industrialization. The textile industry tended to develop either in rural areas, or in less traditional urban centres. The early railway system, however, was based mainly on the state capitals. Several states nationalized their railways at an early stage. Even Prussia, which initially rejected public ownership in principle, exerted close control over developments.[10] The earliest major German railway lines therefore catered mainly for the interests of the court cities, which were served by more than 1,000 of the 1,300 kilometres of track open in 1843.[11]

[8] Wappäus, *Bevölkerungsstatistik*, ii, p. 528.

[9] For the completion of the lines to Danzig and Königsberg, see Henderson, *The state and industrial revolution in Prussia*, pp. 172ff.

[10] *Ibid.* pp. 150–68.

[11] Maps of the early German lines can be conveniently consulted in

The railways helped transform the court cities from parasitic into generative types. Most of the main locomotive and wagon-building firms chose, or were compelled by the state governments to choose, proximity to their markets, and influence over sources of contracts, by locating close to the courts. These firms accounted for disproportionately high shares of workers in the engineering sector in the early stages of German industrial development. In 1861 the two Berlin firms of Borsig and Pflug employed 10.4 per cent of all workers in Prussian mechanical engineering. Maffei in Munich accounted for 17 per cent of the Bavarian mechanical engineering force at that date, Kessler in Karlsruhe for 47 per cent of the Baden force, the Württemberg Company in Esslingen near Stuttgart for 30 per cent of the Württemberg force, Henschel in Cassel for 35 per cent of the Hessian, Egestorff in Linden near Hanover for 48 per cent of the Hanoverian.[12] These firms trained the core of the skilled labour force which in turn attracted other metal firms to their vicinity. Many of the founders of new engineering firms themselves emerged from the older ones. Then, as German industry developed increasingly on the basis of educated and technically trained managerial and labour cadres, the existing court centres enjoyed useful headstarts, particularly as they also tended to be the centres of the technical high schools, fostered on their doorsteps by state officials.

It is therefore to a large extent to the railway that one must trace the growth as engineering centres of many court towns with no particular natural advantages and in many cases with no established tradition of metal work behind them. Of the relevant court centres, Berlin consolidated its prime ranking in the city league. Munich and Dresden, fifth and sixth respectively in 1800, were fourth and sixth in 1914. Karlsruhe rose from about fiftieth to thirty-seventh, Hanover from twenty-seventh to eleventh, and Stuttgart from twenty-fifth to thirteenth. Cassel slipped from twenty-fourth to twenty-sixth place, while Brunswick fell from seventeenth to thirty-second place. Without the court, however, both these centres would almost certainly never have got into the city league at all.

Henderson, *German industrial power*, p. 15 and in Zorn in Léon *et al.* *L'industrialisation en Europe*, p. 387.

[12] Wangenblass, *Der Eisenbahnbau*, pp. 262–3. These were also the biggest mechanical engineering firms in their respective states, except for Maffei of Munich, which was smaller than Cramer–Klett in Nuremberg.

The relative economic importance of the courts within the cities declined dramatically. In 1800 the courts may have provided direct employment for around 25 per cent of the population of many dynastic capitals.[13] A century later direct public employment rarely accounted for more than 5 per cent of the labour force in state capitals. But the dependence of these cities on the court declined only because, in many cases, of the presence of the court in the first instance, which ensured their selection as nodal points on the early railway system.

The diffusion of engineering firms to cater for early railway demand helps account for the remarkably widespread location of the German engineering industry. Engineering counted among the three biggest industries on the eve of the First World War in almost all cities, even in centres like Munich that are rarely associated with this industry. A main reason why regional differences remained surprisingly stable and relatively narrow, despite the classic west–east and north–south gradients, in the course of German industrialization, lies in the location of the engineering industry in general, and in the growth of Berlin in particular.

Berlin's proportion of the city population in general fell from more than 50 per cent in 1800 to less than 25 per cent in 1914. Nevertheless, it is difficult to exaggerate the importance of Berlin's growth in the nineteenth century. With a population of 4 million, it was the biggest agglomeration on the continent by 1914. One-third the size of Paris in 1800, it had outstripped the French capital on the eve of the First World War. Smaller than Moscow or Leningrad in 1800, it was nearly double their size a century later. Within Germany, the railway permitted Berlin to widen the demographic distance between itself and Hamburg. It was only about 30 per cent bigger than the main port in 1800. By 1914 it had nearly treble Hamburg's population.[14] No other major European capital grew at more than half Berlin's rate between 1800 and 1914.

Berlin's location so relatively far east counteracted to some extent the regional imbalance that would otherwise have been accentuated by the rapid development of the Ruhr after 1850. The absolute increase in the population of Berlin exceeded that of all the Ruhr

---

[13] For an excellent discussion of the role of the court in the urban economy in the late eighteenth century see Blanning, *Reform and revolution*.

[14] Agglomeration data from Schott, *Die grossstädtischen Agglomerationen*, pp. 97ff. See also Thienel, *Städtewachstum*.

cities combined in the nineteenth century. The magnet of the Berlin market provided a major attraction for east Elbian agriculture and for Silesian coal. The economic role of Berlin in the east Elbian economy will no doubt attract closer scrutiny than it has tended to receive once moralistic indignation at the role of Junkers, which has vitiated many of even the best studies of the east Elbian economy, begins to abate.[15] It would be tempting to speculate, for instance, on the implications for emigration, or for east Elbian migration to the west, of a more slowly growing Berlin.

It may not be entirely illegitimate to speculate here on the accident of timing in economic history. Had the railway followed a half century of general industrialization, as it did in England, then a number of centres of industrial rather than court capitalism might already have emerged to serve as obvious nodal points on a railway network. Had the unification of Germany preceded the coming of the railway, then it is not inconceivable that the state capitals would have exerted less influence on the planning of the system. One can plausibly argue that had the railways not been built as they were when they were, Prussia would not have conquered Germany, insofar as the campaigns of 1866 and 1870 might either not have been fought at all or might have ended differently. In that case, apart from other considerations, Berlin might have grown less rapidly. One cannot integrate in any coherent manner this sort of consideration into economic history, but that does not mean that it is any less relevant than aspects that can be systematically considered.

The distribution of cities naturally exerted a significant influence on migration patterns. Internal migration assumed massive dimensions as the nineteenth century progressed. Half the population were classified as internal migrants in the occupational census of 1907. The fraction of the city labour force recorded in this category was inevitably higher – about two thirds in 1907. Migration was overwhelmingly local in the earlier nineteenth century and, despite the spectacular east Elbian influx into the Ruhr after 1895, remained predominantly local even with growing industrialization.[16]

---

[15] Much of the work stimulated by the brilliant insights of Hans Rosenberg, for instance, has allowed hostility to the Junkers to distort slightly its perspective on the strictly economic history of east Elbia. An approach, comparable to that adopted by Croon in *Third International Conference of Economic History*, could fruitfully be applied to Berlin.

[16] Köllman, *J. Contemp. Hist.* (1969), pp. 66ff. See also Heberle and Meyer, *Die Grossstädte*.

The implications of migration movements pose some of the most interesting challenges of German urban studies. The sharp variations in the proportions of those born in rural areas between different cities, ranging from 12 per cent in Aachen to 50 per cent in Königsberg in 1907, may help our understanding of their varying demographic, social and political behaviour. In some respects the city seems to belong more to regional than to urban history. Insofar, for instance, as the migration was generally short distance, and insofar as specific regional cultures existed, then migration may not have required as rapid or as traumatic a psychic journey as some models suggest. Urban birth and death rates, particularly infant mortality rates, appear to have depended more on city location than on city type. Dr Knodel's work has reinforced the serious reservations expressed nearly twenty years ago by Dr Wrigley on the utility of rural–urban distinctions in studies of fertility and mortality in late nineteenth- and early twentieth-century Germany.[17] Other observations tend in the same direction. The demographic experience of the coal cities in the Ruhr diverges less from that of the non-coal cities than from that of the coal towns of the Saxon and Silesian fields. The population patterns in the coastal cities diverge more sharply from each other than from those in the surrounding hinterlands. The textile towns of Saxony and Westphalia conform more closely to the demographic norms of Saxony and Westphalia than to each other's experience. Weaning habits, which exerted considerable influence on infant mortality, were likely to be more similar in town and contiguous country, than in different towns or for that matter in different rural areas.[18] It remains to be adequately investigated to what extent the birth rates in different cities, and the varying rates of fertility decline, were influenced by the proportions of those born in rural and urban areas, and by marriage patterns among migrants.

The velocity and volatility of migration movements exerted particular influence on urban residential building fluctuations. The building booms, of 1860–5, 1871–5, 1886–90, 1896–1900, 1903–6, 1909–11, coincided with increased internal migration. The only period of high migration when building failed to boom was 1867–9.

[17] Wrigley, *Industrial growth*, pp. 167ff.; Knodel, *Decline of fertility*, pp. 206–22. General historians have failed to explore the implications of Wrigley's work for the town–country dichotomy so fashionable in traditional historiography.

[18] Knodel, *Pop. Stud.* (1968); Knodel and van de Walle, *Pop. Stud.* (1967).

Conversely, the building slumps, of 1876–85, 1892–5, 1900–2, 1907–1909, all occurred during periods of low migration. This is not necessarily to argue that migrant demand was the crucial component of housing demand. It is, however, to argue that migrant demand was the single most important influence on fluctuations in housing demand. Table 1 provides some indication of the magnitude of fluctuations in rates of population growth deriving from migration.

TABLE 1. Natural increase and net migration in Mannheim, Duisburg and Berlin

	Natural increase	Net gain from migration
Mannheim		
1871–5	2,479	4,368
1876–80	3,664	3,348
1881–5	3,649	4,159
1886–90	4,724	13,061
1891–5	7,337	4,724
1896–1900	12,328	23,404
1901–5	15,362	7,200
1906–10	17,660	7,568
Duisburg		
1872–5	2,600	3,900
1876–80	4,100	—300
Berlin		
1871–5	34,000	155,000
1876–80	69,000	90,000
1881–5	51,000	130,000
1886–90	79,000	185,000
1891–5	72,000	20,000
1896–1900	85,000	123,000
1901–5	81,000	74,000

Reservations may be expressed about the effectiveness of migrant demand for housing. Did not the young, unskilled, unmarried migrants merely increase the demand for sleeping quarters rather than for dwellings? Even where migrants were merely lodgers, of course, their rents may have allowed the family to occupy an extra room which it could not otherwise have afforded. In 1880 25 per cent of families in Breslau and Leipzig, 24 per cent of families in

Berlin, and 20 per cent of Hamburg families took lodgers.[19] It is true, however, that not more than 15 per cent of migrants were household heads, that a high proportion of domestic servants fitted directly, if fleetingly, into existing households, and that many seasonal migrants, particularly building workers, lived very rough indeed. These reservations have considerable validity if one is measuring total housing demand, but they are less relevant to explanations of fluctuations in demand. It is the violence in the fluctuations in migration movements relative to the level of household formation by marriage that is crucial in this respect. If demand for residential accommodation reflected marriage demand alone there would have been much less occasion for severe fluctuations in demand. Except in the later 1870s the absolute number of marriages rarely fluctuated seriously.[20] And in this respect, changes in migration rates, appropriately lagged, accounted for a substantial proportion of fluctuations in the marriage market.

Even if one were to discount this line of reasoning, it is by no means clear that ex-post comparisons of migration demand with marriage demand allots adequate weighting to the role of migration in builders' expectations. Builders tended to guess potential demand by anticipating absolute rates of population change rather than by calculating rates of household formation.[21] As migration largely accounted for variations in the rate of urban population change, this would appear to invest migration movements with decisive importance in builders' expectations.

The chronology of German building activity – peaks in 1843, 1853, 1865, 1875, 1890, 1900, 1906 and 1911, troughs in 1848, 1856, 1880, 1895, 1902, 1908 and 1913 – provides little support for the assertion that the German building cycle 'seems virtually to have coincided with the U.S. building cycle, at least between 1870 and 1900'.[22] Insofar as it coincided with any other cycle, it was, until

[19] Neefe, *Schriften des Vereins für Sozialpolitik* (1886), pp. 198–9.

[20] *Statistisches Jahrbuch für das Deutsche Reich*, 1921–2, p. 37. The number of marriages fell from 423,900 in 1872 (swollen by the return of soldiers from the war), to 335,113 in 1879. Thereafter increases rarely exceeded 10,000 per annum, and the only falls to exceed 10,000 occurred between 1901 and 1902, when the total fell from 468,329 to 457,208, and from 1912 to 1913, when the total fell from 523,491 to 513,283.

[21] *Baugewerks-Zeitung*, 5 January 1887.

[22] Lewis and O'Leary, *The Manchester School* (1955), p. 130. True, some similarity can be detected between the Hamburg series, on which Lewis and O'Leary rely heavily for this period, and their American series. This is

1885, with the British. There were apparent troughs in both countries in the mid-1850s. There were peaks in British building activity in 1864 and 1876, compared with 1865 and 1875 in Germany. Both countries experienced deep slump in the later 1870s and early 1880s. The parting of the ways came when German building activity, unlike British, revived strongly in the later 1880s. It then momentarily appeared as if Germany may have indeed been aligning herself with America. Building in both countries peaked in the early 1890s, and then declined sharply. Another crossroads was reached in the mid-1890s, however, for Germany recovered strongly after 1895 whereas American building remained depressed until 1900.

Migration patterns largely account for the similarities and contrasts between German and British building cycles. Until the mid-1880s the chronology of internal migration movements in both countries was roughly similar. It was high in the early 1860s and the early 1870s, low in the later 1870s and early 1880s. Whereas in Britain emigration continued high, and internal migration low, throughout the 1880s, emigration declined sharply in Germany after 1885, and internal migration revived strongly. Hitherto, emigration and internal migration had been directly, not inversely, related in Germany. Both were high from 1867 to 1873, when America and West Germany boomed together. Both were low from 1874 to 1879, when the American slump choked off emigration as effectively as the German slump discouraged internal migration. An inverse relationship between emigration and internal migration began in Germany in the early 1880s. The huge increase in emigration, as America boomed during continued slump in Germany, contrasted with the low level of internal migration. When Germany revived after 1885 emigration fell by over 60 per cent until 1890, as the migratory wave now began to be diverted from American to German cities. American conditions remained relevant into the 1890s, however. They were reflected in the increase in emigration to a still booming America during the German slump in 1890–2, and still more in the sharp fall in emigration, despite continuing deep depression in Germany, at the onset of the American slump in 1893. Hence-

hardly surprising in view of the Hamburg–American connections. Hamburg, however, was quite unrepresentative of German experience. The data on German building activity summarized in this section are drawn from a more detailed study contained in my forthcoming *Economic history of Germany, 1750–1939.* See also Habakkuk, *J. Econ. Hist.* (1962).

forth, however, German conditions became completely dominant. Emigration dwindled away to a trickle, and there was even a small net immigration on occasions. The depression of 1900–2 brought a sharp fall in the high internal migration rates of the preceding five years, but for the first time no significant increase in emigration despite booming conditions in America.

Discussion of the German building industry can largely ignore the Atlantic cycle, simply because the linkages postulated between emigration and investment in the British case did not exist in Germany. Foreign investment was not a serious competitor for funds, and in any event moved inversely to emigration. Foreign investment fluctuated directly, not inversely, with domestic investment. The German passive investor, like his British counterpart earlier in the century, hoarded his money in slumps until better days should come again.

Consols and, once the Reichsbank acquired control over open market operations after 1889, short-term bills, provided the main competition to mortgage banks for the funds of the potential investors in housing. A virtually perfect market existed between mortgage debentures and consols. The mortgage rate followed the long-term interest rate closely. The mortgage banks, which dominated the supply of capital to urban builders until about 1895, and remained the single most important source of finance until 1913, despite the rapidly growing importance of savings banks and insurance companies, responded fairly promptly to the rise in interest rates after the secular fall from 1875 to 1895. But when the bond rate, for the first time in such circumstances, failed to fall in the wake of the 1907 financial crisis, the reluctance of the mortgage banks to maintain their rates accordingly was a contributory factor to the erratic nature of the subsequent building revival.

Until very shortly before the First World War internal migration accounted not only for the differences in timing between German and British or German and American building cycles, but also provided the key to the relationship between the building cycle and the general trade cycle. Because the building cycle was essentially an internal migration cycle, and because internal migration was a direct function of the trade cycle, the building cycle tended to coincide with the general cycle. The impact of migration on the housing market naturally depended on the rate of vacancies prevailing at the onset of a migratory wave. Berlin builders understandably responded more sluggishly to the impact of the new migration waves in 1867 and 1895, faced with vacancy rates of 5.6 and 6.9 per cent respectively, than in 1871 and 1885, when vacancies were already as low as 1.2 and 2.4 per cent respectively. As a high vacancy rate was itself usually a result of the suddenness and size of the fall in migration in the preceding cycle, this brings one back to migration via another route.

Migration movements changed so abruptly that the builders' margin of predictive error concerning market developments was often very narrow. Little objective economic reason existed why the building industry could not generally adjust output rapidly. The vast majority of builders were small men, operating overwhelmingly on credit, employing little fixed capital. And, in practice, the building industry did achieve striking changes in output over short periods. Completions (living rooms) doubled in Essen between 1905 and 1907, fell by 50 per cent between 1907 and 1909, more than doubled in 1910, rose another 60 per cent in 1911, but then fell by over 50 per cent in 1912 and again by more than 50 per cent in 1913.[23] Output in Frankfurt fell 50 per cent between 1891 and 1892, and again 30 per cent between 1896 and 1897. It doubled from 1899 to 1900 and again from 1901 to 1902.

Even when supply responded promptly in the correct direction to market pressures, the sheer abruptness and magnitude of changes in migration movements made it virtually impossible to adjust to the shifting market situation. Output in Hamburg fell 17 per cent between 1890 and 1891, but the vacancy rate rose from 5.9 to 8.4 per cent. Output in Berlin fell 40 per cent between 1890 and 1892, but this failed to prevent vacancies rising from 2.6 to 4.9 per cent as a net gain of 42,000 from migration in 1889 plunged to a net loss of 2,400 in 1892. A 40 per cent decline in output in Dresden from 1900 to 1902 did not suffice to prevent vacancies doubling from 3 to 6 per cent.[24]

Inadequate adjustment in only one year could create imbalances in the housing market that might take a number of years to correct.

[23] *Statistisches Jahrbuch der Stadt Essen*, vi (1912), table 66, p. 41; vii (1913–19), tables 79 and 93.

[24] Reich, *Der Wohnungsmarkt*, table i, p. 125; tables xiv and xv, p. 135; and *Bericht der Handelskammer Dresden über das Jahr 1901*, pt 2, pp. 2, 126; *ibid. 1902*, pt 2, p. 105. For indications of the variety of pressures influencing Berlin builders in the slump year 1891, see *Baugewerks–Zeitung*, 28 February, 21 March, 24 October 1891.

These were reflected in the wide spread of vacancy rates, usually ranging from 1 to 10 per cent, that prevailed at any given moment in German cities. No obvious pattern existed in vacancy rates even between cities of similar types. Hamburg's rate of 7 per cent in 1910 contrasted with Bremen's 2.9 per cent, Königsberg had a rate of only 0.5 per cent, compared with Stettin's 4.1 per cent.[25]

Rent levels therefore tended to vary far more from city to city than prices of the other essentials, food and clothing. There was no national housing market. Housing densities and conditions in general varied widely, even for groups on the same income levels, between cities.[26] In 1871, to take an extreme case, 825,000 Berliners were crammed within city boundaries smaller than those of Frankfurt, with 90,000 inhabitants. Housing conditions deteriorated sharply in Berlin between 1860 and 1880. The population doubled, by about 550,000, in that period. Over the same two decades, however, 370,000 people went to live in cellars, or on third or higher floors. As many as 34 per cent of Berlin buildings had at least four storeys in 1880 compared with 15 per cent in 1864; 68 per cent had cellars in 1880 compared with 40 per cent in 1864.[27] The proportion of dwellings on the ground floor or on the first floor fell from 49 per cent in 1861 to 21 per cent in 1900. Berlin remained the most densely populated city in Europe on the eve of the First World War, when the negative externalities of housing density were presumably among the highest in the world.[28]

The short-term housing market seems to have been dominated by local idiosyncrasies, which, if anything, became even more pronounced after 1880. The structure of the local building industry and the quality of the entrepreneurship influenced responses to demand, while the peculiarities of local government compounded the housing situation further. Local authorities enjoyed extensive powers in Germany, but how they chose to use them depended greatly on the calibre of the men at the helm, which inevitably varied widely.[29] German municipal authorities enjoyed in one sense the

[25] *Beilage zu den Statistischen Monatsberichte der Stadt Düsseldorf*, 1910, January–March, p. xiii.

[26] Neefe, *Schriften des Vereins für Sozialpolitik* (1886), pp. 174–6, 186. For densities per dwelling 1895–1905 in a range of German cities, see Niethammer, *Archiv für Sozialgeschichte* (1976), which contains a mass of data on a large number of cities.

[27] Neefe, *Schriften des Vereins für Sozialpolitik* (1886), pp. 186, 188.

[28] Dawson, *Municipal life*, pp. 117–18.

[29] *Ibid. passim*; Most in Kaiser Wilhelm Dank (ed.), *Deutschland*, p. 173.

advantage of the late start. In the 1860s English engineers like William Lindley – responsible for the replanning of Hamburg after the huge fire of the 1840s, and for designing the Frankfurt sewage disposal system installed in 1873 – brought the latest infrastructural techniques to German towns in the initial stages of their rapid expansion. German town planners like Hobrecht in Berlin and Stübben in Cologne imitated Haussman's Parisian model. It would be reassuringly schematic to be able to conclude that German administrators took advantage of this late start, and that the pattern of German urbanization reflects an intermediate stage between the British and later patterns, extending a version of the Gerschenkronian model to social as well as to economic developments. But that does not appear to have been, on the whole, the case.

It would also be agreeably schematic to find that housing conditions corresponded in some sense to the several types of city mentioned earlier, and that they could be packaged within the same sort of wrapping. Again this does not seem to be the case. This disparity arises mainly from the heavily localized nature of the building industry and of municipal government. Virtually the only valid generalization that can be hazarded is that east Elbian cities usually suffered from worse housing conditions than west Elbian, due more to historic than to economic reasons.

A glance at three cities, Leipzig, Chemnitz and Frankfurt, in 1880 illustrates the difficulty of closely correlating city types and housing conditions. Leipzig and Chemnitz were both Saxon cities. Leipzig and Frankfurt were mainly commercial cities, the classic fairs cities, whereas Chemnitz was heavily industrial. Leipzig and Frankfurt had both about 150,000 inhabitants in 1880, Chemnitz just under 100,000. All three had grown at roughly the same rate in the previous twenty years, just about doubling in size between 1860 and 1880. Much closer affinity appeared to exist, in terms of size of dwellings, between the commercial cities than between the Saxon centres. In Frankfurt 24 per cent of dwellings and in Leipzig 28 per cent had only one heated room, compared with 70 per cent in Chemnitz. Density per dwelling did not correspond quite as closely – 3.49 in Frankfurt, 3.84 in Leipzig, 4.3 in Chemnitz.[30] Frankfurt and Chemnitz both had 4 per cent of their populations living on fourth or higher floors, contrasting in this respect with Leipzig's 14 per cent. A further feature, for which there

[30] Neefe, *Schriften des Vereins für Sozialpolitik* (1886), p. 188.

does not appear to be convenient data on Chemnitz, concerns household structures. In 1880 35 per cent of Leipzig households included only nuclear family members compared with 49 per cent in Frankfurt. In Leipzig 16 per cent of households had domestic servants living in, compared with 26 per cent in Frankfurt. On the other hand, 25 per cent of Leipzig households had lodgers, compared with 14 per cent of Frankfurt's. On the face of it, Frankfurt appears to have been a rather more comfortable city than Leipzig – but then one notes that its population density, at about 200 per hectare, was somewhat greater than Leipzig's at about 180 and apparently greater than that of Chemnitz at about 120.[31]

There are peculiar difficulties in hazarding comparisons of this sort, arising *inter alia* from the vagaries of local administrative fiat concerning the incorporation of suburbs and alterations in official city boundaries. No finality can be claimed for the figures cited in the previous paragraph, but perhaps enough has been said to make the elementary but important point that the quality of urban housing, which one might use as a crude proxy for urban living conditions as distinct from working conditions, depended on a host of factors independent of industrial circumstances. There is the further important qualification that for the majority of women living conditions were working conditions.

Even the frequently repulsive housing conditions did not suffice to deter the masses of migrants lured to the city by the hope of choice, by the promise not only of economic but of psychic freedom offered, in prospect if not always in retrospect. 'City air makes free' retained its psychological, if no longer its legal relevance, into the twentieth century. If one could measure the energies released – economic, social, political – by urbanization they might be seen to weigh heavily in the scales of modern German economic history.

[31] *Ibid.* p. 186.

12. *Parasite or Stimulus:*
The Town in a Pre-industrial Economy

E. A. WRIGLEY

Life in cities has often stirred the moral passions of observers. Cities have been condemned as sinks of vice where nobler and simpler rural values were undermined, where both moral and physical decay were prevalent, where people learnt to judge all matters in terms of private advantage and monetary gain. Equally, cities have been praised as the best setting in which an advanced culture could develop, as the chief bulwark against relapse into barbarism, and as the only stage upon which a man of talent and energy could find an opportunity to do justice to his gifts. Views about the economic significance of urban growth are almost as diverse as about their effect on morality, for at times they have been depicted as the prime engines of economic change and growth while at others they have been condemned as parasites feeding upon a flow of wealth generated in the countryside but offering little in return. It is true that whereas condemnation of the city on moral grounds has often been sweeping and absolute, comment upon its economic role has usually been carefully shaded. This is a matter in which circumstances are regarded as altering cases, where some cities may be categorized as serving to stimulate economic growth, while others, by absorbing the surplus wealth produced elsewhere without generating a return flow out into the countryside, are regarded as parasites, but the validity of the contrast is widely taken for granted.

My purpose in directing attention to this ancient battlefield is not to suggest a new and better set of criteria for distinguishing between cities which are parasites and those whose net influence upon the economy as a whole is positive. I wish rather to question the value of the dichotomy and the soundness of the arguments which have been used to justify its use.[1]

[1] Twenty years ago the third volume of the journal *Economic Development and Cultural Change* was devoted to papers discussing the role of cities in relation to economic development and cultural change. One of the papers was by B. F. Hoselitz and was entitled 'Generative and parasitic cities'. Since his paper helped to give currency to the use of the terms, and suggested definitions of them, it is interesting to note that he wrote, 'It is not easy to

The archetypal parasitic city is often said to be one in which the power of a ruling group enables them to levy from the dwellers in the countryside a tribute in money or in kind which is consumed in the cities. There the ruling group lives surrounded by such specialist craftsmen as may be needed to minister to their comforts and luxuries.[2] The return flow of tangible wealth may then be very slight, though even in such circumstances there may be intangible benefits accruing to the countryside if the military power of the city rulers secures the country as a whole from invasion, or if the legal and religious services provided by the city to the country are highly valued. Again, the indirect effect of the demands of urban elites in stimulating technological advance, or in causing certain types of social overhead capital, such as bridges and roads, to be constructed, should not be overlooked. If, however, the exploitation of the country dweller by the ruling group is severe, perhaps involving him in giving up as much as a third of his produce each year, the appropriateness of terming the relation parasitic seems at first sight beyond dispute. It seems evident that the material welfare of a peasant in such circumstances would improve if he were not obliged to make over goods for others to consume of which he and his family stand in need.

What seems evident, however, may prove to be delusive. In the context of the study of the relationship between the activities of cities and success in engendering economic growth, a distinction must be drawn between the division of the current flow of goods produced and the creation of circumstances in which the flow of goods can be increased in volume, either from one level to another, or constantly over time. The notion of the city as a parasite can be given greater meaning in the former context than in the latter. It is .. convenient to simplify excessively in order to make plain the nature of the underlying point.

discover actual instances in which the city has exerted long-run parasitic influence on the economic development of the region which it dominated' (*Econ. Dev. and Cult. Change* (1954–5), p. 282).

[2] This conception clearly informs Sjoberg's writing on the pre-industrial city: 'urban *growth* in societies is invariably highly correlated with the consolidation or extention of a political apparatus. . .The crux of our argument is that as a society broadens its political control it enlarges its economic base as well. City dwellers can then tap the resources of an ever-widening hinterland by draining off the agricultural surpluses of the peasantry and utilizing raw materials such as metal ores that the new domains have to offer' (Sjoberg, *Preindustrial city*, pp. 68–9).

Consider an economy in which all wealth is derived from the land and the productive capacity of the land is fixed. The inhabitants of cities may contribute to the total wealth of the community by working up the produce of the land into a form in which it can be directly consumed, as when wool is converted into cloth, but if they do not, or if what they produce is consumed solely in the city, it seems reasonable to describe cities as parasitic. In such circumstances smaller cities would mean a less severely penalized peasantry. Even in these circumstances it may be hard to sustain the view that the parasitism of the city injures the country dweller or the society as a whole. This would only be true if the city population re-absorbed into the country did not affect the prosperity of the original rural inhabitants as severely as by their presence in cities. If the marginal product of the additional population transferred to rural areas were low because of the high density of the existing rural population, the benefit to rural areas would be slight. To remove city populations entirely might improve matters for those in the countryside, but this is a slightly different point to do with the ratio between population size and the productive capacity of the economy. And even if city populations were to be swept away in this fashion it is quite possible that if there were a consequent rise in the living standards of the rural populations, this would simply induce further population growth and so tend to depress real incomes once more by a different path.

Let us assume, nevertheless, that the transfer or removal of city populations did increase consumption in the countryside. Rural populations which possess no means of securing long-term economic growth often treat production in excess of immediate needs as the occasion for a burst of conspicuous consumption. Indeed in many cases they have little alternative but to do so. They display what might be termed a potlatch syndrome[3] where those with control of the surplus enhance their personal standing by making it available to their followers or to the local community as a whole. As Adam Smith remarked:

> In a country which has neither foreign commerce nor any of the finer manufactures, a great proprietor, having nothing for which he can exchange the greater part of the produce of his lands

---

[3] After the term used to describe the elaborate feasts celebrated by Indian tribes of the coastal areas of north-western North America at which objects of value were given away or destroyed in the course of the feasting.

which is over and above the maintenance of the cultivators, consumes the whole in rustic hospitality at home...Before the extension of commerce and manufactures in Europe, the hospitality of the rich and the great, from the sovereign down to the smallest baron, exceeded everything which, in the present times, we can easily form a notion of.[4]

To consume the surplus in the countryside, rather than surrender it for consumption in cities to meet the needs of a ruling urban elite, is no doubt gratifying to those whose bellies are filled as a result, but it is reasonable to view it as a small matter where the surplus is consumed, and a much more serious matter that it is disposed of, whether in town or country, in a way which makes it improbable that the next generation will be any better clad, housed or fed than the present.

If there is to be an advance in living standards measured by an economic yardstick, there must normally be changes whose occurrence is improbable in the absence of towns once a region has ceased to comprise an agglomeration of largely autarchic small areas. Beyond this stage further advance is apt to depend upon the benefits which flow from specialization of function or from technological advance. To oversimplify outrageously, I would be tempted to characterize the former as the chief source of improvement in production and hence income *per caput* before the industrial revolution, and the latter as providing the bulk of such improvement subsequently. Both sources of economic growth tend to stimulate urban growth and both, but more especially the former, are unlikely to occur without prior urban growth. Thus it might be argued that cities are economically parasitic only in a nugatory fashion and very seldom prohibit or render more difficult economic growth, but that they come close to constituting a *sine qua non* of growth whenever it takes place. In short cities may be regarded as a necessary though certainly not a sufficient cause of economic growth. They are unlikely to stifle growth which would otherwise take place.

These are sweeping claims and it will be prudent to attempt both to elaborate them and to consider some of the objections which might be raised against them.

Consider first the circumstances in which higher productivity is attained by increased specialization of function. This is largely a

---

[4] Smith, *Wealth of nations*, p. 182.

question of the size of the effective market area.[5] If the individual village or, in the limiting case, the individual family, has to provide for its need from its own resources turned into consumable objects by its own labour, the scope for specialization is limited and in consequence the range of consumables produced will be small, their quality may in many cases be poor, and production costs (measured in hours of labour and often in money terms) will be high. Corn will be grown perforce in areas better suited to grazing; houses built by men whose lives are mainly spent in the fields; rough cloth laboriously woven on crude looms. Specialized workers tend to be itinerant. If their market cannot come to them, they must seek out a market or abandon their trade for more mundane pursuits. The effective market area is not, of course, the same for all products. Commodities like salt, silk, spices or jewellery may travel great distances even in periods when local autarchy in general prevails. And the effective market area for a settlement on navigable water was very much larger than for a landlocked village. Lübeck was nearer to Bordeaux than to Leipzig in the fifteenth century; Liverpool in the eighteenth was as close to Boston as to Buxton.

To enable a larger market area to develop, there must be better transport facilities. Unless they come into being the full potential of the existing material technology cannot be realized and there will be little incentive to improve upon it. But if the goods are able to move at lower cost and with greater reliability over longer distances the situation is slowly transformed. East Anglia can grow wheat while the clay vales of Leicestershire are used for pasture. Some towns and villages are freed to devote the bulk of their labour force not simply to woollen manufacture in general but to a particular product – fustians, bays, kersies, fine worsteds. The making of pins, to quote the classic case, may be split amongst a dozen sub-trades rather than being the work of a single pair of hands.

Better transport is not, of course, logically prior to the other changes which make up economic growth. It occurs only in response to the presence of the other components of growth. Together they form an interdependent group. But transport is worth singling out in this context because of its especially close connection with urban

[5] This is a key point in Adam Smith's treatment of economic development. It has been used not just in analysing economic growth in pre-industrial societies but has also been adduced as a major reason for the occurrence of the industrial revolution itself. See, for example, the interesting discussion in Berrill, *Econ. Hist. Rev.* (1960).

growth. Goods in transit do not move randomly across the face of a land. The pattern of their movement is normally dendritic and at each node in the network there is a town. Moreover, because the trickles of goods sent or received by each hamlet flow to and from local market towns and between them in turn and larger centres, like the gradual conjunction of many small brooks into larger streams and ultimately great rivers, there is always an ordering of towns and cities into an urban hierarchy.[6] In this hierarchy the intimate connection between specialization of function and urban growth is readily visible since the higher order urban centres contain all the specialized trades to be found in lower order centres and others in addition.

At the bottom of the hierarchy in early modern western Europe even small villages had butchers, carpenters, shoemakers and perhaps a miller and a minister. Larger villages and small towns boasted in addition bakers, innkeepers, a barber, a schoolmaster, perhaps a lawyer and a doctor, weavers, a clothier. The county town or provincial city had a far wider range of those engaged in dealing and administering, representatives of the upper echelons of the church and the professions and finer subdivisions of crafts and trades which appear undifferentiated in smaller centres. A major regional centre, great port, or a fortiori a capital city took the process of specialization a stage further, once more paralleling the degree of differentiation to be found lower down the hierarchy but adding new titles to the list of distinctive forms of livelihood which could find a demand for their services.[7] Characteristically this demand, though most intense within the great city, did not arise exclusively within it. An enclosure negotiation in Lincolnshire might find its way eventually to the Court of Chancery. Spitalfield silk goods commanded a market in Westmorland as well as Westminster. Goods and service flowed in both directions through the channels of trade and communications.

Though the contribution of towns to pre-industrial economic growth was of crucial importance, the nature of the contribution

---

[6] There is a very large literature devoted to this topic stemming primarily from the work of August Lösch. A good short summary of Löschian theory, of more recent developments, and of cognate matters may be found in Berry, *Geography of market centers.*

[7] There is an interesting study of the relationship between size and service provision in the villages and small towns of the Veluwe in the Netherlands in 1749 in Roessingh, *Acta Historiae Neerlandica* (1970).

should not be misunderstood. Urban development within an effective transport network made possible both functional specialization of agricultural production by area and the subdivision of craft operations into a maze of specialist skills which raised productivity per man year and allowed the quality of the product to be improved. But, as Adam Smith emphasized in *The wealth of nations*, the most incisive of all analyses of pre-industrial society, the ultimate source of most wealth remained the land and the most effective way of ensuring that the investment of capital added to productive capacity was to invest it in agriculture.[8] It was because the growth of towns helped to liberate more fully the productive capacity of the countryside that their growth was important. The existence of towns made it both feasible and sensible for agricultural producers to specialize. A dependable market of substantial size for the range of products most effectively produced in a particular locality provided the incentive, while access to other areas and hence other products through the communication network helped to ensure that specialization did not carry the penalty of increased vulnerability. Indeed by averaging out the vicissitudes of the harvest over a considerable area, specialization of function allied to better communication significantly reduced the danger of a local crisis of subsistence.

The opportunity to specialize production in the countryside was not confined to agriculture. Industrial growth in rural areas was often striking. Sometimes it took place at the expense of urban industry because labour was cheaper in the countryside, because of guild restrictions in towns, because of the local availability of raw materials or water power, or for still other reasons. When too much emphasis is laid on the ties between urban growth and urban industrial production, the growth of industry in the countryside is sometimes viewed as in opposition to urban growth. Contemporaries were often vehemently involved in this argument. Weavers' guilds in the towns dreaded competition from the country and often tried to suppress rural rivals by law or by force. But, though the fortunes of

[8] Smith put the matter trenchantly, 'The capital employed in agriculture, therefore, not only puts into motion a greater quantity of productive labour than any equal capital employed in manufactures, but in proportion, too, to the quantity of productive labour which it employs, it adds a much greater value to the annual produce of the land and labour of the country, to the real wealth and revenue of its inhabitants. Of all the ways in which a capital can be employed, it is by far the most advantageous to society' (*Wealth of nations*, pp. 161–2).

individual trades might be deeply affected by the growth of industry in the countryside to the point where there was a loss of population from certain towns, the continued growth of industry wherever sited could not fail to further urban development overall because the growth of functional specialization necessarily involves increased exchange of goods and services pulsing through a network which is also an urban hierarchy.[9]

Anything which served to increase the productive capacity of the land in a pre-industrial economy invariably improved the prospects of industry no less than the supply of food. All major industries of the period depended upon the land for most of their raw materials. The textile, leather and wood industries which provided the bulk of industrial employment used vegetable or animal raw materials. Iron, non-ferrous metals and pottery industries were powerless to transform their mineral raw materials without wood as a source of heat. The building industry, too, used wood in large quantities. All alike could only grow within limits set by whatever gain could be achieved in increasing the productivity of the land. Whatever served to increase the productivity of the land, therefore, not only improved food supply, but also offered the prospect of increased industrial production.

The opportunities for economic growth in a pre-industrial context, whether defined in terms of aggregate production or production per head, are considerable but necessarily limited. The Dutch economy of the seventeenth century epitomizes what is possible while at the same time underlining the constraints that prevented exponential growth continuing for any length of time before the industrial revolution.[10] Pre-industrial economic growth was, in its underlying nature, more like a movement from one plateau or level to another, than a step onto the moving staircase of exponential growth which has been the distinguishing, even in a sense the defining, characteristic of the economic growth of industrial economies. Both the problems springing from the fixed supply of cultivable land, and the limitations on output inherent in any economy largely dependent upon muscle power rather than energy derived from mineral fuels, ensured that economic growth in pre-industrial economies had to be of limited

[9] This generalization appears to hold true of pre-industrial Europe in the main, but it has recently been argued that early modern Japan affords an important exception to the rule. See Smith, *Past and Present* (1973); but see also Rozman, *J. Jap. Stud.* (1974), for further reflections on the same issue.

[10] See De Vries, *Dutch rural economy*.

extent, confined within limits that meant most men lived in or near to poverty if not in misery. Specialization of function could carry economic advance a certain distance but could not sustain the momentum of advance indefinitely.

After the industrial revolution the web of constraints and relationships changed. Technological change was the proximate cause of the bulk of the growth in productivity which took place. Industry broke free from a dependence upon organic raw materials so that the nature of the constraints upon growth imposed by raw material supply changed radically.[11] All mineral raw materials are exhaustible, and this is peculiarly true of fossil fuels since they, unlike metals, cannot be re-used, but until depletion is far advanced the scale of production can be increased without experiencing the type of immediate checks upon production growth which occur with organic raw materials. The supply of the latter can be maintained without term but within relatively narrow limits set by the productivity of the land, whereas production of the former can be built up to almost any desired level for a period of years though ultimately there must be a cessation of all production when the last ton has been mined.

With the radical change in material technology came also fundamental changes in the significance of towns to economic growth and function. Very large urban agglomerations developed, as in the Black Country in England or the Ruhr in Germany, largely given over to mining and to types of manufacture which left them independent of the products of the land apart from food. Such urban areas made immense contributions to the scale of production without being dependent upon agriculture in the manner of all older industrial areas. The harvest no longer determined the prospects of industry for the ensuing year as once it had.[12] As in the past the size and function of towns was not an independent feature of the society of the day but part of an interdependent whole. But now the economy was not constrained by the limited scope for gains in productivity in

[11] See Wrigley, *Econ. Hist. Rev.* (1962).

[12] It is interesting to note how far an intelligent and well-informed contemporary, Thomas Tooke, was prepared to go even in the early nineteenth century in attributing to harvest fluctuations a key role in determining prospects for employment, trade and manufacture (Tooke, *A history of prices*). See, for example, chapter 10 in which Tooke discusses the period 1833–7. Throughout this long work concern about the implications both of the short-term fluctuations in the harvest and of the secular trend in agricultural production is very striking.

agriculture, not only because of the substitution of inorganic for organic raw materials, but also because agriculture benefited as much as industry from changes in technology. Productivity in agriculture no less than in industry increased immensely with technological advance and one man on the land could feed ten or twenty families where once he would have been pressed to feed two. Town dwellers were no longer obliged by the low level of agricultural productivity per man to remain a minority of the population. Instead they came to be the overwhelming majority of the population in all industrialized countries and the question of the contribution of towns to economic growth lost most of its meaning since the economic growth achieved in towns and economic growth in general became largely synonymous. So long as human ingenuity succeeds in discovering and implementing improvements in material technology (and especially in the technology of energy generation) which overcome bottlenecks in raw material supply and maintain the momentum of growing productivity per man, any growth of population will be more than offset by the growth in production. In these circumstances towns attain a degree of economic independence impossible to achieve in the past. The growth of a town by increasing the size of the local market tends *ipso facto* to produce a growth in industry and in employment because access to a large and growing market is itself a prime determinant of industrial location and production.

Before the industrial revolution matters, as we have seen, were very different. Within the bounds set by the nature of a pre-industrial (i.e. an *agricultural*) economy towns could liberate productive forces otherwise likely to remain frustrated. They did so by providing a market which promoted areal specialization, and acting as a focus for a communication network which furthered the process, but the opportunities for growth were limited. Urban growth, however, was important in pre-industrial economies for another reason. If economic growth is considered chiefly in terms of production per head rather than in aggregate, no discussion of economic growth can afford to neglect the denominator in the division sum which defines output per head. If population growth equals or surpasses any growth in output, economic growth occurs without what might be termed economic improvement taking place.

This point should not be lost to sight when considering an extreme instance of a city of a purely parasitic type. If it is the case that the food and other commodities sequestered from the countryside for the city would simply have served to sustain a larger population in the country if they had been left in the hands of the peasants, then it need not follow that the average country dweller would have been better off if relieved of the burden of sustaining a parasitic city. At a given *point* in time no doubt he would benefit, but over a *period* of time, as we have seen, the alternative might prove neutral in respect both of income and production per head. Neither economic growth nor economic improvement, in other words, are necessarily injured by the presence of towns whose economic nature appears parasitic. And corresponding to this shading of the apparently negative effect of 'parasitic' towns, there is a positive point to consider. If economic improvement is to take place (that is economic growth not cancelled out by population growth) any factor which tends to moderate the rate of population growth may be thought beneficial.

In pre-industrial times any growth in the total volume of output from the land, whether gained by the breaking in of new land or by the more intensive cultivation of land already under the plough, was apt to be slow and hesitant. Nor could it be sustained without interruption over long periods. Population growth rates even as low as 5 per 1,000 per annum might be expected eventually to outstrip any possible gain in productive capacity. Such a growth rate means doubling of population in about 140 years, a rate of growth that no pre-industrial economy could sustain for more than a few generations without severe pressure on real incomes. If we assume for simplicity that the productive power of a pre-industrial economy is subject to an upper limit and that as this limit is approached production per head falls, ultimately reaching a point at which the marginal product is less than marginal consumption, it follows both that population growth must at some point cease, and that if it stops growing at an early stage real incomes will be higher than if population had continued to grow for a longer period. The first produces what might be called a low pressure, the second a high pressure equilibrium.

It is sometimes argued that it is mistaken to assume that pre-industrial economies were constrained in this way. As population pressure on the land increased, the land was worked with increased intensity. At one extreme under slash-and-burn cultivation it was in use only for two or three years in each generation. At the other extreme, as in the river basins of China, two or three crops might be raised each year. In between there is a broad band of possibilities with rising population density mirrored by a decreasing percentage of the land in fallow. In general, productivity per man year may be approximately the same across the whole spectrum but productivity per man hour declines as numbers rise. Populations sacrifice leisure in order to eat, adopting more and more intensive cultivation systems under the threat of starvation.[13] While this view of the process of adjustment between populations and the land introduces complications, it does not undermine the significance of the distinction between low- and high-pressure situations. The equilibrium becomes dynamic rather than static and population growth does not necessarily cease but a low rather than a high rate of increase remains beneficial, for it must be remembered that we are only able to observe changes of this type *ex post facto*, which ensures that successes alone are visible. Failure to match an increase in population by an increase in the productive capacity of the land would cause population to revert to its original size, often without trace in the historical record but with great suffering among the population in question. We may therefore continue to consider the simplest case where there is an upper limit to productive capacity in all but the longest term.

The growth of towns tended to increase the likelihood of achieving a low-pressure equilibrium because the high death rates in towns meant that they were normally consumers of men. In most cases only the continuous inflow of new immigrants prevented a decline in numbers. Where agricultural productivity was high and in consequence a large fraction of the population could be supported in towns, a state of affairs existed in which relatively high real incomes per head were not likely to provoke a rapid growth in population which in turn forced down real incomes. On the contrary, once beyond a notional 'threshold' such an economy had some prospects of attaining a 'high level trap' where over-rapid population growth, the bane of pre-industrial societies, was much less likely to occur – Holland in the seventeenth century exemplifies this possibility. Except that the age structure is less favourable economically, this 'solution' to the economic–demographic problems of pre-industrial societies is as effective as a 'solution' via very late marriage or control of fertility in marriage. All are possibilities which produce low-pressure equilibria. Where two or more of the possibilities co-exist the benefits may, of course, be more marked or

---

[13] See Boserup, *Conditions of agricultural growth*.

more stable. High mortality, in short, may paradoxically be a means of preserving relatively high prosperity rather than evidence that the population is on the edge of a Malthusian precipice. At the other end of the spectrum of possibilities facing a pre-industrial society lies the case of an association of, say, partible inheritance, domestic industry in the countryside, early marriage and high fertility, where several generations of rapid population growth may be accompanied by increasing impoverishment and eventually a 'high-pressure' situation with an unfavourable ratio between income and population.[14] In this case increasing functional specialization may provoke demographic changes which more than offset the potential advance in economic improvement.

It may be as well to recapitulate the argument of this paper. Whether or not an individual town, or a class of towns is to be regarded as parasitic is largely a matter of definition. It is not difficult to describe a type of town, such as that depicted by Sjoberg, whose nature seems aptly described as parasitic since it is largely a centre for consumption, levying a tribute upon production in the countryside. If there is a return flow of services in the other direction they may well connote a type of benefit, like religious services, which appear intangible to a pragmatic and secular age, or take the form of the sustaining of an administrative machine whose prime object appears to be the perpetuation of the exploitation of the countryside in favour of the town. Provided that parasitism is appropriately defined, such cases may be defined as parasitic with perfect propriety. But the connotation of the adjective may be argued to make it an unfortunate choice, and the appearance of parasitism may prove deceptive on further investigation.

The danger of any parasite is that it weakens the host and in extreme cases kills it. Describing a town as parasitic implies that it represents a drain upon the resources of the society and that the host would be better off without the parasite. Paradoxically, the first proposition may be true in a limited sense without the second necessarily following. If the surplus creamed off for consumption in towns would otherwise either have been used to sustain a larger population in the countryside or have been used for conspicuous

[14] See, for example, Deprez's description of Le Vieuxbourg in Belgium in the eighteenth century, or Slicher van Bath's remarks about Overijssel in the Netherlands in the same period. Deprez in Glass and Eversley (eds.), *Population in history*; Slicher van Bath in Faber *et al. A. A. G. Bijdragen* (1965), pp. 72–89.

consumption by the community or individuals within it, it is not clear that the countryside would be better off without a 'parasitic' town except in the short term. Only if the surplus would have been devoted to some form of investment or current consumption (such as a better level of nutrition permitting greater physical effort) not vitiated by either of these pitfalls would the removal of the parasite bring long-term benefit to the host. Moreover, quite apart from this consideration, if the growth of towns, however parasitic their nature, leads to the establishment of better communications, it brings into being a facility whose presence makes possible economic improvement (in the sense earlier defined) and whose absence comes close to prohibiting such improvement. Functional specialization was the gateway to economic improvement in pre-industrial times. Between it, better communications and the development of towns (indeed of an urban hierarchy) there was necessarily a close connection. It would be a better characterization of the part played by the town in a pre-industrial economy to describe it as *both* a parasite *and* a stimulus than to seek to class individual towns in one category or the other – and the second role was more significant than the first.

Economic improvement is a complex and intractable topic. The interrelationships between agricultural production, communication facilities, market size, urban growth, demographic characteristics and changes in productivity per head in pre-industrial societies cannot be reduced to a set of simple and unvarying propositions about the effect of urban growth on economic improvement. My intention is not to deny that there were features of the relationship between town and country which might be termed parasitic. It is to suggest that the question of their parasitism is sometimes approached without sufficiently considering whether the term is a happy one, and to try to distinguish between those elements in the pre-industrial economic scene whose relationship to each other is uncertain and contingent and those whose relationship can be viewed with some confidence as more firmly shaped and less subject to frequent reversals or exceptions. I have also wished to stress the wide extent of the differences between pre-industrial society and the new world created by the industrial revolution.

If this view is justified it suggests in turn that a special interest attaches to the period of transition between the old world and the new. Many cities remained important throughout the drastic changes of the transition. In England nothing shook London's pre-eminence. But the second rank of cities – Manchester, Liverpool and Birmingham – had not previously been major provincial centres. Their very different social, economic and demographic characteristics form an instructive contrast with London in the eighteenth and nineteenth centuries, and London itself also underwent great changes. A fuller understanding of the relationship between the town, economic growth and economic improvement in the pre-industrial world, and of the same relationship during and after the industrial revolution would go far towards explaining the nature of the great change from the traditional to the modern world. Urban history, taken in the wider sense to connote the study of the function of the town within the economy as a whole, is therefore a strategic point of entry into the larger question of what stimulated or inhibited growth and improvement in the past.

Consolidated Bibliography

This does not represent an attempt to provide a full bibliography. The works listed are those to which reference is made in the footnotes. They are divided into two sections: those which can be listed alphabetically by author's or editor's name, and other sources. The bibliography is prefaced by a list of the abbreviations of journal titles used here and in the footnotes to the main text.

Abbreviated journal titles

Ag. Hist. Rev.	*Agricultural History Review*
Am. Hist. Rev.	*American Historical Review*
Am. J. Soc.	*American Journal of Sociology*
Am. Soc. Rev.	*American Sociological Review*
Annales, E.S.C.	*Annales: économies, sociétés, civilisations*
Annales d'hist. éc. et soc.	*Annales d'histoire économique et sociale*
Annals Am. Acad. Pol. and Soc. Sci.	*Annals of the American Academy of Political and Social Science*
Annals Am. Assoc. Geog.	*Annals of the Association of American Geographers*
Assoc. Architect. Soc.	*Associated Architectural Societies Reports and Papers*
Beds. Hist. Rec. Soc.	*Bedfordshire Historical Record Society*
Bolletino ligustico	*Bolletino ligustico per la storia e la cultura regionale*
Br. J. Soc.	*British Journal of Sociology*
Bull. Inst. Arch.	*Bulletin of the Institute of Archaeology*
Bull. soc. d'hist. mod.	*Bulletin de la société d'histoire moderne*
Cath. Hist. Rev.	*Catholic Historical Review*
Class. Phil.	*Classical Philology*
Comp. Stud. Soc. and Hist.	*Comparative Studies in Society and History*
Econ. Dev. and Cult. Change	*Economic Development and Cultural Change*
Econ. Hist. Rev.	*Economic History Review*
Econ. J.	*Economic Journal*
Geog. Rev.	*Geographical Review*
Hist. J.	*Historical Journal*
Hist. Meth. Newsletter	*Historical Methods Newsletter*

Internat. J. Comp. Soc. *International Journal of Comparative Sociology*

Internat. Rev. Soc. Hist. *International Review for Social History*

J'buch f. fränk. Landesforschung *Jahrbuch für fränkische Landesforschung*

J'buch hist. Ver. Nördlingen *Jahrbuch des historischen Vereins für Nördlingen*

J'hefte des öst. arch. Inst. *Jahreshefte des österreichischen archäologischen Institut*

J. Asian. Stud. *Journal of Asian Studies*

J. Contemp. Hist. *Journal of Contemporary History*

J. Econ. Hist. *Journal of Economic History*

J. Econ. and Business Hist. *Journal of Economic and Business History*

J. Econ. and Soc. Hist. Orient *Journal of Economic and Social History of the Orient*

J. Eur. Econ. Hist. *Journal of European Economic History*

J. Jap. Stud. *Journal of Japanese Studies*

J. Pol. Econ. *Journal of Political Economy*

J. Rom. Stud. *Journal of Roman Studies*

J. Warburg and Courtauld Inst. *Journal of the Warburg and Courtauld Institutes*

London Rec. Soc. Pub. *London Record Society Publications*

Med. Arch. *Medieval Archaeology*

Nat. Lib. of Wales J. *National Library of Wales Journal*

North Staffs J. Field Stud. *North Staffordshire Journal of Field Studies*

Pop. Stud. *Population Studies*

Proc. Prehist. Soc. *Proceedings of the Prehistoric Society*

Qu. J. Econ. *Quarterly Journal of Economics*

Revue hist. *Revue historique*

Trans. Am. Phil. Soc. *Transactions of the American Philosophical Society*

Trans. Hist. Soc. Lancs and Cheshire *Transactions of the Historic Society of Lancashire and Cheshire*

Trans. Roy. Hist. Soc. *Transactions of the Royal Historical Society*

Univ. Birmingham Hist. J. *University of Birmingham Historical Journal*

VCH *Victoria County History*

Vierteljahrschr. f Soz.- u. Wirtschaftsgesch. *Vierteljahrschrift für Sozial- und Wirtschaftsgeschichte*

Yorks Bull. Econ. and ┆ *Soc. Res.*	*Yorkshire Bulletin of Economic and* *Social Research*
Z'tschr. f. bäy. *Landesgesch.*	*Zeitschrift für bäyerische* *Landesgeschichte*
Z'tschr. f. Geschichts- *wissenschaft*	*Zeitschrift für Geschichtswissenschaft*
Z'tschr. f. Pap. u. Epig.	*Zeitschrift für Papyrologie und* *Epigraphik*
Z'tschr. f. Stadtgesch., *Stadtsoz. u.* *Denkmalpflege*	*Zeitschrift für Stadtgeschichte,* *Stadtsoziologie und* *Denkmalpflege*

Books and articles

Alexander, D. G. *Retailing in England during the industrial revolution* (London, 1970).

Allison, K. J. and Tillott, P. M. 'York in the eighteenth century', in P. M. Tillott (ed.), *VCH A history of Yorkshire. The city of York* (London, 1961), pp. 207–53.

Applebaum, S. 'Roman Britain' in H. P. R. Finberg (ed.), *The agrarian history of England and Wales*, i (Cambridge, 1972), pp. 3–283.

Ascheri, A. *Notizie intorno alla reunione delle famiglie in alberghi in Genova* (Genoa, 1846).

Ashton, T. S. *An economic history of England: the eighteenth century* (London, 1955).

Ashton, T. S. and Sykes, J. *The coal industry of the eighteenth century* (Manchester, 1929).

Atkinson, T. *Elizabethan Winchester* (London, 1963).

Aubin, H. 'Formen und Verbreitung des Verlagswesens in der Altnürnberger Wirtschaft', *Beiträge zur Wirtschaftsgeschichte Nürnbergs*, ii (1967), pp. 1635–41.

Avery, D. *Not on Queen Victoria's birthday* (London, 1974).

Bach, E. *La cité de Gênes au XIIe siècle* (Copenhagen, 1955).

Bairoch, P. *Urban unemployment in developing countries* (Geneva, 1973).

Baker, A. R. H. 'Changes in the later Middle Ages', in H. C. Darby (ed.), *A new historical geography of England* (Cambridge, 1973), pp. 186–247.

Balazs, E. 'Une carte des centres commerciaux de la Chine à la fin du XIe siècle', *Annales, E.S.C.* xii (1957), pp. 587–93.

Balazs, E. 'Marco Polo in the capital of China', in E. Balazs (ed.),

Chinese civilization and bureaucracy (New Haven, 1964), pp. 79–100.

Barker, T. C. 'Lancashire coal, Cheshire salt and the rise of Liverpool', *Trans. Hist. Soc. Lancs and Cheshire*, ciii (1951), pp. 83–101.

Barley, M. W. and Straw, L. F. 'Nottingham' in M. D. Lobel (ed.), *The atlas of historic towns*, i (London and Oxford, 1969).

Barnett, G. E. (ed.) *Two tracts by Gregory King* (Baltimore, 1936).

Bartlett, J. N. 'The expansion and decline of York in the later Middle Ages', *Econ. Hist. Rev.* 2nd ser. xii (1959–60), pp. 17–33.

Battilana, N. *Genealogia delle famiglie nobili di Genova*, 3 vols. (Genoa, 1825–33).

Belgrano, L. *Tavole genealogiche a corredo della illustrazione del registro arcivescovile di Genova* (Atti della società ligure di storia patria, ii, pt 1, 1872, appendix).

Belgrano, L. *Della vita privata dei Genovesi*, 2nd ed. (Genoa, 1875).

Bellinger, A. R. *Dura-Europus. Final Report VI. The coins* (New Haven, 1969).

Bellomo, M. 'Richerche sui rapporti patrimoniali tra coniugi', *Jus nostrum: studi e testi pubblicati dall' Istituto di Storia del Diritto italiano dell' Università di Roma*, vii (1961), pp. 1–25.

Bellomo, M. 'Comunità e commune in Italia negli statuti medievali *super emancipationibus*', *Annali di storia del diritto*, viii (1964), pp. 81–106.

Beloch, K. J. *Die Bevölkerungsgeschichte der griechisch-römischen Welt* (Leipzig, 1886).

Beresford, M. *New Towns of the Middle Ages* (London, 1967).

Beresford, M. *History on the ground*, rev. ed. (London, 1971).

Berkner, L. K. 'The stem family and the developmental cycle of the peasant household: an eighteenth century Austrian example', *Am. Hist. Rev.* lxxvii (1972), pp. 398–418.

Berrill, K. 'International trade and the rate of economic growth', *Econ. Hist. Rev.* 2nd ser. xii (1960), pp. 351–9.

Berry, B. J. L. *Geography of market centers and retail distribution* (Englewood Cliffs, NJ, 1967).

Berry, B. J. L. *The human consequences of urbanisation* (London, 1973).

Bindoff, S. T. *Ket's rebellion, 1594* (Historical Association, 1949).

Blanning, T. C. W. *Reform and revolution in Mainz, 1743–1803* (Cambridge, 1974).

Blanshei, S. R. 'Perugia 1260–1340: conflict and change in a medieval Italian urban society', *Trans. Am. Phil. Soc.* new ser. lxvi (1976).

Blomefield, F. *An essay towards a topographical history of the county of Norfolk*, 11 vols. (London, 1806).

Boeke, J. H. *Economics and economic policy of dual societies* (New York, 1953).

Bog, I. 'Wachstumsprobleme der oberdeutschen Wirtschaft 1540–1618', in F. Lütge (ed.), *Wirtschaftliche und soziale Probleme der gewerblichen Entwicklung im 15.–16. und 19. Jahrhundert* (Stuttgart, 1968), pp. 44–89.

Bolin, S. *State and currency in the Roman Empire* (Stockholm, 1958).

Boserup, E. *The conditions of agricultural growth* (London, 1965).

Braccolini, P. *Opera omnia* with preface by R. Fubini (Basel, 1538: repr. Turin, 1964).

Brandileone, F. 'Studi preliminari sullo svolgimento storico dei rapporti patrimoniali fra coniugi in Italia', in F. Brandileone, *Scritti di storia del diritto privato italiano*, 2 vols. (Bologna, 1931), i, pp. 229–319.

Braudel, F. *The Mediterranean and the Mediterranean world in the age of Philip II*, 2 vols. (London, 1972).

Braudel, F. *Capitalism and material life: 1400–1800* (London, 1973).

Brett-James, N. G. *The growth of Stuart London* (London, 1935).

Bridbury, A. R. *Economic growth: England in the later Middle Ages* (London, 1962).

Bruford, W. H. *Germany in the eighteenth century: the social background of the literary revival* (Cambridge, 1935; paperback ed. 1965).

Brunner, O. 'Souveränitätsproblem und Sozialstruktur in den deutschen Reichsstädten der Früheren Neuzeit', *Vierteljahrschr. f. Soz.- u. Wirtshaftsgesch.* i (1963), pp. 329–60.

Brunt, P. A. *Italian manpower* (Oxford, 1971).

Brunt, P. A. 'The Romanization of the local ruling classes', in D. M. Pippidi (ed.), *Assimilation et résistance à la culture gréco-romaine dans le monde ancien* (Bucharest, 1976).

Bücher, K. *Die Entstehung der Volkwirtschaft*, 4th ed. (Tübingen, 1904).

Buenger, L. R. 'Genoese enterprisers, 1186–1211', unpub. PhD thesis (Univ. of Wisconsin, 1954).

Buer, M. C. *Health, wealth and population in eighteenth century England* (London, 1926).

Bunce, J. T. *History of the corporation of Birmingham*, 2 vols. (Birmingham, 1878–85).

Burke, P. *Venice and Amsterdam* (London, 1974).

Byrne, E. H. 'Commercial contracts of the Genoese in the Syrian trade of the twelfth century', *Qu. J. Econ.* xxxi (1916–17), pp. 128–70.

Byrne, E. H. 'Genoese trade with Syria in the twelfth century', *Am. Hist. Rev.* xxv (1919–20), pp. 119–219.

Caesar. *On the Gallic War.*

Callu, J. P. *Thamusida* (Paris, 1965).

Cam, H. *Liberties and communities of medieval England* (Cambridge, 1944).

Campbell, J. 'Norwich', in M. D. Lobel (ed.), *The atlas of historic towns*, ii (London, 1975).

Carus-Wilson, E. M. *The expansion of Exeter at the close of the Middle Ages*, Harte Memorial Lecture (Exeter, 1961).

Carus-Wilson, E. M. 'The medieval trade of the ports of the Wash', *Med. Arch.* vi–vii (1962–3), pp. 182–201.

Carus-Wilson, E. M. *Medieval merchant ventures* (London, 1967).

Carus-Wilson, E. M. and Coleman, O. *England's export trade, 1275–1547* (Oxford, 1963).

Casson, L. 'New light on maritime loans', *Eos*, xlviii (1956), pp. 89–93.

Casson, L. *Ships and seamanship in the ancient world* (Princeton, 1971).

Cato. *On agriculture.*

Cavalcanti, G. *Istorie fiorentine*, ed. F. Polidori, 2 vols. (Florence, 1838–9).

Chalklin, C. W. *The provincial towns of Georgian England* (London, 1974).

Chaloner, W. H. 'Manchester in the latter half of the eighteenth century', *Bulletin of John Rylands Library*, xlii (1959–60), pp. 40–60.

Chang Ying-ch'ang (ed.) *Ch'ing shih to* ('The Ching bell of poetry') (repr. Peking, 1960).

Clapham, J. H. 'The transference of the worsted industries from Norfolk to the West Riding', *Econ. J.* xx (1910), pp. 195–210.

Clark, C. and Haswell, M. *The economics of subsistence agriculture* (London, 1970).

Clark, P. and Slack, P. (eds.) *Crisis and order in English towns 1500–1700* (London, 1972).

Clavel, M. *Bezières* (Paris, 1970).

Cleere, H. 'Some operating parameters for Roman iron-works', *Bull. Inst. Arch.* xiii (1976).

Cobb, R. *Paris and its provinces 1792–1802* (London, 1975).

Cochrane, E. *Florence in the forgotten centuries 1527–1800. A history of Florence and the Florentines in the age of the Grand Dukes* (Chicago and London, 1973).

Cole, R. E. G. 'The royal burgh of Torksey, its churches, monasteries and castles', *Assoc. Architect. Soc.* xxviii (1905–6), pp. 451–530.

Coleman, D. C. 'Labour in the English economy of the seventeenth century', *Econ. Hist. Rev.* 2nd ser. viii (1955–6), pp. 280–95, repr. in E. M. Carus-Wilson (ed.), *Essays in economic history*, ii (London, 1962), pp. 291–308.

Coleman, O. 'Trade and prosperity in the fifteenth century: some aspects of the trade of Southampton', *Econ. Hist. Rev.* 2nd ser. xvi (1963–4), pp. 16–22.

Conti, E. *I catasti agrari della Repubblica fiorentina e il catasto particellare toscano, secoli XVI–XIX* (Rome, 1966).

Corfield, P. 'A provincial capital in the late seventeenth century. The case of Norwich', in P. Clark and P. Slack (eds.), *Crisis and order in English towns 1500–1700* (London, 1972), pp. 263–310.

Corte, M. della. *Case e abitanti di Pompeii* (Pompeii, 1954).

Court, W. H. B. *The rise of the Midland industries 1600–1838* (London, 1938).

Creighton, C. *History of epidemics in Britain*, 2 vols. (Cambridge, 1891 and 1894).

Crissman, L. W. 'Marketing on the Changhua plain, Taiwan', in W. E. Willmott (ed.), *Economic organization in Chinese society* (Stanford, 1975), pp. 215–60.

Cristiani, E. *Nobiltà e popolo nel comune di Pisa dalle origini del podestariato alla signoria dei Donoratico* (Naples, 1962).

Cronne, H. A. *The borough of Warwick in the Middle Ages* (Dugdale Society Occasional Papers, x, 1951).

Croon, H. 'Die Versorgung der Grossstädte des Ruhrgebietes im 19. und 20. Jahrhundert', *Third International Conference of Economic History, Munich 1965* (Paris, 1968), pp. 131–46.

Crouzet, F. 'Croissances comparées de l'Angleterre et de la France au XVIIIe siècle', *Annales, E.S.C.* xxi (1966), pp. 254–91.

Dannenbauer, H. 'Das Leinenweberhandwerk in der Reichsstadt Nördlingen', *Z'tschr. f. bäy. Landesgesch.* iii (1930), pp. 305–15.

Darby, H. C. 'The age of the improver 1600–1800', in H. C. Darby (ed.), *A new historical geography of England* (Cambridge, 1973).

Davies, O. *Roman mines in Europe* (Oxford, 1935).

Davis, K. and Golden, H. H. 'Urbanization and the development of pre-industrial areas', *Econ. Dev. and Cult. Change*, iii (1954–5), pp. 6–26.

Davis, R. *The rise of the English shipping industry* (London, 1962).

Dawson, W. H. *Municipal life and government in Germany* (London, 1914).

Deane, P. and Cole, W. A. *British economic growth 1688–1959* (Cambridge, 1962).

Dechelette, J. *La collection Millon* (Paris, 1913).

Deprez, P. 'The demographic development of Flanders in the eighteenth century', in D. V. Glass and D. E. C. Eversley (eds.), *Population in history* (London, 1965), pp. 608–30.

De Vries, J. *The Dutch rural economy in the Golden Age, 1500–1700* (New Haven and London, 1974).

Dewey, R. 'The rural–urban continuum: real but relatively unimportant', *Am. J. Soc.* lxvi (1960), pp. 60–6.

Diamond, W. 'On the dangers of an urban interpretation of history', in E. F. Goldman (ed.), *Historiography and urbanization. Essays in honour of W. Stull Holt* (Baltimore, 1941), pp. 67–108.

Dobb, M. *Studies in the development of capitalism* (London, 1946).

Dobb, M. 'A reply', in R. Hilton (ed.), *The transition from feudalism to capitailsm* (London, 1976), pp. 57–67.

Dobson, R. B. 'Admissions to the Freedom of the city of York in the later Middle Ages', *Econ. Hist. Rev.* 2nd ser. xxv (1973), pp. 1–21.

Du Boulay, F. R. H. *An age of ambition* (London, 1970).

Duby, G. *La société aux XIe et XIIe siècles dans la région mâconnaise* (Paris, 1953).

Duby, G. 'La noblesse dans la France médiévale', *Revue hist.* ccxxvi (1961), pp. 1–22.

Duby, G. 'Lignage, noblesse et chevalerie au XIIe siècle dans la région mâconnaise', *Annales, E.S.C.* xxvii (1972), pp. 802–23.

Duncan-Jones, R. P. *The economy of the Roman Empire* (Cambridge, 1974).

Duncan-Jones, R. P. 'The size of the *modius castrensis*', *Z'tschr. f. Pap. u. Epig.* xxi (1976), pp. 53–62.

Dyer, A. D. *City of Worcester in the sixteenth century* (Leicester, 1973).

Ebert, W. H. K. *Die Lodweberei in der Reichsstadt Nördlingen* (Nördlingen, 1919).

Edwards, J. K. 'The decline of the Norwich textile industries', *Yorks Bull. Econ. and Soc. Res.* xvi (1964), pp. 31–41.

Eitel, P. *Die oberschwäbischen Reichsstädte im Zeitalter der*

Zunftherrschaft: Untersuchungen zu ihrer politischen und sozialen Struktur unter besonderer Berücksichtigung der Städte Lindau, Memmingen, Ravensburg und Ueberlingen (Stuttgart, 1970).

Elsas, M. J. *Umriss einer Geschichte der Preise und Löhne in Deutschland*, 2 vols. (Leiden, 1936 and 1949).

Elton, G. R. *Reform and renewal: Thomas Cromwell and the Common Weal* (Cambridge, 1973).

Elvin, M. *The pattern of the Chinese past* (London, 1973).

Elvin, M. 'On water control and management during the Ming and Ch'ing periods', *Ch'ing shih wen-t' i*, iii (1975), pp. 81–102.

Elvin, M. Contribution to 'A symposium on the 1911 revolution', *Modern China*, ii (1976), pp. 193–7.

Elvin, M. and Skinner, G. W. (eds.) *The Chinese city between two worlds* (Stanford, 1974).

Emery, F. V. 'England c. 1600', in H. C. Darby (ed.), *A new historical geography of England* (Cambridge, 1973).

Endres, R. 'Kapitalistische Organisationsformen im Ries in der zweiten Hälfte des 16. Jahrhunderts', *J'buch f. fränk. Landesforschung*, xxii (1962), pp. 89–99.

Epstein, A. L. 'Urbanization and social change in Africa', *Current Anthropology*, viii (1967), pp. 275–96.

Ercole, F. 'Vicende storiche della dote romana nella pratica medievale dell' Italia superiore', *Archivio giuridico*, lxxx (1908), pp. 460–99, and lxxxi (1908), pp. 92–116.

Esperandieu, E. *Receuil général des bas-reliefs, statues et bustes de la Gaule romaine*, 10 vols. (Paris, 1907–28).

Espinas, G. *Le vie urbaine du Douai au moyen-age*, 4 vols. (Paris, 1914).

Evans, J. D. 'The uncrowned iron king: the first William Crawshay', *Nat. Lib. of Wales J.* vii (1951), pp. 12–32.

Everitt, A. 'Social mobility in early modern England', *Past and Present*, xxxiii (1966), pp. 56–73.

Everitt, A. 'The marketing of agricultural produce', in J. Thirsk (ed.), *The agrarain history of England and Wales 1500–1640*, iv (1967), pp. 396–454.

Everitt, A. *New avenues in English local history*, inaug. lect. (Leicester, 1970).

Eversley, D. E. C. 'The home market and economic growth in England 1750–1850', in E. L. Jones and G. Mingay (eds.), *Land, labour and population in the industrial revolution* (London, 1967).

Faber, J. A., Roessingh, H. K., Slicher van Bath, B. H., van der

Woude, A. M. and Xanten, H. J. 'Population changes and economic developments in the Netherlands: a historical survey', *A. A. G. Bijdragen*, xii (Wageningen, 1965), pp. 47–113.

Farr, W. *Vital statistics* (London, 1885).

Fasoli, G. 'Ricerche sulla legislazione antimagnatizia nei comuni dell' alta e media Italia', *Rivista di storia del diritto italiano*, xii (1939).

Favresse, F. *L'avènement du régime démocratique à Bruxelles pendant le moyen age, 1306–1423* (Brussels, 1932).

Fei, J. C. H. 'The "standard market" of traditional China', in D. H. Perkins (ed.), *China's modern economy in historical perspective* (Stanford, 1975), pp. 235–59.

Ferretto, A. *Codice diplomatico della relazioni fra la Liguria, la Toscana e la Lunigiana ai tempi di Dante* (Atti della società ligure di storia patria, xxxi, 1901–3).

Finley, M. *The ancient economy* (London, 1973).

Firmicus Maternus, *Ancient astrology, theory and practice*, trans. J. R. Bram (Park Ridge, NJ, 1975).

Fisher, F. J. 'The development of the London food market, 1540–1640', *Econ. Hist. Rev.* v (1934–5), pp. 46–64.

Fiumi, E. *Demografia, movimento urbanistico e classi sociali in Prato dall' età comunale ai tempo moderni* (Biblioteca storica toscana, xiv, 1968).

Flinn, M. W. *Men of iron. The Crowleys in the early iron industry* (Edinburgh, 1962).

Forbes, R. J. *The history of ancient roads and their construction* (Amsterdam, 1934).

Forbes, R. J. *Studies in ancient technology*, 9 vols. (Leiden, 1955).

Forcheri, G. 'I rapporti patrimoniali fra coniugi a Genova nel secolo XII', *Bolletino ligustico per la storia e la cultura regionale*, ii (1970), pp. 3–20.

Formentini, U. *Genova nel Basso Impero e nell' Alto Medio Evo* (Milan, 1941).

Foster, G. C. F. 'York in the seventeenth century', in P. M. Tillott (ed.), *VCH A history of Yorkshire. The city of York* (London, 1961), pp. 160–206.

Frank, T. *Economic survey of ancient Rome*, 5 vols. (Baltimore, 1933).

Friedrichs, C. R. 'Nördlingen 1580–1700: society, government and the impact of war', unpub. PhD thesis (Princeton, 1973).

Fu I-ling, *Ming-tai Chaing-nan Shih-min Ching-chi Shih-t'an* ('An examination of the economy of the urban population of Chiang-nan in the Ming dynasty'), (Shanghai, 1957).

Furger, F. *Zum Verlagssystem als Organisationsform des Früh-kapitalismus im Textilgewerbe* (Stuttgart, 1927).

Furness, E. S. *The position of the labourer in a system of national-ism. A study in the labour theories of the later English mercantilists* (Boston, 1920).

Gabba, E. 'Urbanizzazione e rinnovamenti urbanistici nell' Italia centro-meridionale del I secolo A.C.', *Studi classici e orientali*, xxi (1972), pp. 73–112.

Gade, J. A. *The Hanseatic control of Norwegian commerce during the late Middle Ages* (Leiden, 1951).

George, M. D. *London life in the eighteenth century* (London, 1925).

Gernet, J. *La vie quotidienne en Chine à la veille de l'invasion mongole, 1250–1276* (Paris, 1959).

Gerschenkron, A. *Economic backwardness in historical perspective* (Harvard, 1962).

Giardina, C. 'Sul mundoaldo della donna', *Rivista di storia del diritto italiano*, xxxv (1962), pp. 41–51.

Gibbs, J. P. and Martin, W. T. 'Urbanization, technology and the division of labour', *Am. Soc. Rev.* xxvii (1962), pp. 667–77.

Gilboy, E. W. *Wages in eighteenth century England* (Cambridge, Mass., 1934).

Gill, W. C. *History of Birmingham*, 3 vols. (London, 1952–74).

Gillett, E. *A history of Grimsby* (Oxford, 1970).

Glaab, C. 'The historian and the American city: a bibliographic survey', in P. M. Hauser and L. F. Schnore (eds.), *The study of urbanisation* (New York, 1965), pp. 53–80.

Glass, D. V. introduction to 'London inhabitants within the walls, 1695', *London Rec. Soc. Pub.* ii (London, 1966).

Gluckman, M. 'Tribalism in modern British Central Africa', *Cahiers d'études africaines*, i (1960), pp. 55–70.

Godber, J. *History of Bedfordshire* (Bedfordshire County Council, 1969).

Goitein, S. D. *A Mediterranean society* (Berkeley, 1967).

Goldthwaite, R. A. *Private wealth in Renaissance Florence* (Prince-ton, 1968).

Goldthwaite, R. A. 'The Florentine palace as domestic architecture', *Am. Hist. Rev.* lxxvii (1972), pp. 977–1012.

Goodchild, R. G. and Forbes, R. J. 'Roads and travel' in C. Singer (ed.), *A history of technology*, ii (Oxford, 1956), pp. 493–536.

Goode, W. J. *World revolution and family patterns* (New York, 1963).

Goria, A. 'Le lotte intestine in Genova tra il 1305 e il 1309', in

Miscellanea di storia ligure in onore di Giorgio Falco (Milan, 1962), pp. 251–80.

Goubert, P. *The ancien régime: French society 1600–1750*, trans. S. Cox (London, 1970).

Gould, J. D. *Economic growth in history* (London, 1972).

Graunt, J. *Natural and political observations*, reprinted in *The economic writings of Sir William Petty*, ed. C. H. Hull, 2 vols. (New York, 1963 and 1964).

Graus, F. 'The late medieval poor in town and countryside', in S. Thrupp (ed.), *Change in medieval society: Europe north of the Alps, 1050–1500* (London, 1965), pp. 314–24.

Green, B. and Young, R. M. R. *Norwich – the growth of a city* (Norwich Museum Committee, 1964).

Greene, K. T. 'The pottery from Usk', in A. Detsicas, (ed.), *Current research in Romano-British coarse pottery*, Council for British Archaeology Research Report 10 (1973), pp. 23–5.

Grenier, A. *Archéologie gallo-romaine*, vols. v and vi, in J. Dechelette (ed.), *Manuel d'archéologie* (Paris, 1931–4).

Habakkuk, H. J. 'Fluctuations in house building in Britain and the United States in the nineteenth century', *J. Econ. Hist.* xxii (1962), pp. 198–230.

Hajnal, J. 'European marriage patterns in perspective', in D. V. Glass and D. E. C. Eversley (eds.), *Population in history* (London, 1965), pp. 101–43.

Harris, C. D. and Ullman, E. L. 'The nature of cities', *Annals Am. Acad. Pol. and Soc. Sci.* ccxlii (1945), pp. 7–17.

Harris, J. R. 'Trends in the industrialisation of Merseyside 1750–1850', in Centre National de la Recherche Scientifique, *L'Industrialisation en Europe au XIXe siècle* (Paris, 1972), pp. 57–73.

Harrison, B. *Drink and the Victorians. The temperance question in England 1815–1872* (London, 1972).

Harrison, C. J. 'Grain price analysis and harvest qualities', *Ag. Hist. Rev.* xix (1971), pp. 135–55.

Harrod, H. 'A few particulars concerning early Norwich pageants', *Norfolk Archaeology*, iii (1949), pp. 3–18.

Hartwell, R. 'A revolution in the Chinese iron and coal industries', *J. Asian Stud.* xxi (1962), pp. 153–62.

Hartwell, R. 'A cycle of economic change in Imperial China: coal and iron in northeast China, 750–1350', *J. Econ. and Soc. Hist. Orient*, x (1967), pp. 102–59.

Harvey, D. *Social justice and the city* (London, 1973).

Haskins, C. *The ancient trade guilds and companies of Salisbury* (Salisbury, 1912).

Haward, W. I. 'The trade of Boston in the fifteenth century', *Reports and Papers of the Lincolnshire Architectural and Archaeological Societies*, xli (1932–3), pp. 169–78.

Heaton, H. *The Yorkshire woollen and worsted industries*, 2nd ed. (Oxford, 1965).

Heberle, R. and Meyer, F. *Die Grosstädte im Stome der Binnenwanderung* (Leipzig, 1937).

Heckscher, E. F. *Mercantilism*, trans. M. Shapiro, rev. ed. by E. F. Söderlund (London and New York, 1955).

Heer, D. M. *Society and population* (Englewood Cliffs, NJ, 1968).

Heers, J. *Gênes au XVe siècle, activité économique et problèmes sociaux* (Paris, 1961).

Heers, J. 'Urbanisme et structure sociale à Gênes au Moyen-Age', in *Studi in onore di Amintore Fanfani*, 6 vols. (Milan, 1962).

Hélin, E. *La démographie de Liège aux XVIIe et XVIIIe siècles* (Brussels, 1963).

Helleiner, K. F. 'The population of Europe from the Black Death to the eve of the vital revolution', in E. E. Rich and C. H. Wilson (eds.), *Cambridge Economic History of Europe*, iv (Cambridge, 1967), pp. 1–95.

Henderson, W. O. *The state and the industrial revolution in Prussia, 1740–1870* (Liverpool, 1958).

Henderson, W. O. *The rise of German industrial power* (London, 1975).

Herlihy, D. *Medieval and Renaissance Pistoia. The social history of an Italian town, 1200–1430* (New Haven and London, 1967).

Herlihy, D. 'Santa Maria Impruneta: a rural commune in the late Middle Ages', in N. Rubinstein (ed.), *Florentine studies* (London, 1968), pp. 256–64.

Herlihy, D. 'Family solidarity in medieval Italian history', in D. Herlihy, R. S. Lopez and V. Slessarev (eds.), *Economy, society and government: essays in memory of Robert L. Reynolds* (Kent, Ohio, 1969), pp. 173–84.

Herlihy, D. 'Mapping households in medieval Italy', *Cath. Hist. Rev.* lviii (1972), pp. 1–22.

Hermet, F. *La Graufesenque* (Paris, 1934).

Hey, D. *The rural metalworkers of the Sheffield region. A study of rural industry before the industrial revolution* (Leicester, 1972).

Hicks, J. *A theory of economic history* (Oxford, 1969).

Higgins, B. 'The "dualistic theory" of underdeveloped areas', *Econ. Dev. and Cult. Change*, iv (1956), pp. 95–115.

Hildebrandt, R. 'Rat contra Bürgerschaft: die Verfassungskonflikte in den Reichsstädten des 17. und 18. Jahrhunderts', *Z'tschr. f. Stadtgesch., Stadtsoz. u. Denkmalpflege*, i (1974), pp. 221–241.

Hill, Sir J. W. F. *Medieval Lincoln* (Cambridge, 1948).

Hill, Sir J. W. F. *Tudor and Stuart Lincoln* (Cambridge, 1956).

Hillery, G. A. *Communal organizations: a study of local societies* (Chicago, 1968).

Hirschmann, G. 'Das Nürnberger Patriziat', in H. Rössler (ed.), *Deutsches Patriziat 1430–1740* (Limburg a.d. Lahn, 1968), pp. 257–76.

Ho Ping-ti. *Chung-kuo hui-kuan Shih lun* (A historical survey of *Landmannschaften* in China) (Taipei, 1966).

Hoffman, H. H. 'Friedrich Staedtler Bleistiftsverleger in Nürnberg 1662', *Tradition*, xxii (1967), pp. 449–56.

Hoffman, H. and Mittenzwei, I. 'Die Stellung des Bürgertums in der deutschen Feudalgesellschaft von der Mitte des 16. Jahrhunderts bis 1789', *Z'tschr., f. Geschichtswissenschaft*, xxii (1974), pp. 190–207.

Holdgate, M. *A history of Appleby*, 2nd ed. rev. (Appleby, 1970).

Hoselitz, B. F. 'The role of cities in the economic growth of underdeveloped countries', *J. Pol. Econ.* lxi (1953), pp. 195–208.

Hoselitz, B. F. 'Generative and parasitic cities', *Econ. Dev. and Cult. Change*, iii (1954–5), pp. 278–94.

Hoskins, W. G. *Industry, trade and people in Exeter 1688–1800* (Manchester, 1935).

Hoskins, W. G. *Local history in England* (London, 1959).

Hoskins, W. G. 'Harvest fluctuations and English economic history', *Ag. Hist. Rev.* xii (1964), pp. 28–46.

Hoskins, W. G. *Provincial England* (London, 1965).

Houghton, J. *A collection of letters for the improvement of husbandry* (London, 1681).

Hughes, D. O. 'Toward historical ethnography: notarial records and family history in the Middle Ages', *Hist. Meth. Newsletter*, vii (1974), pp. 61–71.

Hughes, E. *North country life in the eighteenth century. The northeast 1700–1750* (London, 1952).

Hunter, J. *South Yorkshire* (1828).

Hyde, F. E. *Liverpool and the Mersey. An economic history of a port 1700–1970* (Newton Abbot, 1971).

Imberciadori, I. *Mezzadria classica toscana con documentazione inedita dal IX al XIV secolo* (Florence, 1951).

Imura Kōzen, 'Chihōshi ni kisaiserareru Chūgoku ekirei ryakkō

(A survey of Chinese epidemics recorded in local histories), *Chūgai iji shimpō* (1936–7), 8 parts, pp. 30–9, 263–75, 316–25, 366–76, 414–23, 459–67, 505–8, 550–5.

Jackson, G. *Hull in the eighteenth century. A study in economic and social history* (London, 1972).

Jecht, H. 'Studien zur gesellschaftlichen Struktur der mittelalterlichen Städte', *Vierteljahrschr. f. Soz.- u. Wirtschaftsgesch.* xix (1926), pp. 48–85.

Jefferson, M. 'The law of the primate city', *Geog. Rev.* xxix (1939), pp. 226–39.

John, A. H. *The industrial development of south Wales 1750–1850* (Cardiff, 1950).

John, A. H. 'Aspects of English economic growth in the first half of the eighteenth century', *Economica*, n.s. xxviii (1961), pp. 176–190, repr. in E. M. Carus-Wilson (ed.), *Essays in economic history*, ii (London, 1962), pp. 360–73.

Jones, A. H. M. *The Greek city* (Oxford, 1940).

Jones, A. H. M. *The Athenian democracy* (Oxford, 1957).

Jones, A. H. M. 'Slavery in the ancient world', in M. I. Finley (ed.), *Slavery in classical antiquity* (Cambridge, 1960), pp. 1–16.

Jones, A. H. M. *The later Roman Empire* (Oxford, 1964).

Jones, A. H. M. *Cities of the eastern Roman provinces*, 2nd ed. (Oxford, 1971).

Jones, A. H. M. *The Roman economy*, ed. P. A. Brunt (Oxford, 1974).

Jones, E. L. 'Agricultural origins of industry', *Past and Present*, xl (1968), pp. 58–71.

Jones, P. E. and Judges, A. V. 'London population in the late seventeenth century', *Econ. Hist. Rev.* vi (1935–6), pp. 45–63.

Jones, P. J. 'From manor to mezzadria: a Tuscan case study in the medieval origins of modern agrarian society', in N. Rubinstein (ed.), *Florentine studies. Politics and society in Renaissance Florence* (London, 1968), pp. 193–241.

Jones, R. F. J. and Bird, D. G. 'Roman gold mining in north-west Spain, II', *J. Rom. Stud.* lxii (1972), pp. 59–74.

Kaelble, H. *Berliner Unternehmer während der frühen Industrialisierung* (Berlin, 1972).

Kahrstedt, U. 'Über die Bevölkerung Roms', in L. F. Friedländer and G. Wissowa (eds.), *Sittengeschichte Roms*, 4 vols., 10th ed. (Leipzig, 1919–23), iv, pp. 11–21.

Kammerer, J. 'Die Nördlingen Verfassungsveränderungen vom Jahre 1552', *J'buch hist. Ver. Nördlingen*, xiv (1930), pp. 44–64.

Karmin, O. *La legge del catasto fiorentino del 1427* (Florence, 1906).

Keil, J. 'Vorläufiger Bericht über die Ausgrabungen in Ephesos', *J'hefte des öst. arch. Inst., Beiblatt* (1930).

Kellet, J. R. 'The breakdown of guild and corporation control over the handicraft and retail trade in London', *Econ. Hist. Rev.* 2nd ser. x (1957–8), pp. 381–94.

Kellner, H. J. and Christ, K. (eds.) *Die Fundmünzen der römischen Zeit in Deutschland* (Berlin, 1960–).

Kelly, W. *Notices illustrative of the drama* (London, 1865).

Kent, F. W. 'The Rucellai family and its loggia', *J. Warburg and Courtauld Inst.* xxxv (1972), pp. 397–401.

Kiechle, F. *Sklavenarbeit und technische Fortschritt im Römischen Reich* (Wiesbaden, 1969).

Kiernan, V. 'Victorian London: unending purgatory', *New Left Review*, lxxvi (1972), pp. 73–90.

Kirchgässner, B. 'Probleme quantitativer Erfassung städtischer Unterschichten im Spätmittelalter besonders in den Reichsstädten Konstanz und Esslingen', in E. Maschke and J. Sydow (eds.), *Gesellschaftliche Unterschichten in den südwestdeutschen Städten* (Stuttgart, 1967).

Klapisch, C. 'Fiscalité et démographie en Toscane (1427–30)', *Annales, E.S.C.* xxiv (1969), pp. 1313–37.

Klapisch, C. and Demonet, M. '*A uno pane e uno vino*. La famille rurale au début du XVe siècle', *Annales, E.S.C.* xxvii (1972), pp. 873–901.

Knodel, J. *The decline of fertility in Germany 1871–1939* (Princeton, 1974).

Knodel, J. 'Infant mortality and fertility in three Bavarian villages: an analysis of family histories from the nineteenth century', *Pop. Stud.* xxii (1968), pp. 297–318.

Knodel, J. and van der Walle, E. 'Breast feeding, fertility and infant mortality: an analysis of some early German data', *Pop. Stud.* xxi (1967), pp. 109–32.

Köllman, W. *Sozialgeschichte der Stadt Barmen im 19. Jahrhundert* (Tübingen, 1960).

Köllman, W. 'The process of urbanization in Germany at the height of the industrialisation period', *J. Contemp. Hist.* iv (1969), pp. 59–76.

Köllman, W. *Bevölkerung in der industriellen Revolution* (Göttingen, 1974).

Koselleck, R. *Preussen zwischen Reform und Revolution* (Stuttgart, 1967).

Kraeling, C. H. *Ptolemais* (Chicago, 1962).

Ku Yen-wu (ed.) *T'ien-hsia chün-kuo li-ping shu* ('Documents relating to the advantageous and disadvantageous characteristics of the commanderies and principates of the empire'), Ssu-k'u shan-pen edn (1637).

Lampard, E. E. 'The history of cities in the economically advanced areas', *Econ. Dev. and Cult. Change*, iii (1955), pp. 81–136.

Lampard, E. E. 'The urbanising world', in H. J. Dyos and M. Wolff (eds.), *The Victorian city, images and realities*, 2 vols. (London, 1973).

Landes, D. S. 'Encore le problème de la révolution industrielle en Angleterre', *Bull. soc. d'hist. mod.* 12th ser. no. 18.

Lane, F. C. *Venice: a maritime republic* (Baltimore, 1973).

Laslett, P. *The world we have lost* (London, 1965).

Laslett, P. 'The numerical study of English society', in E. A. Wrigley (ed.), *An introduction to English historical demography* (London, 1966), pp. 1–13.

Laslett, P. and Harrison, J. 'Clayworth and Cogenhoe', in H. E. Bell and R. L. Ollard (eds.), *Historical essays 1600–1750, presented to David Ogg* (London, 1963), pp. 157–84.

Laslett, P. and Wall, R. (eds.), *Household and family in past time* (Cambridge, 1972).

Latham, R. E. *The travels of Marco Polo* (London, 1958).

Latimer, J. *Sixteenth century Bristol* (Bristol, 1908).

Laube, A. 'Wirtschaftliche und soziale Differenzierung innerhalb der Zünfte des 14. Jahrhunderts, dargestellt am Beispiel mecklenburgerischer Städte', *Z'tschr. f. Geschichtswissenschaft*, v (1957), pp. 181–97.

Lauffer, S. *Diokletians Preisedikt* (Berlin, 1971).

Launey, M. 'Inscriptions de Thasos', *Bulletin de correspondance hellénique*, lvii (1933), pp. 394–415.

Law, C. M. 'Some notes on the urban population of England and Wales in the eighteenth century', *Local Historian*, x (1972), pp. 13–26.

Le Bras, G. 'Le mariage dans la théologie et le droit de l'Eglise du XIe au XIIIe siècle', *Cahiers de civilisation médiévale*, xi (1968), pp. 191–202.

Leibenstein, H. *Economic backwardness and economic growth* (New York, 1963).

Leibenstein, H. 'Population growth and the take-off hypothesis', in W. W. Rostow (ed.), *The economics of take-off into sustained growth* (London, 1963).

Leonard, E. M. *The early history of English poor relief* (Cambridge, 1900).

Le Play, F. *L'organisation de la famille* (Paris, 1871).

Lerner, D. *The passing of traditional society* (New York, 1958).

Lestocquoy, J. *Les dynasties bourgeoises d'Arras du XIe au XVe siècle* (Arras, 1945).

Lestocquoy, J. *Aux origines de la bourgeoisie: les villes de Flandre et d'Italie sous le gouvernement des patriciens XIe–XVe siècles* (Paris, 1952).

Lewis, A. W. and O'Leary, P. J. 'Secular swings in production and trade, 1870–1913', *The Manchester School*, xxiii (1955), pp. 113–52.

Lewis, J. W. (ed.) *The city in Communist China* (Stanford, 1971).

Lewis, P. R. and Jones, G. D. B. 'Roman gold mining in north-west Spain, I', *J. Rom. Stud.* lx (1970), pp. 169–84.

Lewis, W. A. *The theory of economic growth* (London, 1955).

Liebel, H. P. 'The bourgeoisie in southwestern Germany, 1500–1789: a rising class?', *Internat. Rev. Soc. Hist.* x (1965), pp. 283–307.

Liebeschutz, W. *Antioch* (Oxford, 1972).

Lloyd-Pritchard, M. E. 'The decline of Norwich', *Econ. Hist. Rev.* 2nd ser. iii (1950–1), pp. 371–7.

Lobel, M. D. *The borough of Bury St Edmunds* (Oxford, 1935).

Lobel, M. D. 'Hereford', in M. D. Lobel (ed.), *The atlas of historic towns*, i (London and Oxford, 1969).

Lobel, M. D. 'Cambridge', in M. D. Lobel (ed.), *The atlas of historic towns*, ii (London, 1975).

Lopez, R. *Benedetto Zaccaria, ammiraglio e mercante* (Messina, 1932).

Lopez, R. 'Le origini dell' arte della lana', in *Studi sull' economia genovese nel media evo*, viii (Turin, 1936).

Lopez, R. 'Nota sulla composizione dei patrimoni privati nella prima metà del Duecento', in *Studi sull' economia genovese nel medio evo*, viii (Turin, 1936).

Lopez, R. 'Aux origines du capitalisme genois', *Annales d'hist. éc. et soc.* ix (1937), pp. 437–51.

Lopez, R. 'Le marchand génois, un profil collectif', *Annales, E.S.C.* xiii (1958), pp. 511–13.

Lopez, R. 'Familiari, procuratori e dipendenti di Benedetto Zaccaria', in *Miscellanea di storia ligure in onore di Giorgio Falco* (Milan, 1962), pp. 227–30.

Loschky, D. J. 'Urbanization and England's eighteenth century crude birth and death rate', *J. Eur. Econ. Hist.* (1972), p. 705.

Ma, L. J. C. *Commercial development and urban change in Sung China* (Ann Arbor, Mich., 1971).

McGee, T. G. *The urbanization process in the third world. Explorations in search of a theory* (London, 1971).

Machiavelli, B. *Libro di ricordi*, ed. C. Olschki (Florence, 1954).

McKendrick, N. 'Josiah Wedgwood: an eighteenth century entrepreneur in salesmanship and marketing techniques', *Econ. Hist. Rev.* 2nd ser. xii (1959–60), pp. 408–33.

McKisack, M. *The fourteenth century, 1307–1399* (Oxford, 1959).

MacMullen, R. *Roman social relations* (New Haven, 1974).

Mair, L. 'Some current terms in social anthropology', *Br. J. Soc.* xiv (1963), pp. 20–9.

Mallett, M. 'Pisa and Florence in the fifteenth century: aspects of the period of the first Florentine domination', in N. Rubinstein (ed.), *Florentine studies. Politics and society in Renaissance Florence* (London, 1968), pp. 403–41.

Mann Jones, S. 'The Ningpo *pang* and financial power at Shanghai', in M. Elvin and G. W. Skinner (eds.), *The Chinese city between two worlds* (Stanford, 1974), pp. 73–96.

Margary, I. D. *Roman roads in Britain*, 2 vols., 3rd ed. (London, 1973).

Marshall, L. M. 'The rural population of Bedfordshire, 1671–1921', *Beds Hist. Rec. Soc.* xvi (1934), pp. 2–65.

Martin, G. *The story of Colchester* (Colchester, 1959).

Marx, K. Letter to Engels, 27 June 1867, in K. Marx and F. Engels, *Selected correspondence* (Moscow, 1956).

Marx, K. *Capital* (London, 1970).

Maschke, E. 'Verfassung und soziale Kräfte in der deutschen Stadt des späten Mittelalters, vornehmlich in Oberdeutschland', *Vierteliahschr. f. Soz.- u. Wirtschaftsgesch,* xlvi (1959), pp. 289–349, 433–76.

Maschke, E. In 'Debats et combats', *Annales, E.S.C.* xv (1960), pp. 936–48.

Maschke, E. and Sydow, J. *Städtische Mittelschichten* (Stuttgart, 1972).

Mathias, P. 'The brewing industry, temperance and politics', *Hist. J.* i (1958), pp. 97–114.

Mathias, P. *The first industrial nation. An economic history of Britain 1700–1914* (London, 1969).

Map, A. *Pompeii* (New York, 1899).

Mauersberg, H. *Sozial- und Wirtschaftsgeschichte zentraleuropäischer Städte in neuerer Zeit* (Göttingen, 1960).

Mehta, S. K. 'Some demographic and economic correlates of primate cities: a case for revaluation', *Demography,* i (1964), pp. 136–147.

Mendenhall, T. C. *The Shrewsbury drapers and the Welsh wool trade in the XVI and XVII centuries* (Oxford, 1953).

Merrington, J. 'Town and country in the transition to capitalism', *New Left Review*, xciii (1975), pp. 71–92.

Middlebrook, S. *Newcastle-upon-Tyne. Its growth and achievement* (Newcastle, 1950).

Miller, E. 'Medieval York', in P. M. Tillott (ed.), *VCH A history of Yorkshire. The city of York* (London, 1961), pp. 25–116.

Miller, E. 'The fortunes of the English textile industry during the thirteenth century', *Econ. Hist. Rev.* 2nd ser. xviii (1965), pp. 64–82.

Minchinton, W. E. 'Bristol – metropolis of the west in the eighteenth century', *Trans. Roy. Hist. Soc.* 5th ser. iv (1954), pp. 69–89.

Minchinton, W. E. 'The port of Bristol in the eighteenth century', in P. McGrath (ed.), *Bristol in the eighteenth century* (Newton Abbot, 1972), pp. 127–59.

Miner, H. 'The folk-urban continuum', *Am. Soc. Rev.* xvii (1952), pp. 529–37.

Minuti, V. 'Relazione del commissario Giovanni Batista Tedaldi sopra la città e il capitanato di Pistoia nell' anno 1569', *Archivio storico italiano*, ser. 5, x (1892), pp. 302–31.

Mitchell, B. R. and Deane, P. *British historical statistics* (Cambridge, 1962).

Moeller, W. O. *The wool trade of ancient Pompeii* (Leiden, 1976).

Molho, A. *Florentine public finances in the early Renaissance, 1400–33* (Cambridge, Mass., 1971).

Möller, H. *Die kleinbürgerliche Familie im 18. Jahrhundert: Verhalten und Gruppenkultur* (Berlin, 1969).

Moore, Barrington. *Social origins of dictatorship and democracy. Lord and peasant in the making of the modern world* (London, 1967).

Moresco, M. 'Note sulla fondazione della chiesa gentilizia degli Spinola nel 1188 in Genova', in *Scritti di Mattia Moresco* (Milan, 1959), pp. 397–411.

Moresco, M. 'Parentele e guerre civili in Genova nel secolo XII', in *Scritti di Mattia Moresco* (Milan, 1959), pp. 429–40.

Moresco, M. 'Le parrochie gentilizie genovesi', in *Scritti di Mattia Moresco* (Milan, 1959).

Morris, R. H. *Chester in the Plantagenet and Tudor reigns* (Chester, n.d.).

Most, O. 'Deutsches Städtewesen', in Kaiser Wilhelm Dank (ed.), *Deutschland als Weltmacht* (Berlin, 1910), pp. 167–80.

Mote, F. *The poet Kao Ch'i, 1336–1374* (Princeton, 1962).

Namier, L. 'Anthony Bacon, M.P., an eighteenth century merchant', *J. Econ. and Business Hist.* ii (1929), pp. 20–70.

Nash, W. G. *The Rio Tinto mine* (London, 1904).

Naujoks, E. *Obrigkeitsgedanke, Zunftverfassung und Reformation: Studien zur Verfassungsgeschichte von Ulm, Esslingen und Schwäbisch Gmünd* (Stuttgart, 1958).

Neefe, M. 'Hauptergebnisse der Wohnungsstatistik deutscher Grossstädte', *Schriften des Vereins für Sozialpolitik,* xxx (Leipzig, 1886), pp. 161–99.

Nef, J. U. *The rise of the British coal industry,* 2 vols. (London, 1932).

Niccolai, F. *Contributo allo studio dei più antichi brevi della campagna genovese* (Milan, 1939).

Niccolai, F. 'I consorzi nobiliari ed il commune nell' alta e media Italia', *Rivista di storia del diritto italiano,* xiii (1940), pp. 116–147, 293–342 and 397–447.

Niethammer, L., with collaboration of Bruggemeier, F. 'Wie wohnten Arbeiter in Kaisserreich?', *Archiv für Sozialgeschichte,* xvi (1976), pp. 61–134.

Nörr, D. 'Zur soziale und rechtlichen Bewertung der freien Arbeit in Rom', *Zeitschrift der Savigny-Stiftung für Rechtsgeschichte,* lxxxii (1965), pp. 67–105.

Oates, W. J. 'The population of Rome', *Class. Phil.* xxix (1934), pp. 101–16.

Olivieri, A. *Serie dei consoli del commune di Genova* (Atti della società liguri di storia patria, i, 1858, pp. 155–626).

Oria, J. d'. *La Chiesa di S. Matteo in Genova descritta ed illustrata* (Genoa, 1860).

Owen, H. and Blakeway, J. B. *A history of Shrewsbury,* 2 vols. (London, 1825).

Pagolo Morelli, G. di. *Ricordi,* ed. V. Branca (Florence, 1956).

Palliser, D. M. 'Some aspects of the social and economic history of York in the sixteenth century', unpub. D.Phil. thesis (Oxford, 1968).

Palliser, D. M. 'The trade gilds of Tudor York', in P. Clark and P. Slack (eds.), *Crisis and order in English towns 1500–1700* (London, 1972).

Palliser, D. M. 'The boroughs of medieval Staffordshire', *North Staffs J. Field Stud.* xii (1972), pp. 63–74.

Parker, V. *The making of King's Lynn* (London and Chichester, 1971).

Pastorino, T. *Dizionario delle stradi di Genova,* 3 vols. (Genoa, 1968).

Patterson, C. C. 'Silver stocks and losses in ancient and medieval times', *Econ. Hist. Rev.* 2nd ser. xxv (1972), pp. 205–235.

Perkin, H. J. *The origins of modern English society 1780–1880* (London, 1969).

Petrucci, A. *Il libro di ricordanze dei Corsini* (Fonti per la storia d'Italia, c. Rome, 1965).

Petty, Sir William. *The growth of the city of London*, in C. H. Hull (ed.), *The economic writings of Sir William Petty*, 2 vols. (New York, 1963–4), ii, pp. 451–78.

Phelps-Brown, E. H. and Hopkins, S. V. 'Builders' wage rates, prices and population: some further evidence', *Economica*, new ser. xxiv (1959), pp. 18–38.

Phythian-Adams, C., 'Ceremony and the citizen: the communal year at Coventry 1450–1550', in P. Clark and P. Slack (eds.), *Crisis and order in English towns 1500–1700* (London, 1972), pp. 57–85.

Pirenne, H. 'L'origine des constitutions urbaines au Moyen Age', *Revue hist.* lvii (1895), pp. 293–327.

Pirenne, H. *Belgian democracy*, trans. J. V. Saunders (Manchester, 1915).

Pirenne, H. *Economic and social history of medieval Europe* (London, 1936).

Pirenne, H. *Les villes et les institutions urbaines*, 2 vols. (Brussels, 1939).

Pitz, E. 'Wirtschaftliche und soziale Probleme der gewerblichen Entwicklung im 15./16. Jahrhundert nachhansisch-niederdeutschen Quellen', in F. Lütge (ed.), *Wirtschaftliche und soziale Probleme der gewerblichen Entwicklung im 15.–16. Jahrhundert* (Stuttgart, 1968), pp. 16–43.

Pizzorno, A. 'Three types of urban social structure and the development of industrial society', in G. Germani (ed.), *Modernisation, urbanisation and the urban crisis* (Boston, 1973).

Platt, C. *Medieval Southampton* (London, 1973).

Poleggi, E. 'Le contrade delle consorterie nobiliari a Genova tra il XII e il XIII secolo', *Urbanistica*, xlii–xliii (1965).

Postan, M. 'Revisions in economic history. ix. The fifteenth century', *Econ. Hist. Rev.* ix (1938–9), pp. 160–7.

Postan, M. 'Some economic evidence of declining population in the later Middle Ages', *Econ. Hist. Rev.* 2nd ser. ii (1950), pp. 221–246.

Pound, J. F. 'The social and trade structure of Norwich 1525–1575', *Past and Present*, xxxiv (1966), pp. 49–69.

Pounds, N. J. G. 'The urbanisation of the Classical World', *Annals Am. Assoc. Geog.* lix (1969), pp. 135–57.

Power, E. and Postan, M. M. *Studies in English trade in the fifteenth century* (London, 1933).

Prince, H. C. 'England *c.* 1800', in H. C. Darby (ed.), *A new historical geography of England* (Cambridge, 1973).

Redfield, R. *The folk culture of Yucatan* (Chicago, 1941).

Redford, A. and Russell, I. S. *The history of local government in Manchester*, 3 vols. (London, 1939).

Reece, R. 'Roman coinage in Britain and the western Empire', *Britannia*, iv (1973), pp. 227–52.

Reich, E. *Der Wohnungsmarkt in Berlin von 1840–1910* (Munich and Leipzig, 1912).

Reissman, L. *The urban process. Cities in industrial societies* (New York, 1964).

Renouard, Y. *Les hommes d'affaires italiens du moyen age* (Paris, 1949).

Reynolds, R. L. 'In search of a business class in thirteenth century Genoa', *J. Econ. Hist.* v, supplement (1945), pp. 1–19.

Richtofen, F. P. W. von. *Baron Richtofen's letters, 1870–1872* (Shanghai, 1872).

Rickard, T. A. *Man and metals*, 2 vols. (New York, 1932).

Rivet, A. L. F. *Town and country in Roman Britain*, 2nd ed. (London, 1964).

Robertis, F. M. de. *Lavoro e lavatori nel mondo romano* (Bari, 1963).

Roessingh, H. K. 'Village and hamlet in a sandy region of the Netherlands in the middle of the eighteenth century', *Acta Historiae Neerlandica* (1970), pp. 105–29.

Rogers, A. 'Medieval Stamford', in A. Rogers (ed.), *The making of Stamford* (Leicester, 1965), pp. 34–57.

Roover, R. de. *The rise and decline of the Medici bank* (Cambridge, Mass., 1963).

Rörig, F. *The medieval city* (London, 1967).

Rostovtzeff, M. I. *The social and economic history of the Roman Empire*, 2 vols., 2nd ed. rev. (Oxford, 1957).

Rougé, J. *Recherches sur l'organisation du commerce maritime en Méditerranée sous l'empire romain* (Paris, 1966).

Rowse, A. L. *The England of Elizabeth* (London, 1962).

Rozman, G. 'Edo's importance in the changing Tokugawa society', *J. Jap. Stud.* i (1974), pp. 91–112.

Rubinstein, N. (ed.) *Florentine studies. Politics and society in Renaissance Florence* (London, 1968).

Ruddock, A. A. *Italian merchants and shipping in Southampton 1270–1600* (Southampton Record Series, i, 1951).

Runciman, W. G. *Relative deprivation and social justice* (London, 1966).

Russell, J. C. *Medieval regions and their cities* (Newton Abbot, 1972).

Rutkowski, J. *Histoire économique de la Pologne avant les partages* (Paris, 1927).

Sagnac, P. *La formation de la société française moderne*, 2 vols. (Paris, 1945).

Salter, H. E. *Medieval Oxford* (Oxford Historical Society, c, 1936).

Salvemini, G. *Magnati e popolani in Firenze dal 1280 al 1295* (Florence, 1899), rep. with introd. by E. Sestan (Turin, 1960).

Sant' Angelo, c. I. di. *Jacopo d'Oria i susi annali* (Venice, 1930).

Sapori, A. In *IXe Congrès international des sciences historiques, Paris, 28 aout–3 septembre 1950. I: Rapport etc.* (Paris, 1950).

Saville, J. 'Primitive accumulation and early industrialization in Britain', *Socialist Register*, vi (1969), pp. 247–71.

Scarfe, N. *The Suffolk landscape* (London, 1972).

Schildhauer, J. *Soziale, politische und religiöse Auseinandersetzungen in den Hansastädten Stralsund, Rostock und Wismar im ersten Drittel des 16. Jahrhunderts* (Weimar, 1959).

Schofer, L. *The formation of a modern labour force: Upper Silesia, 1865–1914* (Berkeley and London, 1975).

Schott, S. *Die grossstädtischen Agglomerationen des Deutschen Reichs* (Breslau, 1912).

Schulten, A. *Geschichte von Numantia* (München, 1933).

Sheail, J. 'The regional distribution of wealth in England as indicated in the Lay Subsidy returns in 1524/5', unpub. PhD thesis (London, 1968).

Sherborne, J. W. *The Port of Bristol in the Middle Ages* (Port of Bristol Series, xiii, 1965).

Shiba, Y. 'Sōdai Min-shū no toshika to chi-iki kaihatsu' ('The urbanization and regional development of Sung dynasty Ming chou [Ning-po]'). *Machikaneyama ronsō*, iii (1969).

Shiba, Y. *Commerce and society in Sung China*, trans. M. Elvin (Ann Arbor, Mich., 1970).

Sjoberg, G. *The preindustrial city, past and present* (Glencoe, Ill., 1960).

Sjoberg, G. 'The rise and fall of cities', *Internat. J. Comp. Soc.* iv (1963), pp. 107–20.

Skinner, G. W. 'Marketing and social structure in rural China', *J. Asian Stud.* xxiv (1964), pp. 3–43.

Slade, C. F. 'Reading', in M. D. Lobel (ed.), *The atlas of historic towns*, i (London and Oxford, 1969).

Smith, A. *The wealth of nations*, rev. ed. J. R. M'Culloch (Edinburgh, 1863; Penguin ed., 1970).

Smith, R. B. *Land and politics in the England of Henry VIII* (Oxford, 1970).

Smith, T. C. 'Pre-modern economic growth: Japan and the West', *Past and Present*, lx (1973), pp. 127–60.

Snodgrass, A. M. 'Barbaric Europe and early Iron Age Greece', *Proc. Prehist. Soc.* xxxi (1965), pp. 229–40.

Soliday, G. L. *A community in conflict: Frankfurt society in the seventeenth and early eighteenth centuries* (Hanover, N.H., 1974).

Sombart, W. *Der moderne Kapitalismus*, 2 vols. 2nd ed. (Munich, 1916–17).

Sovani, N. V. 'The analysis of over-urbanisation', *Econ. Dev. and Cult. Change*, xii (1964), pp. 113–22.

Stanfield, J. and Simpson, G. *Central Gaulish potters* (London, 1958).

Stephens, W. B. (ed.) *History of Congleton* (Manchester, 1970).

Stone, L. 'Social mobility in England, 1500–1700', *Past and Present*, xxxiii (1966), pp. 16–55.

Sweezy, P. 'A critique', in R. Hilton (ed.), *The transition from feudalism to capitalism* (London, 1976), pp. 33–56.

Symonds, G. E. 'Thaxted and its Cutlers' Gild', *The Reliquary*, v (1864–5), pp. 67–8.

Tawney, A. J. and R. H. 'An occupational census of the seventeenth century', *Econ. Hist. Rev.* v (1934–5), pp. 25–64.

Taylor, E. G. R. *The haven-finding art* (London, 1956).

Thernstrom, S. *Poverty and progress: social mobility in a nineteenth century city* (New York, 1971).

Thienel, I. *Städtewachstum im Industrialisierungsprozess des 19. Jahrhunderts, das Berliner Beispiel* (Berlin and New York, 1963).

Thirsk, J. 'Industries in the countryside', in F. J. Fisher (ed.), *Essays in the economic and social history of Tudor and Stuart England in honour of R. H. Tawney* (Cambridge, 1961), pp. 70–88.

Thirsk, J. 'Stamford in the sixteenth and seventeenth centuries', in A. Rogers (ed.), *The making of Stamford* (Leicester, 1965), pp. 58–76.

Thompson, E. P. *The making of the English working class* (London, 1963).

Thompson, E. P. 'Time, work-discipline and industrial capitalism', *Past and Present*, xxxviii (1967), pp. 56–97.

Thompson, J. *The history of Leicester* (Leicester, 1849).

Thomson, J. O. *History of ancient geography* (Cambridge, 1948).

Tooke, T. *A history of prices and of the state of the circulation from 1793–1837*, 2 vols. (London, 1838).

Twitchett, D. 'The T'ang market system', *Asia Major*, new ser., ii (1966), pp. 201–48.

Tylecote, R. F. *Metallurgy in archaeology* (London, 1962).

Unwin, G. *Industrial organization in the sixteenth and seventeenth centuries* (Oxford, 1904).

Vaccari, P. ' "Accomendatio e societas" negli atti dei notai liguri del XIII secolo', *Rivista di storia del diritto italiano*, xxvi–xxvii (1953–4), pp. 85–97.

Vandenbossche, A. *La dos ex marito dans la Gaule franque* (Paris, 1953).

Vitale, V. *Il comune del podestà a Genova* (Milan, 1951).

Vitale, V. *Breviario della storia di Genova*, 2 vols. (Genoa, 1955).

Walker, M. *German home towns: community, state and general estate, 1648–1871* (Ithaca, 1971).

Wallerstein, I. *The modern world system* (New York, 1974).

Wangenblass, H. *Der Eisenbahnbau und das Wachstum der deutschen Eisenund Maschinenbau Industrie, 1835 bis 1860* (Stuttgart, 1973).

Wappäus, J. A. *Allgemeine Bevölkerungsstatistik*, 2 vols. (Leipzig, 1859–61).

Webb, J. *Great Tooley of Ipswich* (Suffolk Record Society, 1962).

Webb, S. and B. *English local government from the Revolution to the Municipal Corporations Act*, ii, *The Manor and the Borough* (London, 1924).

Weber, A. F. *The growth of cities in the nineteenth century. A study in statistics* (New York, 1899; Cornell Paperbacks, 1967).

Weber, M. *The methodology of the social sciences*, trans. E. A. Shils (Glencoe, Ill., 1949).

Weber, M. *The city*, ed. D. Martindale and G. Neuwirth (Glencoe, Ill., 1958).

Weber, M. *Economy and society* (New York, 1968).

Welford, R. (ed.) *History of Newcastle and Gateshead*, 3 vols. (London, 1885).

Williams, G. A. *Medieval London, from commune to capital* (London, 1963).

Williams, R. *The country and the city* (London, 1973).

Williamson, J. A. 'The geographical history of the Cinque Ports', *History*, new ser. xi (1926–7), pp. 97–115.

Wilson, K. P. 'The port of Chester in the fifteenth century', *Trans. Hist. Soc. Lancs and Cheshire*, cxvii (1965), pp. 1–15.

Wilson, R. G. *Gentlemen merchants. The merchant community in Leeds 1700–1830* (Manchester, 1971).

Wipszycka, E. 'The Dorea of Apollonios the Dioeketes in the Memphite Nome', *Klio*, xxxix (1961), pp. 153–90.

Wipszycka, E. *L'industrie textile dans l'Egypte romaine* (Warsaw, 1965).

Wirth, L. 'Urbanism as a way of life', *Am. J. Soc.* xliv (1938), pp. 1–24.

Wise, M. J. 'Birmingham and its trade relations in the early eighteenth century', *Univ. Birmingham Hist. J.* ii (1949–50), pp. 53–79.

Wrigley, E. A. *Industrial growth and population change* (Cambridge, 1960).

Wrigley, E. A. 'The supply of raw materials in the industrial revolution', *Econ. Hist. Rev.* 2nd ser. xv (1962), pp. 1–16.

Wrigley, E. A. 'Family limitation in pre-industrial England', *Econ. Hist. Rev.* 2nd ser. xix (1966), pp. 81–109.

Wrigley, E. A. 'A simple model of London's importance in changing English society and economy 1650–1750', *Past and Present*, xxxvii (1967), pp. 44–70.

Wrigley, E. A. 'Mortality in pre-industrial England: the example of Colyton, Devon, over three centuries', *Daedalus*, xcvii (1968), pp. 546–80.

Wunder, G. 'Die Sozialstruktur der Reichsstadt Schwäbisch Hall im später Mittelalter', in T. Mayer (ed.), *Untersuchungen zur gesellschaftlichen Struktur der mittelalterlichen Stadt in Europa* (Konstanz, 1966).

Zipf, G. W. *National unity and disunity* (Bloomington, 1941).

Zorn, W. 'L'industrialisation de l'Allemagne du Sud au XIX siècle', in P. Léon et al. *L'industrialization en Europe au XIX siècle* (Paris, 1972), pp. 379–92.

Other sources

Adam's chronicle of Bristol (Bristol, 1910).

Annali genovesi di Caffaro e de' suoi continuatori, ed. L. T. Belgrano and C. I. di Sant' Angelo (Fonti per la storia d'Italia, xi–xiv, 1890–1929).

Bengal district gazetteers, by L. S. S. O'Malley and others (Calcutta, 1906–23).

Bonvillano, ed. J. E. Eierman, H. C. Krueger and R. L. Reynolds (Notai liguri del secolo XII, iii, 1939), no.'38.

Calendar of the records of the Corporation of Gloucester, ed. W. H. Stevenson (Gloucester, 1893).

Il cartolare di Giovanni Scriba, ed. M. Chiaudano and M. Moresco (Documenti per la storia del commercio e del diritto commerciale italiano, i–ii, 1935).

Cartolari notarili genovesi (1–149): Inventario (Pubblicazioni degli Archivi di Stato, xxii and xlii, 1956 and 1961).

Chin-shih ('History of the Chin'), compiled by T'o T'o and On-yang Hsuan *circa* 1345, Po-na edn.

Circumnavigation of the Red Sea, trans. and annotated by W. H. Schoff (London, 1912).

Codice diplomatico del monastero Benedettino di S. Maria di Tremiti, ed. A. Petrucci (Fonti per la storia d'Italia, xcviii, 1960).

Codice diplomatico della Repubblica di Genova, ed. C. I. di Sant' Angelo (Fonti per la storia d'Italia, lxxvii–lxxix, 1936–42).

The Coventry Leet Book, ed. Dormer Harris, 4 vols. in 1 (Early English Text Society, orig. ser. nos. cxxxiv, cxxxv, cxxxviii, xlvi, 1907–13).

England in the reign of King Henry the Eighth, ed. S. J. Herrtage (Early English Text Society, extra ser. xxxii, 1878).

Extracts from the records of the Company of Hostmen of Newcastle-upon-Tyne, ed. F. W. Dendy (Surtees Society, cv, 1901).

Giovanni di Guiberto (1200–1211), ed. H. C. Krueger, R. G. Reinert and R. L. Reynolds (Notai liguri del secolo XII, v, 1939–40), no. 390.

Gugliemo Cassinese (1190–2), ed. M. W. Hall, H. C. Krueger and R. L. Reynolds (Notai liguri del secolo XII, ii, 1938), no. 1492.

Inscriptiones latinae selectae, ed. H. Dessau (Berlin, 1892–1916).

L' 'Istoria de Firenze' di Gregorio Dati dal 1380 al 1405, ed. L. Pratesi (Norcia, 1902).

Itineraria romana, ed. O. Cuntz (Leipzig, 1929).

The itinerary of John Leland, ed. L. Toulmin Smith, 5 vols. (London, 1964).

Lanfranco (1202–1226), ed. H. C. Krueger and R. L. Reynolds (Notai liguri del secolo XII, vi, 1953), no. 1738.

Latin Panegyrics, ed. E. Galletier (Paris, 1952).

Letters and papers, foreign and domestic, of the reign of Henry VIII, arranged and catalogued by J. S. Brewer (HMSO, London, ii, pt 1, 1864, iv, pt 1, 1870, iv, pt 2, 1872).

Liber magistri Salmonis, sacri palatii notarii, 1222–1226, ed. A. Ferretto (Atti della società ligure di storia, xxxvi, 1906), nos. 827, 857 and 1015.

The Maire of Bristowe is kalendar, ed. L. Toulmin Smith (Camden Society, new ser. v, 1872).

The manuscripts of the corporation of Southampton and King's Lynn (HMC, 11th repr., appendix, pt iii; HMSO, 1887).

Materials for a history of the reign of Henry VII, ed. W. Campbell, 2 vols. (Rolls Series, lx, 1873).

Methods for population projections by sex and age, United Nations, ST/SOA Series A, Population Studies, no. 25 (New York, 1956).

Monumenta Asiae Minoris Antiqua, ed. J. Keil and A. Wilhelm (Manchester, 1931).

Municipal Corporation Enquiry. A report of the official examination into the existing state of the corporation of Newcastle-upon-Tyne before Fortunatus Dwarris and S. A. Rumball (Newcastle, 1833).

Oberto Scriba de Mercato (1186), ed. M. Chiaudano (Notai liguri del secolo XII, vi, 1940).

Oberto Scriba de Mercato (1190), ed. M. Chiaudano and R. Morozzo della Rocca (Notai liguri del secolo XII, 1938).

Panegyrici latini, ed. W. Baehrens (Leipzig, 1911).

Philippi Villani Liber civitatis Florentiae famosis civibus – et de Florentinorum de litteratura principes fere synchroni scriptores, ed. G. C. Galletti (Florence, 1847).

Records of the borough of Leicester, ed. M. Bateson (Cambridge, 1905).

The records of the borough of Northampton, ed. C. A. Markham, 2 vols. (Northampton Corporation, 1898).

The records of the city of Norwich, ed. W. Hudson and J. C. Tingey, 2 vols. (Norwich and London, 1910).

The register of the Trinity Guild of Coventry, ed. G. Templeman (Dugdale Society, xix, 1944).

Il registro della curia arcivescovile di Genova, ed. L. T. Belgrano (Atti della società ligure di storia patria, ii, pt 2, 1862).

Report on the records of the city of Exeter, ed. J. H. Wylie (HMC, no. lxxiii; HMSO, 1916).

Rotuli Parliamentorum; ut et petitiones, placita in Parliamento, ed. J. Strachey, 6 vols. (1767–77).

Select cases before the King's Council in the Star Chamber com-

monly called the Court of Star Chamber, ed. I. S. Leadam, 2 vols. (Selden Society, xxv, 1910).

The third book of remembrance of Southampton 1514–1602, ed. A. L. Merson, 3 vols. (Southampton Records Series, ii, 1952).

Two tracts by Gregory King, ed. G. E. Barnett (Baltimore, 1936).

Urbanisation in Asia and the Far East (UNESCO, Calcutta, 1957).

York Memorandum Book, part 11 (1388–1493), ed. M. Sellers (Surtees Society, cxxv, 1914).

Index

absentee landlords, 68, 73, 83, 161
agriculture, 36–9, 48, 75, 81, 150–4, 227–30, 236, 257–8, 301, 305
agro-towns, 68
Alexandria, 47, 64
Amsterdam, 31–3, 216
ancient towns, 35–77
Antioch, 46–7, 64
archives, 87, 131
aristocrats, 60, 91–105, 108–12, 140–5, 184
armies, 44–8, 52, 55, 77, 129, 138–44, 225
arms, 47–8
Arras, 100
Arezzo, 44–5, 131, 134
artisans, 92, 123, 124–8, 134, 147–9, 195, 208–11
Asia Minor, 36, 39, 72
Athens, 35

Bach, E., 114, 120, 123, 313
banking, 76, 88, 234, 289
Berlin, 282, 283–4, 291
beggars, 181–2
Beresford, M., 165, 314
Berkner, L. K., 105, 314
Berry, B. J. L., 272, 314
booty, 60–1, 66
bourgeoisie, 187–9, 190–213
Braudel, F., 9, 15, 17, 23–5, 245, 250, 252, 259, 272–3, 315
Bridbury, A. R., 159, 160, 167, 315
Bristol, 163, 168–9, 182, 246, 266–7
Bruni, Leonardo, 140
building industry, 285–90, 302
buildings, 70

Cadiz, 57
Carus–Wilson, E. M., 166, 167, 170, 171, 180, 315
Catasto, 131–54
Cavalcanti, Giovanni, 142, 144, 316
ceremony, 176–7
Chalklin, C. W., 277–316
China, 50, 79–89, 245, 306
Christianity, 39
churches, 111–14

citizenship, 60, 190–9, 204, 210
class formation, 189–90, 195–8, 204–13
cloth trade, 53–5, 200–1, 203–5
coal trade, 230–1, 264–5
Cole, W. A., 229, 248–9, 318
Coleman, D. C., 180–2, 317
Cologne, 29
colonization, 67
commodities, 51, 75
coniurationes, 29
conquest, 36–7, 59–68
consumer cities, 72–4
consumption, 1, 72–3, 222 232, 256–7, 297
corporations, 57, 76, 169, 262, 265
court cities, 280–3
Coventry, 162, 174–5, 177, 182, 184
craftsmen, 93, 189, 195, 199, 202, 206
cultural change, 22–3, 184, 250, 272, 273
cups, 45–6

Deane, P., 229, 248–9, 318
debt, 151, 152–4, 196–7, 204–5
decline of towns, 156, 159–85, 269–70
Defoe, Daniel, 232, 253, 254–5
demographic change, 163, 216–20, 238, 255–7, 276, 279, 297
depopulation, 177–83
Diamond, W., 273, 318
Dinant, 99
Diocletian, Edict on Maximum Prices, 48–54
distribution of towns, 284
Dobb, M., 11–14, 189, 318
Dobson, B. B., 160, 318
dowry, 115–20
dual economy, 3, 5, 81, 251–2
Duby, G., 106, 115, 318
Dyer, A. D., 180, 318

economic growth. 2, 10, 21–3, 35–77, 131, 235–8, 248–50, 272–4, 296–302

341